African Image of the Ultimate Reality

European University Studies

Europäische Hochschulschriften

Publications Universitaires Européennes

Series XXIII

Theology

Reihe XXIII Série XXIII

Theologie

Théologie

Vol./Bd. 237

PETER LANG

Frankfurt am Main · Bern · New York · Nancy

Cosmas Okechukwu Obiego

African Image of the Ultimate Reality

An Analysis of Igbo Ideas of Life and Death in Relation to Chukwu-God

PETER LANG
Frankfurt am Main · Bern · New York · Nancy

CIP-Kurztitelaufnahme der Deutschen Bibliothek

Obiego, Cosmas Okechukwu:

African image of the ultimate reality : an analysis of Igbo ideas of life and death in relation to Chukwu God / Cosmas Okechukwu Obiego. - Frankfurt am Main ; Bern ; New York ; Nancy : Lang, 1984.

(European university studies : Ser. 23, Theology ; Vol. 237)
ISBN 3-8204-7460-9

NE: Europäische Hochschulschriften / 23

ISSN 0721-3409
ISBN 3-8204-7460-9

Printed by Weihert-Druck GmbH, Darmstadt

PREFACE

This book is the outcome of many years of study and is based on two primary studies: "Igbo Ideas of God" and "Igbo Ideas of Life and Death in Relation to Chukwu, God". The studies were submitted as M.A. and Ph. D. dissertations respectively; the former at the "Leopold-Franzens-Universität", Theology Faculty, Innsbruck, Austria, and the later at the "Pontificia Universitas Urbaniana", Rome.

Some of the ideas expressed in the book have been experienced before they were reflected on. A series of interviews were also conducted; and questionnaires were prepared and sent to Igbo people. Ever since I returned to Nigeria in 1971, I have personally interviewed and discussed with many elders-traditional Religionists and Christians - on numerous aspects of the ideas expressed in this book. These have proved most useful.

Written documents-books, monographs, dissertations and colonial reports on the Igbo and other African peoples have been consulted. I have felt free to adapt and adopt these as seemed suitable. Numerous interviews conducted by my students in preparation for their project works were also studied. Many of them were very useful.

The Church's defence of Tradition against heresies, the relationship of its theology to Jewish thought, out of which it developed and to pagan classicism, which it sought to convert, all these influenced much of what the Church has had to say about itself. Indirectly, however, these phenomena have helped to throw light on the Early Church's conception of Non-Christian Religions. In this connection I have consulted much of the writings of the Ancient Christian Fathers. It goes without saying that the book derives much benefit from all these sources.

I wish I could thank everyone who has helped me on the way to the making of this book. But there are a few whom I simply must thank. To my Bishop, the Rt. Rev. Dr. A.G. Nwedo, C.S.Sp., I owe more than can fully be expressed. I also owe great debt to Professor Walter Kern, S.J., of the University of Innsbruck, Theology Faculty. He moderated the M.A. thesis; and without his support and his experienced counsel, I might not have embarked on this book. I am greatly indebted to my "Doktorvater", Professor C. Molari and the co-relatores, Professors J. Vodopivec and V. Maconi who guided the doctoral dissertation with judicious wisdom and tact.

Without the financial aid provided by Rev.Fr. Ulrich Haag and his "Pfarrgemeinde", Grossdorf-Egg, Voralberg, Austria, the onerous and bewildering task of collecting materials for the two theses would have been impossible. The trying years of the Nigerian-Biafra war increased the burden of academic life. And the fatherly and kind advice and the benign firmness of Professor Gottfried Griesl (University of Salzburg, Austria) helped me a great deal. To him, to Rev. Father U. Haag, and to my "Patenpfarrgemeinde" Grossdorf I should like to put on record my deepest gratitude.

I owe a very great debt to Professors G.M. Umezurike, Ikenna F. Nzimiro, both of the University of Nigeria, Nsukka, to Professors Patrick Akoi (formerly of the African Institute, Pontificia Universitas Urbaniana, Rome) and V.L. Grontanelli of State University, Rome; to the Rev. Drs. Ifeanyichukwu P. Arazu, C.S.Sp., for the invaluable documents they recommended and in some cases made available to me.

In the course of my teaching at the Bigard Memorial Seminary, Enugu, I have had to supervise students' project works on one or other aspect of the Igbo people. I have served as an adviser to some others. The discussions I had with these students, their viewes, evaluations and criticisms have often compelled me to carry out more field-work on many aspects of this book. To all these students, and to all the Igbo men and women with whom I have spent hours discussing this or that aspect of Igbo religion, I am immensely grateful.

The Rt. Honourable Dr. Gottfried Feurstein has been financially and otherwise most helpful during the period I spent recasting the theses. Through the aid of Missionswissenschaftliches Institut Missio, Aachen, Western Germany, the publication of this study has been made possible. The

Vincentian Fathers at St.Mary's College, Strawberry Hill, England, and the Rev. Fr. Erich Daxerer, parish priest of Schutzengelpfarrei, Neu-Pradl, Innsbruck, Austria, have most generously provided me with accomodation when the work was being prepared for publication. To them all I am greatly indebted.

I also render my deep appreciation for the helps I received to all the staff of research institutions and libraries where the essential materials are deposited.

Rev. Frs. John Hurley, C.M., Desmond J. McGinley, C.M., Kevin Rafferty, C.M., and Michael Prior, C.M., have expended many hours reading most carefully much of the scripts and spotting and correcting grammatical infelicities. My indebtedness to their comments and their help is in many ways profound.

Mrs Nadine Crépin-Echtermeyer, Absam/Tyrol, Austria, has most kindly expended much time in editing and arranging the bibliography and the references.

To all those mentioned and others who have helped very considerably in one way or another, many, many thanks. Whatever qualities the book possesses derive from many minds. Its defects are all my own.

C. Okechukwu Obiego
Bishop's House, Umuahia - Imo State, Nigeria
13th Dec. 1983

CONTENTS

PART ONE: CHRISTIANITY, AFRICAN TRADITIONAL RELIGIONS AND THE ETHNOGRAPHICAL SURVEY OF THE IGBO

CHAPTER ONE: NEED FOR A SECOND LOOK AT THE TRADITIONAL RELIGIONS

Black Africa's lack of development in science and technology has been attributed to the dominance of religion. This view has been criticized. The critics argue that both the religious thought-systems and the scientific and technological thought-patterns are attempts to explain the cosmic relationships at different levels. Both have common data based on abstract symbols, but they diverge in the way these symbols are transformed. What separates religion from science and technology is the difference in symbolic transformation. Religious thought-systems enjoy psychological prohibitions, which are reinforced by social sanctions. The ritual community often brands as heretics those who question and challenge its beliefs. In consequence its beliefs are not subjected to rigorous examination. On the other hand, scientific and technological thought-patterns have to be proved by strict demonstration.

On the basis of this assumption it is argued that Black Africa developed her distinctive religion, technology and science. Her scientific and technological development was hampered and impeded partly by historical and environmental factors and partly by the absence of written records. These records were essential for the transmission of abstract forms into concrete forms. On the other hand, her religious ideas developed and were transmitted in a non-literate situation. Their transmission involved the transformation of abstract forms into more abstract forms that did not need to be verified[1].

Whatever may be said in favour of or against the argument, the point to be emphasized is that the lack of authoritative documents regarding the Igbo precolonial traditional past, as of the majority of African peoples, presents no small handicap to any Igbo or modern "Africanists" undertaking a study of any segment of their past - what they thought and did, how and why.

Faced with this predicament, one is somehow consoled (a

mixed consolation indeed !), by the fact that, in the last few decades much - indeed a great deal - has been written about the Igbo people. Most of the writers were non-Igbo, and they clearly, one perceives, laboured under very great difficulties. This is all the more reason why the work they had done should be appreciated. Nonetheless one cannot but realise that the measure of success must be proportional to the extent to which the difficulties involved were thereby surmounted.

These writers, no doubt, were at pains to interpret and appraise a people with whose way of thinking, indigenious institutions, habits, customs, and language they were not at all familiar[2]. One is reminded of what Bachofen wrote to Morgan: "German scholars propose to make antiquity intelligible by measuring it according to the popular ideas of the present day. They only see themselves in the creation of the past. To penetrate to the structure of a mind different from our own is hardy work."[3]

And indeed it is a hardy work, for, granted that one might have learnt to speak the Igbo language with some fluency - in fact any foreign language - yet there is still a great deal of difference between speaking it fluently and fully understanding it. In reality it is not infrequently found that though a native and a foreigner may well be using the same words, the connotations are different: they carry different loads of meaning and the two might continue blissfully ignorant of the misunderstanding.

"Religion concerns beings which cannot be directly apprehended by the senses or fully comprehended by reason"; and a great deal of its language "is variously emotive, poetic and mythic rather than fact-asserting"[4].

Fr. Schmidt has contended that "religion is essentially of the inner life" and can only be truly grasped from within. "But beyond a doubt, this can be better done by one in whose inward consciousness an expression of religion plays a part. There is but too much danger that the other will talk of religion as a blind man might of colours, or one totally devoid of ear, of a beautiful musical composition."[5]

Operating from the presuppositions of one's own cultural and theological prejudices and cast of mind, any invective can be uttered against an alien religion. Indeed it can easily be forgotten that every religion is full of "unorthodox" trappings and overlapping and curious mental images of the one and the same God. One is too aware of a variety of overlapping mental images of God within Christianity itself - for example, as the stern and predestinating power, and as the gracious and loving heavenly Father; of Jesus Christ, as a stern law-giver and implacable judge, and as a figure of inexhaustible gracious tenderness; as a divine psychologist probing and healing the recesses of the individual spirit, and as a prophet demanding social righteousness and seeking justice for the poor and the oppressed. He is presented as a supernatural being, all powerful and all-knowing, haloed in glorius light, and as an authentically human figure who lived within the cultural framework of his time: God but in a mythic, poetic and symbolic sense. "He has been pictured both as a pacifist and as a zealot, as a figure of serene majesty and as a 'man for others', who suffered human agonies, sharing the pains and sorrows of our mortal lot...". Ironically and instructively, too, each of these different "pictures" can appeal to some element among the various strands of the New Testament tradition. But in each case communal or individual imagination has projected its own ideal upon as much of the New Testament data as will sustain it, producing a Christ-figure who meets the spiritual needs of his devotees, while behind this gallery of ideal portraits lies the largely unknown man of Nazareth[6].

I recall Pascal's dictum that truth is a fine point never touched precisely by the human mind but covered as a stubby finger covers a dot on paper, thus concealing much that is not truth as well as truth itself. The realization of this fact may well bring home to us the inadequacy of human language for the expression of divine truths contained in the religious faiths of mankind.

Christianity has continually made the tremendous claim that it alone knows God fully. The other religious faiths have only partial and imperfect knowledge of God. Often its adherents refer to other religions as superstitions. Such statements are dangerous; and no matter how they are understood, they create an appaling fog of confusion. And knowingly or unknowingly, it has greatly affected American and European pigeon-holing of African Traditional Religions, as of all non-Christian religions. It has led to the disparagement both of these religions and of their ultimate source - the Divine "ECONOMIA" which is "suited to the practical wants of the multitude, as teaching them in the simplest way the active presence of Him, who after all dwells intelligibly, prior to argument, in their heart and conscience"[7].

This indeed is a grave disparagement of the dealings of Providence with mankind. I should like to think that "the mystery of God's purpose" ("mystērion tou thelēmatos") and "the hidden plan of salvation He so kindly made in Christ from the beginning" ("Oikonomian tou plērōmatos tōn kairōn"), of which St. Paul in his letter to the Ephesians spoke (cf. Eph. 1,9-11), embraced not only the Mosaic and Christian dispensations, but with equal fitness, the general system of Providence by which the world's course is carried on; namely, all those "dispensations" or "economies" which display God's character in action (as opposed to the absolute perfection of the Eternal God, His everlasting and unchangeable quiescence) - His condescensions to the infirmity and peculiarity of human minds; "all shadowy representations of realities which are incomprehensible to creatures such as ourselves, who estimate everything by the rule of association and arrangement, by the notion of purpose and plan, objects and means, parts and whole"[8]. Asked John H. Newman: "What, for instance, is the revelation of general moral laws, their infringement, their tedious victory, the endurance of the wicked, and the winking at the times of ignorance but an 'Economia' of greater truths untold, the best practical communication of them which our minds in their present state will admit ? What are the phenomena of the external world, but a divine mode of conveying to the mind the realities of existence, individuality, and the influence of being on being, the best possible, though beguiling the imagination of most men with a harmless but unfounded belief in matter as distinct from the impressions on their senses ?"[9]

Surely, if God's love is universal in scope; if He is the God of the whole world, we must admit that the whole religious life of mankind is a "dynamic continuum", part of a continuous and human relationship to Him; moments of intersections of His grace, His initiative, His truth, with human faith, human response, human enlightenment. They all display complex relationships of attraction and repulsion, absorption, resistance and reinforcement in humanity's history[10]. Writes St. Irenaeus of Lyons in the second century: "There is but one and the same God who from the beginning to the end and by various dispensations, comes to the rescue of mankind"[11]. "And in each case", says Professor Hick, "the true believer experiences divine revelation, divine activity, divine claim, divine grace, divine love with the same quality of absoluteness. In each case the human capacity for faith and worship is fully activated and a total response of devotion takes place. Why not, then, presume that the ultimate divine reality is in fact encountered and responded to in different ways in all these different streams of religious experience ?"[12]

One often wonders whether the coining and piecing together of special terms to designate African Traditional Religions - such terms as "ANIMISM", "ANIMATISM", "POLYDAEMONISM", "TRIBAL-Gods", "TRIBAL-RELIGIOUS PRACTICES", "CLAN-DIVINITIES", "HIGH-Gods", "NATURE-Gods", etc. - were meant to merely describe the supposed "pagan" religions or to exclude from them the anthropological situation - the "ontic intentionality" or goal, that is common to all human religions ! "The gods of the heathens are devils" !

These curious notions cause some uneasy feelings. Equally disturbing is the position of some modern "Africanists", some of them trained theologians, who fear risking the shelter of inoffensive but unhelpful silence or agnosticism. They object that these religions have no body of written doctrines and no sacred books. Some others tend to give uncriticial credence to what was written in the past by government officials, anthropologists and missionaries as expositions of traditional religious concepts. Writes Professor Evans-Pritchard: "Laymen may not be aware that most of what has been written in the past and with some assurance and still trotted out in colleges and universities about animism, totemism, magic, etc. has been shown to be erroneous, or at least dubious"[13]. And how often one is asked by an American or European friend or colleague: "Do many still worship idols ?" or "Gibt es in Afrika noch Abergläubige oder Götzendiener ?"

This uneasiness is more especially felt among those who were previously members of Traditional Religion, before they became Christians. "When I was a disciple of Plato, hearing the accusations made against the Christians and seeing them intrepid in the face of death and of all that men fear, I said to myself that it was impossible that they should be living in evil and in the love of pleasure". This remark was made by St. Justin Martyr on the falsity of what he heard concerning Christians of his century[14].

In this dilemma another difficulty crops up. Here the ground is dangerous, honey-combed, in fact with snares, a fresh hazard. It is a danger of twin perilous pitfalls. It is easy to read into the Traditional Religion that which is not there and at the same time fail to grasp what is there. Reinterpretation is called for but it itself has its dangers. This difficulty is concomitant with what might well be described as the "pathemata" of one's immediate philosophical and theological milieu, doctrinal truths and prejudices. Yet it scarcely needs be emphasized that a spade must be called by its known name (using the language available to us). Truth and sincerity are called for as two primary conditions, as imperative as they are essential. Exaggerations are as much falsifications of the truth as silence is. It is necessary that I approach this study, and I borrow the words of Major Leonard: "from that most Catholic standpoint of all which sees the good and not only the evil, that is in everything, that tolerant standpoint which sees eye to eye and soul to soul - i.e. without bias and partiality, but with sympathy as well as reason"[15]. And above all respecting that "Divine ECONOMIA" towards all mankind, Divine Providence inculcating in all "the principles of piety and morality, and containing the portions and foreshadowings of the Truth"; or as Clement of Alexandria put it: "all good doctrine in every one... all precepts of holiness combined with religious knowledge..."[16].

Perhaps I should add that this is the time when the good of the Church demands from us at least the gift of plain speaking. As Pope Pius XII said: "The tasks of the Church are too immense today to leave room for petty disputes. In order to preserve the sphere of action of each, it is sufficient that each possess enough spirit of faith, disinterestedness and mutual esteem and confidence."[17]

The following pages deal with the scope, aim and purpose of my work. Everywhere we find man and religion. What is man, this quintessence of dust as Hamlet described him; man, the individual and unique person that each of us knows himself to be; man in his collective aspects and man in his history, his present predicaments and his future prospects ? What is the meaning and purpose of life ? What is the origin and purpose of suffering ? Which is the way to true happiness ? What is goodness ? What is death and life after death ? What, lastly, is that ultimate and indescribable mystery embracing the whole of his existence - his origin and his end ?- all these demand doctrinal answers. Such answers depend upon man's conception of the Ruler of the Universe, while upon the answers themselves depends man's attitude to life. And, even the pattern of life within any given society is an expression of a particular view of man held by that society. The practices of religion and political life are as much the outcome of that society's doctrine of God as it is of its estimate of man[18].

That is, in other words, this study aims at exploring and expanding the Igbo answer to the age-old and enigmatic problem, the question of questions for mankind, the ultimate meaning of human existence as made manifest in their traditional socio-religious life and in relationship to Chukwu, God. Said B. Malinowski: "Of all sources of religion the supreme and final crisis of life - death - is of the greatest importance. Death is the gateway to the other world in more than the literal sense"[19].

In his book, "The Religion of the Semites", William Robertson Smith observed: "No positive religion that has moved men, has been able to start with a tabula rasa and express itself as if religion were beginning for the first time; in form if not in substance the new system must be in contact all along the time with the older ideas and practices which it finds in possession. A new scheme of faith can find a hearing only by appealing to religious instincts and susceptibilities that already exist in its audience, and it cannot reach these without taking into account the traditional forms in which all religious feeling is embodied and without speaking the language which men accustomed to these old forms can understand"[20]. And John H. Newman, rejecting the utter impropriety of ridiculing and satiring of "pagan" religions as a means of preparing neophytes for the reception of the Christian faith, remarked that the mind is often compared to a tablet or blank paper; a state of absolute freedom from all prepossessions and likings for one system or another, as a first step towards arriving at the truth. Infidelity is represented as that candid and dispassionate frame of mind, which is the desideratum. "But in truth, the mind never can resemble a blank paper, in its freedom from impressions and prejudices. Infidelity is a positive, not a negative state; it is a state of profaneness, pride and selfishness; and he who believes a little, but encompasses that little with the inventions of men, is undeniably in a better condition than he who blots out from his mind both the human inventions, and that portion of truth which was concealed in them"[21]. It goes without saying that things we learnt from our very childhood develop with our soul and are part of it.

In recent years there has been intensified study of religions; and this has brought in its train a tremendous awareness of the sheer size and really persistent, abiding, ever new expressions of living religion outside the borders of Christendom, and this after a two thousand years' history of Christianity and Christian evangelization, what Karl Rahner termed "the greatest scandal and challenge for Christianity" ("das größte Ärgenis und die größte Anfechtung für das Christentum"); for no other religion, not even Islam, proclaims itself so absolutely to be "the" Religion, to be the one and only valid revelation of the one living God[22]. The estimated Christian population of the world is 983.6 million, constituting just under a quarter of the world's total population of 4123.9 million[23]. The growth of human population is taking place more rapidly outside Christendom than within it. Remarked W.C. Smith: "The pew, if not yet the pulpit, the undergraduate if not yet the Seminary professor, has begun to recognize not only that the Christian answers on man's cosmic quality are not the only answers but even that the Christian questions are not the only questions. The awareness of multiformity is becoming vivid and compelling"[24].

This problem of the existence of religious pluralism (formerly "more or less interesting footnotes to what was largely a Western debate about other religions" and now being referred to as the "having our Copernican Revolution but not yet our Newton")[25], is especially heightened in our day. Today every man is neighbour to every other man in the world[26], and therefore influenced by communications with every existential, global situation. Every existing religion, in a way similar to all cultural realities of the "other", has become a challenge and a possibility for every "I"; and like the culture of the other, it is experienced as a relativization of one's own, demanding a real and existential response. As Visser't Hooft rightly put it: "The pluralistic world throws us all back on the primary source of our faith and forces us to take a new look at the world around us"[27].

If that new look at "the primary source of our faith" and "at the world around us", has, perhaps, aroused in some people the temptations of relativism, syncretism and agnosticism, and has become for many a stimulus for a greater deepening of their own religious vision of life[28], it is for some others more than a mere theological problem. Catholics and Non-Catholics alike have wondered who could be outside God's plan of salvation for all mankind; the one God, indeed, who desires the salvation of all men and wants all men to reach the full knowledge of the truth. Does not the divine love for all mankind and divine lordship over all life exclude the idea that salvation occurs only in one strand of human history, which is limited in time to the last nineteen centuries, and in space virtually to the western hemisphere ?

Is the restriction of salvation to any one religion or creed or race[29] not, in fact, a restriction of the universal and loving Fatherhood of God, the personal,present, living, active and acting, succouring Reality, who is seeking man, making Himself known to him "multifariam, multisque modis", and revealing to him his (man's) own nature and destiny, and man's responsive soul reaching out for Him according to his native capacity ?[30]

The traditional Christian doctrine is not that there is only one person in God, namely Christ, but really three persons,

God the Father, Son and Holy Spirit. Is God the creator ? If so, then is He not to be known in Creation ? Is God active in history ? If so, is His spirit totally absent from history, including even the history of other men's faiths ? Would all religions, in this light, not have a common ground - and indeed a common goal, in the Unknown, the Future, and perchance in the Beyond ? - in the Divine Spirit ever pressing the finite mind onward towards a further light and fuller consciousness, the Spirit, which "indwells the finite spirit, and whose ultimate union with it is the purpose of the whole many-sided process" ?[31]

For practical purposes we know well enough what is meant by "Revealed Religion". It is the doctrine taught in the Mosaic and Christian dispensations and contained in the Holy Scriptures, and is from God in a unique sense, in a sense in which no other doctrine can be said to be from Him ! Yet if we would speak correctly we must also confess, on the authority of the Bible itself, that all religious knowledge is from Him, and not only that which the Bible has transmitted to us. There never was a time when God has not spoken to man and told him to a certain extent his duty; never a time did He leave Himself without witness in the world and in every nation, and never a time He did not accept those who fear and obey Him. This both the Old and New Testaments tell us.

And again Newman writes: "It would seem, then, there is something true and divinely revealed, in every religion all over the earth, over-loaded as it may be, and at times even stifled by the impieties which the corrupt will and understanding of man have incorporated with it. Such are the doctrines of the power and presence of an invisible God, of His moral law and governance, of the obligation of duty, and the certainty of a just judgment, and of reward and punishment, as eventually dispensed to individuals; so that Revelation, properly speaking, is an universal, not a local gift; and the distinction between the state of Israelites formerly and Christians now, and that of the heathen, is not that we can, and they cannot attain to future blessedness, but that the Church of God ever has had, and the rest of mankind never have had, authoritative documents of truth, and appointed channels of communication with Him...all men have had more or less the guidance of Tradition in addition to those internal notions of right and wrong which the Spirit has put into the heart of each individual.

"The vague and uncertain family of religious truths, originally from God, but sojourning without the sanction of miracles, or a definite home, as pilgrims up and down the world, and discernible and separable from the corrupt legend with which they are mixed, by the spiritual mind alone, may be called the Dispensation of Paganism"[32].

In other words, despite the fact that the divine order is continually deflected by the downward gravitation of human nature to its own selfish ends, God has not abandoned His creation. He communicates to man, by the action of the Holy Spirit, the spiritual power of divine love which alone is capable of transforming human nature. As the natural force of self-love draws man down to "disorder and death", the supernatural power of the love of God draws him back to "order and life". As the centrifugal and destructive power of self-love corrodes his will, so the unitive and divine love moves his will and creates in his soul, in the individual soul, the "City of God". Hence St. Augustine said that there are many who seem to be outside who are within and many who seem to be within who are outside[33]; and, more, that there are those outside the communion of the Church "whom the Father, who sees in secret crowns in secret"[34].

Granted that the Christian anthropological situation is "a supernatural gift, a new creation"; that its special goal is the divinization of man; and its unique knowledge of God is a "gnoseological intentionality": it is the gnosis that God is Trinity and our union is with God in Christ. But surely Christianity will not deny that God wants the salvation of all men and therefore His "grace of newness" somehow descends upon all human beings[35]; nor will it contest that its "ontic intentionality" ultimately is the total realization of human fullness - authentic humanness. Or to put it in another way, losing our humanness in order to acquire godliness ! Writes R. Latourelle: Underlying all the manifestations of God "is one single movement, one single palpitation of love which has its origin in the Trinity and is felt throughout all time culminating in vision... . Revelation is thus not a human doctrine, but a gift of love, a doctrine which stirs up faith, gives rise to life in those who believe and leads them towards vision and immortality"[36]. And Irenaeus would write: "The will and operation of God is the creative and providential cause of every time and place and age and every nature. The reason that is in us is the will of the intellectual soul, as being its self-actuating power. Will is the mind desiring, and desire, and thinking, inclining itself to the object of its desire"[37]. All these are facilated because God "is very near in virtue of that power which holds all things in its embrace... . For the power of God is always present, in contact with us, in the exercise of inspection, of beneficience, of instruction", says Clement of Alexandria[38]. Hence, too, he exclaims: "How can we take up a position of hostility to God ? Knowledge...is characterized by faith; and faith by a kind of divine mutual and reciprocal correspondence, becomes characterized by knowledge"[39].

I should like to add that, because "God is a God that draws near... [though] in essence remote"; because "He is very near in virtue of His power which holds all things in its embrace"; because His "power is always present, in contact with all in the exercise of inspection, of beneficience and of instruction"; because He is the God to whom all men belong, the Teacher "who instructs the enlightened Christian by mysteries, and the faithful labourer by cheerful hopes, and the hard of heart with His keen corrective discipline, so that His providence is particular, public and universal..."; because "He it is who gave to the Greeks their philosophy by His ministering Angels...for He is the Saviour not of these or those, but of all... . His precepts, both the former and the latter, are drawn forth from one fount"; because it is He who led "Greek and barbarian forward by a separate process to that perfection which is through faith"[40] - because of all these and similar reasons the strenuous efforts of some modern Catholic theologians[41] to escape from the unacceptable implications of the older Christian view of looking "at other faiths as areas of spiritual darkness within which there is no salvation, no knowledge of God, no acceptable worship, without feeling entitled explicitly to renounce it", have been criticized. The universalistic role attributed to Christ in all religions (even where he is not accepted), the extension of the Church to include even those who could have nothing to do with her, and the restriction of divine economy of salvation to the mosaic and Christian dispensations have been described as constructing "Epicycles added to a Ptolemaic theology"[42]. Some of the critics argue that the solution does not theologically account for how the fact of man's religious diversity exists at all: "We explain the fact that the Milky Way is there by the doctrine of creation, but how do we explain the fact that the Bhagavad Gita is there"[43].

In other words: why is it an unreasonable notion to hold that there might have been some other poets and sages or sibyls divinely illuminated and organs through whom religious and moral truth was conveyed to their countrymen ?[44]

The uniqueness of the experiences of falling in love, of intellectual illumination or being grasped by some important truth, and of being whole-heartedly loyal to a cause, vary from person to person. In each of these experiences, the uniqueness has not only a tentative or provisional absolute and unqualified character, but may even demand to be expressed in the language of ultimates - the perfect unity of two hearts in love; total illumination; absolute loyalty. Certainly, it is inherently unavoidable that one's own experience may be the normative and everyone else's is seen in relation to this as the centre. But in these non-religious experiences it is quite clear that it is also legitimate to stand outside the experience itself and to describe it, without in any way thereby downgrading anyone else's. In other words one does not need to assume, because one's own love, or insight, or loyalty has the absolute and authentic character that it has, that other people's love, insight or loyalty must be less absolute, less authentic, less assured, or that they do not exist at all. It is equally true that one's absolute and valid experience of a saving encounter with God does not in itself preclude that there are other encounters with the same God exhibiting similar characteristics.

Ernst Troeltsch, the German theologian and philosopher, gave classic expression to this thought in his 1923 Oxford Lecture on the place of christianity among the world religions. He pointed out that christianity has been a manifestation of the divine life to the europeans.

> The evidence we have, [he says], for this remains essentially the same, whatever may be our theory concerning

> absolute validity - it is the evidence of a profound inner experience. This experience is undoubtedly the criterion of its validity, but, be it noted, only of its validity for us. It is God's countenance as revealed to us; it is the way in which, being what we are, we receive, and react to, the revelation of God. It is binding upon us, and it brings us deliverance. It is final and unconditional for us, because we have nothing else, and because in what we have we can recognize the accents of the divine voice. But this does not preclude the possibility that other racial groups, living under entirely different cultural conditions may experience their contact with the Divine Life in a quite different way, and may themselves also possess a religion which has grown up with them, and from which they cannot sever themselves so long as they remain what they are. And they may quite sincerely regard this as absolutely valid for them, and give expression to this religious feeling.(45)

To state it starkly: a comprehensive Christian theology would need to attend to the verification and credibility of the absolute climax of the divine self-communication in the life, death and resurrection of Jesus Christ, and the identification of the Christian (indeed Catholic) community as the people specially guided by the Holy Spirit, and other people's experiences of a saving encounter with God as less absolute, less authentic, less assured.

I should like to think that our theology should take a much closer look as the vital contact with tradition, slough off many of the habits of mind and action peculiar to the defensive spirit of the Reformation and the Counter Reformation and come to grips with the world in which we now find ourselves. Remarks Professor W.C. Smith: "The fallacy of relentless exclusivism is becoming more obvious than is the right way of reconciling a truly Christian charity and perceptivity with doctrinal adequacy"[46]. And Fr. R. Panikkar, I might add, was right, when he warned that "we should beware of the danger of dogmatolatry"[47]. For the mind of man cannot imprison the whole of God's truth in any formula of words. Nor should it be overlooked that creeds and dogmas are designed to meet particular situations and are necessarily affected by the world-view, the psychology and philosophy of the age as also the particular heretical threat of the period. Thus creeds would become idols if they became so sacro-sanct regardless of factual evidence[48].

Catholicism will be nearing, in 1985, its centenary in Igboland (the Protestant Christian Churches have already celebrated theirs in 1957). Yet Catholicism is still to be incarnated deeply in its soil. The religious feelings, instincts and susceptibilities of the Igbo people, "that portion of truth that was concealed in them" and the things they had learnt from their very childhood, and which developed in their religious outlook and are part of it, are being cut off. In their stead new religious dimensions and perspectives are being given to them, but still mostly in foreign categories and also too pregnant with yet-undetermined possibilities. This is most noticeable in the number of people who frequent"prayer-houses" or revert to their traditional ways of life when they have crises of faith. Could this mean that we have not endeavoured to connect Christianity with their previous religious sentiments and susceptibilities and that we do not speak their language ? Perhaps they are pointers that sound evangelization, which is rooted in the theandric Christ (with emphasis on theandric) is badly needed if the Gospel message is to survive and be rooted deeply in our native soil.

As Pope Paul VI rightly observed: We Africans are missionaries to our own people. The task of unfolding more and more the mystery of God in our concrete perspectives, unfathoming the inner nature of the supreme, developing African theologies that would suit these cultural backgrounds, is ours.

If these observations have any significance, then the reason, aim and purpose of this work should be clear. It seeks to open up new horizons or religious springboards which will be of value to the Gospel-carriers in Igboland and above all to inter-faith dialogue.

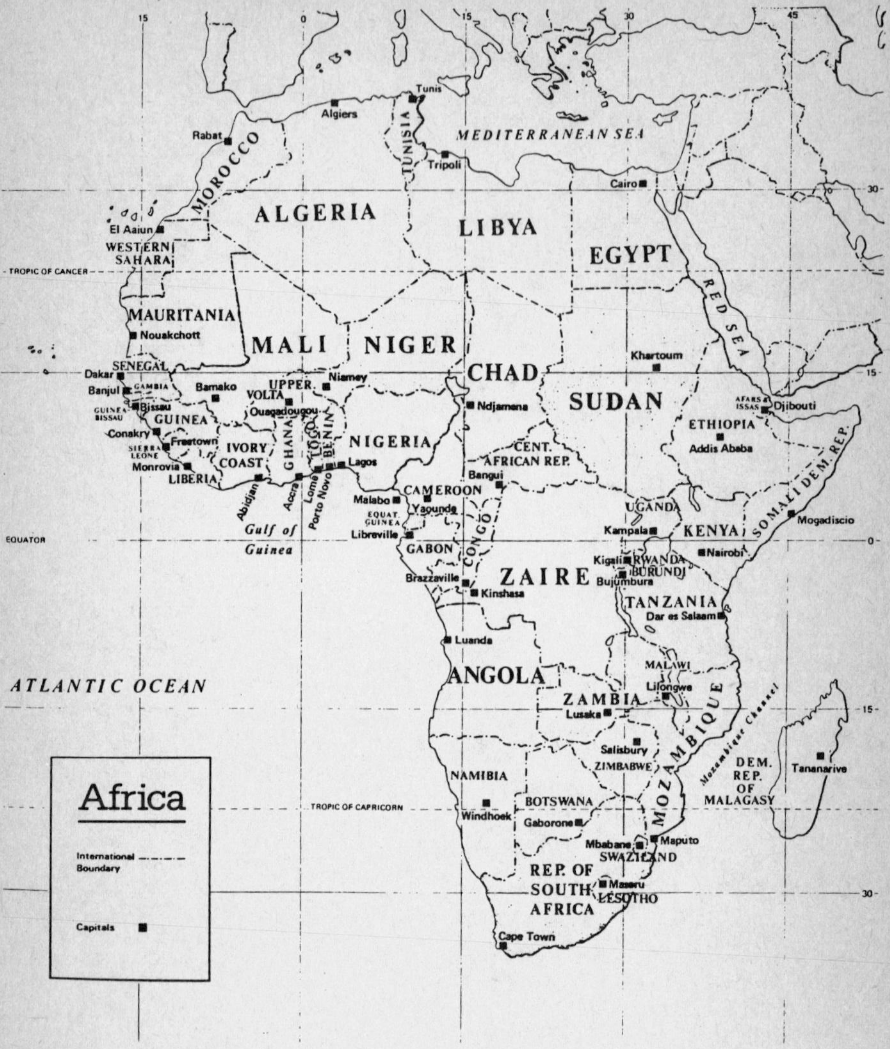
Africa
International Boundary
Capitals
MEDITERRANEAN SEA
ATLANTIC OCEAN
RED SEA
Gulf of Guinea
Mozambique Channel
TROPIC OF CANCER
TROPIC OF CAPRICORN
EQUATOR
MOROCCO
Rabat
ALGERIA
Algiers
TUNISIA
Tunis
LIBYA
Tripoli
EGYPT
Cairo
WESTERN SAHARA
El Aaiun
MAURITANIA
Nouakchott
SENEGAL
Dakar
GAMBIA
Banjul
GUINEA BISSAU
Bissau
GUINEA
Conakry
SIERRA LEONE
Freetown
LIBERIA
Monrovia
IVORY COAST
Abidjan
MALI
Bamako
UPPER VOLTA
Ouagadougou
GHANA
Accra
TOGO
Lome
BENIN
Porto Novo
NIGER
Niamey
NIGERIA
Lagos
CHAD
Ndjamena
SUDAN
Khartoum
ETHIOPIA
Addis Ababa
AFARS & ISSAS
Djibouti
SOMALI DEM. REP.
Mogadiscio
CENT. AFRICAN REP.
Bangui
CAMEROON
Yaounde
Malabo
EQUAT. GUINEA
GABON
Libreville
CONGO
Brazzaville
ZAIRE
Kinshasa
UGANDA
Kampala
KENYA
Nairobi
RWANDA
Kigali
BURUNDI
Bujumbura
TANZANIA
Dar es Salaam
ANGOLA
Luanda
ZAMBIA
Lusaka
MALAWI
Lilongwe
MOZAMBIQUE
Maputo
ZIMBABWE
Salisbury
NAMIBIA
Windhoek
BOTSWANA
Gaborone
SWAZILAND
Mbabane
LESOTHO
Maseru
REP. OF SOUTH AFRICA
Cape Town
DEM. REP. OF MALAGASY
Tananarive

FIG. 1

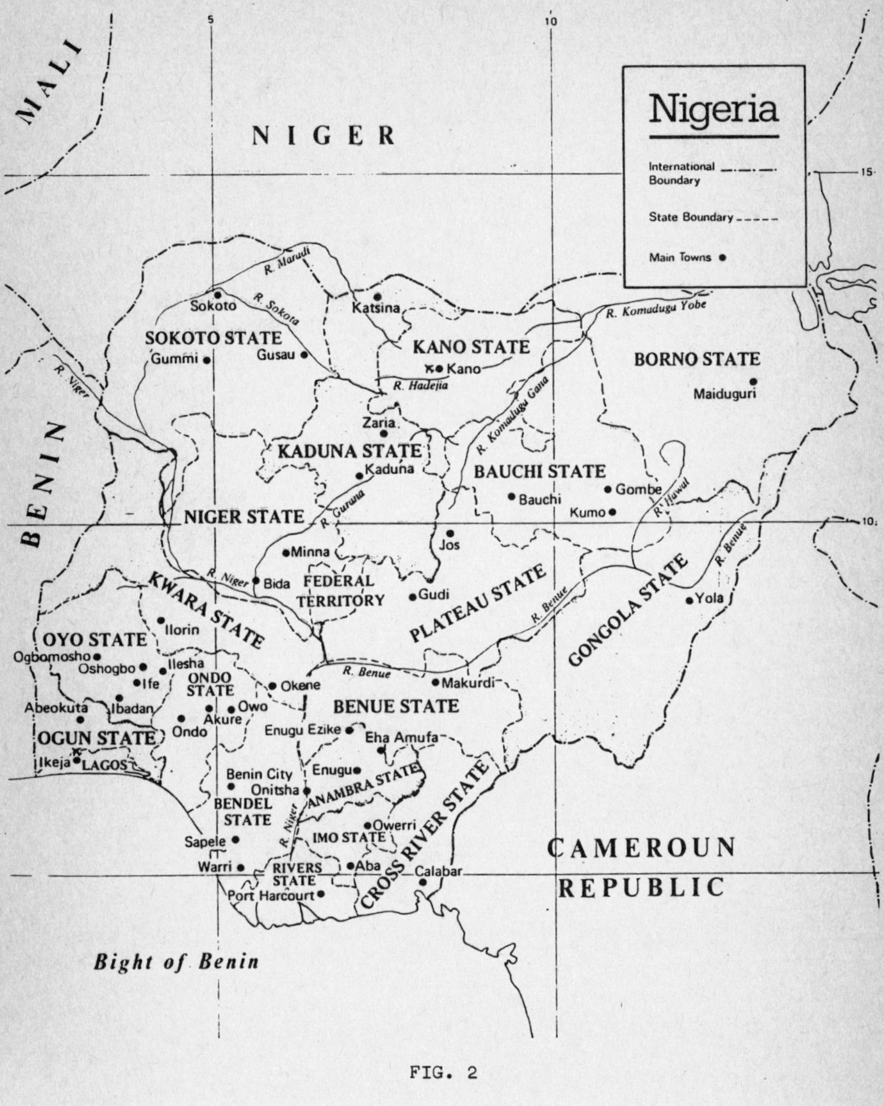
Nigeria
International Boundary
State Boundary
Main Towns
MALI
NIGER
BENIN
CAMEROUN REPUBLIC
Bight of Benin
SOKOTO STATE
KANO STATE
BORNO STATE
KADUNA STATE
BAUCHI STATE
NIGER STATE
KWARA STATE
FEDERAL TERRITORY
PLATEAU STATE
GONGOLA STATE
OYO STATE
ONDO STATE
BENUE STATE
OGUN STATE
LAGOS
BENDEL STATE
ANAMBRA STATE
IMO STATE
RIVERS STATE
CROSS RIVER STATE
Sokoto
Katsina
Gummi
Gusau
Kano
Maiduguri
Zaria
Kaduna
Gombe
Bauchi
Kumo
Jos
Minna
Bida
Gudi
Yola
Ilorin
Ogbomosho
Oshogbo
Ilesha
Ife
Okene
Makurdi
Abeokuta
Ibadan
Owo
Akure
Ondo
Enugu Ezike
Eha Amufa
Ikeja
Enugu
Benin City
Onitsha
Owerri
Sapele
Warri
Aba
Calabar
Port Harcourt
R. Maradi
R. Sokoto
R. Niger
R. Hadejia
R. Komadugu Yobe
R. Komadugu Gana
R. Guruna
R. Hawal
R. Benue
5
10
15
10

FIG. 2

CHAPTER TWO: ETHNOGRAPHICAL SURVEY

2.1 Igbo: Culture area or land, language and people

The Igbo of South-East Nigeria speak the same language, though with some dialetical differences. They also occupy a continuous geographical delimitation of areas and have in common the same dominant and significant cultural traits, complexes or elements developed around socio-cultural, political, economic, ritual and other cultural themes; again with understandable varieties among the different groupings[49]. Because of these factors we speak of them as a single people and the territory they occupy as Igboland or Igbo Culture Area. This lies between 5° and 7° north of the Equator and between the 6° and 8° east of the Greenwich meridan, spanning the river Niger about midway between the Niger-Benue confluence to the North and the Atlantic to the South. It embraces an area of some 15,800 square miles[50]. The Igbo live on both sides of the lower Niger with the greater territory and population (which had been variously estimated: some say 8.5 million; some other 9 million)[51], concentrated on the Eastern sector - in Anambra and Imo States. The rest live in the north and east of the Rivers and Bendel states respectively.

Traditionally they are predominantly farmers and traders. They exploit the palm produce in the equatorial forest and cultivate yams, coco-yams, maize and cassava. Domestic technology in bronze-casting, iron-work and pottery dates back to the 9th century A.D. as the Igbo-Ukwu archaeological finds indicate. Excellent craftsmanship still exists in wood and ivory carvings, woodwork and pottery[52].

Politically, the Igbo were not formally unified in this sense: before the advent of the Europeans there was no all-territorially pervasive and politically centralized organization among them. But "their highly political organization developed along its own unique lines" and certain interconnections - principal among them being rituals, economy, politics and exogamous marriages - linked them horizontally one with another in all directions like "a well-articulated sheet of chain of mail"[53].

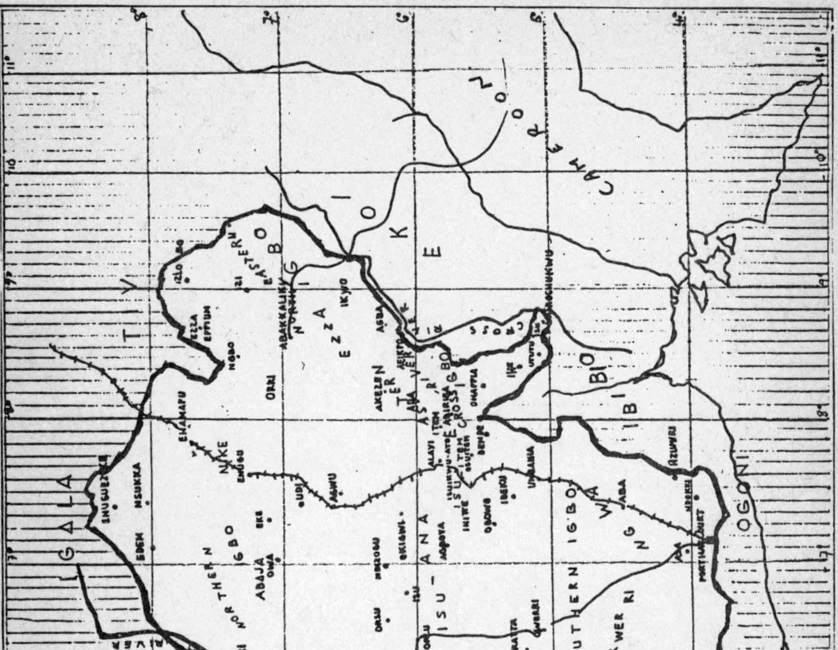
NORTHERN IGBO
SOUTHERN IGBO
ISOKO
IJAW
OGONI
BINI
ONITSHA
ABAKALIKI
ENUGU
NSUKKA
AGBOR
OWERRI

FIG. 3

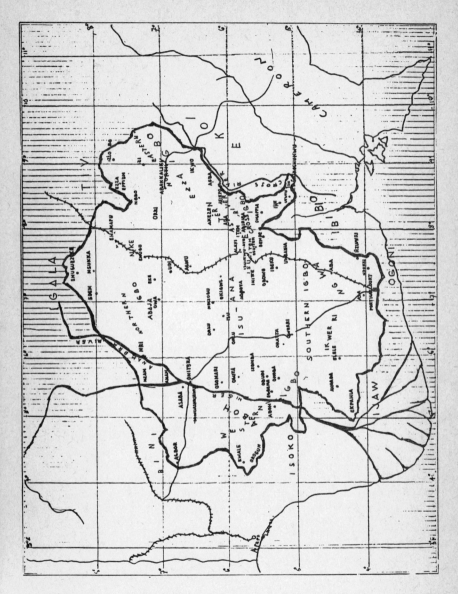

Linguistically according to Greenberg's classification of African Languages the Igbo Language is one of the speech communities in the Kwa sub-family of the Niger-Congo family[54]. Igbo language is marked by a complicated system of tones used to distinguish meaning and grammatical relationships; a wide range of dialectical variations that is a source of difficulty to Westerners; and a tendency to vowel elision which makes it difficult to express a few of the spoken words in writing. "If we follow a longitudinal dialectic profile, we encounter mutual intelligibility between the communities at the centre and those at the poles" but between the polar communities intelligibility varies from partial to almost nil. These polar dialects are the results of greater marginal isolation rather than survivors of a previous dialectical cradle-land[55].

When and from where the Igbo came into their present territory is not known. Their historical origin is a subject of much speculation. The people have no common tradition of origin[56]. "Americans know", says Ojike, "that their contemporary society began when in 1620, the Mayflower docked. This is precise whatever one can make of it"[57]. As regards the Igbo with no written words or permanent buildings, proofs are hard to come by, and therefore no one can utter with historical authenticity, how, when and whence the indigenuous Igbo communities emerged. Both about them and their neighbours little is known. What local traditions the Igbo have do not provide clues to their origin or migration, if any ! The most one can say is that for centuries they had lived in their present homeland[58]. A French correspondent of "L'Express", as if echoing this says: "Ils semblent avoir toujours été là, c'est le seul des grands peuples de Nigeria qui n'ait aucune tradition de migration"[59].

It is because of this obscurity concerning their historical background that some early Western writers during the colonial era treated the Igbo as "a people without history"[60]. This view has been criticised; the critics argue that a people with a culture are a people with history. The Igbo have a culture; they have also a history - an unwritten history which the historian of culture has to piece together[61].

In fact recent archaelogical evidence[62] and studies[63] reveal that Igbo land has been under continuous occupation for at least 3,000 years and that her people developed an ancient civilization a thousand years ago, which is about half a millennium before the emergence of the Kingdom of Benin. One can only hope that the scientific researches going on will continue to throw some light on what is now obscure.

In this regard it may be remarked that there is an observable tendency of some of us Africans - some of them with scholarly niceties - trying to glorify our largely uncharted past and to indulge in wild and mythical speculations about some respectable ancestry for it in Egypt or even in Mesopotamia. Others had aimed to prove the influence of Hebraic or some other oriental religions and customs on West Africa and perhaps thereby to trace the origin of any cultural development of the latter to the former[64]. These tendencies, to say the least, seem to savour unconsciously the notion of the so-called "natural and inherent inferiority" of the negroids - a notion favoured by some "Africanists", and "has settled", as Davidson put it, "like a layer of dust and ashes on the minds of a large number of otherwise thoughtful people and is constantly swirled about "despite all factual evidence to the contrary". Though it has vanished from open "serious discussion, these opinions still retain a kind of underground existence"[65].

Irresistible and attractive though such hypotheses may be, it must be borne in mind that correct knowledge is more important than theory. Besides no human being need have a methusalem sort of historical origin and culture in order to be treated with dignity and humanity.

IGBO SOCIO-RELIGIOUS STRUCTURE

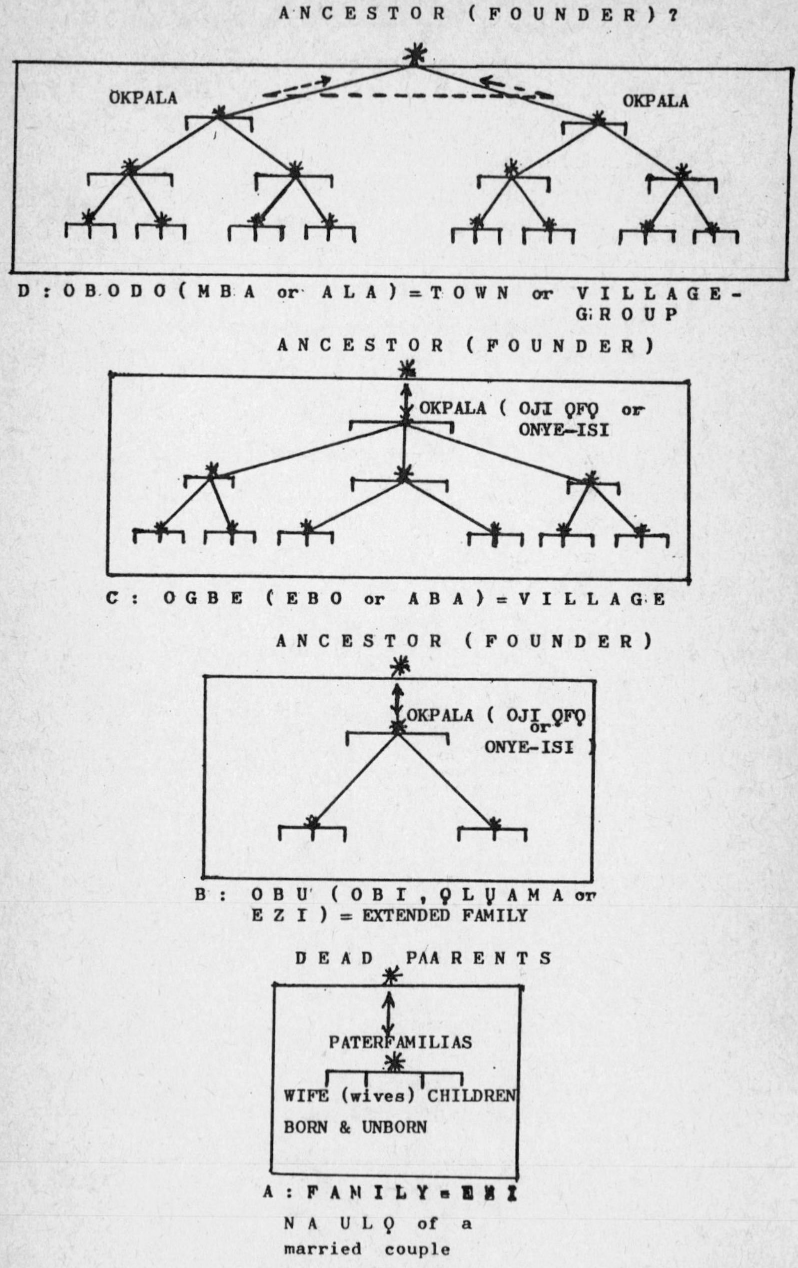

FIG. 4

2.2 Socio-religious structure in traditional Igbo society: Maintenance of Law and Order

2.2.1 The Igbo socio-political system stresses social mobility

The Igbo "uncommonly among Africans, have been markedly success orientated; egalitarian but individualistic, they have thought it an essential aspect of the 'right and natural' that talent should lead to enterprise, and enterprise to promotion, and promotion to privilege. They have insistently stressed social mobility"[66]. Thus"they have been poles apart from their neighbours across the Niger, the aristocratically governed Yoruba, whose hierarchies were laid down in heaven and have ever since persisted in supremely complacent assurance of their worth and value. Encased in such hierarchies, the Yoruba built urban states of imposing rank and ceremony, and an Empire that was at one time among the largest of its kind. But not the Igbo: their clamorous and personal democracy was based on dispersal of authority"[67]. They have always been jealous of their legislative authority and are not willing to surrender it to a small group of individuals[68].

Mazi Mbonu Ojike called the Igbo system of political organization "gerontocracy-ohachi"[69]. Professor J.C. Anene preferred to describe it as "village-democracies" and remarked that subtlety and complexity and stability characterized the manner in which the Igbo communities organized their political life[70]. Mrs. Sylvia Leith-Ross describing the structure says that the organization which did actually exist was "tenuous and intricate"[71]. And indeed the Igbo system of social organization is harder to analyse, and so harder to define, than the kind of social system which unites upwards to a king or supreme chief, for it rested on complicated arrangements and distribution of political power[72].

Perhaps it needs be said that in the past the Igbo traditional system of social organization as well as those of their neighbours south-east of the Niger - the Efiks, Ekoi, Ibibios and Ijaw (Ijo) had been described as lacking in cohesion and as being low in the scale of political organization, especially when compared to the highly centralized monarchies and states of the Western pattern. But modern ethnographers and historians have criticized such comparisons as having no scientific basis, because, they argue, "no universal criteria for comparisons of this sort exist"[73]. Professor M.J. Herskovits has said: "Scholars drawing comparisons of this nature have merely reacted to their own conditioning which has given them a predisposition to favour their own customs and place differing cultures on levels which are deemed less advanced"[74]. And Piddington emphatically remarked: "No human community is any lower, earlier or more ancient than any other. All represent highly specialized human adaptations, the product of millennia of traditionalized cultural life"[75].

With this in view it suffices to observe that our aim here is not to prove that the Igbo, before their contact with the West, have had their social organization, however unique. Rather what we intend to do here is to study this traditional system which, as J.C. Anene remarked was the product of evironmental and other circumstances peculiar to their communities[76]; and "it served well the needs of their days"[77].

2.2.2 Why socio-religious ?

We have termed this section "socio-religious" because in traditional Igbo communities both social and religious units were often rolled in one. It is (1) social or socio-political because they are traditionally reputed to be built on a foundation of kinship, and always have had some recognized authority - a council of elders or other body, who "made" its laws and saw to their enforcement, controlled the use of its land and generally managed its affairs. It is (2) religious because in the traditional Igbo societies "OMENALA" or "ODINANI" (which is a generic term for the body of Igbo socio-religious laws, customs and traditions passing from generation to generation) is believed to have been handed down to the people's ancestors from God, Chukwu, through the Earth-spirit, Ala (Ana). Thus Igbo Omenala is related to ancestralism and the cult of the Earth-spirit, and eventually, to the cult of God[78]. Consequently making new laws or better when emergency laws were promulgated, they were always ratified by the elders and given a divine sanction by invoking the approval of the ancestors. Further the head of each such socio-religious grouping is ipso facto a priest, a principal intermediary between his people and the ancestors in one capacity or the other. Secular and ritual roles are combined. Also the elders (or the ozo-title holders, "institutionalised natural rulers" with more secular roles, who also sometimes displaced the elders) were/are still fundamentally the representatives and mouth-piece of the ancestors. Their sacred staff of office, called "ofor", symbolizes the authority of the ancestors and is venerated as the embodiment of the supernatural world and all the spirits of the ancestors. Thus each unit-head possesses domestic authority (quasi socio-political) as well as religious and is an intermediary between his unit and the ancestors on whose good will the members of the unit set great store. Thus it is clear that there is no clear cut or rigid distinction between the religious and purely social organization or act. Rather in these two realities - religion and sociology - the Igbo, as other Africans, always seek their ultimate good[79]. And so these two realities, though distinct in principle are yet very closely interwoven, such that social life is a religious affair and a religious cult is a social act[80].

2.2.3 <u>The structure</u>

Generally it can be said that the Igbo share a common political system based on decentralization of power and delegation of authority exercised by the holder of the staff of authority, ofo. This is epitomized in the hierarchy of lineages called "Umunna". But there are also those with centralized authority superimposed on the hierachies of the patrilineages (as in Aboh, Agbor, Aguleri, Aro-Chukwu, Nri, Oguta, Ogwashi-Ukwu and Onitsha)[81]; and some with a gerontocratic centralized system (as in Ibusa, Okpanam)[82].

Among the traditional instruments of government are the Age-grade associations, title-making societies, Dibia fraternities (priestly and medicine-men's associations), secret societies and

Aluse i.e. powerful spirits which have been institutionalized by a community to serve as a medium by which hidden knowledge and divine will might be ascertained; and resort to these when human tribunals had failed (Oracles).

It may be observed that the role of each of these associations in the political processes of a given village or village-town differs markedly. Despite these differences there emerges a general pattern of socio-religious process which is shared by all the Igbo communities. So we can to a very great extent speak of some homogeneity of Igbo socio-religious structure[83].

There are two layers of political structure : village and village-group or town (or "village-town" according to some authors)[84]. At the village level it is direct democracy, autonomous and sovereign; at the village-group or town level, it is representative with "equal sharing of kola"[85].

However, in order to get a thorough and clear insight of this "tenuous and intricate" organization, I propose to discuss it stage by stage. This method, it must be remarked, will entail some repetitions. So we begin with the smallest - the "nuclear" socio-religious grouping; this is the family, the "EZI NA ULO" of a married couple[86].

2.2.3.1 The nuclear (simple or elementary) family or nuclear socio-religious grouping: Ezi na ulo (Di na nwanyị + umu)

The "nuclear family" in the traditional Igbo society is made up of a man and his wife (wives)[87], their sons and their daughters as well as their dependants, if any[88]. So long as this man lives, all his issues (less the married daughters) are regarded by the Igbo law and custom as his dependants. He represents them both collectively and individually according to need in their relationship with like social units. He is their spiritual head and he offers sacrifies on their behalf and blesses them.

His political (better, quasi political) authority as well as his priesthood is symbolized in his ofo-staff[89]. He acquires this as soon as he establishes his household. He may acquire more as he advances in his social status placement[90].

Thus every paterfamilias combines two offices in one person. At his death, the family may or may not break up. If the adult members of the family fail to agree among themselves they will partition the family land according to Igbo law and custom[91].

2.2.3.2 <u>The Obi (Obu, Oluama, Ezi or Ovu) alias extended-family structure</u>

When a son of the nuclear-family has reached the age of maturity and has a prosperous future or his parents are rich, his parents or he himself may suggest that he marries and establishes his own household[92]. In like manner, all other male children of the family establish theirs. In this way the nuclear family increases and becomes what is called Obi, (Obu, Ovu, Ezi) or extended (or joint) family[93]. All these male descendants of the nuclear family, their wiwes and issues (less the married daughters) who in turn might as well have married and begot children and their dependants form what we call in Igbo, "Obi" (Obu, Ovu, Ezi). This is the so-called extended family. It is sometimes called compound, hamlet or ward. It is so called because in the past, these 'families' lived in a vast walled - in or fenced premises with one entrance on the front and a tiny exit at the back. So the extended family or compound strictly speaking consists of a number of economically independent households each with a man or woman as a householder (e.g. a widow with her children)[94].

All the householders and their dependants have a compound head. This man is called the Okpala (Okpara or Diokpa). He is the eldest living male descendant of the eldest son of the nuclear family[95].

"Onye nwe ezi or obi" (as this compound Okpala is sometimes called) has numerous ritual, moral and legal rights and obligations. He offers sacrifices for the welfare of his compound members "whom he helps to extricate from their ritual, social and legal problems"; his symbol of authority and priesthood is the Ofo[96].

Ofo is the instrument of communication between the priest (including any paterfamilias) and ancestral spirits. Whoever takes charge of the ancestral ofo is regarded as the embodiment of the ancestral spirits. Thus this is the symbol of his office. The family's religious objects (e.g. the ancestral ofo) the family house or its site, and any property common to members of the family are in his care[97].

The Okpala settles the internal problems (for instance, matrimonial cases, pilferings and the like) of the members and confers a special name on each child born in the compound. "He is the eyes of his compound members and they are his ears", says an Igbo idiom. He represents them in their external dealings with other like social groups. An injury inflicted on any member of his group without his having been first notified is considered a personal injury for which he makes a personal repraisal if need be. Likewise if any member from his compound offends another like social grouping he should first be notified before the offender be revenged upon. In return the compound head receives respect, obedience and material tokens of good will from the members[98].

Victor Chikezie Uchendu says that all the householders and their dependants recognize the authority of the compound head and would not make a major political decision without first consulting with him[99].

Perhaps it needs be mentioned that the okpala is the head. But the extent of influence he wields within the group depends "on his personal qualities, powers, wealth, sagacity and personal charm". And though in theory the task of "legislation" and administration, as well as maintenance of law and order within the group rests on his shoulders, in practice whether "political" or legal or "merely social", he works in fullest collaboration with the council of elders (or the ozo-title-holders) Ndi Nze (Eze - where it is in vogue) agegrades (Ogbo or otu) and masquerades (whose importance here is very minimal) of the compound. Decisions are always taken after fullest possible consultation, formal and informal on a scale approaching universel "adult suffrage". Hence, S.N. Chinwuba Obi remarks, "we are now approaching a stage in the history of Ibo society, where there was and still is something of the nature of the early Greek democracy"[100].

2.2.3.3 The Umunna-unit, the patrilineal grouping

At the higher level than the compound units, we have the Umunna units. "Umunna" is a 'fluid term' in Igbo language. Its narrowest referent is the children of the same father but of a different mother i.e. in contradiction to Umunne (children of the same father and mother or of the same mother but not of the same father). Its widest referent is the group of localised patrilineal members, real or putative whom one cannot marry. And it is in this context we are using it in our discussion. Sometimes it is very loosely applied to members of a village or village-group in contradiction to all other like villages or village-groups[101]. Obi has remarked that the Umunna unit cannot "at this stage be called an extended family no matter how extended"[102].

Umunna unit comprises of all the compounds, Obi or Ezi or Oluama or Ovu of the descendants of the "nuclear paterfamilias" (the original founder) occupying the same territory and recognize the same immediate authority. The group is known by the name of their ancestor - one of the sons of the nuclear paterfamilias e.g. Umueze or Umuosu - children of Eze or Osu. From this it is clear that the constituent members of Umunna regard themselves as blood relatives. Thus the group is, too, exogamous and any "sexual relationship between its constituent members whether by birth or by marraige, is strictly forbidden". To go against this taboo is an abomination - Aru or Alu or Nso - which requires ritual purification before forgiveness is accorded[103].

But in most cases the ancestral founder is now so long lost in the midst of time that it is quite impossible to say how long ago he lived or to trace the relationship between the present members of the group in the terms of cousins and nephews and the like. It must be noted too, that there is often an immigrant intelement in the Umunna grouping who has been sufficiently integrated in the fabric as to cease to be treated as strangers[104].

Though every male head of each localised sub-patrilineage is termed Okpala and holds his personal ofo or his ozo-title - ofo (a symbol of priesthood and domestic authority)[105], in the Umunna unit, the most important ritual head or figure is the

Okpala. He is the eldest living male descendant of the eldest son of the original founder (he need not be the oldest man in the group so long as he belongs to the senior branch of it and is the oldest man therein)[106].

He holds the localised patrilineal ofo (ofo-umunna) which in Igbo political processes is very important. He derives his authority from the belief or fact that he is regarded as the intermediary between the lineage and the ancestors; and this authority-symbol (ritual-authority symbol) is the lineage ofo[107].

The Okpala is thus chief priest, principal intermediary between the "quick and the dead, the visible and invisible". He offers sacrifices to God through the Earth-spirit on behalf of all the members of the lineage[108].

His political power and the extent of his influence within the unit follow the same principle we enunciated in the "Obi" structure. The same principle holds for the maintenance of law and order within the group[109]. It needs be mentioned that in those societies where the ozo-title-holders (ndi nze or ndi eze) displace the Okpala and the elders, the Okpala should be made aware of what action is planned for he must give his opinion on matters conflicting with custom and tradition, Omenala. Sometimes, even when he does not belong to the actual ruling body (i.e. if he is not an "onye eze") he is made a ceremonial head whose activity concerns mainly divinely sanctioning what is agreed upon. Also the various associations (esp. the age-grade and masquerader play a much greater role in the Umunna unit than in the Obi unit; but a much less important role than in the village grouping. The Okpala cannot interfere in the internal affairs of the component members. Social and economic pressure, however, may well be used as effective way of forcing conformity with established norms as well as effective sanctions for voluntary deviation therefrom[110].

2.2.3.4 Village-unit

Higher than the localised patrilineal socio-religious units is the village. This term suffers greatly from ambiguity when translated. However various Igbo communities use "Ogbe" (mostly the Oru people, the Riverian Igbo) "Ebo" or "Aba" for village[111].

A village consists of a number of "localised patrilineal groups" (Umunna-units). It is founded on a number of ties and a claim of an ultimate common descent. But like the umunna unit the founder is now lost in the midst of time so that it is quite impossible to say how long ago he lived, or to trace the relationship between the present members of the group. The members occupy a common territory; have a common religious unifying patron or guardian, and common economic activities. Invariably they speak a common dialect. These factors greatly enhance the feeling of being a real unit; and in fact they are more effectively and closely pervading among the villagers than in the village-group unit[112]. A village is believed to be an offshot of the ancestral tree - a unit founded by one of the sons of the original founder of the village-group. For this reason the villagers use the term "Umunna", sometimes among themselves. Perhaps this might well explain why some foreigners use the name Umunna for a village[113]. But as Dr. Obi rightly remarked: "It is this all-pervading idea of blood relationship plus the Iboman's incurable habit of playing up the fact (or the fiction) of his close kinship ties with everybody else in his group that tends to blur the distinction between these various groupings"[114].

Because of the 'blood tie' (or should we say the supposed blood tie) between the villagers, villages in most parts of Igboland are exogamous units. But to this rule there are exceptions[115]. The area a village covers and the population it supports vary from place to place. The average population may well be somewhat over a thousand[116].

The village, like the Umunna unit, has its senior branch, the subdivision which represents the descendants of the eldest son of the founder of the village-group. The eldest man in this branch is again normally the holder of the senior - village - ofo. As usual his title is Okpala (Diokpa or Okpara). Like the Okpala of the Umunna unit, he need not be the oldest man in the village. Indeed he may be a baby in arms, provided he is the eldest living descendant of the original diokpala of the village[117].

Generally succession to the office of Okpala follows the

adelphic principle. It passes from the incumbent to his next brother in line rather than from father to son. For instance: Let us say that Okafor and Okonkwo were brothers; and Okafor was the elder of the two, when their father (whom we may call Okeke) died, Okafor would take over the headship of the group. After him, his brother, Okonkwo; and after Okonkwo, Okafor's first son; and after Okafor's son, Okonkwo's first son; and after Okonkwo's son, Okafor's first grandson; and after Okafor's first grandson Okonwkwo's first grandson would take over and so on[118]. Even in this principle it is not an automatic succession. Character is the overriding factor and a candidate qualified by the age-order principle, may be turned down because he is considered to have a questionable character for, as Mazi Mbonu Ojike emphasised: "The people are one and the same public. They vote, not on the basis of campaign oratory and promises but on the principle of the best man for all... Rulers are considered father of their people...and public office is a social responsibility rather than a privilege"[119].

However the effectiveness of the office depends on the personality of the office-holder, again on his prowess, wealth, sagacity and personal charm[120].

As was said earlier, government at village level is an exercise in direct democracy. It involves all lineages and requires the political participation of all the male adults. Though it forms part of the village-group (the town), the widest political community, the village is autonomous in its affairs and accepts no interference or dictation from any other group[121]. Even where the town or village-group has a recognized political head, in practice each village has a large measure of local autonomy. The rights of the Obi (King) and his council are so regulated by custom, that when they exceed their rights the offended village boycotts the Obi's palace; its Ndichie holds his own village court, presides over the government of his village[122].

The institutions which are utilised in the political processes of the village include "Amala" (Oha) - a general assembly, the title-making societies, the Dibia fraternity (a priestly association), the secret society, oracles and the age-grade associations[123].

Leadership is provided by the ofo-holders (or the titled men), men and women of wealth who have risen spontaneously in the village and have developed their power and influence gradually[124]. So the Okpala belonging to the actual ruling body depends on his physical, mental and temperamental endowments for effective leadership. Otherwise he remains a figure head with his official duties limited to ceremonial occasions[125].

Legislative activities are performed by all males meeting in ad hoc general assembly called the Amala, or Oha. The meeting place may be in an open square where all the paths of the village converge. Every villager who can contribute to the discussion is given a hearing. When the matter had been thoroughly talked out, the heads from each Umunna in the village retire for "izuzu" (consultation). After "izuzu" a spokesman is chosen - not necessarily because of age but because of his talents and his ability to put the verdict in perspective - to announce the decision. When a decision is accepted by the Amala, it is followed by general acclamation; when rejected, by shouts of derision. In the later event the view of the assembly prevails[126].

Once a decision has been thus acclaimed into law it is given a "ritual binder by the ofo holders", who invoke this formula: "This Iwu', law, is in accordance with our custom and must be obeyed and respected. "Those who refuse to obey the law, may ofo kill them". Each time the ofo is struck on the ground (mostly four times) the assembly assents with "iha - ise" (let it be so). This done it becomes a duty of each adult male and householder to explain the legislation to his household group and to see that the members respect the law[127].

It can hardly be over emphasised at this stage that neither this meeting in ad hoc general assembly (the amala) nor the council of elders (or ozo-titled men) is a legislative body in the orthodox sense of the word.

The meetings whether of elders or of the ad hoc meeting are neither formal nor frequent. They meet when it is necessary to take a common action like sacrifice or war or to settle an internal dispute which if allowed to continue would undermine the solidarity of the community. Nor is it necessary to prescribe formally any laws as deterrents against bad behaviour, for as was said earlier, every one accepted implicitly that any departure from the behaviour approved by God, Ala and the ancestors, was likely to incur the displeasure and vengeance of the ancestors to whom these laws were handed on by God, through the Earth-spirit[128].

Consequently, there was no institutionalised judiciary. Judicial proceedings are informal and are aimed, too, at restoring solidarity, and often are ad hoc affairs[129]. The injured party takes the initiative in most cases. He may appeal to the head of the compound of the offender or to a body of arbitrators (In those societies with ozo titled men he may appeal to them)[130]. And since the arbitrators have no means of enforcing their decision, for it to be respected it must be acceptable to both parties. If this fails, special friends of the litigants are invited to help resolve the matter. Recourse for judicial opinion may also be made to the age-grade society or to the dibia-fraternity. And finally when all human tribunals fail to give the litigants satisfaction such supernatural tribunals as the oracles are approached. This is the final court of appeal[131].

Because a breach of the standard of behaviour would evoke the displeasure of the spirit world, the police and the secret service, services so characteristic of modern society, formed no part of judicial control among the Igbo[132].

The institutions of age-groups (organised according to ages) were the nearest to formalised groups the Igbo ever found necessary for the services today performed by the executive organs of government. The senior age-grade (including members of titled societies where it is in vogue) was usually concerned with the vital questions of war and peace. From among the members, there usually emerges the kind of personality to provide the leadership necessitated by the exigencies of external danger[133]. The junior age-grade of young men is charged with social services which included sanitation and related services. There are lower age-grades for music, play and so on, which are important agencies of socialisation. These age-grade associations are very jealous of their prestige. They ostracised a member who through continual misbehaviour brought his or her grade into disrepute. Thus they play an important part in upholding standards of behaviour so vital to stability and peace in Igbo communities[134].

2.2.3.5 Village-town or village-group or town-unit[135]

Higher than the village is the largest unit in most parts of Igboland - "Obodo" (MBA OR ALA), village-town, village-group or town. Towns vary in size and population[136]. This socio-religious grouping is also founded on a number of principles[137]. First, it is a local unit in that its inhabitants occupy a common territory, e.g. Egbema. Secondly, it is a "mythical" kinship unit. Many towns have legendary accounts to "substantiate" how their unit took its origin or how its founder arose and begot children[138].

The name a town bears is usually the name of the founder. The villages constituting the village-group are the sons' descendants of the nuclear pater-familias. Often there are stranger elements; and mostly they constitute seperate villages of their own within the village-group[139].

Thirdly there is a central patron or a recognized guardian of the whole socio-religious grouping. This may be the "Earth-spirit", Ala whose "parochiality" in this case becomes a wider symbol of solidarity. The visible symbol of solidarity for the town would be the priest of this spirit[140]. He is called Ezeani (Ezeala, Okeyiala), Chief priest of Ala. In some cases the water-spirit is the central and recognized guardian, for example, in Okija it is Ulashi, at Obosi the Idemili, at Ukpo, the Kisa; and at Oguta it is the Uhamiri[141].

Some towns have recognized political heads for the whole unit, e.g. Onitsha, Oguta, Agbor, Aboh, Ogwashi-ukwu, Nri, Aguleri[142]. Otherwise in the bulk of Igboland, there is no recognized political or socio-religious head for the whole town. In those towns with recognized political heads - the Obi of Oguta, Onitsha and among some communities of the western Igbo-political authority lays with him in Council[143]. For example, the Obi is the official title of the King of Onitsha. His prime minister is called Onowu. Below the Obi are three colleges of titled men called Ndichie, namely, Ndichie Ume, Ndichie Okwa and Ndichie Okwa-Aranze. Each college has a hierarchy of officials who have achieved their present status by taking a costly ozo title. Adult males are organized into age-grades and age-sets association. From these organizations the Ndichie draw men who perform police functions in the various villages. In theory the government of the town (Onitsha) consists of Obi and his Ndichie Ume, but in practice, each village has a large measure of local authority. The rights of the Obi and his council are regulated by custom. When they exceed their rights, the offended village boycotts the Obi's palace. Each Ndichie holds his own village court, presides over the government of his village, leads his men to the king's war, may act as the King's ambassador, and represents the interests of his village in the king's council. The office of the Obi is elective and not hereditary. It has given rise to a lot of abuses and heated disputes in the recent years[144].

It might well be that the kingship system is intrusive, but it is adapted to Igbo democratising tendency in those places where it became an accepted system. "Ndi Igbo enweghe Eze" - The Igbo have no kings, is a popular Igbo proverb. It contrasts with other systems.

In every village-group there is a senior branch. This represents the descendants of the eldest son of the original founder of the town. The eldest man in this branch holds the village-group - ofo (the senior ofo). He is the head - normally a ritual figure or head with only a presidential function among equals.

Unlike the village affairs, the government system of the town is representative. Let us take a sample government: the Aro-Chukwu. The people of Aro-Chukwu occupy a territory about twenty-five square miles, approximately nineteen miles from the eastern bank of Cross River[145]. They became notorious because of their oracle - Ibini - Okpabi, which became an instrument of exploitation among Igbo communities in their sphere of influence. Due to their manipulation of this oracle for their own ends and to their depredations, their power grew. Their employment of such head-hunting mercenaries as the Abam, Abiriba, Edda and Ohafia furthered greatly their manipulation of this trade[146].

The early history of the Aro is obscure. According to

tradition they claim that they grew from two village-groups, Amuze and Ibom-Isi, to nine, the process of segmentation resulting in the present nineteen village in Aro-Chukwu. Matters of common interest to these nineteen villages are discussed in a general assembly in which each is represented. No village "could be bound by a law or decision made at a meeting in the absence of its representative"[147]. The principle of equal sharing of rights and privileges is sacred. To be effective decisions must be unanimous, since there is no sanction strong enough to coerce any dissenting member into submission.

The Eze of Aro (chief) has only a presidential function at the meetings of the nineteen villages. Although young men are allowed a voice, the government of the nineteen is dominated by "elders" from each village because of the need (perhaps !) to keep the manipulation of the oracle secret. At the village level Aro-government is a direct democracy (as was described in the village unit). The affairs of the village are decided by a general assembly in which men and women can participate. However, effective control is in the hands of elders, members of an age-set whose turn it is to govern the village at a particular period in their age-grade cycle[148].

2.2.3.6 Conclusion

Summarising we can say: Igbo socio-religious structure - despite some marked regional differences - creates a society (a socio-religious society) that is clamorously and personally democratic; a society where its unit-heads called Okpala or Ofo-holders are fundamentally the representatives and mouthpiece of the ancestors. Thus each head for his unit becomes a rallying point; a society in which the oneness of the community is not an abstract idea but a concrete fact realisable in a solidarity of which the eldest ofo-holder of each unit is the rallying point - a rallying point in so far as he occupies the senior position traceable to the first (putative) ancestor and eventually to God from whom the ancestor obtained his power; a society in which the conduct of public affairs is a sacred undertaking, and a society where the attainment of material progress and economic growth as well as the welfare of the members of the community depends on conformity to the "Omenala" as it is done from "Mgbe Ndichie" (conformity to laws and tradition); an undertaking the reward of which is the realisation of the entire raison d'être of all its constituent members namely: at once heavenly and earthly, eternal and temporal, collective and personal[149]. Needless to say this explains why sin is first and foremost a social evil - a distortion of or a threat to the existing equilibrium[150].

This society, on account of its ideological principle of equalitarianism allows for social mobility - aspiration to any hierarchy possible within the community (a hierarchy which one carries with oneself to life beyond the grave)[151]. But this hierarchy is to be achieved by personal efforts[152].

This structure attaches politico-religious sanctions to the office of each-unit head (ofo holders), being also a socio-religious unit. But these ofo-holders in order to "institutionalise" themselves as natural "leaders" of their people must respect this fundamental principle: "that talent should lead to enterprise, enterprise to promotion, and promotion to privilege" - likewise all other leaders to be[153].

Because of the 'mythical' conceptualisation of blood-tie between the unit members, the society repudiates the use of force, especially capital punishment[154].

Trial becomes a matter of conciliation and a purification ceremony[155]. Political cohesion is achieved by rules rather than by laws, and by consensus rather than by dictation. Finally with its age-old respect for age-status (tendency to preserve the ranking by birth - order) and realisation of a social hierarchical order, it establishes the 'seniority - juniority principle' which regulates behaviour and grade-association both between kinsmen and non-kinsmen. Seniors are thus made moral agents of the young. The latter in turn owe the former respect and obedience. Those who have utilised the principle of social mobility are accorded respect and privileges; thus it creates some hierarchical order of social status placement.

Perhaps one could say that Igbo traditional society structurally follows a somewhat hierarchico-democratic pattern, where all share the same egalitarian ideology: the right of the individual to climb to the top, and faith in his ability to do so, and has a right to his actual social status placement on his achieving a hierarchical order through his personal efforts.

I have devoted much space to this aspect for it is hoped, it will help us appreciate Igbo approach to God, what has often been misunderstood and misinterpreted.

PART TWO: IGBO RELIGIOUS BELIEF

CHAPTER THREE: CHUKWU AND HIS ACTIVE ATTRIBUTES

3.1 Assertion of Chukwu's Existence and Igbo Cosmogonical Traditions

3.1.1 The Igbo - A deeply religious people

Like all Africans, the Igbo are naturally and profoundly religious[156]. "Their religion is their existence and their existence is their religion"[157]. It permeates into all the departments of life so fully that it is not easy or possible to isolate it.

Their "Weltanschauung", their vision of the world is a unifying fact: and so no clear-cut line can be drawn among them between the "sacred" and the "profane", between the natural and the spiritual, the strictly social and the religious. It simply "impregnates" the whole life of the community: it is the beginning and end of everything[158].

In fact, for the Igbo, religion "is an ontological phenomenon"; "it pertains to the question of existence of being"[159]. And they are in all things so truly and deeply a religious people that Major Leonard in 1906 writing about them found it necessary to remark: "It can be said of (them) as has been said of the Hindus, that they eat religiously, drink religiously, bathe religiously, dress religiously and sin religiously"[160]. An Nri Chief voiced out the same idea when he told Rev. Fr. I.A. Correia: "Chez nous est religieux même nos marchés et nos repas"[161].

However, Igbo religion, like the majority of African religions, was not and is not formulated into a written and systematic set of dogmas which a person is expected to accept. Yet it is so fundamental for all they do, think and say. For them, to live, is to live in a religious universe. They see the Universe and all in it through a religious meaning and understanding[162]. Thus in their view the living and the dead, the visible cosmos and the invisible world merely constitute one and the same universe and the antinomes of good and evil; life and death which spring from antagonisms inherent in existing beings do not vitiate the unity of this world-vision[163].

Therefore, to understand their behaviour, their problems, their thoughts, their customs - in short everything about them - one must grasp this. It is no exaggeration to say that religion probably exerts the greatest influence upon all they do, think and say[164]. This world-vision does not seem to be based on a seeking after the laws governing the universe, in the manner of scientific study. It is rather an empirical experience, a system of thought having its own coherence between its constituent elements[165].

Their religion controls their lives and so much so that one could rightly say they are caught up in a religious drama in all of their activities. It expresses itself in many ways. It forms the themes of Ukwe (hymns), Uri or Nkwa (dancing music); it provides topics for minstrelsy and ritual mime (songs); it finds vehicles in myths and folk-tales (Ifo, akuko ilo or akuko ani - literally stories of the earth and historical legends), proverbs (ilu), and sayings (agwu-gwa); and it is the basis of their philosophy.

The Archdeacon of Onitsha, Dr. Basden, was right when he called this extraordinary faculty of Igbo spiritual perception (and one is compelled to maintain that this is the root of their religiosity) "a prime elemental force, that might quite fairly be described as a sixth sense, as much alive and as keenly active as the normal five"[166].

3.1.2 Omenala (Omenana) or Odinani - Igbo generic name for the body of answers to fundamental existential questions

The Igbo have left no written records of their remote past to their descendants, and so to trace the processes of their religion is difficult. All that has been preserved of their myths, philosophy, liturgies, songs and sayings, have come down to their descendants by word of mouth from generation to generation. These give a clue to what they thought and did. All these together form what the Igbo call Omenala (Omenana or Odinani).

Ome-na-ala has its starting point or beginning from "mgbe gbo" (in diebus illis) or "Mgbe ndichie" (the time of the ancestors). The body of omenala is often, if not always, linked with ancestralism and the cult of the Earth-spirit (Ala, Ani or Ana). It is believed that the ancestors received laws (which they passed on to their descendants as traditions and customs) from God, Chukwu, through the Earth-spirit, Ala. Ala, the Earth-spirit, helped them (ancestors) establish their stand on Earth and directed them to erect the first shrine to the Earth-spirit, Ala, on the Earth.

Hence all Igbo laws, customs and traditions came to be termed omenala. It is worth-while noting that all these are always socio-religious, because in the two realities - religion and sociology - the Igbo, as other Africans, always sought their ultimate good. Thus though these two realities are distinct in principle, yet they are very closely interwoven so that social life is a religious affair and a religious cult is a social act[167].

Ome-na-ala (Ome-na-ana) comes from "ome", "na" and "ala" (or ana). "Ome" means as it is done (3rd person, impersonal from "Ime" meaning "to do", "to happen", "to obtain"). "Na" is preposition and it means "in". Ala (ana,ani) means land, earth, ground. Omenala, therefore means that which is done or obtains in the land; and conventionally Omenala, in general is a generic term for the body of Igbo socio-religious laws, customs and traditions passing from generation to generation and having its origin as far back as from the time of the ancestors. And related to Ancestralism it becomes a means whereby not only the doctrine of lineage continuity is expressed and upheld but also a means by which social and eternal control is maintained by the elders over the younger generations. Further it is manipulated to perpetuate and sustain the social order in time and space[168].

Omenala, in so far as it is handed on from generation to generation becomes tradition (dynamic aspect of omenala)[169]. Omenala, as an accepted practice becomes custom (the static aspect of omenala)[170]. Omenala as a tradition is liable to change in accordance to the changing conditions of the generation to which it is handed on. But what is left of it is true, "not merely useless baggage"[171].

Omenala, as custom (odibuadibu), is sacred and is normally linked not only to ancestralism but also to the cult of the Earth-spirit (Ala) and as such unchangeable and must be respected[172]. Thus it is not infrequent that one hears the Igbo give as their sole reason for doing this or that, such emphatic assertion as: "Our Fathers (nna anyi) and great-grand-fathers (nna nna anyi or nna anyi ochie) did it so. It worked for them; it should also work for us". Or in refusing any untested innovation say: "This was never heard of since the time of our fore-fathers". And as long as the Igbo continue to keep and respect the sacred ofo - the politico-religious symbol of authority of their ancestors among them, this wonderful influence of the ancestors as guardians of law and morality will be assured continued endurance[173].

This Omenala is the only means of knowing any thing at all of their theodicy, their theogony as well as their cosmogony. They give a clue to what they thought and believed about these; and the relationships between heaven and earth. It enables one to see that fundamental questions to religion have been asked and answered in the past, and that it is in consequence of these questions and answers that the body of Omenala now available to us has come into being[174].

For, no doubt, the very facts of man's confrontation with the physical universe and his awareness of a world, which, though unseen, is yet sufficiently palpable to be real to him pose to man multiple questions which need answers[175]. For example, questions relating to the common occurrence of human existence, questions regarding "serious riddles" like those involved in the phenomena of birth, human life in all its phases and death; questions with reference to that "awesome immanence of the wholly other" - "das ganz Andere" of Rudolf Otto - which is outside him and stronger than him; questions regarding the very whence and wherefore of the unseen world in which man feels himself enveloped and which he feels rules, guides or molests him; in short the whence and wherefore, why and how of all things; all these demand answers[176].

Needless to add that the mind of man, however "naive" or "untutored" or "prelogical" has always been an explorer into the mysteries of existence, ever roaming and recounting the results of its exploration. And his natural curiosity must be given something acceptable by way of answer[177].

The Igbo, like all human beings, thus confronted with these questions namely "the why and how of all things" - who made this world and all its fullness ? How all the affairs of the world are managed ? - asserted that Chukwu (Chineke), God is the origin and ground of all that is.

It does not seem (or at least we have no written data to prove) that they really thought further back than Chukwu, though there could scarcely be any doubt they might have had their occasional worries like all believers and thinkers down the ages with regard to the very origin of Chukwu himself. But this question does not seem to be relevant. They took for granted, and for all practical purposes, the eternal self-existence of Chukwu as a fact beyond question. This fact seems to impress itself upon everybody who has been among them or has had contact with their omenala as with the force of something incontrovertible[178].

This assertion warrants the famous Igbo phrase "Na oge gbo" - "in diebus illis" - which, apart from the fact that Chukwu is called Chineke, i.e. "the creating chi" (Deus creans) and the consequently logical conclusion that he must be the origin of things, starts their story of the cosmic origin of things.

3.1.3 The Myth of Origin

And the story is: "At the beginning of things when there was nothing: neither man nor animals nor plants nor heavens nor earth, nothing, indeed, nothing was; only one very powerful person was and his name was Chukwu. Then He came and created the Heavens and Earth.	'N' oge gboo ihe obula adighi: Mmadu, Umuanumanu, Osisi, igwe (enu) ma ala, onweghi nke obula denu; soso otu onye di; o siri ike nke ukwuu; aha ya bu Chukwu. O bea kea igwe na ala.

Chukwu and Ala brought forth water above and water beneath, animals, plants: everything as we see it today on earth. Afterwards Chukwu created man (Mmadu). Mmadu was the head of all things; but Chukwu and Ana own man. After a long time death entered the world and began killing men. Men sent a messenger to Chukwu asking him whether the dead could not be restored to life and sent back to their homes. They chose a dog as their messenger. The dog, however, did not go straight to Chukwu; rather he dallied on the way[179]. The toad[180] had, however, over-heard the message and he wished to punish mankind; he overtook the dog and reached Chukwu first. He said that he had been sent by men to say that after death, they had no desire at all to return to the world. Chukwu declared that He would respect men's wishes and when the dog arrived to Chukwu with the true message, Chukwu refused to alter His decision. Thus although a human being may be born again, he cannot return with the same body and the same personality."[181]

Chukwu na ala weputa miri di n'elu na miri di n'ala, mmadu, umuanumanu, Osisi ga: ihe nile di n'uwa taa.

Emechaa Chukwu kea mmadu. Mmadu bu onye isi ihe nile di n'uwa; mana Chukwu na ala nwe mmadu dum. Emekata o onwu wee bata n'uwa bea gbube mmadu: mmadu ewere nwuwa onwu. Ka mmadu nwuwara onwu o zipuga nkita ka o gaa ngaa Chukwu juta ya ma ogaemee ka ndi nwuru anwu dikwa ndu ozo ma chiatakwara ndi nke ha. Nkita ejeghi nke Chukwu ozigbo, kama o bara ngaa di ichi iza oku ana akpo ya, (iri nsi). Mgbe mmadu na-ezipuga nkita ngaa Chukwu, awo nuru ozi ahu. Ya achoo ka ya taa mmadu ahuhu. O wee turipu, ntente, ntente, wokom; ntente, ntente, wokom, gawa nke Chukwu. O gafeaa nkita n'uza burukwa ya uzo ruta ngaa Chukwu; o siri Chukwu na ndi mmadu zitara ya igwa ya yabu Chukwu na ha achoghi ichighatakwa ozo n'uwa ma ha nwuchaa. Chukwu wee si ya riea-nu mmadu ka a siri kwu. Mgbe nkita beara gwa Chukwu ozi mmadu siri ya, Chukwu hiekee isi si na ihe mmadu choro ka o nwetara, na ya, enweghi ike igwughari ihe ya kwuru n'mbu. O bu ya butara na mmadu adighi eji otu ahu na mkporo-obi mbu ya abea ozo n'uwa.

Before I go further it must be noted that Traditional Igbo Society was not a "literate society" and therefore no two Igbo would tell a story or myth in exactly the same way. Insofar as the

Igbo have been notable as adaptors and have not possessed "institutionalised literati" or "specialised groups" such as among Dahomey, Manding, Tswana and Yoruba it will then not be surprising that "an extensive body of culturally dispersed oral literature" is "shared by members of Igbo communities" and less so that this "traditional literature" is always subject to modification where necessary[182]. The most important thing to bear in mind is that what is retained after the modifications, contains at least, a kernel of truth[183].

3.2 Chukwu and "ife obuna adeghe (n'uwa)": Cosmic origin

And now back to the story. According to this story there was absolutely nothing - Ife obuna adeghe n'uwa: God alone was; and from nothing - this non-existence of anything - God, CHUKWU, created everything that is on earth today. From other Igbo traditions he created first the heavens (IGWE) and then the earth (ANA); some other sources imply that God's abode was in the heavens (n'enu) and that not only He but also some "strange" or non-corporeal beings or even "men" (!) were with Him[184]. What exactly the Igbo meant by this vague and undefined assertion "Ife obuna adeghe n'uwa" is difficult to define. It is, as far as we are concerned today, lacking in precision (perhaps for them very pregnant in meaning !). Were they expressing here the so-called "creatio ex nihilo" - an expression which today presupposes an abstract philosophical conception of nothing, and which entails discursive thought and rationalisations and above all a philosophy of nature - the concept of complete nothingness ? Whatever interpretation one may be inclined to, is open to question. We have no data to incline us either to a categorical YES or NO !

But it is not improbable that this statement enunciates what came within the scope of the knowledge and ordinary perception of a normal and "prescientific" man[185]. The Igbo described the natural objects and realities just as they appeared to their immediate and unbiased perception; and without further explanation, namely, that the material world (uwa) has been arranged by the author in an orderly and indeed transparent manner, so that we see the whole rich and varied world, which we know today only as complete-growing, as it were, and being formed in God's "hands". In other words: everything we see today has been formed by Chukwu's creative initiative (What promoted this initiative ? Again the sources are silent). There is, however, this insinuation that He created the heavenly bodies to be His messengers[186].

To do this effectively, however, the Igbo tell how "things were" before the creative initiative of CHUKWU. Their method of telling their children this is not that of scientific knowledge. Theirs was rather the method of contrast-namely the very antithesis of their own experience. The starting point was the actual world of their own experience in which things were ordered from "a formless waste", "a void" and "empty desolation".

That is from the absence of any definite form of life or of any particular thing, CHUKWU started to "form the Universe as we know it today". Yes "Ife obuna adeghe" is just the anthesis of what now is.

Thus they prepared the way for the assertion that follows: "God alone was (Soso Chukwu de) whereby they emphasised the absolute independence and supremacy of God as well as his eternal existence (This shall be treated later).

The tradition we are treating and some other complementary ones tell that Chukwu created the Universe in two parts namely IGWE (the HEAVENS) and ANI (ANA) earth. According to some other traditions God sent IGWE to "pregnant" ANI[187]. IGWE in Igbo language is a fluid term, rather ambiguous. As a physical reality, it may mean "blue dome" of heaven or firmament; "the highest heaven" above where God Himself is believed to dwell; and also the whole of the "court of heaven". It may also simply mean the "atmosphere" or the "sky" (We shall treat Igwe as a spirit later).

ANA (ANI, ALA, ALE) is sometimes used to mean quite specifically "the dry land" as opposed to the sea. Often it is used to signify UWA - i.e. the Earth and this includes everything that is visible and tangible, e.g. man, animals, forests and sea or rivers. It may, too, mean the Earth-Spirit (We are leaving this aspect for the next section). So, Chukwu created Igwe na

Ana (the Heavens and the Earth) means that God created all things, both those that are above and those that are below; all those things that fall within the scope of ordinary human perception. Some traditions even explicitly say that God created Anyanwu and Oñwa (the Sun and Moon) to be his messengers and Akpukpando (the Stars).

The enigmatic statement: "Chukwu na Ana (Chukwu and Earth) brought forth (weputa mmadu) Man, plants (Osisi), animals (umuanumanu), miri de n'enu na miri de n'ana (Water above and water below), and everything we see on Earth today...", would seem to contradict the supremacy, the independence and lordship of CHUKWU in His creative initiative; perhaps it may even lend flavour that apart from CHUKWU there were other distinctive and independent "creative powers" as some had been wont to insinuate[188] (I shall go into this fully when Chukwu will be treated). For the moment it suffices to observe that this seems no more than a symbolic expression - namely the productivity of Earth (ANA), her co-operation in helping the ancestors establish their stand on earth and in bringing forth Umuaka - children (i.e. progeny to continue the group on earth) and nwanyi (wives)[189], as well as her role as an intermediary between God and the ancestors and their descendants on earth. The Igbo included Ana as a creature of Chukwu, they have never called Ana any name which would make her an independent creative force[190]. She is never regarded or referred to in Igbo belief as a rival to Chukwu. On the contrary all her powers are believed to be given to her by Chukwu. And in sacrifices her name scarcely, if ever, precedes Chukwu's.

Then there is the expression "Chukwu and Ana brought forth water above and water below". This again is a symbolic expression - a natural and picturesque conclusion of what comes into the ordinary, uncritical and immediate perception. Let me say this by way of example: we all know that seas and lakes are fed by rivers and rivers in turn have their beginning in springs and streams. It is also a common experience that if a man digs deep enough he comes to water; and if he walks far enough he will eventually come to a place where the land comes to an end, and water begins. All water has a common origin and is connected in surround the whole and likewise to be found under the earth. Perhaps this is what the Igbo meant by "the waters beneath" - "Miri de n'Ana" !

The phenomenon of rain (Rainfall) makes it appear, as if, there are also water above with the natural conclusion that above the sky there is (conceived to be) "a great mass of water" held back by the "great metal dome of heaven", which at certain times "opens" its windows and lets down some of this water through so that "the water from the Sky" becomes mixed with the water beneath ! Thus below and above we find some "element" - water. No doubt all these give food for thought, especially to an innocent child and the natural or picturesque conclusion would be that Chukwu (as far as He is identified with Igwe) and Ana brought forth water above and water beneath.

The universe is believed to have been created in four days. According to the reasoning behind this: God created Anyanwu and Oñwa as his two messengers (We are concerned here with the "physical" aspects of these two phenomena).

The Sun (Anyanwu) is to travel daily across the sky by day and the moon (Oñwa) by night. Both are to bring back news to Chukwu of what happens on the earth. Because the Sun and moon pass over the face of the earth in different directions, they cut it into four quarters. And since the Sun does its travels across the world in the day time cutting it into two; and the Moon at night time cutting it into two and since both travel in different paths, so the world is divided by Chukwu into four parts; hence too the four days: Olie (Orie), Afor, Nkwo and Eke - the Igbo four-day-week. This is also why the number 4 (four) is sacred (Nso) to the Igbo. As the world is divided into Earth and Sky (Ana and Igwe), Sun (Anyanwu) and Moon (Oñwa) so also do they respect the number two as sacred. Some traditions tell that the names of these four days (Olie, Afor, Nkwo and Eke) were revealed to man by a "man sent from Heaven"[191].

3.3 Chukwu and Mmadu (man): Igbo anthropological notions

3.3.1 Mmadu's origin and nature

Igbo traditions have always regarded 'Chukwu' as the originator of Mmadu; and Mmadu owes his being to Him. Chukwu created man: the different parts of the body - the head, feet hands, eyes, the stomach and the other members. When he had completed all, he placed them in a beautiful garden and gave them certain laws to observe, the chief of the laws was they should be liberal in almsgiving and show kindness and hospitality to all strangers[192].

As regards the exact time of creating man, Igbo oral traditions are silent. Some traditions say however, that Chukwu brought man into existence after he had created heaven and earth. Those traditions which join the story of the cosmic origin with that of the origin of death seem to confirm this sequence: they insinuate that man was created after 'something' has been accomplished i.e. at or towards the end of the creation of all things.

Man was at the head of all things, though 'Chukwu' and "Ana" (the Earth Spirit) own man[193].

To speculate on when Chukwu brought man into existence will be a sheer waste of time, for there is no written data; oral tradition on the point is scanty, let alone the "Dürftigkeit mystischer Berichte"[194].

Regarding how man was created, Igbo common parlance seems to insinuate that Chukwu is an "uzu-na-akpu-nwa": "Chukwu is a smith who moulds, forms or fashions children i.e. Mmadu. Some parents, as if to inculcate this idea, name their children "uzuakpunwa" - a smith can mould everything but a child. As we shall soon see, Igbo ontology is basically anthropocentric: not only animate but inanimate objects have life - ndu. Mmadu is at the centre of existence. He is an 'in-between', a 'common denominator'[195] and the Igbo see everything else in its relation to this central position of Mmadu.

Mmadu[196] is the Igbo word for human being (homo, 'adam, anthropos). It makes no particular reference to sex. Etymologically, the composite parts of the term are "MMA" and "DU" (DE).

MMA means goodness, order, beauty, peace, depending on the context in which it is used. DU (De) is the imperative of "dee" or "du" meaning "to be". So the word is Mmadu (e) and should be pronounced MMÁ DỤ (dê): let there be goodness, beauty, order or peace[197].

Ezenwadeyi, when interviewed by Father Arazu, said: "What Chukwu created was MMA DU (let there be goodness and peace). But Mmadu himself emptied the phrase, which is Mmadu's nature, of its original meaning i.e. he called himself Mmadu but without reflecting on the significance of the name"[198].

It is interesting to note that when people are quarrelling, the elders who settle the disputes often recall to the litigants the meaning of their being, as men: let-there-be-peace and goodness. And in some areas (in Egbema) Mmado is the usual way a junior greets a senior.

So Mmadu according to the Igbo man - concept is the synthesis, the sum total, the climax, the culmination of all that Chukwu created, and created beautifully, and is good[199]. Mmadu is valuable (Mmadubuife). He is greater than all wealth (Mmaduka-aku, ego); in effect greater than other things created (Mmadukaife, Mamadukauba).

The innate resourcefulness of man cannot be compared with any other created object, for man is both strength and power itself (Mmaduwuike). Man's resourcefulness, power and strength are found in his hand (Akam), in his strength (Ike); in his work (olu), in his intelligence (Ako) and in his will-power (Uche); all these come from Chukwu, God (Osinachi)[200]. In all respects "mmadu" is the pride of the society (Mmadubuugwu); he is the sunlight and priceless gift from Chukwu to parents and to society (Mmadubu anyanwu, ibe ya). Indeed he is the image of Chukwu, God (Ohirichi). Man's destiny is focussed towards the Divine from whom he originated (Uwasinachi or Mmadusinachi, Nwasinachi).

In fact Igbo conceptualisation of Mmadu reminds one of Shakespeare's description of man as spoken by Hamlet : "A piece of work, noble in reason ! infinite in faculty ! in form, and moving, how express and admirable ! in action how like an angel ! in apprehension how like a god ! the beauty of the world ! the paragon of animals"[201].

But despite this high position which man occupies among creatures the Igbo realise that man is not and cannot be Chukwu. They name their children as if thus to remind man of his basic nature: a creature. Hence Mmaduabuchukwu, Man is not and can never be God. He cannot create either (Mmadueke), not even be another's Chi (Mmaduabughichi ibe ya). So for the Igbo the basic conception of man is that of a creature - he lives as long as Chukwu does not recall or take back his "recharging" life - principle, the breath of life he has given man[202]. His life is not his. He must yield it at any time God wants it back. Under Chukwu, however, man is supreme in the universe - he remains the common denominator between the visible and invisible world and must maintain a "get-even" between the two[203]. In short Mmadu is a creature and the crown of God's creative act in the midst of the world; he is a creature who is rooted in history and yet can never determine with any note of finality the history in which he finds himself, for the ultimate meaning of history always remains under the free enactment of God's command (We shall see more of this when we shall discuss God and man's destiny).

3.3.2 Mmadu: Cause of Evil on Earth

And Igbo proverb often cited by elders and judges suggests, however, that "Mmadu makes the world wicked", Mmadu bu njo ala. It is Mmadu who caused the evil on earth and not the spirits, "the people emphasise"[204].

And Igbo anecdote also gives the basis of this maxim. It is told of an Igbo leader and philosopher who was engaged in an informal discussion with a distinguished foreign visitor who made some disparaging remark about his host's country. This remark upset the philosopher, who thought about it for a while and then made this reply: "Do you say that my country is bad ? Can the earth or trees or mud or walls speak ? How do they offend ?"

"No", answered the visitor, "as far as I know, they don't". "Well answered", the philosopher replied, "never speak badly of my country again; should any of my people offend you, accuse them directly". As if to leave no doubt in the mind of the visitor, the philosopher called one of his sons, by name Mmadubunjoala, and requested him to bring okwa - a carved wooden bowl for presenting pepper and kola nut. After his son had left the philosopher explained: "To mark the intrigues of some of my enemies in this country, I named the Child (pointing after his son) Mmadubunjoala (MAN makes a country wicked). It is people not the spirits who make a country wicked"[205].

But when exactly man became responsible for the wickedness on earth is not known. Some Igbo myths, however, seem to imply that God kept man (endowed with all his bodily parts) in a beautiful garden and gave him a set of laws to observe. All the parts of man with the exception of the stomach failed to observe the precepts that God commanded them to keep. So they were punished. The puzzle about this story as narrated by Basden's informant was that the stomach chose willingly to share with the other parts the punishment meted out to them. Perhaps it is an allusion to Igbo lineage solidarity ! It is worthwhile nothing that some versions of the same story say that from that time on men began to die[206].

At this juncture, one would be tempted to ask: "But what makes Mmadu different from the rest of creatures that Chukwu had created ? Why his lowliness and exaltation, his distress and grandeur ?" In other words in what does his greatness consist ? Here we must pause a while to examine the Igbo psychology of man.

3.3.3 Igbo psychology of mmadu: Mmadu's Chi

In our examination of Igbo ideas of life (see Chapter 4) we shall learn that everything that exists has a "Chi" - an "apportioned-life-principle" given it by the Supreme Chi, the "Life per Se". Though this self same "apportioned-life-principle" is given to man, animals and plants, it differs, however, in degree. For just as Chukwu is higher than Mmadu (man) man is above the animals and distinguished from them by virtue of the fact that man gets a higher degree of this divine life; and the animal is also above the vegetable. Similarly the latter is distinguished from the inanimate[207].

Mmadu: A psycho-physiological composite

The Igbo conceive Mmadu as one single psycho-physiological composite made up of "Aru (ahu) and Mkpulu-obi" elements. Aru or ahu is the flesh or body. It is the concrete manifestation of the Mkpulu-obi i.e. "the visible expression of the 'real' man"[208]. It is scarcely, if ever, conceived independently of Mkpulu-obi; for, for the Igbo, Mmadu is a well-integrated organism which has both physical and spiritual aspects. They know Mkpulu-obi through the Aru (body); and the various parts of the body are regarded as corresponding to various "faculties" relating to and recapitulating the Mkpulu-obi: they are merely the Aru (body) concentrating the whole person - the "real" man - for an instant. Thus sickness or illness is viewed by the Igbo as a state of imbalance "onye ike adighe" or "onye aru na anwu" while recovering of health implies that one is filled with "ike" (life) again - "onwetala ike" or "ahu adina ya". A weakling is called "onye adighi ndu" - "one who is not alive" or "onye ike gwuru" - "one who lacks energy" - "an exhausted person".

The human psyche: A tripartite structure

MMADU in his totality is endowed with mkpulu-obi. Here the Igbo make rather subtle distinctions. There is a tripartite structure. First, man has an "obi". Obi for the Igbo signifies both the physical heart as well as the seat of the emotions of love, hate, joy, happiness, fear and courage. A kind man is "onye obi oma" (a man of good heart). A bitter person is "onye obi ofu". A man whose dispositions have always shown bitterness, quarrelsomeness, inaffability is referred to as "onye obi ya fere azu" (his heart is at his back); or "onye molu obi n'azu".

To be happy is "Inwe obi añuli", to have a joyful heart; "Onye oke obi" is a man of greedy heart or a man of courageous heart, meaning a greedy man or a courageous man depending on the context. "Onye obi oku" is a man of fiery heart i.e. a hot-tempered man; and a wicked man is often referred to as a man whose heart is dry i.e. "onye obi tara miri" or "onye ajo obi" or "onye afo tara mmiri". A remorseful person is referred to as "onye obi ya na apia utali" - his heart smites him; whilst "onye obi ya kwu ekeresi or oto" is a man with a clear and good conscience.

Besides the Obi, Mmadu has also the mkpulu-obi, which literally means the seed or kernel of the heart. This is a subtly more spiritual element of the human psyche. Its function is to unify the psycho-physiological composite and make it a well-integrated organism. Mkpulu-obi is really the living being itself; the self, the person or the "real" man. It is the centre of self-awareness, the centre of unity of man's live-forces; the individual person animated by basic dynamism. Hence when an Igbo receives a shock he puts it in a forceful expression: "Mkpulu-obi (or simply obi) agbafugo m" - "my heart or the seed of my heart has run away from me". This means I am a good as dead. So while obi is the affective element, mkpulu-obi is the spiritual element of Mmadu's psyche. It is the "spirited-soul".

In addition to these two elements the Igbo make another distinction: they add a third element. This is the mmuo. The difference between Mmuo and Mkpulu-obi is rather difficult to express. It is very subtle; and worse still both terms are sometimes used synonymously. Nonetheless, as Major Leonard says: "In their dense way they can appreciate and discriminate between them all the same"[209]. And perhaps, he too, I think, gave the best or almost best explanation when he wrote that the difference is best defined by the position occupied, by the soul (Mkpulu-obi) when confined in the human body (Aru), and being the spirit when at large, or when confined to an object or organism outside the human, the actual texture of the essence being the same, irrespective of its situation. "The meaning attached to the word is, in fact, that of the living or life-giving essence, i.e. the essence which not only gives but which is life, and which also gives a man that intelligence and reason which raises him above the brutes"[210].

The infusion of Mmuo into Aru - Mkpulu-obi produces an existential union: Its ontic intentional substratum

So for the Igbo, the Mmuo when infused into the Aru - Mkpulu-obi composite becomes the source of the stability of the Mkpulu-obi - aru composite: it becomes the cause of continuation of man's day-by-day existence. Without it Aru-Mkpulu-Obi composite would not have life. It would be devoid of consistency. It is also a life-force bestowed from above - from the Supreme Chi - which keeps the living being alive and gives it consistency. Hence the Igbo speak of a "dead - Aru-Mkpulu-obi" composite as a man whose "mmuo" or "mkpulu-obi" is gone away - "Mmuo ya anago or arapugo"; and of a dying man as a man whose mmuo is going away - "mmuo ya anabana or anabago".

In other words it is that divine-apportioned-life-principle, divine "aposposma", that offshoot from God (Chi) which when infused into that 'moulded shape', into that "edifice" unites it: gives it life and makes it a mmadu - a creature sharing in a higher degree in the self-same divine life than any other terrestrian being. And I would call this union an existential union, for none of the elements, aru, mkpulu-obi (or mmuo), alone can be termed mmadu strictly speaking nor does any alone possess its own perfection except in union with the rest. By virtue of this union all the elements become in some sense both corporeal and spiritual. Perhaps one would be bold enough to say that by virtue of this union mmuo, the divine-life from above (the divine "aposposma") becomes flesh and thus making mmadu according to the Igbo, a being in whom nothing is purely material, purely physical, purely biological nor purely spiritual, but rather an organic life which in all its dimensions, including the involuntary functions, is partly determined, shaped, "formed" by the spiritual centre of decision in the personality by free human attitudes towards the world, above all towards the social environment. In short man's ontic intentional dispositions derive from this fact. Hence for them Mmadu shares in a higher degree in the divine life than all other creatures and becomes as it were, more like God towards whom his whole being, its "ontic intentional substratum" tends i.e., to possessing the full life. This explains, too, why man is a common denominator, a bridge between the invisible and the visible, an "in-between".

Mmadu's chi "a god-towards" tendency

And this mmadu's chi (Chiukwu - within - man, as Professor Shelton would have it)[211], Mazi Mbonu Ojike tells us, is, as well "a personal guard to which God entrusted every man"[212]. As an image of God in man credited with some radical capability of responding to secret illumination of the creator-God, the Igbo name it "ULI MMU" (or fully ULI MMU NKE CHUKWU or ULI MMU CHINEKE), that is "the will-o'-the-wisp", "a luring, warning and guiding beacon", that shines in the heart of each man[213]. "It belongs to Chukwu", though it is a "God-within-man"[214] and as such necessarily tends towards God. And on it and man, as the Igbo say, depends man's destiny[215].

But this brings us into an apparent difficulty, one would be inclined to object, that this is determinism regarding the individual's destiny, or even fatalism, of which the Igbo had been accused[216]. This seeming difficulty is answered by pointing to the fact that the Igbo defends the liberty and freedom of man in his actions. This is clear from their names and proverbial sayings, as well as their mythical tales.

The Igbo say that proverbial sayings "provide the oil with which speech or conversation is eaten and digested" - "Ilu bu abu eji eri okwu". The Rt. Rev. Dr. Obiefuna rightly remarked: "Proverbs draw from all aspects of life its maxims and meanings"[217]; they are "aphoristic sayings enjoying a traditionally handed down currency and having protean powers of interpretation" and "essentially reveal the cultural attitudes and the systems of values of the society in which they exist"[218]. They "express the moral and the ethics of a society; "they contain moral uprightness, moral excuses and condemnations"; "they are convenient standards for appraising behaviour in terms of the approved norms and because they are pungently, sententiously and wittingly stated, they are ideally suited for commenting and correcting the behaviour of others irrespective of their age and dignity"[219].

Thus for example, we have the following proverbs which

give us an insight into the moral conscience of the Igbo.

Injustice and Partiality

(1) Efi obele onye mualu ibua, asi n'obulu alu. - A small (poor) man's cow gave birth to twins and so it was stigmatized as an abomination. In other words, if it were the "big man's" - rich man's cow, it would not have been so.
(2) Azu kalia azu owelu azu noo. - When one fish surpasses another it swallows it.
(3) Onye ka onye n'emeli ya. - One who is bigger than the other wins against him (Might is right).
(4) Ogbenye bu nwata. - A poor man is a child. Therefore big men decide things. (This means when a poor man speaks in an assembly, his wisdom may be blown to the winds. Even there, where age is respectable, youth backed with wealth may stand a better chance of getting a hearing ! There is a ditty which explains this proverb: "Ogbenye enwero onu okwu makana onwero ego: obulu n' o'nwelu ego, okwu obuna ga abu eziokwu". - The poor has no speaking mouth because he has no money. Should he become wealthy, every word he utters would be true !)
(5) Ikpe adighe ama eze. - The king is never guilty.

All these proverbs in one way or other express the Igbo's moral conscience on justice. They show that the people recognize but do not approve the vices. Some express regrets and lamentation like Nos. 1 and 4; others show how a person's status comes into the decision of a case for or against him, for example Nos. 3 and 5.

Sin and Pardon or Punishment

(1) Emesia ta onu kwulu njo ekwua mma. - In the end or at long last, the mouth that spoke sin will speak good i.e. a wrong-doer in the end begs for mercy or owns up his guilt.
(2) Onya naa apa ya ada ana. - The wound heals but the scar remains, i.e. every evil has its repercussions.
(3) Njo dili onye melu ya. - Evil remains with the evil-doer.

(4) Ife onye kolu na amili ya. - What one sows, one reaps.
(5) Isi kote ebu, ya gba-a ya. - The head that touches the wasp must be stung by it - Whatever evil one commits, let him bear the consequences.
(6) Usa gwu onye ochu na onu, obia kelu ohiho. - Only when the murderer has exhausted himself with all sorts of excuses does he finally hang. In other words, the murderer must hang; blood for blood.

Conscience

(1) Afo n'enwero otobo ifilifi k'obu. - Stomach that has no navel is a mass - There are no men without consciences.
(2) Onye n'enwero ife iyi ada atu egbe igwe egwu. - One who did not swear falsely an oath does not fear thunder - A clear conscience fears no accusation.
(3) Egbutulu ojutulu. - If you cut down a tree it affects the others (collective responsibility).

There are also innumerable Igbo names with excellent moral principles[220]. "Whether these proverbs are put in the mouths of sages or of the foolish; whether they are applied to human beings or to animals, they are modes of speech which are drawn from the cultural attitudes and values of the Igbo society for their potency"[221]. They enuntiate what are morally upright principles among the people (whether or not in "our moral ideas" they are good or bad is here immaterial). All that interests us is that they give us an insight into their moral conscience. And no one can uphold moral principles unless liberty and freedom of actions are also recognized !

This freedom of action can also be deduced from some Igbo myths, such for example, is that which explains the origin of death, and why the stomach is fed by the other parts of the body[222]. From the myth on the origin of death we learnt that men sent a messenger to Chukwu, namely the dog (nkita) with all his speed-facility being the fastest domestic animal; and the toad, slow in movement decided to go to Chukwu with a contrary message for the sole purpose of punishing man; whoever reached

Chukwu first would bring "good news" (life) or "bad news" (death) back to man. In other words, if the dog had reached God first, men would be living for ever ! or rise again after death ! But alas, the toad reached Chukwu first and the result was death for ever.

The dog reached Chukwu too late not because it had not the facility of speed but rather it deviated from the purpose of its course. The toad on the other hand, slow enough in movement, jumped its way slowly but steadily and without any one moment's deviation from the apportioned course and reached Chukwu first.

Applying the myth to Igbo man's conceptualisation of man's march towards Chukwu - his seeking "the full life", we may say that Chi (Chiukwu-within-man) is a "God-toward" tendency, a "God-achieving-and-God-arriving" tendency. Perhaps one could call it a Directive, "a luring, warning and guiding beacon" or "good moral - prompting" that directs or reminds man of the need to achieve "the full goal" - the abundant life, of which his Chi, "God-within-man" is, as it were, a "miniature". It is a light that shines in the heart of every one, and the way one reacts to it determines one's destiny. If one avails oneself of the "prompting" and decides to act accordingly, one's Chi - (the "God-toward" tendency) becomes "efficacious" and one will attain the "full life". But if one neglects the prompting it becomes "inefficacious" and one may miss the chance of attaining the goal. Hence the Igbo says: "Onye kwe chi ya ekwe" - if one wills, his Chi wills too, or "Onye mewe emee ma chi tiri ya aka" - Begin to do and your Chi will help you to finish. "Nga onye no bu nga chi ya no" - one is where one's chi is or where one is, there, too, is one's Chi. "Akpo onye oku chi ya aza" - if one is called, one's chi answers". "Onye kwadobe ije chi ya akwadobe" - when one gets ready for a journey, his chi gets ready also".

In this explanation of Chi, I have tentatively attempted to explicate Chi as the Igbo understand it and thus combining the two ideas of Chi as the "personality-soul" i.e. "a portion of the divine life in man" (God-within-man) as well as Chi's role as a guardian - all of which loom large around Igbo use and conception of Chi. I do not pretend, however, to have exhausted the obscurities about the term and its role in Igbo religious conception. And therefore much could still be discovered about it by careful studies.

3.3.4 Conclusion

From the above, it emerges that for the Igbo, everything - the reality of the whole existence (without any attempt to set down a long and tiresome description of how and when they came into being) is ascribed to the creative initiative of Chukwu, who "went to work" in an orderly manner. The orderliness of the world - the antithesis of the Igbo's immediate and ordinary perception, i.e. the actual order - comes into its present completeness by the work of God, God's creative act without any element of struggle on the cosmic level. The crown of the creative initiative of Chukwu is Mmadu - the "Let-there-be-goodness-and-beauty" - the crown, because he becomes the synthesis of all, a creature in whom nothing is purely material, purely physical, purely biological nor purely spiritual, but rather an organic life which in all its dimensions, including the involuntary functions, is partly determined, shaped, "formed" by the spiritual centre of decision in the personality by free human attitudes towards the world, above all, towards the social environment.

This "forming", as it were, becomes "a generic order" i.e. how the various natural phenomena within this world came to acquire their respective roles and functions assigned to them on earth; and from this starting point of a particular picture of the world - a world where "IFE OBUNA ADEGHE", which expression gives (or seeks to give) the general impression of "formlessness", indeed, "the absence of any definite form of life or any particular thing - a "condensed" account of creation has been constructed to correspond to this particular picture by our ancestors and handed on to their descendants. Thus a particular cosmology which turns out to be more of a cosmogony, but a cosmogony in which God is believed or portrayed as having simply formed everything by "imposing Himself on all with effortless supremacy". This cosmogonic-tradition narrative (that is all that is left of the original story whatever it might have been) is made to correspond to the structure of the finished creation as it is perceived immediately, empirically and uncritically.

But nevertheless our ancestors believed - they were indeed conscious that what they handed on to their descendants is true; but this truth is to be sought not on the basis of physics but on that of metaphysics - i.e. the principle and presupposition which did in fact lie behind the tradition, namely belief in the supremacy and lordship of Chukwu's initiative. To this being we shall devote the next chapter.

CHAPTER FOUR: CHUKWU - HIS NATURE

4.1 Chukwu's Existence

It has just been mentioned that the Igbo asserted the eternal self-existence of Chukwu. In very precise language when the Igbo describe Chukwu's eternal self-existence, they say that he is "Chigbo". This is, as if to say: He is the chi that is made by no other chi; the unmade chi, the chi-that-exists-of his own and beyond whom there is none, for he is the totality of being (CHUKWUBUNDU, CHUKWU-IS-LIFE; Chinwendu, the Chi-to-whom-life-belongs; the Chi-who-is-life). And upon this basic faith rests the superstructure of their belief. - Now we want to examine whether there is any indication to the effect in their traditional vocabulary.

4.1.1 The existence of theophoric names implies belief in the existence of God

The fact that there exists theophoric names among the Igbo implies, of course, belief in the existence of God. "Der Hochgottglaube", writes D.J. Woelfel of Igbo religion and theophoric names, "ist bei ihnen noch ganz lebendig, und sie schreiben ihm als dem allmächtigen Schöpfer und großen Gott auch die Bestrafung der Sünden zu... . Es gibt eine Reihe von theophoren Namen, die mit dem Namen des höchsten Wesens zusammengesetzt sind."[223]

And, indeed, such names are numerous[224] (e.g. Chukwudifu, Chukwukere, Chinelo, etc.) and go quite often to the immemorable past - long before christianity came to Igboland[225]. All these names are fruits of man's experience of the divine. Nothing is asserted of God which is not first felt. The assertions came about by means of God's interventions, not in their history as a people chosen by him, but in individual and analogous situational experiences shared with other members of their group, and embedded in their common religious culture which as a precious heritage they preserved and handed on down through their history[226].

Perhaps it would be superficial to argue from the mere existence of theophoric names among a people to their belief in the existence of God. Among other peoples theophoric names abound also and are used by "believers" and "non-believers" (atheists ?) alike. The meaning of the name seems not to be of vital importance in this case !

We must bear in mimd that among the Igbo names are not mere tags to distinguish one thing or person from another; but are expressions of the nature of that which they stand for; they contain memories of human experience, every shade of human sentiments and emotions in the struggle for existence, indeed, an everlasting and imperishable record of their life and death-struggles and their attempts to live in harmony with other men under the ubiquituous eye of providence[227]. In fact with them the meaning of a name is of prime importance; and this explains why serious reflection is required before the choice of a name, and the Igbo ask a man to change his name if his life contradicts the import of his name. The name and reality should agree as much as possible.

Moreover, for an ordinary Igbo (as with any other group of mankind on earth) the demonstration for God's existence does not begin with the gamut of metaphysical reasoning or the "five ways" of "the Angelic Doctor". On the contrary, it begins from God's providential care for men - from men's experience of that "awesone immanence of the wholly other" - i.e. men's experience of God coming as providence - good and thoughtful of men, giving children to the barren, food to the hungry, perseverance to the despairing, justice to the afflicted, and peace to troubled households. All these shades of human experience are expressed in Igbo names in one form or the other. Given this mentality and background, one is then in a position to argue from the existence of theophoric names to Igbo belief in the existence of God.

4.1.2 Igbo names asserting God's existence

But, even if this does not suffice, there are also certain Igbo names that positively assert that God exists. Such a name is:

"Chukwudi" which means: "God is". "Idi" is the verb "to exist". "O di" is the third person singular meaning "he/she/it exists" or "is". In the above name, it is stated simply that "Chukwu di" - "God is"; and "Chukwudifu" - "God still exists". This is a more emphatic form of the first name, "Chukwudi". "Fu" is added for emphasis as if to assure a "doubting Thomas" that the fact is beyond doubt.

I. P. Anozia remarked that these two names are generally given by parents who have had some difficulties in which they found themselves, and were, abandoned by all, even apparently by God; and quite to their surprise succour came to them when they least expected. This reasurance that God was not forgetful of them is thus expressed in an emphatic assertion: "Chukwu di" - "God is; Yes God still is"[228]. Eugene Azorji, commenting on Chukwudi, noted: "When this name is situated within a historical context, it appears to be more meaningful, since it is now a reflection of past experience. It could be a man escaped from death narrowly or won a just case or had been favoured by fortune and the only way to summarize this experience was by asserting God's existence, God really is - Chukwudifu"[229].

Two other names assert God's existence in a rather peculiar way. They seem to "localize" God. One of these names is "Chukwuno". It means "God is but in a sense, as it were, of being in a place". "Ino" is the Igbo verb for being in a place. "Ino ani" (or Inodi ana) means: "to be seated"; "ino na ulo" (uno) means "to be in the house" or "at home". However, there is no mention in the name as to the place where God is said to be. Like Chukwudifu, it is a more emphatic form.

Another is "Chukwunofu" - "God is still". In Igbo imagery this is more assertive of a conviction of God's existence as felt by man, even if philosophically it may be fraught with misunderstanding.

4.2 Chukwu - The Name

Hitherto, we have seen that the Igbo assert the eternal self-existence of a supreme being. This they call Chukwu or Chineke. He is the origin and ground of all that we see on earth today.

We shall do well to look more closely at this supreme being, first by examining the meaning and implications of his name. The guiding question for us is: What do the Igbo mean when they pronounce the name Chukwu ? What idea does the name connote for them ?

4.2.1 Classification and significance of names among the Igbo

At this point it will be very rewarding for us to pause awhile and learn briefly the pregnant significance of Igbo names in general. I.P. Anozia has made an illuminating study of this subject[230]. And E. Azorji has studied the socio-religious significance of Igbo traditional personal names under my supervision; he has unearthed some unsuspected dimensions in Igbo religious feeling[231]. So the subject can only be mentioned here by way of introduction to our theme.

It was hinted that among the Igbo, names were and are not considered as mere tags to distinguish one thing or person from another: they are expressions of the nature and significance of that which they represent and stand for[232]. Every name has a character and significance of its own. The Igbo, like many africans, do not give names to children without a cause; "and that cause", as Professor E.B. Idowu would have it, "is not the bare, inevitable one that a child must be born before it can receive a name"[233]. Rather, and in the words of Major Leonard: "To every name itself is attached a significance of expression and an intensity of human emotions, the depths of which it is quite impossible for us to sound, much less to fathom"[234]. And not only is this attachment a living personal memory, but it is a record of persons and events that have been associated and connected with it: whether it be of the circumstances surrounding the child's birth, the state of the parents or of the family affairs when it is born; or a remarkable event in the town or the general world into which it is born[235]. Thus every Igbo name is invariably either a sentence, a clause, a phrase, an abbreviation or even a proverb; and it tells many a time a clear story[236].

4.2.1.1 Natural names

Traditional Igbo personal names can be classified into natural, theophoric, historical, social and proverbial names. In Igbo tradition there is a gradation of personal names given to an individual, as he develops from child-birth to manhood. The first natural name a child receives after birth is called "AHA-OMUMU" (birth-name). It is generally derived from the day of birth, that is EKE, ORIE, AFOR and NKWO. Hence such names like Nwaeke, Okeke, Nwaorie, Okorie, Nwafor, Okoroafor, Nwankwo, Okoronkwo, Okerenkwo, etc. are given to the male children. The female children are called Mgbeke, Nwanyieke, Mgborie, Nwanyiorie, Mgboafor, Nwanyiafor, Mgbokwo, Nwanyinkwo, etc. The second natural name a child gets is called "Aha-Ezi" or "Aha Obiri" (family name). Some Igbo communities call it "Aha Onuezi" or "Aha-Okpesi", because it is given in front of the family shrine or at least in the "Obi" (Ovu or Obiri) in the presence of the family members. This name is a family name and it usually expresses the innermost feelings of the family-members. The third natural name a child may receive is called "Aha-Chi" or "Aha-Uwa". This name is given after " Inyo mmadu rite", that is after a diviner or fortune-teller has been consulted. He usually reveals what spirit(s) in particular played a leading role in the conception and birth of the child in question, namely, Amadioha-spirit, Agwu-spirit, Ifijioku (yam-spirit), Ala (earth-spirit), etc. Hence also such names as Nwagwu, Nwammuo, Nwamadi, Nwala, Njoku, Ajoku, Mmaji, etc. These names may be termed revealed names [237].

4.2.1.2 Historical names

Besides these three natural names, there are a number of historical names, which are given to children. These names sum up the past experiences of the family: their fortunes and misfortunes, their joys and sorrows, their happiness and sadness, their hopes, expectations and aspirations. They are situational names surrounded with circumstantial experiences. Some examples may help to illustrate the point. A young and newly married couple named their first male child, "IHUOMA" - literally "good face" (but the real interpretation is "good luck" or "good fortune"). The background suggesting the name shows that a young couple in dire need of a child were not only blessed with an offspring but also a male issue. The parents express their joy by calling the child "IHUOMA", to document how fortunate and lucky they are - at the beginning of their married life. Other names with similar background are "UZO-OMA" (the good way), "Uzodimma" (the way is good), "Ezi-Uzo" (the right way). All these names echo the happy expressions of a woman who is blessed with a child in her marital home and tell the story of how she came from her parental home to experience good fortune in her marital home, which indicates that the future seems promising, "Nkeiruka".

On the other hand the misfortune that befalls a family may be expressed in the name "Egwuonwu", "the fear of death". This illustrates the sad experience of death that had occured and how death instills fear into the family. A family that witnesses successive deaths in its life, may give vent to such feelings in names like: Beeluonwu (provided death spares), Onwuasoanya (death is no respector of persons), Onwuasomba (death respects none, not even a nation), Onwubiko (please, oh death !).

These names further illustrate how man is psychologically affected by death. Death is here personified and prayed to not to interrupt again the smooth running of affairs! Hence "Onwuegbule" - "may death not kill"; "Ozoemena" - "may it not happen again". The hazards of death are dreaded because its consequences are numerous. Expressing such feelings are Onwumere, death is responsible; Onwujiuba, death retards progress and brings sadness to the family (Onwudiwe).

Historical names also express various concepts in Igbo worldvision. The Igbo idea of justice or righteousness, the idea of life and death, the idea of man and his destiny, the concepts of love and hatred, the hardship of having to live in human society, the idea of co-operate personality, etc. Let us take a few names and analyse the backgrounds that suggest them. EJIOFOR (EJIMOFOR) (I have truth and justice on my side); Nwa-ofor (the son of justice); Nwaogu (the son of righteousness); Ejiogu (the holder of righteousness). Ofor and Ogu are Igbo emblems or symbols of justice, truth and righteousness. A person who holds Ofor or Ogu has justice and equity on his side. "EJIM OFOR EJIM OGU; OFOR KA IDE JI AWA ANA" is an Igbo saying. When parents give their children such names they are declaring their innocence and righteousness and are protesting against some unwarranted calumny, slander or false accusation.

Ndu (life) and Onwu (death) are the beginning and the end of the ontological rhythm of man. Life is the basis of every other development: "Onweghihekandu" - "nothing is dearer than life". It is "Iheanacho" - what is sought for, because "Ndu-bu-isi", "life is the first principle" in every human endeavour. Hence all are admonished to protect and guard life (Zobandu). Indeed always to think about it (Uchendu), because ideally it is greater than both wealth and riches (Ndukauba or Ndukaku).

Death, on the other hand, is beyond history and puts an emphatic end to all of man's endeavours. Hence it is "Onwuamaghi-Oge", death has no appointed or due time; it does not give notice or information. Because of its "timelessness" the Igbo, curiously with a certain tinge of overt rhetoric, asks "Onyema" (who knows ?), for he knows the morrow is uncertain (Amaechi). The uncertainty of death makes it deeply mysterious (Onwudiegwu), in fact simply unpredictable (Onwudiomimi, Amaghi-oge onwu). Because onwu (death) is mysterious, puzzling and powerful everywhere (Onwudike, Onwuasoanya, Onwuasomba, Onwuamaeze), it is dreaded (Egwuonwu), for it destroys both wealth and riches (Onwujiuba) and is the cause, at the same time, of all untold humiliations (Onwujiariri or Onwubuariri).

For the Igbo life and death cut across the whole of human existence and Ndu (life) cannot be considered in isolation, that is, without the conception of death. This interaction of life and death explains why this life for the Igbo is a promenade (Iji-uwa-bu-oriri); man is ontologically destined, therefore, to shade off his "humanness" in order to gain "full life" or "full godliness" ("Onwu bu ina ulo" or "ina Chukwu" - death is a going-home or a returning to God).

Beyond that point the individual's history comes to a close, realized or unrealized, leaving behind his personality, his fortunes and misfortunes, his ups and downs in life. This is why the Igbo pray for life (Adindu), for as long as there is life there is hope (Onwukwe). Man can always hope for a better future and he can only do so, if he lives. This vision of life and death synthesizes the whole of human existence. It seems the Igbo belief that God "gives life" and "takes it back" helps them to appreciate the value of human life (We shall see more of this when we discuss the Igbo idea of life; Chukwu and Mmadu's destiny. Regarding historical names describing Igbo conception of man and his destiny see the same section).

4.2.1.3 Social names

Social personal names are those which depict the individual's social status. They are associated with title-taking, puberty, initiation and other religious rites. Some describe a person's peculiar outstanding characteristics in the community; others describe his exceptional valour in war or as a leader in the community, as renowned wrestler, hunter or an expert of the occupation. Such names are Igwe, Obi, Ezeala, Okeyiala, Ofala, Owelle, Ezeji, Diozo, Dimkpa, Dimgba, Agu, Dike, Akajiagu, Omemgbeorji, etc..

4.2.1.4 Proverbial names

Igbo proverbial names are a mark of wisdom effectively used for oratorical effect in the form of epigrams and thus capable of summarising a piece of ordinary prose. While historical names are situational, drawing from circumstantial experience, Igbo proverbial names are guided by practical experience in life and they serve as a collection of centuries of experience, and an accumulation of the experiential wisdom of generations within a given culture. Take the name ONUOHA as an example. Onuoha (public opinion) is a shortened form of "Onuoha egbunam" - "may public opinion not kill me". The name is given as a protest by someone who had been a victim of an unjust public reproach, victimisation, abuse, discredit or unwarranted calumny from neighbours or community[238]. It may also be equivalent of the latin "vox populi, vox Dei". It is correct, because the people say so; and therefore it says satirically: "I am at fault, because it is public opinion". Another similar name is "EBOSIE" - "after all the accusations". It is a name that indicates a sigh of relief by one who had been accused falsely when the accusation is proved false.

> This was verified in the case of a new wife whom the relations and villagers of her husband had falsely accused of deceiving her boy-friend into putting her in the family way so that he would be obliged to marry her. The villagers continually remarked that she did not play fair. But after the marriage things took their course. The time came when her pregnancy would have appeared if the accusation was founded, but nothing was seen and the period of delivery was just when it would be evident to all that there was no foul play before. All were ashamed and the woman with a tone of exaltation called her first son EBOSIE. The name reminds her of the false accusations and reminds all that false accusations will in the end be false (239).

Igbo proverbial names express how things are or should be or that the "status quo" is imperfect. Examples of such names are "Uwadiomimi" or "Uwadiegwu" - the world is a mystery or is a riddle; but at the same time imperfect - Uwaezuoke; Nwabuogo, a child is a favour; Nwaamaka, a child is beautiful; Nwabugwu, a child is an honour; and a gift (Onyinye), as well as a blessing (Ngozi).

Proverbial names may be used to justify a position. IFE-EYI-NWA (Nothing is like a child) is one of such names. "In Igbo moral and social life the question of offspring is of paramount importance. Its priority is such that it tends to tone down other moral demands. No matter what happened or what event surrounds the bearing of a child - was it through adultery, was it by concubinage, was it by one whose husband has died - all these may and are sometimes reprehensible but in the face that a child is forthcoming or is already born, we must tone down our moral sensitiveness because nothing is like offspring - IFEEYINWA"[240]. A child is scarse (Nwadiuko); it is precious (Nwadimkpa); it satisfies the need (Nwagbolumkpa), and it should unite the family no matter what odds there are (Nwajikolu).

Proverbial names may serve as a vocal warning and a reminder that some endurance in the face of provocation is necessary and worthwhile. ABOKA is again one such name. Aboka is the abbreviation of "Aboka atunye isi" - if one insists much on revenge and retaliation one runs the risk of losing one's head (life) in the process. While it is given by a family as a vocal warning to an untiring avenger and persecutor, it also indicates what the family has had to endure[241].

Proverbial names may be used to draw attention to certain facts of human existence - the ominousness and the uncertainty of the morrow and the need for extra vigilance. Such names are: Adiele (let us watch and see); Echewozo or Ariwodo, while one is expecting one thing another thing may happen; Echidime, the morrow is portentous and no one can forsee the events of the morrow (Amaechi). Both the will of God (Uchechi) and the actions of one's follow men are uncertain (Amaucheora).

There are also proverbial names that evaluate and satirize human situations and actions and caution prudence: "Achinihu" (to laugh before a person's face or in his presence - "oculus serviens" and "Ochionu" (to laugh with the mouth - lip-service) are such names; and they describe the hypocritical attitude of some people towards their neighbours or "friends". They pretend to be friendly or concerned in their neighbour's presence but mock and caluminate them as soon as they turn their backs. Experience teaches (Anukam - I have heard [and seen] enough) that such people should not be trusted for they speak only words (Akalefu). Unless they correct their ways (Ekwugha) and begin to practise what they say (Akalonu), they will always bring about quarrelling and distrust in the community (Okwulehie).

From this brief description of some of the backgrounds that suggest Igbo names, it is clear that traditional Igbo personal names - their experiential wisdom - not only kept alive and dynamic the essentials of their faith in their ancient beliefs, but also enshrined in themselves the whole music of their human heart, the lyrical bursts of their love and tenderness, the depth of their hate, the pathos of their sorrows, the triumph of their victories and achievements, the firmness of their confidence, the rapture of their assured hopes, aspirations and ambitions. In short their names present the anatomy of all parts of the human heart and soul; and comprise "the sunrise and sunset, birth and death", "promise and fulfilment", hope and despair - the whole drama of their humanity. No wonder Major Leonard remarks of their names: "From a natural standpoint, there is more in a name - more joy and more sorrow, more pathos and more passion, more tragedy and more comedy, more humanity and inhumanity than it is possible for the civilized unit to realize."[242]

More, their names are but pages in the life-history of every house; more than this, they are the diary or daily record either of its progress and development or of its deterioration and downfall. Consequently in Igbo names are found "every colour of human experience, every shade of human sentiments and existence, and in the attempt to live in harmony with other men under the ubiquituous eye of Providence"[243]. Rightly, indeed, did Leonard comment: "...these human beings...have utilised the flesh and blood of their own children...so that they might leave behind them an everlasting and imperishable record of their life and death struggles"[244].

Igbo names are also considered as expressions of the human personality in so far as they express man's programme of life, his aspirations and emotions. "If you want to know what a man is ask him for his self-chosen names", is an Igbo saying. And another Igbo saying is: "Agua onye aha chi ya anuru" - "if you give someone a name, his 'God-within, Chi' hears, sanctions and accepts". Every person is unique and each has his or her own destiny and role to play in life. To grasp "how the Igbo man understands his uniqueness", his destiny, what he does hope to make of his short span of life, and how he intends to realise his dreams, "go to his name". These express his human personality[245].

With this, we return to our question: "What do the Igbo understand by Chukwu ?" What ideas does the name connote for them ?

4.2.2 Etymology of the name, Chukwu: Concept of Chi

Etymologically, Chukwu is made up of two words: "Chi" and "ukwu". The meaning of the latter word is "great", "big" or "supreme". But regarding the original meaning of the first term, "Chi", our written sources are confusing. I.P. Anozia, commenting on this, says: "Of no other" 'spirit'[246] has so much that reeks with confusion and misunderstanding been written"[247]. So, before we go further, we would like to examine first the concept of "Chi".

4.2.2.1 Earlier writers and criticisms of their opinions on chi

In 1926, P.A. Talbot in his book: "Peoples of Southern Nigeria" calling "Chi" "over-soul" writes: "...the essential idea appears to be that of a spark of Divinity or a monad, which exists in a very high spiritual state with God, as it is put; an Ego which sends down emanations through various planes and finally unto the Earth..."[248]. Later he says: "In Ibo belief, 'Chi' is a kind of group-self, or multiplex-Ego able to manifest itself in several individualities at the same moment, so that many facets of the Ego are evolved and able to contribute their quota of experience simultaneously..."[249].

With respect it must be said that Talbot's description of "Chi" is fraught with misunderstanding and confusion. For him "Chi" is a monad or a spiritual part of God which exists outside man. The second statement, "In Ibo belief, 'Chi' is a kind of group-self, or multiplex-Ego..., makes for an understanding which gives some inclination towards, if not wholly pantheistic, at least polytheistic tendency. To accept "Chi" as meaning "a group-self" or "multiplex-Ego" destroys the distinction of persons and the principles of individuation that follows the nature of "Chi". It forces us to run against Igbo saying: "No one Chi is like another, because no two persons are identical; a rich man's Chi is rich and a poor man's Chi is poor. A man's Chi is masculine and a woman's Chi is feminine. A man's Chi is equal to that man."[250]

On the other hand, if we were to accept "Chi" as denoting "a spark of divinity", the group-self should be distinct from God; and if it were to manifest itself in different ways in different individuals at the same time, we have to accept the possibility of at least two gods - the divinity and the group-self. And this seems contrary to the Igbo idea of God, which is strictly monotheism (i.e. "Chukwuism"). - More on this point will be discussed later.

Some have treated "Chi" primarily as a guardian-angel or are inclined to do so, though to do justice to some of them it must be said that they frankly admit that "Chi" plays a greater role than the christian guardian angel. Thus C.K. Meek in 1937, after a painstaking research which lasted for three years, describes "Chi" as follows: "One of the most striking doctrines of the Ibo is that every human being has associated with his personality a genius or spiritual double known as his 'Chi'. He goes on to compare this conception of a transcendent self to the Egyptian notion of "Ka", which was the double or genius of a man, an ancestral emanation apparently, which guided and protected him during his lifetime and to which he returned after death."[251]

This approach, though partially correct, seems to me to be defective and does not express exactly what the Igbo "Chi" stands for. For this opinion fails to note that besides the duty of guiding, the "Chi" has some direct power over the individual, even if, as some would have it, such power is "only over material life and matter"[252]. Again it fails to account for the fact that the individual "abilities, faults and good or bad fortune are ascribed" to "Chi"[253]. Hence the Igbo speak of "onye chi oma" (a man of good chi) and "onye chi ojoo" (a man of bad chi); "eke-di-na-chi" (in one's chi is his portion or share or destiny, "okike chi nyere m" (the share [okike] given me by Chi); "okike chi nyere nna" (okike given to father by chi); "Chi - ekeghem" (chi has given me); "onye na akpali mmadu n akpalikwazi chi ya" (to offend or insult a person is likewise offending or insulting that person's chi); "onye ajo chi gbulu oji okulu na ata" (a person of evil chi cut down an iroko-tree, but while falling it remained suspended on a needle grass); "Chi bulu ililo onye ilo ekwolu ya" (if a man's chi were grass, the enemy would uproot it).

4.2.2.2 Chi - A spark of divine life in being or "God-within-everything": Igbo ideas of life

In an article by Professor A.J. Shelton (formerly of the University of Nigeria, Nsukka) more light is shed, though indirectly, on the concept of Chi. Here are some of the interrogations and answers from his field-work.[254].

Question: Who made all things ?
Response: Chukwu.

Question: Who made Alusi (spiritual forces) ?
Response: Chukwu.

Question: Who is Chukwu (Chineke) ?
Response: The invisible living soul (Chi), the same as Chukwu.

Question: What is man's chi ?
Response: Chukwu and Chi mean the same thing. Chi is also the first person the man is related to, the Ndichie (ancestors) who came back in him.

Question: How do men come into the world ?
Response: We come from Chukwu, because we get the Chi from Chukwu and we cannot be people without Chi.

Question: What happens to a man's Chi when he dies ?
Response: Chukwu takes it back, because it is Chukwu and it belongs to Chukwu.

From the foregoing interrogations and answers it appears that Chukwu is the invisible living Chi who made everything including man and the spiritual forces (Alusi); and that men are people because they possess Chi which is given them by Chukwu and which upon death returns to Chukwu to whom it belongs. So Chi is w i t h i n man, not outside him nor external to him. This explains, too, why the treatment of Chi as a guardian angel primarily is defective (Cf. Igbo psychology of man, Chapter III).

But what exactly is the nature of Chi, we are not yet fold. C. K. Meek, however, gives us a clue. He tells us that according to the Igbo, not only men have Chi but also animate and even inanimate things have their own Chi[255]. To grasp the significance of this statement one has to grasp the Igbo concept of life - Ndu.

Life - Ndu, for the Igbo is the greatest, the most precious and holiest gift from God[256]. All Igbo love it and love to live it long and abundantly. They say: "Ndu bu aguu; ona agu onye, ona agu ibe ya" (Every human being has an innate desire to live just as he instinctively longs to eat). Even in some areas in Igboland, they make it the object of daily salutation. They simply greet one another with "Anwula" (Do not die; live on or live to the full); or "Anwuchula" (Do not die early or prematurely). And there is a curious identification of life with power, strength or force (Ike); whereas sickness or illness is viewed as a state of imbalance[257].

The key to understanding Igbo concept of life lies in one of their common names; "Chukwubundu" (God is life), or "Chibundu"

(Chi is life). Other variants of this name are "Chukwunwendu" or "Chinwendu" and these signify "Chi-who-owns-life"; "Chi-to-whom-life-belongs" or Chi-who-summons-(into being)-life, strengthens and preserves it. In other words, God does not receive life from anybody. He is life (Ndu); life in himself and life itself. He gives it to every being that exists - i.e. Chukwu is life "in abundantia", from which every other being participates[258]. Yes, everything, not only animate but even inanimate things, each has life. All things existing outside God receive life. They have life. But they are not life. God alone is life.

It is this life that Chukwu "apportions" to everything when he brings it into being. And the Igbo echo this whenever a new baby is born. People visiting a mother after child-birth usually lift the child and salute the mother invariably with "Olisaemeka" or "Chukwuemeka" - "God has done well". This is, as if to say, God has done well in apportioning life to this baby - i.e. allowing it a share of his "Big-Life"[259]. Joseph P. Jordan records this ancient belief of the Igbo:

> Yes, the natives were right, the trees had spirit, the spirit of life put in them by God, and by this they grew and blossomed and throve; the animals had a spirit, the spirit of life, also put in them by God, which caused them to move and growl and grew; man too had a spirit, called a soul, given by God and responsible for his manifestations of life. And why did all this happen ? Because God himself was life. Yes, that is what God is. He is life, and therefore all life comes from him, for tree, animal and man...(260).

From these examples it emerges that Chukwu is the "Big-Life", the "abundant life"; the "life per se", the "life par excellence". Every other being has a life in so far as God "apportions" or allows it a share of the "Big-Life". To put this in other words: "Everything has a Chi" is tantamount to saying everything has a "share" or a "portion" of the "Big-Life" in it. So then Chi is the "life principle", the "Mmuo", which is given to everything that exists by the "Big-Life", principle par excellence[261], or "Chi" is "an apportioned life" in everything, a "small Big-Life" in everything; a miniature, as it were, of the "Big-Life" in every thing - nay a "Chukwu-within-every-thing". It is that portion in everything which is derived from the "Big-Life", "Chi-ukwu".

At this juncture, one would be tempted to ask: What then is the difference between the "life" in the "Alusi" (spiritual forces), in man, in animal, in plant, etc. ? The Igbo see no contradiction in this. They see all these "apportioned" lives - all these "Chukwu - within", higher in some creatures and in others lower. For them these "apportioned lives" have an ascending order. There is a hierarchy. That is why also there are different beings - different in the sense that each being has a "particular share" of the "Big-Life", in it - i.e. a precise "Chi".

"Chi" both distinguishes being of various species and individualises being in the same species[262]. In the words of Mbonu Ojike: "There are as many such Chi as there are personalities; and through it the individual becomes visible[263].

In the light of this analysis the Igbo saying becomes intelligible: "Ofu nne na amu, ma ofu Chi adighi eke" - one mother brings forth children, but they are not "created" by one Chi - i.e. though we are all of the same species (human beings, animals, plants, etc.) and we derive our "apportioned - lives" from the same source, nevertheless we are individuals and have our personal or particular characteristics. In other words, each and everything that exists has its or his or her own particularly specific portion of the "Big-Life", his or her or its own Chi. Likewise, the full significance of "Onye ka mmadu ka chi ya" - he is greater or stronger than a person, who is stronger or greater than that person's Chi; or "Ebe onye dara obu Chi ya kwaturu ya" - a man falls where his Chi pushes him down. In other words, a man falls into the category to which his Chi belongs. "Onye Chi ututu kelu" (a man created by an early morning Chi); "onye chi mgbede kelu" (a man created by an evening Chi); "Onye ajo chi kpatalu nku, ewu ta ya" (a person of bad chi fetched firewood and a goat ate it); "Okike kelu onye bu chi ya" (the okike or eke (share) of a person is of that person's chi); "oke chi onye nyelu ya ka oga ara" (the portion or share given to one by one's chi, that he must take); "Mbosi nne mulu nwoke ka omulu chi ya" (on the day a woman gives birth to a baby boy, that same day she gives birth to that child's Chi).

It must also be borne in mind that the Igbo, like other Africans, in some ways consider man as a "in-between", the centre of the universe, the "common denominator"[264], and this egocentricism makes them interpret the universe, that is all things that exist, both anthropocentrically and anthropomorphically. It is hardly surprising, then if their ontology is also anthropocentric.

4.2.2.3 Chukwu is the head-source-life par excellence, the supreme Chi

Coming back to our analysis of Chukwu: we have seen that Chi is equivalent to "the apportioned-life-principle" "a small-Big-Life-in-everything"; a Chukwu-within-everything; that portion in everything which is derived from the "Big-Life", Chi-ukwu".

"Ukwu", as was mentioned earlier, is "supreme", "great" or "big". So "Chukwu", or "Chi-ukwu" is the "Big-Life", the "abundant life", the supreme-life or supreme-Chi. In short, Chiukwu is the superlative, most perfect life, the pure life par excellence, the great-head-source-life and being, the immense and endless source of life from which every other life is derived[265].

4.3 What or who is Chukwu ?

4.3.1 Anthropomorphisms in Igbo conceptualisation of Chukwu

The etymological significance of the name, Chukwu, has been examined. The analysis brought to light that "Chukwu" is the "head-source-life" in which every other being has its source. This participated or "apportioned life" is "Chi" or "a small-Chukwu-within-every being"[266]. The present examination will describe more fully the nature of Chukwu. The question of first importance, then, is: "What or who is Chukwu ?" It has already been remarked that the Igbo see man in some ways as the centre

of the universe, a common denominator, an in-between[267]. This egocentricism makes them interpret the world both anthropocentrically as well as anthropomorphically. They look at God and nature then from the point of man's relationship with them. Many expressions, therefore, attribute human nature to God: their conception of the nature of Chukwu is laden with anthropomorphisms. And rightly had E.B. Idowu rhetorically asked: "But what worshipping people can wholly divest their thought of antropomorphism in a matter such as this" ? Even in more "developed" religions as well as in christianity, he went on to say, one finds it difficult to make God "comprehensive in abstract term to the worshipping and praying mind"[268].
And the prayer of the Indian sage Sankara is:

> O Lord, pardon my three sins.
> I have in contemplation clothed in form Thee who are formless;
> I have in praise described Thee who are ineffable;
> And in visiting temples I have ignored Thine omnipresence[269].

Need it be added: But this is natural and human ! For man finds really little satisfaction but in a deity "who lives", "who hears", "who has a heart", "who speaks", etc.. Not even centuries of the gamut of metaphysical thinking has succeeded (and may, perhaps, never succeed) in curing man of anthropomorphisms in his private thoughts about God. Man will always project something of himself and his environment into his thinking about God in order to make the unknown intelligible, by analogy, from that which is known[270].

It goes without saying that these anthropomorphisms are aids, at least, to the people's conceptualisation of God, whom they have not seen and about whom they confess to know in so far as they feel his existence and presence in daily life. Therefore the Igbo picture of Chukwu reflects their "Alltagsleben" and is a carbon-copy of their socio-religious structure: it is that of a personage, venerable and majestic, aged but not ageing (Chigbo), who speaks, commands, acts, rules and judges. In short he does all that a person of the highest authority does; a person in whose control everything is and everything depends. Now let us examine in details some of these.

4.3.2 Chukwu as Creator

We have already learnt that the Igbo assert the eternal-self existence of a supreme being to whom everything in heaven and on earth owes its origin. In Chukwu's capacity as the origin and ground of all, creator, he is known as "Chineke" ("Chileke"), "Chiokike" or "Chukwu-okike", "Ezechitoke", "Chukwu-abiama", "Anyanwu-Eze-chitoke"[271], and sometimes as "Akpuchukwu". A cursory look at all these names shows that in all but "Chukwu-abiama" and "Akpuchukwu" (the head-source-chukwu), the word "ike" (verb), meaning"to share", "to divide", "to apportion" is found. "Oke" (noun) means "a portion", "division", "lot". The underlying thought in these names is the idea of "creation"; in them God is portrayed as the One "who apportions" something to creatures. And as we saw in the examination of the name, Chukwu, the thing God "apportions" or puts into creature is life, which becomes "God-within" (Chi).

In some areas of Igboland one hears Chineke or Chileke more often used than Chukwu; and, mainly as a result of the influence of mission schools and christianity, Chukwu and Chineke are today more commonly used all over Igbo country. "Eze-Chitoke" - i.e. "Chi-the-chief-of-creation" or "the chief-creating-Chi" is the name used by the elders and it only survives among them for the supreme being especially in parts of Nsukka Division and is rapidly falling out of use[272].

"Chukwu-okike", "Chukwu-abiama", "Anyanwu-Eze-Chitoke" and "Akpuchukwu" are almost relegated to liturgical usage, especially in sacrificial rites. "Akpuchukwu", however, survives still in a few names, especially among very old men, for example in Egbema, in Ohaji/Egbema/Oguta Local Government Area.

In order, however, to grasp the full implication of 'Chukwu' as creator, may we split the name "Chineke" (Chileke), which is today commonly used among the Igbo, into its component parts. The word, "Chineke" (Chileke) is made up of three syllables namely "Chi"[273] "na" and "eke" - (Chi-na-eke). This has two possible translations: First, if we take "na" as a conjunction, we have "Chi" and "eke" (Chi na eke); and we would have two beings, perhaps two authors of creation, namely "Chi" and "eke" ! This translation is possible, but the implication that there are two creative powers is yet to be proved[274]; secondly if, however, we take "na" to signify the copulative "is", then our sentence would be "Chi-is-creating" or "Chi-who-creates" - i.e. the creating Chi (Deus creans). This is the popular and normal way of understanding the word in Igbo society.

"Chi-is-creating" underlines the idea that creation is a continuous activity. Hence they call the "Creating-Chi", "Osebuluwa"[275] (he-who-is-carrying or supporting-the-world, including man) and were the creating-Chi to relax his hold, the world would relapse into "nothingness" (ife obuna adeghe). Chi is continually creating - i.e. his creative activity is believed to be constantly at work. Hence he is called in this respect Chukwu-Abiama, because as for the Igbo every manifestation of the forces of nature proves to human experience that these forces are not static nor are they mechanical and they need continual and continuing activity of the creating-Chi, a re-enactment of the drama of creation. In other words, just as the creating-Chi brought forth everything we see today from "ife-obuna adeghe" (nothing) at the beginning, so also does he continue his activity in the daily appearances of all that we see today.

The above meaning, applies to the rest of the names used to describe Chukwu as creator. Chukwu-okike, means "the big-Chi-who-creates"; Eze-chi-toke means "Chi-the-chief-of-creation", Chukwu-abiam(a) means "the big-Chi-creator of everything", the Creator who comes to clearer light as he apportions life (cf. also Chukwu as the unique God); and Anyanwu-Eze-Chitoke means "the sun-the-Lord-Chi" (or God) - "the creator". Akpuchukwu "the-source-supremen-chi-the-creator" (Akpu-genuine). This name, Anyawu-eze-chi-toke, exists in places "where Chukwu is commonly identified with the sun"[276].

With the above explanation of "Chineke" one would feel compelled to remark that the normal translation given to Chineke, etc., namely, the creator, voices out incompletely the more profound truth the Igbo intend to convey in the work of Chineke. For, though the creating-Chi is conceived as the living personality above and beyond, surpassing all and transcending completely the cosmic forces (Chukwu-abiama)[277] or (Eze-Chitoke), he is nevertheless conceived as the continuous and continuing force, "the head-source", (Akpuchukwu or simply Chi-ukwu), the full-life par excellence operating in nature.

A fuller message is conveyed in the following names. The Igbo for some reasons - to distinguish it from "akamere, man-made" name their children "Chimere" or "Chikere" or "Akachi" (God-made); they thereby accentuate Chukwu's act of causing existence and him as the living being who dispenses life; "Chinwe", "Akuchi" or "Chiechi" (Chi or God-owns [possesses]) by which they stress that Chukwu owns everything that he has caused to be; and Chidube(m) or Chukudube(m)[278] or Chibunna(m) or Chichebe(m) when the stress is on his fathering of all that he has made. In short in these names they assent that in Chukwu all begin and end.

From these names it emerges that there is a deep-rooted conviction of sustained divine providence; and this refutes totally such theories as speak of the God of the Igbo people as a "high God, which is also a sky God. But he is often a withdrawn high God, a deus otiosus"[279]. E.B. Idowu calls this theory of "the high gods of primitive peoples" "erroneous" and says:

> If ever there is a god who is a figment of man's imagination, it is this 'high god'; for he is only an academic invention, an intellectual marionette whose behaviour depends upon the mental partiality of its creators. Therefore he could be made to withdraw from the life and thought of the people, could be lent features and a face, could be made to be just everything that could preclude the slightest suspicion of a revelation from the living God. These scholars have furnished us with an unnecessary artificial pluralism. For they do not hesitate to concede to each nation, people or 'tribe', its own 'high gods' of various brands.(280)

4.3.3 Chukwu as the Omnipotent

For the Igbo, Chukwu is the omnipotent God. This concept is the fruit of existential experience, not of speculation. It is articulated in their names, proverbs and sayings; and in Chukwu's exercise of power over nature. For example, some Igbo often refer to Chukwu as "he who makes the sun set" - (Chijiekeanyanwu).

Chukwu-wu-ike (God is power) is one such name. The verb "wu" (bu) is a verb of identification. It is really stronger than its English rendering "is". A proud man is often asked by the Igbo: I bu (i wu) Chukwu ? - Are you identical with Chukwu ?

"Ike" (not to be confused with the verb "ike" signifying to divide, etc.) means power, energy, strength or force[281]. Chukwu is the source of all these (Akpuchukwo or Chulwuwuike or Ilechukwu). He alone is "Ike" (or "Ile" or "Ire") in any living thing or form.

From the Igbo concept of Chi we learnt that they associate Chukwu with everything that is. God is the "Chi-within" everything. This indicates, too, their belief that Chukwu is life (Ndu) in everything. He is involved in his creation. There is no space or time where or when he cannot be found, since he is contemporaneous with all things. Everything is "Nkachukwu" or "Akuchukwu", an act of God. It needs to be remarked that this is not pantheism. There is no evidence that the Igbo consider Chukwu to be everything and everything to be Chukwu.

Philosophically speaking, Chukwukere (or Chikere, it is God who created or creates all things) expresses still better the Igbo concept of God's omnipotence; because from it follow many truths, such as the uncreated creating-Chi; the unreceived-big-life, etc. (Chigboo, Chukwudigboo, Chiagbaoso)[282]. As if summarising this belief of theirs, the Igbo left expressed these ancient sentiments in such names as, "Chukwunweolu", "Chukwunaru" (Activity-(work)-belongs-to-God); every type of operation belongs to Chukwu; and "Chinwendu" or "Chukwunwendu" meaning "to-Chi-belongs-life" or "life-belongs-to-Chi".

The strength of the Dibia, Agwu's servitors (i.e. various categories of traditional doctors) is well known and not gain said among the Igbo. They are highly respected and cherished in each society; and they are even often feared. But in spite of this the Igbo consider their strenght and power nothing before God. The Dibia with all their skill and charms, etc. cannot do all things. Chukwu can and does all things. He is "Chukwu-ka-dibia" (God's power is greater than that of the Dibia). Everything that the Dibia do and can do is through "Ikechukwu", "Irechukwu" or "Ilechukwu"m through the power or efficacy of Chukwu, for he is "Chukwu di ike" - God is powerful; indeed he is "Chukwuwuike" (God is strenght and power).

"Ifeanyichukwu" or "Ifeakachukwu" or "Iheanyichukwu" is another picturesque name, affirming, though negatively, the absolute power of Chukwu. To summarise their experience of God's universal omnipotence the Igbo often refer to Chukwu as "Agalaba-ji-igwe": literally, "the-pillar (agalaba)-which-supports (ji)-the-heavens (Igwe)" or "Ogaranya-bi-enu-ogodo-ya-n'akpu-n'ala" - "the chief who resides in the heavens and yet his loins touch the ground". In these expressions, God is conceived not only as the origin butthe sustenance of all things. He is outside and beyond his creation, on the one hand, and on the other personally involved in his creation, so that it is not outside of him or his reach. Should we say: God is thus made simultaneously transcendent and immanent ! (cf. Chikere, Chimere, Chinwe, Chiechi, Akuchi, Chukwudebe, Chidube, Chibunna, Chichebe, Chukwubunna).

Osebuluwa (or in full Orisa-/Orisha - Olisa/-bulu-uwa) means Olisa or Orisha-who-is-carrying-the-world (uwa)[283]. Orisha (Orisa) or Olisha (Olisa) is a foreign word, whose origin is probably Yoruba, and it means "Lord" "head", "source"[284]. It is commonly used among those Igbo communities who claim descent from Benin; such for example are the Onitsha, Asaba, Oguta, etc. But the spread of Nri ritual hegemony would seem to have helped the spread of the term in other areas of Igboland, or even the eastward movements of peoples between 1750 and 1755 might have spread the term into Igboland[285].

In these names God is portrayed as carrying the world, supporting it. Chukwu is similarly personally involved in all his creation, in the spirits, and the natural phenomena. To grasp the full implication of these names it must be noted that to the Igbo the world is wonderfully mysterious, awe-inspiring. The world is stupifying; the world is fearful, lofty and incomprehensible (Uwadiegwu, Uwadiomimi). It needs therefore a being who is not only courageous but omnipotent to carry it. Such a being can be no other but Chukwu who is "O di egwu kpomkwem" - i.e. "who is himself that wonderful mystery - the incomprehensible". He it is, whose support is essential for the very existence of the world. An Igbo ditty, as if to inculcate this idea, has it thus:

Oyoyo uwa di ya.	Speak of beauty, the world abounds in it.

Oyoyo uwa di ya.	Speak of beauty, the world abounds in it.
Ma Chukwu sere aka uwa agwu.	But if Chukwu withdraws (his hand) his hold, the world goes back to nothingness (i.e. collapses).

In other words Chukwu alone is the one who set the machinery of the universe in motion. He can bring it, in part, or as a whole, to a stand-still; and set it going again if need be; in short God's supremacy is absolute. Yes, Chukwuagbaoso - Chukwu cannot run. (See note 282)

4.3.4 Chukwu, the omnipresent and the omniscient

"Onwero ife gbalu Chukwu anya ghari" - Nothing puzzles (the eye of) Chukwu - is an Igbo proverb expressing the Igbo belief in divine omnipresence and omniscience, the highest possible position of honour and respect. For among the Igbo, as in other African societies, wisdom commands great respect[286]. In so doing the Igbo admit that man's wisdom, however great, is limited, incomplete and acquired. On the other hand Chukwu's omniscience is absolute, unlimited and intrinsically part of his eternal nature and being, for he is Chigbo (the eternal self-existing-Chi). To inculcate this belief, they name their children "Chukwufuzulu" (God sees everything), both inside and outside (of man). Seeing and hearing are metaphors which explain the Igbo concept of God as omniscient in the concrete way which is easy to grasp.

Some Igbo communities - the North Igbo groups - refer to Chukwu as the omniscient by calling him "Anyawu" - the eye of the sun which beams its light everywhere and sees everything; the eyes of the sun from which nothing is hidden, since nothing can escape his vision. This is a symbolical visualisation of God's omniscience as well as of his omnipresence. No secrets are hidden from him, not even the hidden secrets of the heart; for "Chukwu-ma-Obi" (Chukwu knows the hearts of men). No veil is so thick and dark as to hide anything from Chukwu, that he cannot see through, for he is "Chimauche" (God knows our thoughts). He knows all because he sees all - both inside and outside. He is the discerner of hearts, however much a person may try to conceal his deeds, being "Chukwumaije" (Chukwu knows journeys), "Ifeanyichukwu" (Nothing is impossible to God), "Eze-bi-n'igwe-ogodo-ya-n'akpu-n'ala" (the king whose abode is in the heavens while his loins sweep the ground) i.e. his surveillance is effective everywhere and at any time.

Often "in this valley of tears" people are falsely accused and unjustly tried. Such people may in some circumstances have absolutely no hope of fair play or retribution here on earth. An Igbo under such circumstances often rests "consoled" with the hope of receiving justice from him who knows all things, by saying "Chukwu ma" - God fully knows (that he is unjustly victimised) even the secrets of the heart.

Even the very fact that Chukwu is regarded as the "small-chukwu-within" every existing being implies not only his omnipotence but also his omnipresence as well as his omniscience. Ezenwadeyi has vividly brought out this when he told Fr. Arazu: "It is of the same Chukwu all speak. If Agwu-Nsi is mentioned, it is Chukwu... We cannot mention any and leave Chukwu behind"[287].

4.3.5 Chukwu as the just Judge

According to the Igbo, Chukwu has a personality and in this personality there is a will which governs the universe and the life of mankind. It is an immutable will and men generally have to invoke it or accept it in situations that seem beyond human power. This will is exercised, however, in a just way and the Igbo consider it to be just. No matter what befalls them they believe that God is always right. They hold that God evens things out, rewarding good to those who follow good conduct, and evil to those who follow evil conduct, and overlooking breaches done accidentally[288].

The justice of God is felt or invoked in judicial situations, swearing and pronouncing formal curses, "all of which are taken seriously by African peoples"[289]. Chukwu is the ultimate judge and executes judgment with justice and without partiality. He is "Chukwujekpe" (ikpe) or "Chukwujekwu" (God will judge or God will the last word). He is "Chukwumaije(m)" - God knows (my) journeys or (my) ways. He knows everything and he will eventually give justice where it is due, for he is "Chilagorom" (God denies for me = Chiagoro); he is "Chukwunweugwo" - to reward belongs to God. The retributive justice of God is inescapable for man, for no man can run faster than God (Mmadu adagbanari Chukwu n'oso). He is the final disposer of all (Chinweokwu) - the final word belongs to God; He is the ultimate judge, "Chinweobo", to whom it belongs to revenge[290]. He controls man's destiny and each will receive from him as he deserves, because he is "Chukwuatuugha" (God does not tell lies) and equally "Chukwualafu" God does not deceive anybody. Yes ! - He does not have to compete with either man or spirit to have anything, being Lord of all, "Onyedikechukwu ?", "who is like God ?" - None, for God is the head (Chukwubuisi). Therefore the common experience of deception and infidelity rampant both among men and spirits is not in him, because he is completely otherwise and selfless. Indeed he is "Chukwualafu".

Even here on earth this judgement has already begun for every man according to his character. It is Igbo belief that misfortunes, illness, etc. are sometimes punishments meted out for sins known and unknown. This also explains the distinction between the Igbo "Ichu aja" and Igo mmuo[291].

Since God is all-wise ("Izuchukwu")[292], all-knowing ("Chukwumaobi", "Chukwumauche", "Chukwumaokwu"), and all-seeing ("Chukwufuzulu"), his judgement, too, is the final word because he is "Chukwujekwu" ("Chukwu will give the word"). Even the uttered words of men, the sound of which has disappeared into the air, and are later on reported falsely or distorted by false accusers, even those are known to Chukwu: "Chukwu ma fa(ha) nine" (God knows all) because he is "Chukwumaokwu" (God knows the words), our thoughts expressed in words ("Chimauche"), that is God knows all thoughts. In short God is an impartial judge because he knows "our sitting down and our standing up"; and "Mmadu ada-agbanari Chukwu n'oso" - Man can never run faster than God. He is "Chukwufuzulu" - God sees everything both inside and outside (of man).

4.3.6 Chukwu as the unique

The Igboman is not pre-occupied with the unicity of God (die Alleinigkeit Gottes). By this it is primarily meant that Igbo pre-occupation is not to assert that there is only one God (ein alleiniger Gott). In other words the Igbo do not concern themselves with monotheism as it is understood today in Western philosophy. What they primarily assert is that there is no other being like Chukwu, an assertion that flows from human experience.

For them Chukwu is the only effective and perennially reliable God, powerful everywhere and in all things (the Chukwu-within-everything). He is the creating-Chi and Lord of everything, the "Ama-ama-amasi-amasi"[293]. Spirits may fail. They have human attributes as well as frailties and may, in effect, be manipulated by men[294]. But not Chukwu; he cannot and is not influenced by any other being. Though often spoken of anthropomorphically, he excels in all human characteristics.

He is "Onyedikechukwu" - who is like Chukwu ?; as well as "Odionye buchukwu" - is there anybody or person who is Chukwu ? These are two Igbo proper names expressing their concept of Chukwu, as unique[295]. Dr. Anozia has described some circumstances known to him in which the former name was given to a child by his mother. He writes: "A 'pagan' [296] couple known to me lived for five years after their marriage without any issue. People began to gossip as is a common custom of the Igbos in such circumstances. The natural victim was the wife who was supposed to be barren. The husband was induced by his relatives to take a second wife. He did. But soon after, the first wife conceived and bore a boy. She gave him two names: 'Onyedikachukwu' and 'Obujurum' meaning may my heart now be calm and pacified."[297] So for the woman, whatever men may say, no one is like Chukwu who dispenses his benefits as he pleases; who as Lord and creating-Chi, effectively comes to the succour of all when all hopes are despaired of; who is an impartial judge (Chukwujekwu); who is merciful (Omerebere or Chukwu diebere); who does not deceive, is selfless, because he does not have to compete with either men or spirits to have anything, being the Lord of all (Chukwualafu); whose time of visitation is best, though sometimes humanly speaking painfully trying i.e. whose apparent delay does not compromise his fidelity (Ogechukwukamma); in short, who is everything and does everything at the right time when and if he "thinks" fit. (Izuchukwu, Oseloka, Osegbo, Oseka /Olisaemeka/ Chukwukanero /Kanelo/[298] or Chukwueloka - God has been most thoughtful /in this case/).

For lack of a better terminology I would call Igbo belief in the uniqueness of Chukwu, God's "Einzigkeit" (i.e. their monotheistic belief) "Chukwuism" or "Chinekeism". By this belief they acknowledge Chukwu as supreme over all on earth and in heaven (both men and spirits); he is recognized by all the spirits as the head to whom all authority belongs and allegiance is due. He is not one among many (Chukwubuzo or Chibuzo); not even "Chukwu-in-Council" or "Chineke-in-Council". His status of uniqueness is supreme, and his supremacy is unique and absolute (Chichinile). Things happen when he approves; things do not come to pass if he disapproves (Beeluolisa or Beelueke, Chijioke, Chinwuba, Chikwe, Chikaodili, Chinagu,Osakwe, Olisakwe). He is the first and last (Chukwubuisi and Chigbo)[299], the ultimate pre-eminent being.

4.3.7 Chukwu, as the transcendent, the sublime and the immense

Ontologically viewed, Chukwu is the origin and sustenance of all things. He transcends all boundaries, i.e. all things were made by him and he is the Chigbo, the aged, but not ageing Chi, who sustains or supports all. He controls all, not only spirits (human and non-human) but also all men as well as natural phenomena. He is sublime in status, beyond all spiritual and non-spiritual beings. His power is immense.

He is "Chukwudiegwu" or "Chukwudiomimi" - Chukwu is a mystery (Riddle). The word "egwu" is used variously. It may mean "that which is stupefying wonderful, mysterious, fearful, lofty or incomprehensible". In describing something exceedingly beautiful, the Igbo sometimes say in praise of it: "O di egwu". "Chukwudiegwu" may then connote either of these expressions to a man depending on what circumstances motivated the exclamation. But Chukwudiegwu when given to children by parents is more often than not an expression of gratitude (by the parents) to Chukwu whose inscrutable ways they have experienced[300]. So Chukwudiegwu is a name expressing the transcendence and sublimity of God.

"Does anyone know the will of God ? - "Amauchechukwu" or "Onyemauchechukwu" - is another Igbo name asserting God's transcendence as well as his sublimity. Likewise "Amauzochukwu" - no one understands God's ways. May I narrate an incident known to me under which the name "Onyemauchechukwu", was given to a child. Perhaps it will throw some light on the above names, as well as on the subject ! There was a non-christian man whose wife gave birth to twin boys (May 2nd., 1948). It was customary in the locality at the time that such children be done away with. More understandably so since the man's relatives were also non-christians. By insinuations they were forcing their will on him, for they dared not openly say so, since the same had officially been forbidden; and there could be a spy to bring up the matter to the knowledge of the authorities. The father of the twins stubbornly objected that anybody should tamper with either his wife or with the children. He even threatened reporting the case to the authorities. And so the people desisted from their plans. Eventually came the naming day. He called one of the twins, "Onyemauchechukwu" - who knows the will of Chukwu, God ? As if to tell his people why he gave him such a name; he called the second of the pair "Chukwuma" - God knows. In other words, for this man, God's ways are inscrutable; his thoughts are impenetrable. He is "Ama-ama-amacha-amacha" (ama-ama-amasi-amasi) - one you can know but never "finish" comprehending (incomprehensible - Amaobichukwu).

The "obi" is the seat of human emotions, sentiments and thoughts. The qualities usually attributed to the soul and human conscience are also predicated of the "obi". "I malu obi m ?" - Do you know my heart ? - is the Igbo way of asking: "Do you know what is hidden in the depths of my thoughts ?" Therefore Amaobichukwu is a concrete and picturesque way of saying that God's thoughts are impenetrable by men, therefore transcendent and sublime.

The Igbo, as if summarising their belief in Chukwu's transcendence, his sublimity and immensity, call him "Obasi-di-na-enu" (elu) or "Chi-di-na-elu"[301] or "Ogaranya-bin'elu-ogodo-ya-akpu-na-ala". In the first word they express that Chukwu is the Lord, Obasi[302], who resides on high. "Elu" or "enu" (igwe) means high, height, or the sky, the firmament. When the Igbo speak of Enu or Elu, they are referring more to the all-pervading presence of the sky than to the simple fact of a sky above the human head. The sky is regarded as completely "wrapping up" the earth, that is the earth is seen as a ball in the immense bowels of the sky. Hence the sky is sometimes spoken of as "Igwe-ka-ala". And if "Chukwu" is the Lord of the immense sky ('Igwe-kaala'), then he himself (Chukwu) must transcend it and notwithstanding exceedingly immense[303].

God is, too, "Chi-di-na-enu" or "Chi-ukwu", that is to say, Chukwu is the most abundant reality of being, is immense and sublime; for he alone is "Chukwuka" (God is greater than everything); to him who is "Chukwuebuka" (God is very, very big or great), no one is comparable. He is Chukwuagbaoso or Chiagboso[304] both in power and in any other quality. He is simply the great one. "Who is greater than Chukwu ?" - "Onyekachukwu ?" Surely none is greater than him, whose abode is in the heights inaccessible to man (Afuluchukwuanya or Afuluenuanya).

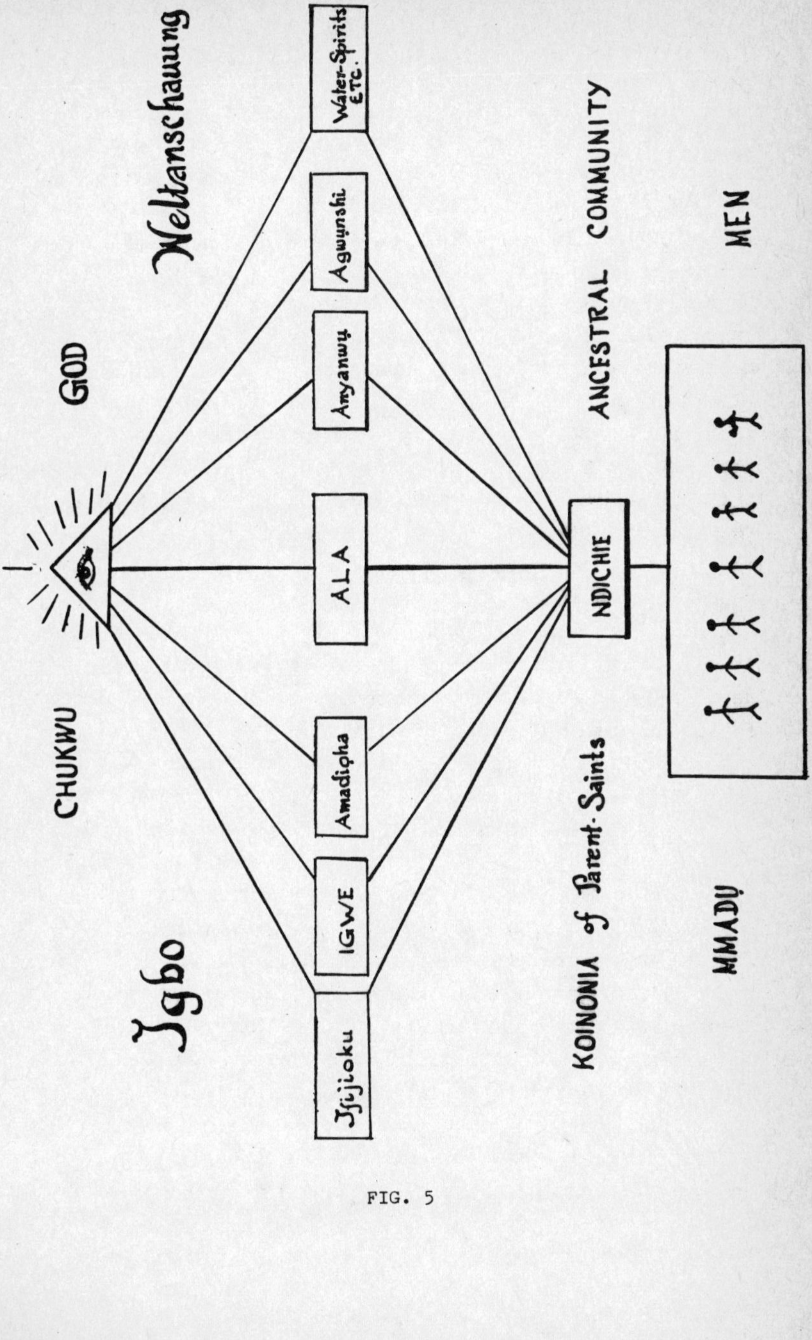
Igbo Weltanschauung
CHUKWU GOD
Ifijioku
IGWE
Amadioha
ALA
Anyanwu
Agwunshi
Water-Spirits ETC.
NDICHIE
KOINONIA of Parent-Saints ANCESTRAL COMMUNITY
MMADU MEN

FIG. 5

CHAPTER FIVE: CHUKWU, THE SPIRIT-WORLD AND SPIRITUAL BEINGS

5.1 The Spirit-world, a manifestation of God's being and presence, and a reality of empirical experience

John S. Mbiti in his book, "African Religions and Philosophy", has observed: "Traditional African Societies have been neither deaf nor blind to the spiritual dimension of existence, which is so deep, so rich and so beautiful"[305]. In another book of his he rather humorously remarks: "When a missionary asked Africans in Zanzibar to tell him something about their concepts of God they simply said: 'God thunders !' The man has crossed the waters to come as he so sincerely believed to tell the 'heathen' about God. But for these and many African people the tropical thunder is the most powerful thing that they know. In it they discern not merely the sound of natural phenomena but the almighty power of God himself. Thunder is not simply an impersonal force of nature. It is the mighty voice of God, which nothing can silence..."[306].

These two remarks are very true of the Igbo. For them the universe is a religious "arena". Nature in the broadest sense of the word is not an empty impersonal object or phenomenon. "It is filled with religious significance."[307] They give (or seem to give ?) life even where natural objects and phenomena have no biological life. Chukwu is seen in and behind all the objects and phenomena of nature. They are his creation. They manifest him; they symbolize his being and presence[308]. The invisible world is the counterpart of the visible. It is symbolized or manifested by visible and the concrete phenomena and objects of nature. It presses hard upon the visible; one speaks of the other; and the Igbo "see" that invisible universe when they look at or feel the visible and tangible world. Both are dimensions of one and the same world: they dove-tail into each other to the extent that at times, and in places, one is apparently more real than, but not exclusive of the other. And the Igbo exclaim: "Uwa di egwu" - the world is profoundly mysterious, full of mysteries beyond man's comprehension.

The invisible dimensions of existence are essentially metaphors for him (Chukwu) - it is the same Chukwu that all speak of. "If Agwunshi is mentioned, it is Chukwu, if Ubu is mentioned, Chukwu. We cannot mention any spirit or phenomenon and leave Chukwu out."[309]

As for most Africans this is one of their most fundamental religious heritages[310]. But this "Weltanschauung", this world-vision, the reality of this spiritual world is not an academic preposition: it is rather an empirical and common-place experience. It is perhaps a world-vision, unique, but by no means lacking in coherence. It is a world-vision based on the harmonious and profound appreciation of the "ama-ama-amacha-amacha" nature of Chukwu, the prime elemental force and source of their religious consciousness[311].

This fact practically all who have studied them or worked among them (missionaries, government officials and anthropologists) have in one way or another acknowledged. Thus in 1938 Dr. Basden, the Archdeacon of Onitsha, after some 35 years of evangelical work among the Igbo wrote:

> It is essential to understand something of what, it is true, constituted the controlling principle in all old Ibo "tribal"(312) life. We have been accustomed to speak of . this dominating spiritual force as "religion", but it is something much more incisive and comprehensive than what that conventional word commonly implies. The conception of spirit is deep and powerful, operating from within, and is not merely an outward conformity to religious observance although it might quite fairly be described as a sixth sense as much alive, and as keenly active, as the normal five. Due regard for this spiritual sense must have foremost place because herein is found the motives of action and the key to the solution of many problems... Without this faculty of spiritual perception much in native thought and custom remains obscure if not completely unintelligible. (313)

The Rev. Father Jordan, recounting the experiences of the great apostel of Igbo land, Bishop Shanahan, and his own-two-score of years as a missionary remarks in his book, "Bishop Shanahan of Southern Nigeria": "The average native was admirably suited by environment and training for an explanation of life in terms of the spirit rather than the flesh. He was no materialist. Indeed nothing was farther from his mind than a materialistic philosophy of existence. It made no appeal to him...

Every Ibo believed that an invisible universe was in action around him and that his term of life was short if he happened to fall foul of its denizens. He felt that it was up to him therefore to propitiate them with courtesy and deference."[314]

And Dr. Uchendu, himself an Igbo anthropologist, after his careful field work sums up the Igbo world as follows:

> The Igbo world is a world peopled by the invisible and visible forces, by the living, the dead and those to be born. It is a world in which all these forces interact, affecting and modifying behaviour; a world that is delicately balanced between opposing forces, each motivated by its self-interest, a world whose survival demands some form of co-operation among its members, although that co-operation may be minimal and even hostile in character. It is a world in which others can be manipulated for the sake of the individual's status advancement - the goal of Igbo life.
> It conceives reincarnation as not only the bridge between the living and the dead, but a necessary precondition for the transaction and transfer of social status from the world of man to the world of the dead. It is a world of constant struggle which recognizes that conflict situations exist and therefore demands from the individual constant adjustment; and although leaving some of the rules of adjustment rather vague, still insists that "good citizenship" demands "transparent" living and that human interdependence is the greatest of all values. It is a world that is spoiled by man and not by spirits, yet man is allowed a wide latitude in his behaviour - an important factor in the dynamics of Igbo culture...(315).

From the passages cited it clearly appears that the belief in the reality of the spiritual dimension of existence is deeply and profoundly rooted in the people. These two dimensions of existence are one and the same universe. They "dove-tail" into each other. The question, however, is: "Who are the inhabitants of this spiritual dimension ?"; and what is their nature ?

Before I go further, it must be noted that it cannot be over-emphasized that in dealing with the Igbo (as well as with the other Africans who have not been influenced notably by western culture in their traditional environment), one must bear in mind that one is dealing with people for whom the traditional heritage has the force of law. Their most important reason for believing what they do believe and doing what they do is that it is handed down to them; their fathers (NNA FA /HA/) and their grand-fathers (NNA FA OCHIE) believed and practised those things, and any deviation from them would be inviting trouble from the invisible world. "It is this unshakable faith in the tradition handed down that explains the baffling ignorance exhibited by some of those questioned when scholars try to find out the why and wherefore of things they believe and practise" says Dr. Ezeanya[316].

5.2. The inhabitants of the spiritual world

5.2.1 Alusi (Arusi, Arushi, Umuarobenagu), Non-human spirits

According to Igbo belief, Chukwu created not only the physical universe, Uwa, and all therein, but also spiritual beings[317]. These spiritual beings inhabit the invisible world. This world is, too, the abode of their creator. Of these spirits, some there are who were never human. It is also the abode of the spirits of the deceased human beings[318]. Some of the spirits are good and benevolent, hospitable and industrious, others are wicked and malignant, unmerciful, fraudulent, treacherous and envious.

The spiritual beings in general belong to the ontological mode of existence between God and man. Broadly speaking, we can recognize two categories of spirits: Those who were created as such (therefore never human) and those which were once human beings. The first category - the non-human spirits - the Igbo call ALUSI, (ARUSI,ARUSHI) or UMU AROBENAGU. Chukwu brought them into existence so that they might be his messengers in carrying out, each in his own office, the functions connected with the theocratic government of the world[319]. But as to when they began to be, there is no information. They were first introduced in connection with the creation and government of the world[320]. The Alusi are "metaphysical forces", that have human attributes but they are neither human beings(mmadu) nor deceased human beings (mmuo). They are "being forces"[321]. The old man already mentioned, Ezenwadeyi described them: "...those, whose nature is power in comparison with man who has a body, must be called 'Spirits': ...Nde mmuo (bu) ihe sili mmadu (mmadi) ike na ahu"[322].

If we analyse this definition and bring out its implication we can grasp the meaning more fully: Ihe means that which ..., the thing, or a thing, something, or simply thing (res); isi ike means "to be strong", "to have energy or power" (sili: in other dialectal variation would be "silinari": it means to be stronger i.e. the comparative of strong = ike). Mmadu means man, adam or anthropos. Ahu is body i.e. the entire body of man from head to toe.

So in the first instance the entire body of a man from head to toe is strong or is the effect of strength ! Secondly, strength is distinct from the body as cause is from its effect. It would seem that in Ezenwadeyi's definition, 'Matter' as 'materia secunda', existing and palpable and therefore strong, it has these positive qualities because it has what makes the universe a unit, without being itself part of the universe. And the differentiation of things in the universe is the effect of power, distinct from the things that fall within our sense perception but sustaining them and keeping them firm, in all their varied structure of "genus" and specific differences.

Earlier, during the interview he argued from the phenomena of sense experience to the existence of invisible beings who could be greeted as persons. And when he was asked: "Do you want to say that 'Ana' is invisible ?", he retorted: "Where can you see it ?" Fr. Arazu replying said: "Is this not Ana on which we are standing ?" And Ezenwadeyi gave this reply: "We look up to the heavens and point upwards to say there is Chukwu, God; Do we see him there ? Do you think that you can see Ana, the earth-spirit, because you are standing on Ana ?"

Thus one sees that Ezenwadeyi was very conscious of the spiritual dimension of our physical existence. Another peculiarity in his definition is that it seems to say that spirits are not distinct from "where they are", for this was the actual question he was asked[323].

5.2.1.1 What does Alusi mean ?

But what does the word used to designate these beings mean ? Some people interviewed said that ALUSI is a shortened form of

"Alukwana Nso ndi Mmuo", others said it is an abbreviation of "Alukwana nso". They explained that "new spirits", when they first enter into a village or take possession of someone, they usually issue stern warnings regarding their likes and dislikes. And the possessed people (or the villagers) to remind themselves of the warnings, usually erect something - a stick, a heap of mud, a hut; and whatever is erected to this effect becomes ALUSI - ALUKWANA nso - No one should violate, desecrate, profane or polute it or trespass.

Onwubia Mmara of Umueze-Anam narrated a legend to drive home this message. He said that there were spirits called "Okpu-uzu". They made moulds and other equipment, for farmers on a certain island. These spirits normally did the work at night so that nobody would see them. A native was so inquisitive that he climbed a tree at moon-lit night in order to see OKPU-UZU at work. The following morning he was seen dead and dried up on a tree. Okpu-uzu, O. Mmara concluded, had punished the man for not heeding the warning of the spirits[324].

Etymologically and apart from the above explanation, however, the term Alusi is not without its difficulties. Alu (aru) is the Igbo word for abomination, sacrilege, desecration, defilement or heinous crime for which a ritual purification is needed before forgiveness is accorded. The verb to commit an abomination or sacrilege, to defile something that is holy (descrate), is ILU or IRU: and normally with a cognate object, e.g. ilu ala. Thus, for example, the second person imperative of "ilu ana" would be "Alu-sina-ala". ALU-SINA YA ogu: Do not fight him (her or it) or "do not defile (it, her or him) by fighting". ALUSI-NA YA AKA means "do not touch (it, him or her) with (the) hand". "A" is the prefix for the 2nd person. So, etymologically, ALUSI or ARUSI (if it comes from this root ILU or IRU) would seem originally to mean: "Do not defile", or, "commit no irreverence...". Thus it implies that the subject or object which must not be defiled or descrated, whose defilement is forbidden, is holy or sacred (NSO). Hence too we hear of IRU (IHU) ALUSI (ARUSI), the face of the not-to-be defiled or not-to-be descrated object or subject. It is ironic that what originally was a representation now stands as a generic name for the non-human spiritual beings. All ALUSI are ontologically regarded to be superior to man - MMADU; whether they are ethically superior as well is not clear. However, they are believed to be nearer to God, CHUKWU in terms of communication.

They are described sometimes as kind, hospitable and industrious; at other times, as fraudulent, treacherous, unmerciful and envious. They are in general subject to human passions and weaknesses. And according to Igbo belief they can be controlled, manipulated, and in fact used to further human interests[325]. When they visit men with painful calamities, it is generally believed that they were duly deserved as punishment for sin, known and unknown[326]. They are also all looked upon as intermediaries.

They include IGWE (very often associated with CHUKWU)[327], the Sky-spirit; ANA (ALA,ANI or ALE), the Earth-spirit[328]; ANYANWU, the Sun-spirit (often too identified with CHUKWU); AMADIOHA or KAMALU, the Lightning-spirit (not to be confused with physical lightning which the Igbo call AMUMA); ONWA, the Moon-spirit. They also include the forces that control the days and from which the days derive their names (EKE, NKWO, OLIE (ORIE), and AFOR)[329]; ARO, the year-force; IFE-JI-OKU, the Yam-spirit; AGWU, the divination-force; the river-forces[330].

The organisation and power structure of all these Alusi mirror the Igbo social structure. And like the Igbo social structure all these, are not to be conceived of as forming a hierarchical pantheon. There is no seniority or authority implied in the conception of them. Though some are conceived as being "more uncompromising and more wicked" than others, yet this trait does not make them rank higher or lower than the others. Hence it is Igbo practice to appeal to one or to a number of them simultaneously without any consideration of their rank or status. And the Igbo demand from them "effective service" and "effective protection", in which duty, if they fail, they "are always threatened with starvation and desertion". But if they give "effective protection", the Igbo are very faithful to them[331]. Here we are face to face with the Igbo "markedly success-orientated", egalitarian and individualistic principle - namely, that essential idea that it is "right and natural" that talent should lead to enterprise, and enterprise to promotion, and promotion to privilege, i.e. "social status placement"[332]. From this point of view, I think, Elizabeth Isichei was right when she remarks: "In the very act of intellectual analysis we tend to falsify the nature of Ibo, as of other religions. One discerns a hierarchy - from lesser spirits to the supreme God - yet this rigid structuring seems to be alien to the religion we analyse."[333]

5.2.2 The place of some of the spirits in Igbo religious psychology

At the same time, though these "spirits" are not normally ranked in importance (except the importance they "achieve" by making use of the Igbo principle of "sucess-orientation") the Igbo regard some of these beings as "nearest" and "dearest" to them[334]. So we shall consider and describe some of these spirits according to the role they play in Igbo religious life.

5.2.2.1 The Ala (variously termed Ana, Ani, Ane, Ale)-Spirit, Earth-Spirit

John Mckenzie remarks that man's sense of his dependence upon the divine is nowhere more apparent than in his quest for food. In ancient agricultural societies this sense developed into the fertility cult. The succession of the seasons was for these ancient agricultural societies not an effect of "physical laws", but of the determination of a superior will which could, for reasons unknown to man, alter its decision. Hence the importance of the fertility cults in the ancient Semitic world. He concludes by saying that the forces of fertility in human and animal life are also subject to the same arbitrary will[335].

And writers on the Igbo people usually bear witness to the importance of ANA (Ala) in Igbo religion. That ANA assumes such paramount importance is psychologically understandable: the agricultural Igbo villages were practically dependent on crop cultivation, and festivals are largely determined by the cycle of the agricultural year[336]. Thus, perhaps, with the possible exception of the ancestors (we shall deal with these shortly) ANA, the Earth-Spirit, is "regarded as the 'nearest' and 'dearest' to the Igbo"[337].

She is the great mother-goddess, the spirit of fertility - the mystic power of which every body stands in awe. She is a merciful mother who intercedes for her children with God and the other spirits; a mother whom the other spirits ask to "warn" her children on earth before they take action against them; but a mother, when she has decided to punish, no other spirit may intercede or intervene; a mother, nevertheless, who does not punish in haste but quite reluctantly, after a series of warnings had gone unheeded[338]; the great mother of all: of plants, animals and men both quick and dead. Hence the Igbo call her ẠNA NWE MMADU NINE ! ANA NWE ANYI !, ANA, the owner of all mankind, yes ANA is the owner [339].

As the spirit of fertility, she is believed to be responsible for increase of fertility both of man and of the land. Without her, life would be impossible. Public sacrifice is made to her before hoeing and planting the land; and at harvest, the Igbo offer her their first fruits[340]. Her role in Igbo socio-religious life is such that the Igbo do nothing without first asking for her help[341].

Ana is the queen of the underworld. As such she is connected with the cult of ancestors. She is the unseen president of each Igbo community, the "parochial" symbol of the common origin and solidarity of the community - a common bond of humanity[342]. Being the unseen president of the community, she is responsible for public morality. Thus offences against her are regarded as defilement of the earth, an abomination (ARU OR NSO ANI); for example, such sins as incest, murder of a member of a socio-religious unit, sexual intercourse between persons for whom marriage is prohibited[343]. For all these offences and the like, ritual purification is needed before forgiveness is accorded[344]. If such people die before purification is performed (in which case it is believed that this is a sure evidence that ANA killed the person (in question) such people are denied ground burial, the worst social humiliation for any Igbo[345].

Ana is believed to have helped the ancestors (Igbo patriarchs or the "canonised" fathers) to found the land - i.e. towns or villages. She is believed to have got the laws from God and handed them on to the ancestors. The ancestors "made" all subsequent laws under her direction, as did their descendants. Hence Igbo laws are always socio-religious laws and are believed to derive their sanction primarily from Ana. They are called OMEN-ANA, that which obtains in the land. The ancestors were responsible for the erection of the first ANA-shrine (of course under her direction)[346]. That is why each Igbo community is incomplete without an ANA-shrine (place of worship for the localised social group)[347]. This Ana-shrine is normally a tree with a pottery dish in which offerings are placed. This tree is in a great part of Igbo land, Ogirisi (a dolichandron tree). Sometimes stones or pieces of iron are placed there also[348]. Some of her statues (esp. those in Mbari temples in Owerri division) depict her with a child in her arms or on her knees and a halo round her. Dr. Talbot remarks that all these "are reminiscent of some Italian madonnas and still more of Ast or Isis, with her son Horus. The attitudes of the two goddesses are very similar. Often also, as with the Cretan goddess, snakes are modelled in attendance on her."[349]

Igbo communities invariably have myths or legends about their settlements. These myths or legends aim to validate their claim to the piece of land they inhabit. Some communities claim that their founding parents were created by CHUKWU on the spot; others lay claim to priority of settlement. Thus in each Igbo socio-religious unit (apart from the family-OBI, or UMUNA-earth-shrine where the senior man in each of these unites, the Okpala or Onyisi, offers daily sacrifices for his people)[351], there is always an "IHU ALA" - the face of the Earth-spirit. This is the putative shrine erected by the first settlers of the group or ancestor[351]. The priest, taking charge of this shrine, is known as Okeyih-ala (in Egbema), EZEANI or EZEALA and he is the visible symbol of the solidarity for the group[352]. Here before IHU ALA, all major decisions take place, e.g. like going to war, summarily disptaching a sorcerer, or giving a democratically-reached decision a ritual binding. Dr. Uchendu says: "The Igbo are fond of changing their mind, but decisions taken at IHU ALA are not lightly treated and are often respected."[353]

With all this mystic and "numinous awe", reverence and

respect for the Earth-Spirit, it is not surprising that the Igbo are ideologically opposed to the sale of land (ALA). In fact they feel guilty and ashamed to have to sell their land. And if there is a "sale" of land, ANA must be ritually pacified in order to consummate the transaction[354].

In many ways Ana can be said to be very important - indeed the "nearest and dearest" of all the spirits - to the Igbo. She helps them with many things: they ask her for children, for prosperity in trade and for increase in live-stock. As the source of strength, she must be notified before her children go to war. She is the "parochial symbol of brotherhood" being the common "mother" of all. It is a great privilege to be a priest of ALA. This requires a "DIALA-STATUS", which is ascribed to all children born of a free-man and a free-woman. Every DIALA is therefore a potential priest of ALA. One can rightly say that the cult of Ala is largely connected with material needs[355].

5.2.2.2 The relationship of Ana to Chukwu and to the other spirits (especially the so-called minor spirits)

As Horton rightly remarked, the concept of ANA among the Igbo is by no means simple[356]. Igbo religious inward consciousness regarding her and her relationship to CHUKWU, as well as to the other spirits, especially to what is normally designated "minor spirits" is subtle, complex and intricate. I am inclined to think that no one in whose religious psychology this belief does not exist can adequately express Igbo conceptualization of ANA.

Even sometimes the fact (or the assertion) that "religion is essentially of the inner life and can be truly grasped only from within", and more, "by one in whose inward consciousness an expression of religion plays a part, may well be true[357]. But more often than not this is again difficult, for "religion concerns beings which cannot be directly apprehended by the senses or fully comprehended by reason" and therefore can sometimes defy expression by accurate images and words[358]. Nonetheless, let us see what Igbo tradition, and those in whose inward consciousness this belief finds an expression, can tell us.

According to the Igbo tradition, to which Ezenwadeyi constantly alluded while he was being interviewed by Fr. R. Arazu, CHUKWU AND ANA brought forth everything as we know it today. This tradition, in fact, "OMENALA IGBO" has always retained in the formula: CHUKWU NA ANA (CHUKWU AND ANA); ENU (sky above, CHUKWU), and Earth beneath, ANA. Both own everything, even the lesser spirits[359].

With regard to the relationship between CHUKWU and the minor spirits there is no difficulty. Ezenwadeyi remarked that they are all subordinated to CHUKWU, more, that "all are essentially metaphors for CHUKWU. It is the same CHUKWU that all speak of, if AGWU NSI is mentioned, it is CHUKWU, if UBU is mentioned, CHUKWU, if ARO (AHO) is mentioned, CHUKWU, if OGWUGWU is mentioned CHUKWU. We cannot mention any and leave CHUKWU behind[360]. The question arose when Ezenwadeyi was asked: "CHUKWU and ANA, which of the two is the greater ?" - He seemed inclined to say that ANA was greater but emphasised that tradition did not give any clear indication on this point[361]. Later he remarked that tradition has it that ANA is also above[362]. One wonders whether this is an identification of CHUKWU with ANA ? At this juncture others who joined in the discussion claimed that CHUKWU was greater than ANA. One of them, EPUNAM, went to the extent of adducing an argument from the phenomenon of death. He said: "Watch an man who is dying: He breathes in and in. When he breathes upwards (in and in and in) it means death. He is blown upwards. But when he breathes down (out) it means coming back to ANA. So we belong to both of them - CHUKWU and ANA. It is the truth. But CHUKWU is greater, because he takes the dying man first (i.e. he takes us back first) before we go into the earth"[363], i.e. before we are buried.

It would seem that this physical act of "breathing in" is viewed ontologically as "a spiritual movement" away from ANA, the Earth-spirit ! If the breathing out, the downward movement back to ANA does not follow, the man has been received first by CHUKWU. This is why death is called in common parlance "INA CHUKWU", "going-home-to-CHUKWU". But yet the dead are also referred to in daily language as "NDI ANI JI" - "those who are held by ANI". An Igbo adage has it thus: "EKWE EKWETEZIH IHIE ANA JI" (the tom-tom cannot recall what ANA has in her grip)[364].

Later on Ezenwadeyi tells us that "CHUKWU AND ANA" are supreme. They are the principle from which we start to enumerate every else. Both own everything on earth, including the minor spirits. For him it would seem that the essence of religion lies in a dualism between CHUKWU and ANA (sky above, ENU and earth beneath, ANA); the transcendental and the material. "There is nothing that is not split into two in the cosmos"[365]. And in the same interview, answering the question who the priest of CHUKWU was (e.g. at IHIEM-BOSI), he emphatically said: "The priesthood of CHUKWU is like this: Wherever men establish a shrine to ANA (IHU ANA) there they establish one to CHUKWU". He repeated this statement to show his conviction and the validity of the principle enunciated.

Certain questions arise from this interview and from the statements of earlier writers on Igbo religion[366]. Does this signify that the Igbo believe in an eternal dualism, an ultimate dualistic principle, the twofold lordship of CHUKWU and ANA ? What exactly does this tradition about "CHUKWU and ANA" intend to convey to us ? What is the "traditional" Igbo concept of the relationship between CHUKWU and ANA ? Is the Earth-spirit (ANA) only a personification of natural objects and phenomena, which are mythologically "characterised" as God's agent or even associate ? Igbo customs, laws and institutions are often linked with ancestralism and the cult of the Earth-spirit, and whatever is in accordance with local custom (Omenala), is natural, right and lawful, and therefore morally binding. Is the Igbo conceptualisation of the Earth-spirit then a subsequent attempt to "historicize" what is otherwise "timeless - i.e. explaining customs, laws and institution, whose origin is otherwise lost to historical sight, in the oblivion of "DUDULUDU" (i.e. time immemorial) ?

Against accepting any ultimate dualistic principles are the evidences or strong belief among the Igbo that everything took its origin from CHUKWU, the ultimate ANI inclusive[367], and the difficulty of interpreting Igbo symbolism. Also there is the fact that Igbo conceptualisation of these beings shows remarkable parallelism with their social structure. Thus in practice they appeal to one or a number of spirits simultaneously without any consideration of their rank or status[368].

Perhaps it would be of interest to investigate more, whether the "CHUKWU-ANA-Supremacy-tradition" does not embody two alternative philosophies; and if so, which of the two concepts, CHUKWU or ANA is older in Igbo religious psychology.

However, it must not be forgotten that Igbo world has never been seen in the modern way as a passive, at most, a mechanistic system, a background for human energies, mere matter for the human mind to mould. The traditional Igbo man sees the world as a living system of mysterious forces, greater than his own, in the placation and service of which his life also consists. The first need for him, no less vital than food or weapons is the psychic equipment or armament by which he fortifies himself against the powerful mysterious forces that surround him. He does not only learn to make the earth fruitful, to raise flocks and herds and children, both as a practical task of economic organization and to perpetuate his being. He relies on his enterprise and handiwork and strength, but he views them also as a religious rite by which he co-operates as priest and hierophant in the great cosmic mystery of the earth - the fertilization and growth of nature and humanity. Human strength and knowledge and harmony must exist side by side with the divine cosmic powers. And harmony is only attainable by moral rectitude and sacrifice.

5.2.2.3 Anyanwu - The Sun-spirit

Another spirit that figures often in Igbo religious life is the Sun-spirit, Anyanwu and for manifold reasons among various communities. Etymologically the word comes from ANYA AND ANWU and these mean "EYE" and "SUN" respectively. So "Anyanwu" is the "eye of the sun". Homage is most commonly paid to the Supreme Being, CHUKWU or CHINEKE by some Igbo communities (in the Nsukka area) through ANYANWU, the Sun-spirit; these communities regard him as one of God's most powerful agents[369]. Such offerings very often take place at dawn or at sunset; and it is the sun that is asked "to present it to CHUKWU", to "sweep away evil with its morning rays and substitute in its place good fortune and divine blessings; UTUTU TUTURU NJO, IHE OMA MEE, IHE OJOO EMELA"[370].

Dr. Ezeanya described one such sacrifice he witnessed at OKPATU in UDI division.
At the shrine of Anyanwu called "ONUANYANWU", literally "the mouth of ANYANWU", there were pieces of stone, an ofo (the symbol of justice, authority and communion with the ancestral spirits), an OGBU tree, a woven palm-frond, one small earthen pot (which must not be painted in any way, it must be free of any artifically applied colour; the people say its colour is "white"). While the rites are performed the people say: "We offer sacrifice to Anyanwu and we ask him to present it to CHUKWU (CHINEKE), GOD"[371].

Some communities identify ANYANWU with CHUKWU, manifesting himself as the author of light and knowledge[372]. These commonly call CHUKWU, ANYANWU and often describe him as "EZE ANYANWU, EZE-OKIKE, i.e. the sun, the lord, the lord God, the creator[373].

The sun's position as the intermediary nearest to God - in connection with fortune and prosperity - has had such influence on some Igbo people, that the sun is identified with CHUKWU himself. Some regard him as the Son of God. Hence, we hear sometimes the sun spoken as "Nwa Chukwu" - "Son of CHUKWU" or Son of God[374].

Some think of Anyanwu as the spirit that makes crops and trees grow[375], while other communities associate him with good fortune, success, wealth, good luck and prosperity. Because of this the sun often figures metaphorically in Igbo language. For example if one undertakes an arduous expedition (e.g. to an unknown country) or sets out for a marriage negotiation, one is wished by one's relatives "a bright day". If by mishap the enterprise fails, one needs but tell the relatives "MMIRI AMARA M - I have been beaten by rain". This means I have failed in my undertaking. Thus it is that "a person's sun is cited as the ultimate explanation of his good fortune or misfortune"[376].

Some people bear the name ANYANWU. They are supposed to have been conceived through ANYANWU's intervention; and as such the name is meant to remind them of this. But this status is normally confirmed by divination. There does not seem to be any specific ritual attached to it. Mostly this name is given to children born on Afor day - the second day of the Igbo - week[377].

Traces of the cult of the sun among the Igbo differ in

intensity from north to south. In some areas "the sun-cult is a purely private cult"; while in other places "as with the Igbo of the Nsukka division, it is common, with every householder having a shrine of Anyanwu in his compound[378]. So, besides the daily invocations which the family head makes to the sun during his morning kola petition, there are also direct sacrifices to Anyanwu before his shrine, asking for protection[379].

M.D.W. Jeffrey's claim that the Igbo borrowed the sun-cult from the Near East (Egypt) needs more authentic and convincing proof. His etymological analysis of ANYANWU and the linguistic affinities of ANWU and ANYA with "ANU" or "NYUNU" or "INU", "IWNW", seemed to be too far fetched, if not dubious[380].

5.2.2.4 Igwe and Amadioha - The Sky-spirit and the Lightning-spirit

The Igbo view the position of Igwe in two ways. First, IGWE is said to be the "place of residence" of the Supreme Being, CHUKWU, as is evident from the names given, sometimes, to CHUKWU: CHUKWU-DI-NA-IGWE; OBASI-DI-NA-ELU or CHI-DI-NA-ELU; EZE-BI-NA-IGWE OGODO-YA-ANA-AKPU-NA-ALA or OGARA-NYA-BI-NA-IGWE-MA-AKPA-YA-ANA-AKPU-N'ALA; AGALABA-JI-IGWE (or ENU)[381]. Secondly, IGWE is regarded as the husband of the Earth-spirit. They say it is IGWE who fertilises the earth, with rains, and makes it possible for men to reap abundant harvests[382]. IGWE, the sky, is believed to be larger than ANA, the earth, hence, the name IGWE-KA-ALA. Though IGWE is believed to be the spirit responsible for rain, it is seldom appealed to for rain. Rain-makers claim the power to make and drive away rain at will, and their services are always bought on big feast days to keep off rain[383].

The Igbo distinguish two aspects of this spirit: IGWE as the source of rain, and IGWE as the Lightning-spirit. This latter is called KAMALU or AMADIOHA. (This should not be confused with the physical phenomenon which the Igbo call AMUMA.) The thunder which often accompanies rain is regarded by the Igbo as a manifestation of IGWE's or God's anger. Thus when, during the rain, it thunders and thunders, the people see it as a sign of IGWE's anger. Many Igbo people identify these two aspects and simply call the spirit

Igwe. Some Igbo communities, on the other hand, regard IGWE and AMADIOHA as two brothers. IGWE (the sky) they see as a pacific spirit, whose main function is to send down rain to the earth, while AMADIOHA or KAMALU is the punitive spirit. The role of this latter is thus explained by the AMADIOHA priestess, CHIOMO MADUME: "AMADE-OHIA (AMADIOHA is the right spelling), like ALE, and ARO-CHUKWU JUJU, is against all those who act contrary to custom. The thunder God sends down, his bolt, to strike such sinners. So, when a man is killed by lightning, people always know that he had done some bad thing. Witches and wizards specially dread his power and never dare to go out during a storm"[384]. And indeed when anyone is struck dead by lightning the people believe that either the victim is punished for a sin he himself comitted or for a sin, committed by some near relative of his. Thus AMADIOHA is "a symbol of terror for all criminals"[385]. Dr. Talbot suggests that this punitive power of AMADIOHA may account for some people's abandonment of the cult of IGWE (as the giver of rain[386]. Generally every Igbo community recognizes the existence of KAMALU or AMADIOHA. But its cult is usually "the affair of a lineage or lineage-segment". Such a lineage or lineage-segment has the prerogative of appointing a priest who ministers to the needs of other people requiring the service of the spirit[387].

In pre British days the cult of IGWE-AMADIOHA developed into a big oracle which had its centre at Umunneoha in Owerri. It is known as IGWE-KA-ALA at Ozuzu. Like-wise at Diobu near Port Harcourt, where it is called AMADIOHA[388]. The managers of these cults, especially that at UMUNNEHOHA, in time took it on themselves to impose death-penalties under the guidance of IGWE" on supposed criminals. The government eventually intervened and had the oracles destroyed. These oracles played in many an Igbo community the role of the final court of appeal and forged links among many communities in Igbo-land through the institutionalised network of an intelligence service[389].

In general one can say that both Anyanwu, IGWE and AMADIOHA are very often identified with the Supreme Being (CHUKWU). They are metaphors either as personifications of his activities and manifestations or as the spiritual beings in charge of the major objects or phenomena of nature. They are, as such, regarded as "associates" with God, being the nearest intermediaries between him and other creatures. But at other times they are conceptualised as separate entities[390].

5.2.2.5 Ifejioku (Ifijioku, Njoku, Ajoku, Aha Njoku), Yam-spirit

Etymologically the word (words) is (are) very difficult to analyse and leads (lead) us not much far into deciphering the inner meaning of the term. With various accentuations of the term, one has the following meanings: either the things that hold (or pertain to) oku (fire), or, the thing that holds (wealth, farm) oku[391], or (here 'u' is a little longer than the rest) may things (wealth) fill the earthenware container.

If on the other hand, "Oku" (Joku, Njoku, Ajoku) were formerly a proper name, the term may mean: The thing or things that pertain or belong to "Oku" (Joku, Njoku or Ajoku). In this sense, Talbot's remark would be right: "It would appear more probably that "Njiokku" refers to the deified ancestor, who occurs so often in Ibo myths, is portrayed in white colour - to show that he is dead - by statues in houses, and is perhaps connected with Jok, the God of the Lango and still probably with the ancestral spirits among the Dinka"[392]. However, for many ages now Ifijoku has been believed to be the particular Aluse who, under Ale, is in charge of the plants on farms, especially the yam[393]. The Yam-spirit is universally recognized by the Igbo to be responsible for the growth of yams. No one who knows the position yam occupies among the Igbo will wonder at this. Yam is the staple food of the Igbo. "To be derived of yams", writes Dr. Basden, "creates a condition of acute distress. Whatever substitute may be offered, it cannot satisfy the native's desire for this favourite food... The yam is a tuber; as a foodstuff and as an agricultural product, it is equivalent to the potato in Ireland"[394].

"Yam is not indigenous to the country", says Basden. "Tradition says it was introduced by the Portuguese"[395]. But there are legends telling how Chukwu gave men yams and coco-yams and taught them how to cultivate them[396]. Perhaps these were attempts to historicize what is otherwise lost to historical sight.

In traditional Igbo society (and even today to a great extent), yam occupied a very important position; it is round it that much of the social and religious life of the people centre[397]. Yam-spirit acts as a social sanction which controls the behaviour of women in the home, in the farm and the "oba", the storage place for yams. Women are obliged not to throw away yams in anger. It is believed to offend Ifijioku. If they do, they must appease Njoku before they eat yams; otherwise they will have dysentery or cholera[398]. Quarrelling or fighting is not allowed on the farms; this binds both men and women. And when a quarrel breaks out, the farm must be appeased: an egg is usually broken on the spot to ask for forgiveness[399].

Within each agricultural cycle sacrifices are made to Ifijioku before clearing the bush, during planting season and soon after the harvesting of new yams. In some communities it is forbidden to eat yams until sacrifice has been made in thanksgiving to Njoku; and some devout priests do not eat yam until a formal sacrifice is made to Aha Njoku[400]. The biggest of those thanksgiving sacrifices is the communal rite known as Iro Ofo or Ofala, Igwaji (Egbema), Ogwugwu-ji (Agbajah) in which the whole community participates[401].

For traditional Igbo communities yam stealing, "whether of fresh seed or mature roots, was punishable by death". This was because of the respect for the Yam-spirit. Coupled with fear of capital punishment, yam theft was greatly minimised. But "since the introduction of English Criminal Law, this sort of robbery has increased greatly", writes Dr. Basden, "as the penalties do not inspire sufficient fear"[402].

Njoku features in some Igbo names. These are the so called Yam-spirit oriented children. Male children are called Njoku, Ajoku, Agbaraji, Nwosu, Osuji or Ifijoku, while Mmaji refers to female children. They are regarded as human representatives of the Yam-spirit. As such they have some social privileges: they have the right to any yam they may demand from the oba, the storage place for yams. The yam-chief, called "Eze-ji", has the privilege "to sire" these children. These privileges have proved a ritual burden in recent years, and many a time caused friction and envy between the yam-oriented children and the less privileged, either of the same family or of the same locality. A Njoku must marry a Mmaji. A Mmaji must be the first wife of her husband as well as the only wife with her ascribed status, i.e. other co-wives must not be Mmaji. This belief persists even among Christians who happen to be Njoku and Mmaji[403].

At their deaths the heads of Njoku and Mmaji may not touch the ground. At burial there is a raised platform to which a solid receiver is attached in order to collect the head as it falls off after decay. The head is then ritually dug out, washed and put away in a box which is placed on a raised platform built for the purpose. From this moment, a taboo is put on yam automatically; no member of the family may eat yam until the head is ritually buried, a very costly affair. It is then not surprising that some Igbo developed an ambivalent attitude towards yam-oriented children[404].

5.2.2.6 Agwu-spirit (Agwunshi or Agwu-isi)

Agwu or Agwunshi, is the spirit that gives knowledge in matters pertaining to: the medicinal value, power, quality and use of different herbs, roots, leaves, fruits, grasses and various objects like minerals, dead insects, bones, feathers, powders; objects used in cures and prevention of diseases and other forms of sufferings (such as barreness), failure in undertakings, misfortune, poor crop-yields in the field; magic, witch-craft, sorcery and how to combat (or use) them; the nature and handling of spirits and various secrets; power to divine hidden phenomena; and to reveal to human beings through their servitors (specialists)[405] the complicated nature of cosmic relationships.

Dr. Uchendu remarked that the Igbo exhibit much ambivalence towards Agwu-Isi (Head-spirit). "They discuss Agwu with horror and refer to it as Onye ukwu-a (the big one). The only Igbo willing to discuss Agwu extensively are its servitors, who talk of their early horrible encounter with Agwu, their long struggle to avoid it, and how they finally agree to serve it"[406]. Agwu is indeed a most proselytizing spirit, always in need of servitors ! It is very envious of people's wealth, which it paradoxically claims to bring. To serve Agwu, is to enter the long rites of ordination which makes one eventually a specialist, a "Dibia", either "Dibia-na-agba-afa" (a diviner, fortune-teller, or medium) or "Dibia-naachu-aja" or "Dibia-na-ago-mmuo" (priests - professional priests in contradistinction to normal family priests) or "Dibia-na-agwo-ogwu" (traditional doctors of various kinds, the so-called medicine-men, herbalists, witch-doctors)[407], "Dibia-na-agha-mmiri" (rain-makers), or "Ndi Amuma", (prophets, prophetesses[408] and magicians)[409].

To specialize for any of these offices entails a long and arduous period of training, costs much money and demands a great deal of patience. Some stop after the initial rites or at any stage of the ordination process[410].

As in all traditional African societies, these servitors of Agwu are the greatest gift and the most useful source of help to traditional Igbo communities. Every village has one or more of them within reach; they are the friends of the community; they are accessible to everybody and are all times ready to play their part in individual and community life[411]. To understand their important position in the society one has to bear in mind what was said about the Igbo world-vision, a world-vision where nothing is purely physical. Everything has its spiritual or religious dimension; even disease and misfortune are religious experiences. They therefore require a physical as well as a religious approach for a cure[412].

One often regrets that these Agwu-Servitors - these "Specialists" - and their specialized offices have not been given the careful study they deserve; and worse, that the traditional societies are daily disintegrating. It is no exageration to say that all these servitors of Agwu belong to a special category of their own. In fact they have a language, symbolism, knowledge, skill, practice and what one may call "office personality" of their own, which are not known or easily accessible to the ordinary person, whether he is a villager or a scholar in search of knowledge. They are in effect the repositories of knowledge, practice, and symbolically of the religious life of their communities. They make the history of Igbo traditional societies both sacred and religious. They are symbolic points of contact between the historical and spiritual worlds, concrete symbols and an epitomy of man's participation in and experience of the religious universe, such that without them society would lose sight of and contact with religion. In them are to be found the continuity and essence of Igbo religious thought and life. And as long as these specialists and their specialized offices (i.e. what remains of them) are not given the careful and due study they deserve, much, in fact a great deal of inner information, will remain ungathered and unaccessible to the public[413].

5.2.2.7 Water-spirits

Among the Igbo, not only the major objects of nature like the sun, mountain or hill, but also seas, lakes, rivers, rivulets and streams have become subjects of great veneration. It is Igbo belief that a big river or lake has a spiritual principle which animates it[414]. "In a prescientific environment", remarks Professor Mbiti, "this form of logic and mentality certainly satisfies and explains many puzzles of nature and human experience. Through the centuries it has become an institutionalised part of 'looking at the world'; so much so that it colours the subconscious corporate and individual thinking and attitude of African peoples".[415]

Whether it is just the fish or some other inhabitants of the river, such as crocodile, water-snake, etc. which are regarded as sacred or spiritualised, or the water itself, i.e. the principle supposed to animate the river, stream or lake, is rather a difficult question. Basden seems inclined to think it is just the fish or some other creature inhabiting the water[416]. In some communities, indeed, there is no doubt that this is the case. They regard some creatures of the water such as fish or crocodiles as sacred, either because of some mystic or mythical connection with their ancestors or because of some other similar reasons or belief. In such cases they often refer to these creatures as "Nne Anyi" - "our mother"[417]. No such creature which is reverenced may be taken away from the stream, or be killed by anybody. This is the case at Amaiyi, a small stream in Ihitte-Amakohia. It is not infrequent that a great conflict arises between those who uphold the sacredness of these creatures and other Igbo or non-Igbo communities which show no respect for them[418].

In some communities, it seems to me, it must be admitted that it is the river itself the principle animating it, that the people believe to be sacred. Such is the case with Iyi-Igu, a small stream at Obiakpu-Egbema. The fish and other inhabitants of this stream may be killed, the water can be drawn. But whatever falls either into the water while crossing it or on the ground regarded as the "territory belonging to Iyi-Igu-spirit", must not be touched. It is believed that Iyi-Igu desires such. Likewise other articles of whatever kind used in sacrifices to him must not be taken by anybody. Many people report of their encounter with him. He is represented as an elderly man in white colour.

In some other communities both the water and everything inhabiting the water are regarded as sacred. In such cases it seems the sacredness of the creatures inhabiting these waters is more or less an "attributed sacredness" - i.e. these creatures are sacred because the water which they inhabit is sacred or spiritualised.

Among the Igbo there are numerous such water-spirits[419]. But as it is to be expected these are naturally locally recognized, and likewise the cults paid to them. The Southern Igbo communities on both sides of the Imo River respect Imo-Miri very highly. This gives rise to a communal rite in which people participate annually. The rite is held during the annual flood, which occurs between May and July. At this rite the Imo-Miri is requested to bestow more favours, children, an increase in wealth, for example, and to protect her worshippers during the next season. People may swear their innocence before an Imo-shrine. It is believed that those who swear falsely are liable to drown in the river or suffer from water-logging disease. People who die in this way are denied ground burial. Likewise those who die by drowning (either by suicide or otherwise) are buried on the banks of the river. They are believed to be taken away by Imo-Miri during her annual flood[420].

A similar cult obtains among the people of Oguta, who live on the banks of a very beautiful lake. The spirit of the lake is called Uhamiri, but is often referred to as Ogbuide, the lady of the lake. Ogbuide is an attribute of Uhamiri and means "she that gives in plenty". Many Oguta girls bear this name. Stories abound of people who have seen, or spoken with her[421]. Some people even claim that Ogbuide is responsible for their wealth. Such people give themselves such greeting and dance names as

"Egosinamiri" - wealth from the water[422]. On Orie day all those whom she has chosen as her favourite may not go to the lake to fish. They "go on a special diet and eat plantain which is the favourite of the woman of the lake"[423].

The River Niger is paid a similar cult by various Igbo communities. She is referred to as Osimiri or Oshimiri or Orimili. At Oguta, she and Uhamiri are regarded as the wives of Olashi - a river that runs through many Igbo communities e.g. Oboroto, Mmahu, Abacheke, Okwuzi (in Egbema village-group), Osu (Ezi-Osu), Ihiala, Ihiembosi and Okija. In all these places cults are paid to Olashi.

5.2.2.8 Remarks

(a) The organisation and power structure of all these "Aluse" mirror Igbo social structure. And like Igbo social structure they are not conceived of as forming a hierarchical pantheon. There is no seniority or authority implied in the conception of them. Though some are believed to be "more uncompromising" and "more wicked", and, some still "nearer" and "dearer" to the Igbo than others[424], yet this trait does not make them rank higher or lower than the others. Actually it is in Igbo practice to appeal to one or to a number of them simultaneously without any consideration of their rank or state. The Igbo, further demand from them "effective service" and "effective protection" in which duty, if they fail, "are always threatened with starvation and desertion". But if they give "effective protection", the Igbo are very faithful to them[425]. Here one is face to face with the Igbo "markedly success orientated", egalitarian but individualistic principle - namely that essential aspect of the "right and natural" that talent should lead to enterprise, and enterprise to promotion and promotion to privilege i.e. "social status placement"[426]. A rigid structuring, therefore, of these spirits would do harm to this principle[427].

(b) A careful reflection on Igbo conceptualisation of these created but non-human spirits, apart from the fact that they all are essentially metaphors for Chukwu; it is the same Chukwu that all speak of, and we cannot mention any and leave Chukwu behind[428], compels one, nonetheless, to make the following observations.

Psychologically these spirits are semi-physical and semi-spiritual entities: men imagine that there is a spiritual being activating what otherwise is obviously physical, which form of logic and mentality, in pre-scientific environment "certainly satisfied and explains many puzzles of nature and human experience". This has, through the centuries, become an institutionalised way of looking at the world, so much so that it colours the sub-conscious corporate and individual thinking and attitude of African peoples[429]. In other words, they are mostly the creation of man's imagination. But this does not cancel their reality. On the contrary they are "real beings", as far as the people are concerned. They are in effect "timeless", i.e. in the eyes of the people they have always been there, and are constantly experienced in the physical life of men, as "Ale", "Igwe", "Anyanwu", "Amadioha", as "Ifijioku", etc. In a way they appear "closer" to men than God, whom they manifest and symbolize. Men feel them nearer both to themselves and to God. Little wonder it is then, that men regard them as intermediaries and even pay cult to them as an indirect way of approaching the Supreme Being.

(c) Sociologically, one would be tempted to view them as men's attempts to "historicize" what is timeless and what man experiences in another context as spiritual beings. They use them to explain (perhaps unconsciously ?) customs, ideas or institutions whose origin is otherwise lost to historical sight, i.e., to "historicize" for their descendants customs, ideas and institutions which are either difficult to grasp or are shrouded in the mystery which covers them as they sink deeper and deeper into the oblivions of the "duduludu" period[430].

(d) The sacrifices the spirits receive, the devotion, the honour and the reverence the Igbo pay them - the cults of the spirits, including that of "Chi", "Ikenga", and all the other cults of individual achievement and advancement: "Ukwuije" or "Ukwu-na-ije" (the cult of the feet), "Iru" (the cult of the face), "Uho" (the cult of the tongue" and "Umu-oku" (the cult that conserves accumulated wealth)[431] - all are ascribed to what Pius Anyadioha Ibeawula[432] termed "Ikele Chileke na ndi mmuo nile n'enye aka" - Thanking God and all the spirits that help. From his explanation there seems to be a deep-seated twofold dimension of religious inward consciousness, often too subtle to distinguish.

First, Chileke (Egbema dialectical form for Chukwu, God) he emphasized is the Be-all and End-all (Chi-Chinile) who created and controls the spirits, gave them power over men and the world. At the same time there is the awareness that sacrifice, honour, devotion and reverence should be given to these spirits, for they are present to protect and help men, and present to them not merely by accompanying them and by watching over them, but also by reporting all the activities in the world to Chukwu (this even when they visit men with calamities). In doing all this the spirits obey Chukwu with such faithfulness and help men in such great need. In paying honour, devotion and reverence and in sacrificing to the spirits "we believe that, not only are we not ungrateful to the spirits, but also, at the same time, we sacrifice, honour and worship God from whom all the spirits and men derive their being"[433].

5.3 Ndichie, Akaliogeli (Dead Human-spirits), generically Mmuo

5.3.1 General characteristics

Apart from the Alusi, the Being forces, which we have hitherto been describing, the Igbo have another category of spiritual beings. These are the remains of dead human beings who once lived in Uwa - the earth of men, animals, rivers, seas, etc. Whatever remains of human beings when they die physically the Igbo call Mmuo[434]. To become Mmuo is the "ultimate status of men". It is a destiny which men must necessarily and inevitably reach when they die physically[435]. Mmuo are ontologically nearer to God, i.e. in terms of "communication" with God they need no intermediaries, as men would. "Ibu Mmuo" is then ontologically higher than "Ibu Mmadu".

All Mmuo are invisible and ubiquitous. But the Igbo in common parlance designate the subterranean regions, the underground, the nether world to them, which is believed to be under the presidency of the Earth-spirit - Ale[436]. Perhaps the idea of the subterranean regions, the nether world, seems to be suggested by the fact that the bodies of the dead are buried and the ground points to, or symbolises, the new-home-land of the departed[437].

5.3.2 Various categories of Mmuo

There is a subdivision between Mmuo and Mmuo. Some are regarded as good Mmuo; others as bad Mmuo or evil Mmuo (Ajo Mmuo or Akaliogeli).

5.3.2.1 Ndichie ("canonized spirits")[438] and their role

If men, while on earth "founded lineages", were "good and popular"[439], die without blemish after a good "old age" and "received proper burial"[440], they become what the Igbo call "Ndichie" i.e. "canonized spirits" (I shall return to this later). This is similar to canonization by acclamation in early Christendom. These, too, are intermediaries between their families on earth and God. They intercede for them before God; and intervene with all Alusi on their families' behalf; prevent evil spirits from carrying out devilish designs against their descendants on earth. On their good will, indeed, their families set great store[441].

"The Ibo", writes C.K. Meek, "believe that their lives are profoundly influenced by their ancestors /i.e. the "canonized spirits"/, and this belief has far-reaching sociological consequences. Any departure from custom, for example, is likely to incur the displeasure and vengeance of the ancestors. The ancestors under the presidency of the Earth-spirit, Ala, are the guardians of morality and owners of the soil."[442]

Such is indeed the influence of the ancestors. They are thought of as the invisible segment of the lineage. The Igbo regard them as ever interested in the affairs of their descendants, and because they are now "Ndi Mmuo" - spirits - they enjoy more power, which they can effectively utilize in interceding for their children before God. It is their particular concern, that their descendants should thrive and prosper indefinitely and create a big name on earth; and any honour or glory the family acquires belongs to the entire unit, in both its segments, visible and invisible[443]. Afamefuna and Obiefuna, (meaning, may my name live interminably in my descendants, or may my name not be lost; and may my "Obi", house-hold, or extended family, not perish respectively), are two Igbo names echoing this ardent wish.

Since the ancestors were responsible for the creation of the first shrine to the Earth-spirit, Ala, being the founders of the land, village or town, they become for their descendants the best interpreters of the mind of the Earth-spirit. They are regarded as tuteledge of law, customs and morality[444]. Hence Professor Ilogu remarks: "It is by being loyal to the traditional code of morality, that the tribe or extended family could survive. The concept of society among the people, therefore, is a perpendicular one in which the present are rooted in the past through respect and obedience to the wishes of dead ancestors, and the future is assured of stability through obedience of the present generation."[445]

5.3.2.2 Bad-spirits, Ajo-Mmuo or Akaliogeli

When, on the other hand men who lived in this world, though they may have founded lineages, but were "bad" and "unpopular" or "unsuccessful", die physically, what remains of them is regarded as Akaliogeli, Ajo-Mmuo or Ekwensu[446], i.e. mischievious, cruel or wicked spirits[447]. They are said to be wanderers. Likewise those who left no male issues are invariably included in this category. The logic behind this is that the Igbo are a patriarchal people and if any man leaves no male issue at his death to succeed him, his "Obi" or his "Afa" will be then extinguished (We shall return to this later).

Also people who died of what the Igbo call "Ajo Onwu" or "Onwu Ekwensu", as some Igbo communities term it, are thought of as Akaliogeli. Such are all whose deaths are caused by lightning or who die after swearing on oath (for this is evidence of punishment for grave sin), and all who commit suicide; often, too, people who die of small-pox or paralysis. None of these has a place in the spirit world among the community of "good spirits". They are believed to be wandering about perpetually, doing mischief to people (especially to their lineage members). They cannot return to the world by reincarnation - "fa ama noo uwa". They are thought of as wicked and cruel and as such are regarded with tremendous fear.

They "intrude" into the life of their living lineage members. The Igbo endeavour to avert the danger they may do to them by "Ichu Aja"[448] a drive - away offering made with rotten and worthless things. But the extent to which they can influence the lives of those on earth depends on the permission of God and the neglect of the canonized spirits.

If must needs be mentioned that all the spirits so far examined receive homage and "worship" from the Igbo on what may be described as a "contractual basis"[449]. Fidelity to them is assured when they play their part well. When they grow negligent of their "clients" they receive the same attitude in return. An Igbo adage has it, "Ka ana enye ndi mmuo nri, ka ikpe na ama fa", which means "let us continue feeding the spirits, so that guilt will be theirs !" When this guilt after a considerable time is not atoned for with diligence on the part of the spirit, the Igbo desert their cult. This may account for many shrines of spirits being left in dilapidated condition[450].

In fact one would be right to describe the cult the Igbo pay the spirits as "religion based on reciprocity". For if the contractual partners, the spirits, are guilty of negligence, i.e. show no diligence on their part, the Igbo are quite often forced, indeed they feel themselves justified and obliged, to change contractual partners in order to get the better of a difficult situation. This again agrees with their "success-oriented ideology", the essential aspect of which is that it is right and natural that talent should lead to enterprise, and enterprise to promotion, and promotion to privilege"[451].

More-over, in the Igbo conceptualisation of these spirits, they are all intermediaries, "ladders" to God and "bridges between him and men" (This will be treated at length later). The "triumph" of evil spirits over men and the effective and continued helps the good ones render to men are always in accordance with and in the measure the Supreme Being permits them. And this one perennially all-powerful Being before whom the Igbo have always to bow under all conditions, is Chukwu or Chineke. To his worship we shall now devote the following pages.

CHAPTER SIX: CULT OF CHUKWU: HIS PLACE IN IGBO RELIGION

6.1 What is the place of Chukwu in Igbo Religion ? Views of earlier writers

We have seen that Chukwu is the origin and sustainer of all things. He is the all-knowing, the all-powerful, who introduces order into the chaos of the universe. He is the final arbiter of right and wrong. He is the Lord of the visible and invisible world. All beings, both spirits, men and all forces of nature, are under him. Each in varying degree shares in his being[452].

What is the effect of this recognition ? What is the place of Chukwu in the religious life of the Igbo consequent upon this recognition ? What is his relationship to the spirits and the world of men ? In other words, has this theoretical recognition any practical consequence ? In short, is Chukwu worshipped by the Igbo ? There would have been no difficulty in categorically saying yes: He is worshipped. But there have been a few things written on this theme, all of which seem to agree in making him of little account in the religious life of the people.

Thus in 1938, the Archdeacon of Onitsha, Dr. Basden after forty years of evangelical work among the Igbo remarks: "Although there is a universal belief in a Supreme Being and His inveterate enemy, the Devil, the effect of such belief is negligible. It is purely theoretical and has no marked influence on life or character... There is no symbol erected to the Supreme Being, neither is there a figure (Alusi) to represent the Author of evil nor does there appear to be any trace of actual Devil worship ... Knowledge concerning him is vague and confused; it is as incoherent as that connected with the Supreme Being..."[453]. Meek, writing on same observes: "But he is a distant God of a vague personality and sacrifice is seldom offered to him directly."[454] Bishop Mark Unegbu made a similar observation: "The strange thing was that while the place was full of idols, while an altar of worship was dedicated to any god that claimed to exercise some influence over man, there was none to the 'Unknown God' of the Greeks or the Great God of the Ibos."[455]

James O'Connell, writing on West African religion in 1962 remarks as follows: "Most West African Religions have a high god who is also a sky god. But he is often a withdrawn high God, a deus otiosus... ; in spite of these attributes the high God is not usually directly worshipped; he has no priests and no shrines are dedicated to him; people may make a token offering to him in every sacrifice but hardly ever do they offer a sacrifice exclusively to him"[456]. And Le Roy Ladurie seemed to hold that God for the African is "en effet trop grand, trop puissant, trop bon et trop loin"[457]. Uchendu, writing in 1965, thought that this traditional viewpoint of the paradoxical "withdrawal" of Chukwu, "his otiositas", his remoteness has become such an "accepted fact" or shall I say "axiomatic" that he must needs toe the line. And so he writes: "The Igbo high god is a withdrawn god. He is a god has finished all active work of creation and keeps over his creatures from a distance. The Igbo high god is not worshipped directly. There is neither shrine nor priest dedicated to his service. He gets no direct sacrifice from the living..."[458].

Perhaps these writers are not all to be blamed, for to any casual observer, the "objective phenomena" in the religious life of the Igbo seem to be the spirits and the cults attached to them. Nonetheless one cannot help remarking that this "traditional view-point" does not do justice to facts. Despite Chukwu's transcendence, his "en effet trop grand, trop puissant, trop bon et trop loin", he is not so "far". He is no "deus otiosus" or a "withdrawn god", not even a "high God". On the contrary he is immanent, he is so "near", that men can and do in fact establish contact with him[459].

6.1.1 Chukwu is psychologically and immediately present to the Igbo in their names

That Chukwu of the Igbo is not conceived as a "withdrawn" God is clearly evident from their personal names. In Chukwu's hands is everything (CHUKWUKAODINAKA); and nothing happens when he disapproves (CHUKWUKWE, Osakwe, Oseloka). Had it not been for his mercy (EBERECHUKWU, Osegbo); were it not for God, something might have happened (BEELOLISA). Chukwu keeps us, even to this very day (CHINEDU, CHUKWUDEBELU)[460]. He has thought kindly of us all (CHUKWUEMEKA, Chukwueloka), and he has done well (OLISAEMEKA, Oseka).

As noted already, the most important and joyous occasions in Igbo life is when a woman brings a new babe to the world. IFEAKANWA is a popular Igbo name. It means "nothing is more precious than a child". For the Igbo a child is a "priceless pcssession"[461], "a woman's glory"[462], the "highest goal in life"[463], "the greatest joy of every Igbo man and woman"[464]; and the lack of children in an Igbo family is a "central tragedy"[465], culminating in a man being "written off the dynasty"[466]. "No one", writes M. Fortes, "is so unfortunate or so unhappy as a woman who has no children"[467]. And how often do visitors who come to welcome the child, congratulate the mother who brings such into the world, and say as they take up the child: "Chukwuemeka" or "Olisaemeka" - God has done well because he imparts life into the child for he is Chukwunwendu or Chukwujindu (Life belongs to Chukwu) and it belongs to him to apportion it. Thus the whole gratitude goes to Chukwu who has done well and has been very thoughtful of us all (Chinelo); the mother, however, is indirectly congratulated[468].

6.1.2 The gratitudinal response to Chukwu's providential care as an acknowledgment of his presence in the religious life of the people

Divine providence is so constantly alluded to in Igbo daily life that it has been made a salutation - greeting. Salutation among the Igbo is an elavorate affair and a mark of good breeding. A mere "good morning" or "good afternoon", does not suffice. One inquires about the health of the members of one's friend's family or his relatives. An invariable answer to this inquiry is nearly always an expression of gratitude to God; "Thank God, we all woke up this morning; we are well; we have only hunger to fight".

In some places, to have salutation-names very like and sometimes identical with personal names is a perennial custom and many of these names are theophorically conceived. After salutation with these names, there follows the traditional question as given above. And how many times will a man or a woman be greeted during the day with this name ?

Also how often does one hear an Igboman facing hard fortune console himself (or is consoled by others) with this Igbo adage: "Onweghe ife gbara Chukwu anya ghari" - Nothing puzzles (the eye of) Chukwu; He knows why He has let me suffer this. No one knows His times (Amaogechukwu) and His time of visitation is best (Ogechukwukamma). "He holds both the knife and the yam; whom ever he gives a slice, let him eat" (Chukwu ji mma, jide ji onye o nyere ya rie). Perhaps the imagery in this proverb may not be familiar to any one who does not know the importance of yam (ji) among the Igbo !

6.1.3 The immediate presence of Chukwu in Igbo conception of life

As we saw in Igbo ideas of life, Chukwubundu - God is life; and everything that exists has a "chi-ukwu-within", man inclusive; therefore because each man possesses chi (God-within), which is created and given him by Chukwu, and which upon death is reclaimed by Chukwu, the High God is always in one sense immediately present to the Igbo: "the villager participates in the High God through the possession of Chi"[469].

All are acts of religion. They are spontaneous prayers - the essence of cult and "religion in act"[470]; "the commonest acts of worship; some of which may be long and formal, but most of them are short, extempore and to the point"[471]. They are some attempts of elevating the mind, heart and sentiment to Chukwu; and thus establishing some kind of communion with him. They are Igbo responses of their mind, heart and sentiments to a divine person. And all these are born out of their internal conviction and awareness of their contingency and dependence on a power recognized as personal and divine, and, notwithstanding, concerned about each and every one of them.

6.2 Why the spirits loom large in Igbo religious psychology

Besides these religious or prayerful expressions which

permeate Igbo daily life, it must be borne in mind that the Igbo approach to God reflects their socio-religious structure. As one author would have it: "We may expect that social organisation will be reflected in religious belief and practice of the Africans."[472] For "sociologically speaking, African Religion is one element of African culture. No one element in the cultural complex can be understood in isolation from the rest. Religion permeates their life and therefore any full explication of it involves complete exploration of their social and political organisation, material culture, law and custom, as well as the physical environment."[473]

6.2.1 Religion, an affair of the group

Among the Igbo religion is not primarily for the individual, but for the group of which he is a part. It is communal: an affair of the family, the 'OBI-UNIT', the 'UMUNNA-GROUP', the village-unit and the town-grouping[474]. In fact, with regard to the Igbo, Professor Mbiti was right when he states: "Chapters of African religions are written everywhere in the life of the community; and in traditional society there are no irreligious people. To be human is to belong to the whole community, and to do so involves participating in the beliefs, ceremonies, rituals and festivals of that community. A person cannot detach himself from the religion of his group, for to do so is to be severed from his roots, his foundations, his context of security, his kinships and the entire group of those who make him aware of his existence."[475]

But the community as in all of its group activities, religious activities inclusive, speaks and makes its petition through a leader. In the family, the father leads; in the Obi, the Obi-unit-head; in the Umunna, the Oji-ofo of the Umunna-unit; in the village, the village-unit-head; and in the village-group, the Okpala of the town-unit or the Obi (the King) for those towns with central heads. Is it any wonder, then, that the practice of speaking through a mouth-piece forces its way, too, into their approach to God, that they establish contact with God through mediators, the spirits, who are looked upon as intermediaries?

6.2.2 Igbo approach to the worship of God reflects their socio-religious structure

In our analysis of Igbo socio-religious structure, we saw that there is in each grouping a unit-head called Oji-ofo or Okpala (ofo-holder), who is fundamentally regarded as the representative and mouth-piece of the ancestors: he is a rallying point in so far as he occupies the senior position traceable to the first ancestor and eventually to God from whom the ancestor obtained his power[476].

In each of these units, the individual member may not approach the unit-head except through a legitimate mediator i.e. through a representative of the subdivision of the unit or some one who is somehow equal to the "onye-isi", the unit-head. If one applies this principle to the Igbo man's approach to God, one finds that for him it is right and fitting to go to God through the messengers God created to carry on the theocractic, governmental affair of the Universe or through their "Ndichie", the ancestors who, now ontologically higher than ordinary human beings on earth, in turn direct the individual's requests to God either as personal intercessors for their lineages on earth or through the appropriate spirit[477].

6.2.3 Igbo approach to the worship of God reflects their age-status principle

The age status (seniority - juniority) principle regulates behaviour both between kinsmen and non-kinsmen[478]. It provides a recognized and institutionalized behaviour pattern. "Junior sets are expected to obey and respect senior ones, and it is on this behaviour pattern - the fear of the aged - that the whole political and social organization is founded."[479]

It is of such paramount importance that this etiquette be respected. Seniors lose no time in reminding juniors who do not respect this principle[480]. Thus in Igbo social etiquette it is considered discourteous, in fact, a thing "NOT-DONE", that a junior approaches an elder directly when he wants a special favour or to apologise for an offence. Not even a son may in such occasions go directly to his father[481]. The young person must approach the elder on such occasions through an intermediary, a friend or a peer of the one to be approached. If it is a thing considered "NOT-DONE" in inter-human relationship that a junior should approach his human and visible elders directly, logically it is all the more to be considered so for mortal men to go directly to "the-who-is-like-Chukwu" (Onyeḍikachukwu); who is "O di egwu kpom kwem" (the "mysterium tremendum" of Rudolf Otto)[482].

6.3 The cult of the spirits

6.3.1 Indirect worship of Chukwu (Chineke)

We have so far seen that among the Igbo Chukwu is psychologically and immediately never withdrawn from the people. It is also seen that their approach to Chukwu, the Supreme Being, reflects their conceptualisation of religion as a group-affair, their socio-religious structure as well as their social etiquette. Now the question is: apart from this reflection, is there any factual indication that homage is paid to Chukwu in the cults attached to the spirits ? To this we shall devote the following pages.

We shall, however, select those spirits which figure prominently in the religious life of the Igbo. These are the Earth-spirit (ALA), the Sun-spirit (Anyanwu), the Igwe-Amadioha, the Sky-spirit and the Spirit of Lightning, and the ancestors. (We shall not consider the ancestors here). It suffices for the moment to observe that the Igbo on their part, have their ancestors for "saints". They know no other who could listen to, and understand them, with the same patient interest. And that (they ancestors) are anxious to intercede for them before Chukwu and the spirits is beyond question.

6.3.1.1 The Earth-spirit and her cult

For the Igbo the whole earth is sacred. "In importance, it takes after the Supreme Being"[483]. And since the whole earth is sacred, every part therefore is sacred in a general way and is treated as such. So literally the people lived in the midst of the sacred. "They moved and had their being in an environment", says Dr. Ezeanya, "in which the sacred and the profane were closely interwoven but not mixed up; sacred persons, animals, trees, hills and streams."[484]

This abundance of the "sacred" makes it easy for the Igbo to pray to the Earth-spirit and swear by her anywhere and at any time. They need not travel long distances in order to get a sacred-place (a church for instance). But one interesting thing to note is that while the Igbo recognize the whole earth as one mighty spirit in a general way, there is no single shrine dedicated to the universal Mother Earth. There are, however, offences which are recognized as desecrating the earth no matter where they are committed. There exists a multitude of local Earth-spirit all over Igboland. Every town has its own particular Earth-spirit with a special shrine dedicated to it. Likewise every village within a town, every Obi within an Umunna-unit, and even a family has its Earth-spirit and shrine dedicated to it. This is known as ANI-EZI to which prayers and offerings are made[485]. At these shrines prayers - both private and communal - are offered to the Earth-spirit. Such prayers include daily invocations which every family-head or any unit-head makes for the welfare of his group. There may be also purification rites or sanctioning of new laws made by the community (which as is said already are given a ritual binding by sacrificing to the Earth-spirit).

Beginning the day

In Igbo society heads of families or any other unit-head, are priests; and as such, being aware of their privileged positions, are bound by Igbo custom to pray for their families, their relatives and friends[486]. This morning prayer the Igbo call "Ikpa Nzu" and "Iwa Oji" (powdering with chalk and breaking of kola). It precedes every other activity. No head of any unit may speak to anybody until this is said. Mr. Alutu referring to this remarked: "An Nnewi man who rises from bed does not begin day's work if he does not do them, and before however they are done, he must earlier have washed his hands."[487]

The family-head on getting up in the morning clothes himself and goes to the OBI[488]. Here he sits with his legs out-stretched and between them he places the family ofo, kola-nuts, white chalk and a cup of water. He breaks the kolanuts, chews a piece and spits a part of it on the ofo and throws out another piece to the invisible spirits and reserves the rest for visitors who will come to him during the day. He cleans his mouth with water and spits it out with force thereby producing a sound which onomatopoeically pronounced, is "TUFIA". Then he begins praying thus:

Ututu tuturu njo !	May the dawn dispel evil !
Chukwu (Chineke, Obasi)	God (Chukwu, Chineke, Obasi)
bia taa oji !	Come and eat kola !
Ala (ani) bia taa oji !	Earth-spirit come and eat kola !
Nna anyi... bia taa oji !	Ancestors (...names are mentioned) come and eat kola !
Mmuo nine bianu taa oji !	Ye Spirits come and eat kola !
Ihe Oma mee, ihe ojoo emena !	Let good, never evil happen !
O wetere oji wetere ndu	He who brings kola, brings life !
Ndu m, ndu ndi be m !	My life and that of my household !

God is then specifically thanked for preserving his family during the past night; for protecting them against enemies both known and unknown; and that they are offering this morning sacrifice of chalk and prayer to ask him to continue to guide and guard them for the day. Chukwu is invoked "to bless their hands that they make good"; their hearts "that they may think good"; their tongues "that they may speak right", he should not let their "children step against thorn or their pregnant wives bear children prematurely"; "them who think or do evil", he should "visit with destruction", but to their families and people, may he give good things, health and prosperity[489].

Annual sacrifices to Ala (Earth-Spirit)

Apart from these morning prayers and kola and chalk offerings at the shrine of Ala, there are also annual rites to Ala. The first of these is the "Sacred Week" or "Sacred Month" of Ala. This week precedes the planting of new seeds in the farms. It is a period when men should practise peace and good-will or as Talbot would have it, a time when:

No war or battle sound
Was heard the world around,
The idle spear and shield were high uphung[490].

During this period the Igbo observed meticulously absolute peace knowing that "should the peace of the Earth Mother be broken, she would permit the ground to bring forth but scanty harvest; whereas did but universal good-will reign at such a time, crops would spring forth with luxuriance, and flocks yield great increase and a multitude of strong and healthy babes be sent to gladden happy hearth."[491]

At the rite, before the planting of new seeds, on an appointed day, every house-holder brings to the central Ala shrine - IHU ALA[492] - his farm implements, knives, hoes etc. The family-heads having assembled, the Okpara takes some kolanuts, splits them into pieces and lays some before the shrine saying: "Ala, our beloved Mother, we the sons [the name of the village is mentioned] have gathered here, imploring you on our knees[493] that you may look favourably on us, your poor children and give us a rich harvest this year. When we plant our little yams of this size [he shows his fist] may they yield yams as big as this [he indicates the lenght of his leg]. A man's occupation is always his preoccupation ! It is ours to plant the crops, yours however to give the increase. When we plant our yams, we only see the outward signs, the green leaves. These leaves may be healthy but this does not mean that the harvest will correspondingly be big. We see the outside, you see the inside. It is your side of the rope that matters, for there hangs our very lives ! Save the yams from their infernal foe, the white ants, and may we reap them fat and unscorched !" "Eat this kola and help the yams in the small farms that if the rain be too much they may not drown and if the sun gets too strong he may not cause them to wither."[494] "Ala, our dear Mother, save us from harm. May we finish planting our crops safe from knife-cuts and other injuries. May all who are here today come back at the harvest to thank you for your graces." All present answer: "Ihaa" or "Ise" - may it be so ! He distributes the remaining kola to those present and when all have eaten, he makes a libation of palm-wine. All drink the wine and with this rite begins the planting season. The people begin their work hopeful of a successful output since they have in peace lived with their fellow men and have now the good-will of the Mother Earth !

The next popular rite to Ala among the Igbo is the harvest feast. This feast is known as Iro Ofo, or Ofala, Iriji or Ikeji or Igwa-ji, Ogwugwu-ji - i.e. the yam festival. This festival was mentioned in the section dealing with the Yam-spirit, Ifijioku, And as is noted, Ifijioku is believed to be the particular Alusi who, under Ale, is in charge of the plants in the farms, especially the yam. So the yam-festival is really sacrifice made to Ala as president of all the spirits connected with agriculture.

The chief-priest of Ala announces the date through his assistants, each in his village[495]. On the appointed day, the village is alerted by sounds of "Odu agwu" - the ivory horns used by priests. Rams, sheep and chickens are slaughtered by the compound and household heads, Ifijioku receiving the blood in a portable altar known as "ugbo aha (afa) Njoku". At about ten in the morning the communal meal prepared at Obu (Ovu, or Obi) - a reception hut - is ready. Children are given yams dipped in fresh palm oil. They are asked to take a bite of the yam and drop some crumbs as they run along the village paths. They are enjoined, however, not to look behind (perhaps for fear of scaring the spirits !)[496]. Then comes the rite at Ihu-Ala (Ala shrine). There the chief-priest of Ala (ezeani) places his ofo (staff) and a dish of palm-wine before the symbol of the Deity (which is a pot containing an egg) and, holding a kola-nut in his right hand and a chicken in his left speaks as follows: "Ala, I come to you on behalf of all the people to offer sacrifice. Do protect and prosper us all, and grant that we may live in peace with one another !" He breaks the kola, places a fragment in the pot, another on the ground, eats a third and gives a portion to the seniors present. Then he pours some palm-wine over the pot and ground, drinking the remainder himself[497]. It is pertinent to note that this festival "provides an occasion for women who have had children during the year to give thanks; those who have had male children present cocks and those who have had female children present hens"[498].

6.3.1.2 <u>The cult of Anyanwu - The Sun-spirit</u>

We saw that Anyanwu, the Sun-spirit, is commonly identified with the Supreme Being under the name of Anyanwu-Eze-Chukwu-okike (the Sun-the-Lord-the creator). Some communities speak of him as the Son of Chukwu[499]. The cult of Anyanwu differs from north to south in intensity. In some places it is primarily a private cult, while in other places, e.g. with the Igbo of Nsukka division, it is common with every Igbo householder having a shrine of Anyanwu in his compound[500].

Before this shrine daily invocations are made to the Sun-spirit during morning kola-prayer by the family-heads, during which they pray to the Sun for life and prosperity for themselves and their families. Then the kola is shared with all present giving the Sun his share, thereby manifesting the unity between them and the Sun-spirit[501]. But besides these daily invocations there are also regular sacrifices offered to Anyanwu at his shrine. Such sacrifices take place at dawn or at sun-set. During this rite the Sun is asked to sweep away evil with its morning rays and substitute in its place good fortune and divine blessing: "Ututu tuturu njo, Ihe oma mee, ihe ojoo emena"[502].

Dr. Meek describes one such sacrifice. Before the shrine of Anyanwu which "consists of 'Obo' tree, with a mound of sand built round the base of the tree", the family-head makes his offering of kola to the Sun. He splits a kolanut and lays two pieces on a stone-altar of the shrine and says: "Anyanwu, Eze Chukwu oke, protect me and my people". He then hands other fragments of the kola to all present in order of seniority, and all ate. After a minute or two a small boy handed a platter of palm-oil to the officiant who poured the oil over the kola saying: "I do not offer sacrifice to you with an evil heart. Protect me therefore and protect my family". His senior wife, standing in the background, added: "Protect us all"[503].

In "Biblical Revelation and African Beliefs", Dr. Ezeanya describes a similar sacrifice at Okpatu in Udi division. There the shrines of Anyanwu are called Onuanyanwu (the Sun's mouth). The component parts of such a shrine are pieces of stones, ofor (the symbol of justice and an essential cult object of the Igbo), Ogbu tree, woven palm-frond, one small earthenware pot which must not be painted in any way; it must be free of any artificially applied colour (the people describe its colour as white). Rites are performed during which the people say: "We offer sacrifice to Anyanwu and we ask him to present it to God"[504]. At Ukana, a neighbouring town to Okpatu, a similar cult is performed.

6.3.1.3 The cult of Igwe-Amadioha - The Sky-spirit and the Lightning-spirit

The sky-spirit (Igwe) and Amadioha (the Lightning-spirit) have been treated already. Likewise the subtle distinction the Igbo make between them. Both, however, are commonly recognized as agents of the Supreme Being, Chukwu; and are in fact often identified with Chukwu[505]. There are also cults attached to them.

In land cases, in disputes involving false and malicious accusations, Chukwu is sometimes called upon to arbitrate through his agent, Amadioha. The ritual for such is simple: "A white cock is taken to the shrine of Amadioha; tied to a bamboo stick which is then stuck in the ground before the shrine. The offender is asked to declare his innocence and then break an egg before the shrine of Amadioha. This part of the ritual is called "itu-ogu". "If he is innocent, it is believed that thunder and lightning will fight his cause. The head of the cock is torn off the body and placed at the shrine. The Supreme God is expected to act unfailingly through his agent."[506]

Dr. Talbot in his book, "Some Nigerian Fertility Cults", describes a shrine of Amadioha as "a house on whose door are carved two strange woman figures". Their functions are explained thus: "These are the servants of Amadioha. Their names are Omogwa and Otamelli. The first - with spread tresses - is calling upon the tempest by striking on her mouth. The second is about to loosen her hair which floats around her in the storm-wind darkening all the earth - a possible picturing of the rain-bearing cloud."[507] At this shrine he told us that offerings are made to Amadioha through small holes near the figures described. When people come "to bless the shrine" or to ask for personal favours, they place offerings of kola through theses holes[508].

Annual sacrifices are made to Amadioha before harvest. At such occasions "each householder is expected to take an offering of four lumps of pounded yam to the shrine, wave them round his head and deposit them before the cultus-emblem. The priest then sacrifices a chicken (brought by the householder) and makes petition for the welfare of the householder. The body of the chicken is taken home by the householder, cooked and eaten on the following morning, one leg being sent to the priest."[509]

All these are samples of indirect prayers and sacrifices offered to Chukwu. And as Dr. Ezeanya remarked: "During these sacrifices, God may be mentioned and his help invoked explicitly. Sometimes he is not mentioned at all; but whether he is mentioned or not he is generally believed to be the 'ultimate recipient' of offering to the lesser 'gods' who may be explicitly referred as intermediaries."[510]

Now we shall examine direct sacrifices to Chukwu. For just as there are occasions when citizens feel compelled to think, that heads of departments of a government, who are charged with such authorities as permit them to take far-reaching, executive action with reference to the affairs of the citizens, and to all intents and purposes are "almighty", but are, after all, men under a superior authority, must be brought under discipline, and they make appeal against an action on the part of such heads of departments to their superiors, so too the Igbo in distress or in serious crisis of life feel compelled to approach God directly without any mediation.

6.3.2 Direct cult and worship of Chukwu

6.3.2.1 Direct worship of Chukwu through prayers

"In time of great distress", when God becomes "the final resort, the last court of appeal", the Igbo turn to God; they pray to Chukwu directly without intermediaries[511]. Thus for example: "Often, barren women", writes Ojike, "go to God with gifts asking him to give them children. They do not think that God purposely made them barren; rather they say that they sinned against God and are being punished just as a mother punishes her disobedient child. Under such an anxiety, an Ibo woman can be heard praying: 'O Great God, Keeper of Souls. What have I done to anger Thee ? Look upon me ! Behold ! I bring gifts and beg Thee to have pity upon me and give me a child. Grant this prayer and all my life I will be Thy servant'."[512]

Sometimes such prayers may be only simple gesture of the hand, a gesture, however, which symbolises and implies an appeal to the Supreme Being. "It may be a mother who behind her hut in the early morning when the village is still quiet, raises her first-born to heaven to present it to the Supreme Being, while murmuring a prayer of offering of filial request; or again, a father who when his son is leaving the paternal roof for a long journey, invokes the help and protection of the Most High during the journey till the day of return home."[513]

For the Igbo Life is the priceless gift of God; and the protection and prolongation of it form every morning's object of prayer. And so writes Talbot: "Every morning among most Ika as with many other Ibo, every man or woman, on rising, raises his hands to heaven, rubs them together and says: 'God, I thank you for long life' and if a child has just been born, 'I thank you for my child', etc - and prays for help for the day"[514]. As Dr. Nwokocha rightly observed: "The most solemn and most official of these morning prayers is the Kola-offering-prayer where the family-head, the Onyisi, Oji-ofo, etc, invites God to come and eat kola: 'Chukwu eat kola, ancestors eat'."[515] And Dr. Ezeanya records for us the morning prayer of a Nnewi priest while offering kola-nut. Here is the prayer:

Chukwu taa oji	God, eat kola-nut.
Mmuo taanu oji	Spirits, eat kola-nut.
Igwe taa oji	Sky, eat kola-nut.
Agbala taa oji	Agbala (one of the local spirits) eat kola-nut.
Ayi aya anwu	May we not die.
Ayi aya efu	May we not perish.
Ekwena k'any yaa	May we not be sick.
Ekwena k'anyi dudue	May we not be tormented with maladies.

Another prayer addressed directly to Chukwu is the following recorded from an elderly non-christian man of Ukana:

Chineke kelu mmadu !	God who created man !
Ndum, ndu ndi nkem	My life, the lives of my relatives.
Onye sim di, nya di	Whoever wishes me to live, let him live also.
Onye sim nwulu, nya nwulu	Whoever wishes me to die, let him die too.
Onye sim nweta, nweta	Whoever wishes that I should get good things, let him have them.
Onye sim elina, onu kpo ya nku	Whoever says that I should not eat, let his mouth dry up[516].

6.3.2.2 <u>Direct worship of Chukwu through sacrifices</u>

Apart from prayers addressed directly to Chukwu, the Igbo offer direct sacrifices to Chukwu too. These sacrifices may differ in names much as in ritual procedures from one community to another, but their end is the same - man's humble approach to the Omnipotent God to ask him for favours, or thank him for those received. For the sake of brevity the sacrifices to God will be studied under two headings: calendrical worship and non-calendrical sacrifices. But first the irregular sacrifices or non-calendrical sacrifices.

6.3.2.2.1 Non-calendrical sacrifices offered directly to Chukwu

These are offered by the individual or by a group, "when there is a bad harvest, or serious sickness, or an accident, or a calamity, that is, when some one is in trouble or in need of some help which he feels cannot be supplied by man, then a diviner prescribes a sacrifice to Eze-Enu."[517] And as Jack Goody remarks: "The rationale of such rituals and the function ascribed to them by the actors themselves (express or manifest purpose) is solving specific problems."[518] This sacrifice is called "Aja Eze-Enu", sacrifice to the King of the above. Though irregular it is "perhaps a more significant and more widespread sacrifice to the High God"[519]. It is of frequent occurrence in Agwu division and in parts of Awka, Onitsha and Afikpo, etc. [520].

The sacrifice is offered at sunrise or at sunset in the evening. The main elements of this sacrifice are a bamboo stick which can be of any lenght between ten and thirty feet, one white cock, a strip of white cloth[521], some leaves of "ebenebe" tree, some kola-nuts and, in places like Afikpo, some seed-yams[522], whereas in others phallic chalk (nsu)[523] are used. The cock is not killed but tied to one end of the stick; the strip of cloth and the "ebenebe" leaves are also fastened to the stick which is then fixed upright in the ground. Where seed-yams are used they may also be attached to the bamboo stick. The kola-nuts are left at the foot of the stick. "This sacrifice may be offered in front of a person's compound or within the precincts of a deity. Nothing used for the sacrifice may be eaten. The priest who offers it may be paid for his service with a few cups of wine. An adult may offer the sacrifice on behalf of himself and his family, but no female may set it up."[524] The offerer of the sacrifice assumes a squatting-position, facing the sun and prays: "You Anyanwu who are coming forth (or going home) receive this chicken (or seed-yams) and bear it to Chukwu. Protect my life and that of my family and avert all forms of evil. May sickness be kept at a distance and grant that I may obtain children, male and female". "And when he has finished", remarked Dr. Meek, "he leaves the chicken to die ultimately rot"[525].

There is another type of direct sacrifice which one comes across occasionally. This type is not offered at any special shrine. Such a sacrifice was witnessed in IHE in Agwu Division by Monsignor Ezeanya. The formula of the prayer which will soon follow was tape-recorded in the vernacular and translated by him almost literally. He writes: "The relatives of a young girl, who was about to get married, consulted a diviner and were told that a sacrifice had to be offered to God for the success of the proposed marriage by a priest at the shrine of Ana-Ihe /the principal Earth-spirit shrine in Ihe, a town in the Agwu-Division/ square, but not before any shrine, even though there were at least ten minor shrines within the square. The priest, seated on his traditional stool in the open and surrounded by the clients, offered the cock and then killed it, sprinkling the blood over the receptacles, yams were peeled and boiled and a meal prepared".

"The following prayer was addressed to God by the priest: 'God, behold Ugwuaka (the prospective bride) my child; protect her for me. Offspring is the main thing in the world. God, who acts according to his designs, give her children, preserve her husband-to-be. Give him means of giving me wealth to eat. If she gives birth to a female child, it will live, if a male, it will live. May she not have difficulties in child-birth. May her health be good; may the health of her future husband be good. Prayer obtains both among the spirits and among men. God, treat me well ! I am asking for goodness. My son-in-law shall give me things and I shall eat. Love will exist between us. God, that is what I ask for. Ihe land ! Sprits of Ihe ! God the creator ! I thank you. I have finished'."[526]

Dr. Ezeanya remarked that "when it was suggested to the priest in question that he might have borrowed his ideas about the High God from Christians, he retorted immediately and emphatically: "Chineke dili be anyi duduludu[527], anyi na akpalu Ya ugbo" (God has bee̩n among us from time immemorial; we weave sacrifical boat for him)[528].

6.3.2.2.2 Regular or calendrical worship of Chukwu through sacrifices

Regular worship of God may be daily, annually or seasonally according to the custom of the people. For the sake of clarity, we shall examine this under three-headings, namely, the regular worship by the family-head, the regular worship by the Onyisi (either of an Obi-unit, Umunna-unit or village-unit); and that by the Village-group.

Worship of Chukwu by the family-head

This may take place every day or during annual festivals before the individual's personal altar to the Supreme Being. Among the Nsukka people are the following types of altar: the small cone-shaped earthen altar such as those at Umani-village and elsewhere: a life tree called Ogbu or Alagba such as those at Umunne-Gwa village; a very small house type structure, usually unwalled, with a thatched roof such as those at Alor-Uno. At Alor-Uno, the family-head conducts his prayer to Chukwu twice daily: at dawn and at dusk. A.J. Shelton observed that Mr. Ugwu-nwa-ugwu-ani, whose shrine is referred to as Eze Chukwu Okuke (Lord God the Creator) twice in the morning and twice in the evening chant the following prayer before the altar, to which he sacrifices either kola-nut or palm-oil (after striking a small Ogene or iron conical bell four times):

Eze Chukwu 'Okuke: taa oje
Eze Chukwu 'Okuke: eat kola
Ka ndu ya dili
Preserve life, his, - i.e. that life may continue. (It appears he is praying for someone.)
Taa bo (name of market, usually): Eke (bo = bu)
Today is Eke[529].

This is equivalent to the kola-offering-prayer to Chukwu where the family-head asks for life and divine assistance during the day.

Worship by Onyisi (of Obi-Umunna or Village-unit)

This is more annually or during the year's feast than daily. Shelton has still another account of the worship by the Onyisi among the Nsukka. He writes: "The Arua ceremony is conducted by the Onyisi of the clan for he is the 'keeper of Arua', or the set of staffs and symbols through which the clan maintains close relationship between the ancestors (spiritualised Ndichie, and thus closer to Chukwu, the High God) and the living. Briefly preceding the Arua ceremony the Onyisi usually offers a short prayer to Eze Chitoke: Eze Chitoke, bea welu oje, Eze Chitoke, come have kola.

Mmuo nine di ebea bea welu oje	-	All spirits here come have kola
Wetebe umu aka		Bring forth 'children' i.e. villagers.
Wetebe nwayi		Bring forth women i.e. wives
Wetebe ego na ife oma		Bring forth money and good things." [530]

Worship of Chukwu by the village-group

This is done annually. In some places this worship also includes the intermediary spirit i.e. this sacrifice is offered to God through them. But Umugoje in Oba, Nsukka, has a day set aside annually for the worship of Eze-Chitoke. Here again we have Shelton to describe one such sacrifice: "For instance at Umogoje village in Oba there is a communal shrine in the village square called Onu-Chukwu (the place of God)[531] to which prayers and sacrifices are made annually on designated Eke day. At Umunne-Gwa village on the festival day for Chukwu (Eze Chitoke), each householder makes a sacrifice according to his personal economic ability at his house-hold altar (the 'life-tree' or Ogbu). On this day no sacrifices are made and no prayers offered to any other Alusi, for the day is dedicated to the High God alone. The prayers to Eze Chitoke on annual festival day in Umunne-Gwa are as follows:

Eze Chitoke: biko zogide anyi	Eze Chitoke, please protect us
Ketebe umu, ketebe ife, isi gi dibe	Bring forth 'childern', bring forth goods to please you.
Zogide umu ndi ikenyelu	Protect the people, the one you have made,

Biko zogide anyi	Please, protect us.
Ekwene ife obuna ka ome anyi".	Do not let things unexpected happen (to) us". 532

A similar sacrifice is offered annually in honour of Ezechitoke by the people of Okpuje. Here too almost every home has an altar dedicated to Eze-chitoke. "These shrines usually consists of a few flat stones with two bamboo sticks fixed some two feet apart and a strip of cloth streching across, tied to the ends of the sticks. From this strip of cloth hang smaller strips of various colours, with white predominating"[533].

Besides offering kola-nuts, food and fowl to Ezechitoke occasionally on this spot, there is a feast termed "Ili agba Chukwu", eating of the covenant of God; and it is celebrated during the yam-festival. Here is an example of the formula of prayer used by the priest as accompaniment to the presentation skywards of the gifts to Ezechitoke who is asked, in the company of other spirits, to accept the gifts:

Ezechitoke, Ana, Ugwuokpuje	Ezechitoke, Earth-spirit, Ugwuokpuje (Hill-spirit)
mulum, nyem ife olili;	that gave me birth, give me
nyem omumu; nyem nwanyi;	things to eat; give me offspring;
nyem ego; gozie madu nine.	give me wives; give me money; bless all men[534].

So far, I think, it is evident that Chukwu is worshipped in many parts of Igboland. Though there are no images or statues representative of the Supreme Being, Chukwu, yet there are specific offerings to him, such offering varying in frequency from place to place. And therefore God is never 'withdrawn' from the Igbo.

PART THREE: CHUKWU AND MMADU'S DESTINY

Every religion has to face the question of man's relationship to the power that rules the universe. Whereever we find man and religion "what is man ?" and "to what end was he made ?" are questions that demand doctrinal answers. Such answers depend upon man's conception of the ruler of the universe[535], while upon the answers themselves depends man's attitude to life[536]; and even the pattern of life within any given society is an expression of a particular view of man held by that society. Thus the religious practices, the shape of political life are in part much the outcome of that society's doctrine of God as of its estimate of man[537]. To these questions the next three chapters will be devoted.

CHAPTER SEVEN: WHAT IS DEATH, ONWU, IN ITS RELATION TO CHUKWU ?

7.1 Death of Mmadu: a natural event, a non-natural event or both ?

We have seen that for the Igbo life is a participation by a variety of existing beings in the Big-Life, who is the Chi-Ukwu; and the life-giving principle which Chukwu gives to every being is the MMUO (his breath of Life). This MMUO is generally the source of stability of every existing being and it gives that being its consistency. This source of stability when infused into that edifice called ARU-MKPULU-OBI composite assumes a peculiar form; it makes it MMADU - a creature sharing in a higher degree in the divine life than all other creatures and becomes, as it were, more like God, to whom man's whole being always tends. But in order that any being continues its day-by-day existence, Chukwu has continually to 'recharge' it as it were, with life. And when this 'recharging' with life is stopped, that being ceases to be (see Chapters 3 and 4).

So generally speaking, ONWU, death is the 'withdrawal' of the life-giving-principle, which is given to each being from above by the Big-Life-principle, a life-giving-principle which makes that being move, grow, thrive, growl and exhibit all sorts of manifestations of life. In other words, ONWU occurs when

Chukwu takes back the chi-ukwu-within-everything, which 'recharges' it day-by-day and keeps it alive. This separation of life-giving-principle from any existing being, be it plants, animals or men is in a certain sense common to all beings; hence the Igbo speak not only of ONWU MMADU but that of animals as well as of plants.

With animate beings ONWU means "becoming stiff". This "stiff-becoming" is most apparent in the immobility of the lifeless body, an element common to both men and aninals, and which can even be observed more readily in the cadaver of a dead animal. But is this immobility - this cessation of breathing and heart-beating i.e. this "common stiff-becoming", the characteristic thing when the Igbo say that "mmádu anwuala" (man is dead) or when they say "Okonkwo is dead" (Okonkwo anwuala) ? In other words "what element or who dies" ? What actually happens when a man is dead ? And why, if this "common-stiff-becoming" is the characteristic thing in the dying of man, is "ONWU MMADU", death of man, "ARIRI" - a sorrow deeply felt (Onwubuariri or Onwudiariri); the most painful calamity (Onwudiwe); a misfortune, a disastrous destruction (Onwudinjo); a most violent separation, the thought of which leaves mmadu frustrated (Ncheta onwu) ?[538]

To grasp how the Igbo conceive and feel about "onwu mmadu" (death of man) we must explicate more the meaning of MMADU. We must bear in mind that for the Igbo MMADU is the "Let-there-be-goodness or beauty", i.e. a synthesis of all that Chukwu created and created beautifully and is good (See Chapt. 3.3). MMADU, being then a synthesis of all creation is a being in whom nothing is purely biological, and nothing purely spiritual. It is rather an organic life whose component parts are existentially united and constitute the single and unitary living being; an organic life which in all its dimensions, including the involuntary functions, is partly determined, shaped, 'formed' by the spiritual centre of decision in the personality by free human attitudes toward the world and above all toward the social environment (See Chapt. 3.3 and Chapt. 4.2). Hence MMADU in Igbo belief shares in a higher degree in the Big-Life than all other creatures; and possesses its nature more perfectly in union and as such is not only more human but also more like God.

And if, for them, the interrelationship of ARU and MKPULU-OBI (Body and Soul) really constitutes the existence of the living man, constitutes the single and unitary living man, death is then not merely a 'neutral' process. It is a violent separation of something that belongs together by nature, a destruction, a disastrous misfortune. Thus in death what is called MMADU - MAN in the full and unadulterated sense of the word - simply ceases to exist, for man only exists as living being. In other words once these elements (Mkpulu-obi, Aru) are separated then the dissolution of this unity follows. MMADU no longer exists. Death is thus eo ipso the end of MMADU'S existence. With it is the downfall of what man is bent on life. It robs MMADU of what is the most lovable and precious gift, NDU, and this NDU as MMADU. That is why the Igbo regard it as a downright, "anti-natural" or "non-natural", a senseless break, i.e. something opposed to natural impulse and particularly to the natural impulse of human consciousness (Onwuelo). They do not wish it to reoccur (Ozoemena or Ozoemezinam), because it is responsible for the sad state of affairs both in the home as well as in the country (Onwumere; Onwumechiri).

But is this all the Igbo think Onwu is ? Would we be fair to stop here ? To stop here would give us an incomplete picture of the Igbo idea of Onwu. For despite the fact that they see Onwu as a dissolution eo ipso of Mmadu's existence, anti-natural, (Onwumechiri), they still speak of Onwu as 'a going-home' e.g. Okonkwo anago or arapugo (Okonkwo is gone home) or 'Ina Chukwu', "A going-home to Chukwu". (See also Classification and Significance of Igbo names: Chapt. 4.2).

So in order to grasp really what happens in the death of mmadu as the Igbo see it, we must also understand all the questions concerning man - not only of the questions of man's nature but also of his history, of the "pathemata anthropou" as Plato calls it - in other words all that has happened to man, and all that he has undergone since the very beginning of his historical existence[539]. These words "pathemata anthropou" were used in Aristophane's speech on love: "You understand absolutely nothing about the things of love if you do not consider what has befallen the human race" - by which, as it then turns out, he meant principally the primordial fall of man, his loss through guilt of his previous wholeness. The same thing is true of all our thoughts and discussion about the Igbo on death. If we mean to treat of fundamental existential matters, we cannot shirk the task of considering the implicit meanings of their mythical tales.

7.1.1 Onwuzuligbo - Universality of death

Empirically onwuzuluigbo (onu), i.e. death extends the whole length and breadth of Igboland. This is Igbo concrete and picturesque way of expressing that death is universal to humanity. "Igbo" here stands for the human race. The same usage is made of Igbo in the name - Igboefechukwu - meaning all men put together are not higher than God. Therefore death is a universal human experience[540]. This experience is both an abstract, conceptual as well as existential knowledge, as such names as EKENYENI-Onyeonwu and ENWEONWU (ENWE) suggest. The former name means "Is there anybody who alone inherited death (as his unique inheritance) ?" The latter is "Does anybody own death ?" These names are as if to say, though everything else about us, good as well as evil, is uncertain; death alone is certain. When a child is conceived one can always say: perhaps it will be born, perhaps there will be a miscarriage; perhaps it will grow, perhaps not; perhaps poor; perhaps rich; perhaps honoured; perhaps humiliated; perhaps it will marry and have sons, perhaps not. This "perhaps" can be said practically of whatever other good or evil one may name on the face of the earth: "perhaps it may be, perhaps not", but of no one through the length and breadth of Igbo land can one say "perhaps he will die; perhaps not". For as soon as one is born, it must at once be said and that necessarily too: "He cannot escape death".

Onwu is therefore a necessity, an absolute necessity, that awaits every one at an absolutely unknown moment (Igbapuni-onwu, Onwuferemugwu). Death knows no king (Onwuamaeze), respects no warrior, all become weak before onwu (Onwuamadike, Onwuasoanya, Onyekaonwu, Onwuegbufor). In the grave all men become equal, even the rich and powerful will die (Amadiaso-onwu), because onwu is afraid of none (Onwuatuegwu or Egwuakaonwu, Onwuasoanya).

In fact come what may, onwu must nevertheless be, it will never be lacking (Onwuako)[541].

7.1.2 Onwu, as "punishment" and therefore non-natural ?

But despite all this conceptual and existential knowledge of death, namely, that death is universal to mankind, everyone must necessarily die (shall I say that death is a biological necessity, which man must undergo), the naturalness of which some Igbo daily expressions as well as names seem to confirm, we have mythical tales which narrate that death is a punishment or "something"[542] which was imposed on mankind consequent upon a previous culpability, which culpability even, as was noted earlier, some Igbo names, such as Mmadubunjoala, seem to insinuate. Others attribute it to the maltreatment or failure of the messenger of immortality, thus implying the "non-naturalness" of death or its contrariness to nature ! Here we are necessarily faced with an enigma. And another Igbo name calls death an enigma (Onwugbaramuko) - and forced necessarily to ask: Is death for the Igbo after all a natural event or mainly a non-natural event or is it both ?

If we were to answer this question from what has been said so far beginning from Chapter Three, one would be inclined to say that the Igbo conception of death (onwu) is, that it is both natural and non-natural (a punishment ?). First onwu is natural. From Igbo cosmological concept, mmadu is a creature. Only "Chukwu bu ndu" (God alone is life). He owns life: to be is his nature (Chukwunwendu, Chibundu or Chinwendu). Every other being receives its being, man inclusive, from him. And it is inherent in the concept of creation that the "Creatura" - i.e. "a being receiving its own existence entirely from outside", can never by itself effect a fundamental change in its own state of being and its own existential goodness - not even given the premise of freedom to oppose the divine purpose[543]. Man is in that position and because he is a "creatura", he is absolutely incapable of remodelling his created being, his "nature", either for good or evil, even if he were to desire passionately to do so (and one is tempted to ask: is such desire really possible ?) And therefore no fault, no crime, no matter how 'inhuman' can so profoundly change man that he could even cease to be really human with all the natural endowments that belong to man: personality, physicality, spirituality and so on[544].

This basic fact of the createdness of mmadu is expressed by the Igbo in some of their names: MMADUABUCHUKWU, Man is not and can never be Chukwu, God. He cannot create - i.e. he can never effect any fundamental change in his nature nor in another's; not even be another man's Chi: MMADUEKE and MMA-DUABUCHI (Ibe ya). Therefore come what may death will nevertheless be; it will never be lacking (ONWUAKO, ONWUFEREMGBURUG-BURU, ONWUFEREM). If on the other hand, the Igbo in their mythical tales, etc., speak of death as a punishment, then there is an implicit admission that there is something in the phenomena of mmadu dying, which was formerly not there: Shall I say, something 'non-natural' ! And the most that one can say at this juncture is that there must be something in human death as it happens 'now' which was (probably) not there 'before', i.e. 'before' the 'guilt', for which mmadu was punished and sentenced to die; or before the 'maltreatment' or 'failure of the messenger of immortality', otherwise it would not be possible to speak meaningfully of a punishment. But what this 'before' is, Igbo tradition is silent.

Already it appears that for the Igbo, physical death, on the one hand, is inevitable and 'natural' to man; and on the other hand, it is a 'something' imposed on man because of some 'guilt' or on account of 'maltreatment' or 'failure of the messenger of immortality', and therefore in their concept, it seems to be both natural and non-natural that mmadu should die. But curious enough, for this physical death, there are often, if not always, immediate causes, such as witch-craft, magic, sorcery, and possibly the departed. Occasionally Chukwu himself (or another spirit) may be considered as causing or allowing death as a punishment to the individual (especially those killed by lightning or where one contravened an important custom, prohibition or taboo; or where there is no satisfactory cause)[545]. At other times (especially deaths which occur at a ripe age and are a cause for joy, being an index of a high status among the ancestors)[546], it is "Onwuchi" - natural death[547].

Perhaps it needs be remarked that these 'so-called immediate causes' of death, as the Igbo conceive them, should not be taken arbitrarily - i.e. they should not be considered in isolation. They should be examined in connection with their world-vision, a world-vision where both the visible and invisible 'dovetail' into each other to the extent that at times one is apparently more real than the other, but not exclusive of the other; a world-vision where each presses hard upon the other, manifesting and symbolizing each other; and as such there is nothing that is purely physical. Everything has some religious significance[548]. Also 'death', says Robert Hertz, "does not confine itself to ending the visible bodily life of the individual; it also destroys the social being grafted upon the physical individual and to whom the collective consciousness attributed great dignity and importance. The society of which the individual was a member formed him by means of true rites of consecration, and has put to work energies proportionate to the social status of the deceased: his destruction is tantamount to a sacrilege, implying the intervention of powers of the same order but of a negative nature. God's handiwork can be undone only by himself or by Satan... This is why primitive peoples do not see death as a natural phenomenon: it is always due to the action of spiritual power, either because the deceased has brought disaster upon himself by violating some taboo or because an enemy has 'killed' him by means of spells or magical practices"[549]. (We shall see more of this in Chapt. 9). Thus the paradoxical phenomenon that some scape-goat is often brought into the picture as the immediate cause of death and thereby satisfying the people's psychology.

7.2 Death and Immortality

7.2.1 Evidence to the factum of Igbo belief in survival after death

Professor Mbiti writing on death and immortality in traditional African religions remarked: "As far as one has been able to find out, the belief in the continuation of life after physical death exists among all African peoples though certainly with varying degrees of emphasis."[550] Talbot on the peoples of the Southern Nigeria observed in 1926: "Perhaps nowhere in the world is the influence of the dead stronger than in West Africa; nowhere is the dividing line between the dead and the living less definite. The ancestral shades play a full part in the life of the community, passing almost at will from one plane to the other. No one can hope to appreciate the thoughts and feelings of the black man who does not realise that to him the dead are not dead but living, in full command of all their faculties including memory endowed with greater abilities and power than when on earth... No doubt ever enters their minds as to the continuance of life after death..."[551]. And Archdeacon Basden of Onitsha in 1938 wrote of the Igbo belief in the life-after-death: "To him the unseen world is a reality: he is conscious of its nearness always. He knows that the end of this life will come in due course, and his one anxiety is that he be granted a worthy entrance into the land of spirits when the call comes."[552]

When that end comes the Igbo refer to it as "a going-home" - ina uno , or "going-to-the-spirit-world", or Ina CHUKWU - "a returning-home-to Chukwu"; and the mourning of the survivors is that of those who have said farewell for the time being only[553]. An Igbo song compares this life to a market place: "We are all buyers and sellers on earth"; it says, "whether we buy all we need or not when the market day comes to an end, we must pack our commodities and go !" (Afia ka anye biara na uwa; azujuo abo, azujughi abo, mgbe oge ruru onye obuna eburu abo ya naa)[554]. And a proberb calls life on earth a promenade, Ije uwa bu oriri.

Inherent in all these statements is the idea or belief that there is something in man himself that arrives somewhere after termination of this earthly course (NDU na uwaa), and that therefore persists undestroyed through the event of death and inspite of it; they purport that, though death puts an 'END' in a most emphatic sense to our life in this world, there is nevertheless an element in the concept of death that proclaims itself 'NON-END', that insists on transition, future continuance, even a new-beginning. In other words within the Igbo description of death, there inevitably arises the question of imperishability and indestructibility of some element of man's composition. The question, however is what element of this composition remains undestroyed and what is its nature ?

7.2.2 Igbo idea of Immortality

7.2.2.1 Onwu is ina Chukwu or ina ulo

The Igbo idea of the immortality of man is tersely expressed in their terming the phenomenon of dying (Onwu) "a going-home-to-Chukwu" (ina Chukwu) or "ina uno" - simply "home-going"[555]. To grasp the implication of these phrases, we have again to review Igbo idea of life.

In our examination of Igbo idea of life we saw that for them "Chukwu bu Ndu", "God is life itself". "Ya nwe ndu", "he owns life". He is "Chukwu Okike", the creating Chi; and he creates, i.e. apportions life to all existing things. In other words, all other beings are creatures. Of all creatures, man is the "let-there-be-goodness or beauty". He is the synthesis of all that Chukwu created and is good and beautiful[556]. Therefore implicitly the Igbo affirm that the whole creation is good. In fact an Igbo ditty expresses this thus: OYOYO UWA DI YA: OYOYO UWA DI YA - Speak of beauty or goodness the world abounds with it[557]. In their notion of cosmic origin, we saw that all creatures proceded from the Absolute existence-determining will or initiative of Chukwu. Thus every thing that is, receives its being from this creative-source, i.e. Chukwu summoned all forth into existence from "ife obuna adeghe"[558]. Also we saw that in their conception of a creature, it is one that is incapable of maintaining itself in being by its own powers. It must continually be "recharged" day-by-day with life[559]. To be sure, it likewise cannot take any step of returning into "ife obuna adeghe" (nothing ?) by its own powers, no matter how much it may long to do so. In other words, in apportioning life to beings (creation), something happens that absolutely cannot be undone again; the creature which has once entered existence can never again vanish totally from reality. There is some indestructibility in the life-giving-principle ("small Chukwu") given to each being; and this indestructibility inherent in creatureliness alone rules out the idea that after death everything can once again be exactly as it was before, i.e. before Chukwu brought it into existence.

So in a sense creatures according to the Igbo are "incapble of not-being' though they could return to 'ife obuna adeghe', just as they emerged from it, provided that pleased Chukwu. For none but he could evoke and undo the act of apportioning life (creating)[560]. Therefore in a sense according to the Igbo no created being can be called absolutely perishable, since all creation is Chukwu's work, who is Chigboo - a Being existing in eternity, i.e. the aged but not ageing Chi. And so his works persist also in eternity, unless he otherwise so wished ! Hence death (especially of Mmadu) is paradoxically called by the Igbo INA CHUKWU - a going- home to CHUKWU.

So despite physical death, as it is most apparently observable in the cadaver of man and animal when there is a cessation of heart-beat and breathing and the body becomes stiff, man is not annihilated. He still retains some relationship to its former being. He does not experience a total disappearance of being. Rather he 'lives' on, though it may be an attenuated form of life, life in a very feeble way. Thus it is intelligible for the Igbo to speak of a man continuing his life in the beyond among the group with which one was once associated here on earth[561]; to speak of the dead as being an invisible member of the family on earth[562]; their survivors on earth in the ancestral cult to address their dead not as Mmuo or soul of (let us say Okeke), but as Okeke; to speak to them as they would speak to a person living. Thus, too, it is understandable why a dead man is thought of as carrying over with him his social status placement and personal qualities to the world beyond. This is most apparent from the dialogue between Father Shanahan (later Bishop of Southern Nigeria) and a condemned murderer whom he wanted to baptize before his execution: MURDERER: 'If I accept baptism, Father, will it prevent me from meeting my enemy in the next life ?'

FATHER: 'Well, No, you will probably meet him in one way or the other'. MURDERER: 'Then baptize me by all means, and as soon as I do meet him, I'll knock his head off a second time'[563].

Also significant in this context is the formular some Igbo communities e.g. the Ngwa people and their neighbours, used to announce the death of a married woman to her people. When a married woman dies messengers are sent to her people to announce her death. After the sharing of kola-nut the messengers announce through their leader:

"Ogo i meela !
Nkea bu udu mmanya nabo (aboo)
Iji gwa gi na onwere onye ahu (aru) na anwu.
Nkea bu udu mmanya nabo (aboo).
Iji gwa gi na mmadu nwuru".

This may be rendered as: "Father-in-law, thanks for kola ! These are two jars, two pots of wine to tell you that mmadu (man, somebody, some-one) was sick; these are two jars, two pots of wine to tell you that mmadu (somebody, someone or man) is dead". The use of 'mmadu' is impersonal. And it implicitly enunciates their belief, namely that their daughter (let us say Adama) has gone home to join their ancestors in the Ani mmuo, leaving that which one used to see (the aru, body). We shall say more concerning this in Chapter nine[564]. From the above it goes without saying that according to the Igbo, it would be better to speak of the immortality of the whole man than just of the soul.

7.2.2.2 The religious significance of marriage and procreation

But Igbo concept of immortality is incomplete without a word on their social consciousness and the religious significance of marriage and procreation. The Igbo, like all other Africans, have always emphasized 'existence - in relation'[565]. They believe in maintaining a close relationship with their kith and kin[566]. As with most Africans, the Igbo 'feels himself incomplete when he is alone'[567]. For them life here on earth is not a private adventure but must be shared and lived with the community. This concept is carried over to the life in the beyond; and they would even reject "heaven" if going there means separating them from their kith and kin[568]. In fact a "visio beatifica" where they would probably be without their kindred is a shocking thought, a "taboo". This is palpable from the story Bishop Shanahan, the great missionary of the Igbo, told us of an Igbo chief whom he wanted to "convert". Here, in his own words is the dialogue: "This time after much sparring, I found the opening I sought, and began to talk about the next life. The chief listend gravely to rough - etched exposition of heaven; and what it meant. He heard me through and then, seriously: That is Heaven, you say. But tell me, will all the other chiefs be there too ? Or... ? They all live the same way as you do yourself, I suppose ? Yes, they do ! Well I'm afraid... 'T will be doubtful anyhow if they shall get to heaven at that rate. "Umm-m-M...". - Here was a difficult hurdle. You see... if I go to heaven and they all go off somewhere else ... I'd be up there in heaven all by myself ... while my brother chiefs would be down in this other place you speak of ... No ! I'd rather be with my own"[569].

And which traditional Igbo man, not yet influenced by Westernism, will blame the old man ! The Igbo on their part believe that the members of the village-and town-units, at the end of this life, when they go home - die - will congregate with their ancestors according to their families, villages and village-group-units in the ANA MMUO (spirit-world) to continue life as usual but in another mode[570]. This was why it was shocking for the chief to learn of a "visio-beatifica" where he would be separated from his kith and kin; it sounded like a taboo to him, indeed[571].

In the traditional Igbo society, like most African communities, "marriage", its economic and social significances notwithstanding, "is a duty, religious and ontological"[572]; "a sacred undertaking and obligation which must neither be abused nor despised"[573]; "a responsibility for everyone", to get married; and if a man has no children or only daughters, he finds another wife so that through her, children (sons) may

be born who would survive him and keep the name of the kindred interminably alive[574]. It is a 'sacred drama' in which everybody is a religious participant and he who fails under normal circumstances to get married is looked upon with misgivings by his kith and kin[575].
Even an Igbo proverb has it thus: Onye nulu nwanyi akwugu umunna ya ugwo; i.e. a man who marries has paid his um-unna (the localised patrilineal group) the debt he owes them. And how many Igbo Catholic priests and seminarians were, and to some extent, are still, regarded by their people as 'rebels and law-breakers' just because they chose to live celibate lives ? But what is the logic behind all this ? Is it as Basden and Onuora Nzekwu oversweepingly remarked and would have us believe that 'celibacy is an impossible prospect' for the Igbo ? I would be reluctant to comply with such an opinion. I would be more inclined to think, that it is because when a man is married and procreates a new 'focus of existence' is formed; 'a focal point where all the members of his given socio-religious unit meet' is constituted[576]. Or to put it in the words of an elderly non-Christian Igbo during a ritual act: he asked rhetorically: "Gene bu ndu ebe-ebe ?" - i.e. "What is life eternal or life interminable ?" "Ndu ebe-ebe bu onye amutala, ya mutakpa onye ozo", i.e. "Life eternal is when a person is born, let he also bring forth another person". In other words through marriage and procreation an Igbo believes that he lives on in a manner in his name which is formed, "renewed and revitalized", as it were, by his sons; he believes that "the torch of life for his group is not extinguished". In short he implicitly believes thereby to be "recapturing" at least partially or "attaining" in some degree the lost immortality or ability to rise again after physical death. On the contrary an Igbo who dies childless or has no male descendant to succeed him regards it as the utmost disaster, for he believes the fire of his life is in effect quenched and dead forever. His line of physical continuation is blocked[577].

This mysterious sense of continuity and solidarity enables the Igbo to think of themselves as living on as long as the group with which their life had been linked continues to live.

And this is the full implication - the religious yearning - of the prayers: "Afam efuna" - "may my name live on interminably"; and OBI(m) efuna, meaning may my household (obi), my kith and kin, live on interminably - i.e. may they not perish. In other words, may they live on and contribute the seeds of life which will continue man's struggle against the loss of original immortality[578].

Needless to remark, this is not, however, a personal immortality in the sense of the Christian teaching, but it is also not an absorption into the absolute, nor is it entirely irreligious[579]. Nevertheless it needs supplementation. But it should not be a cheap form of evangelization which simply 'sells' the Gospel by promising believers a utopia in heaven where an essentially carnal life of pleasure and leisure replaces this present life of sorrow and pain; and thus promising "heavenly mansions and other items which individuals may lack but wish to have in this life" - "a form of escapism" and "a cheapening of the Gospel" which "turns Jesus Christ into a purveyor of souls from this to the next world". What we need is a supplementation that is rooted in sound evangelization and coupled with "a comprehensive and biblical christology"[580].

CHAPTER EIGHT: LIFE-AFTER-DEATH

"But where a human being is concerned", says Robert Hertz, "the physiological phenomena are not the whole of death. To the organic event is added a complex mass of beliefs, emotions and activities which give it its distinctive character. We see life vanish but we express this fact by the use of a special language: it is the soul, we say, which departs for another world where it will join its forefathers. The body of the deceased is not regarded like the carcass of some animals: specific care must be given to it and a correct burial; not merely for reasons of hygiene but out of moral obligation."[581] In fact what becomes of man after death, is a question which has haunted Igbo religion, as every other religion, all down the ages. After death, what ? This is a poser on the face of life itself; and all religions each in its own way and according to its conception of the essential constitution of life has found an answer. And this, for "if you have reverence for death, then you have reverence for life"[582].

The Igbo on their part, are definite in the answer. For them death is not the end of life. It is only a means whereby the present earthly existence is destroyed. But in spite of the event of death, something in man himself persists undestroyed: an element in that concept of human death proclaims itself 'non-end'; it insists on transition, future continuance, even a new beginning. In other words, despite death life is not annihilated. It is changed for another. After death therefore, man passes into a 'life-beyond' which is called 'Ndu na Ani Mmuo' (life-in-the-Spirit-world) or 'a gathering into the community of the forefathers' (commune with ancestors), 'a going-home-to-Chukwu' - ina Chukwu[583]. This belief is attested in several ways.

8.1 Igbo belief in Life-after-death

8.1.1 Joy or fear of anticipation

The Igbo aged, look forward with longing or dread in anticipation of what may be awaiting them in the new life where they are bound to fare according to their deserts. This has often warranted during death-throes detailed confessions of past wickedness[584]. It is a common occurence to hear the aged saying: 'I am ready or prepared to go home' ('Oge m erugo' or 'oge erugo m ga eji ana'), meaning 'I am prepared to die and enter into after-life'[585]. When an ageing person is heard talking absent-mindedly or abstractly, it is generally believed by the Igbo that the person is talking to his associates or relatives who have gone before. Even sometimes some of them confirm this if asked. And often the Igbo speak of such aged people that they no longer hear what we say here; their conversation being with those who are on 'the other side'.

8.1.2.1 Burial and final rites

"In our society death has always been regarded with awe, as the most important of all the stages in passing through the world. It was surrounded by elaborate ritual, some of it quite beautiful."[586] And so "holding the most profound" and "exceeding tenacious belief" "in the spiritual" and "with it a profound conviction of the existence of a future state", the Igbo is deeply conscious of its relationship to the unseen world[587]. They believe that "when men have run their course in this world they return to their master - the Supreme Being - and live with him in the Spirit-world. In their spiritual state they are endowed with never-ending life". But this only occurs when a person is buried with due and proper ceremonies[588].

Before we go further it must be remarked that no proper mortuary and funeral rites (ini ozu and Ikwa ozu, either of 'ozu ndu' or 'ozu okponku' - the so-called 'second burial') are accorded to any one whose moral life while here on earth was, in the concept of the people, 'bad'. Likewise all those who died what the Igbo call 'onwu Ekwensu' (the death of the Devil) or 'Onwu-ike', forceful or wicked death; those who committed suicide or died after swearing, etc. - All these are thrown away into 'ajo ofia' - 'bad bush', or disposed of without delay[589]. They are regarded eo ipso as bad and disgruntled spirits. They remain forever wanderers, living a miserable and restless life and doing mischief to human beings. They will never join the community of the ancestors (Ndichie). Their 'existential abode' is known by some Igbo communities as 'Ama-ani-mmuo-ama-ani-mmadu' - those inhabiting - 'a not-spirit-nor-a-human-being's-world'. In short they are doomed forever[590].

8.1.2.2 The rites: Preliminary remarks

Igbo 'Ini-ozu' and 'Ikwa ozu' (burial and funerary rites) are a complex and intricate ceremony to which many an author had devoted a number of pages to describe. Ahunanya has written his doctoral thesis on this theme. But one regrets to say that all the writers concerned themselves mainly with the outward signs of these rites. Father Ahunanya seemed to dwell very much on the social aspects of them. The religious significances connected with these ceremonies have not been given the due attention they deserve[591]. These burial and funerary rites are observed in varying details from place to place; and according to the status of the deceased[592]. The underlying motives as well as the general routine are the same. And the main object of these rites are the following: first, they are all such as make it plain that the survivors strongly believe that the deceased is making a journey, though a final one, into another life. Secondly, there is also inherent in the rites the common belief that at the moment of death, the 'Aru-mkpulu-obi' composite splits into two parts: the marrow of the soul, the essential element of the personality-soul (the life-giving-principle which Chukwu gives man and which gives it consistency and stability, recharges it day-by-day and keeps it alive) - i.e. the 'Mmuo' or 'Mkpulu-obi' (the spirited soul) - separates from the 'physical heart' or 'corporeal-soul' (Obi)[593]. The former goes to 'Ani-Mmuo' or 'returns-home-to Chukwu' (Ina Chukwu)[594]; but its life is somewhat unstable and it does not feel at ease in these regions nor has it got yet its appropriate place among the ancestors; it is, as it were, sad; and as though lost, it pines for its other half since despite death, according to the Igbo, it still retains some relationship to its former being as 'Aru-Mkpulu-obi' composite[595]. So these rites apart from giving burial to the remains of the deceased are also meant to ensure the soul's peace and solemn access to the land of the dead: i.e. they are meant to aid the soul to regain its existential relationship to its former human existence, and enable it to be solemnly admitted into 'Ani-Mmuo' (the spirit-world). In other words, they serve to incorporate the deceased into the invisible community of its forefathers[596]. Thirdly, the rites (esp. the final rites - 'ikwa ozu') are designed to declare officially and definitively that such a one has led a life here on earth without 'blemish' and is now inscribed into the community of the ancestors and that his life is accordingly worthy of imitation and that the deceased should be venerated with ancestral cult[597].

8.1.2.3 Mortuary rites and burial

Immediately a person dies there is performed a series of ritual killings. First a cock or a goat (for a male) and a hen (for a female) is killed and the blood is sprinkled on the symbol known as 'Ukwu ije' or 'Ukwu-na-ije'. This rite serves to notify the ancestors of the deceased that he/she is coming on his/her way to joining them[598]. Death by striking the individual, makes him an object of horror and dread. Everything that surrounds him becomes polluted - i.e. not only the people but also objects that have been in physical contact with the deceased[599]. So his belongings may no longer freely be used, they must be stripped, by appropriate rites, of the harmful quality they have acquired. Hence some articles of the deceased's personal belongings are collected and broken or cast away into 'ajo ofia' (bad bush); some others are dedicated to his 'use' in his life in the 'Ani Mmuo'; the earth, too, is ritually cleansed[600]. At the spot where these articles are broken or gathered for casting away, the head of the deceased's kindred takes a kola-nut, breaks it and appeals to his/her predecessors in office not to harm him/her for he/she is the rightful priest/priestess, their successor. This is essential for he/she is doing a dangerous job: that of dispatching a soul to the spirit-world. The cotyledons of the kola are deposited beside the articles on the ground. After this he/she is handed a cock/hen, which he/she holds by the legs and strikes on the ground to die. This rite serves to despatch the released spirit of the deceased and give it protection during its journey to the spirit world.[601] The hair of the deceased is shaved at the same spot where the belongings are collected, and the corpse is bathed (formely in a large sized calabash). After bathing the corpse, it is annointed with canwood dye (ufie), dressed in its best attire, and laid out or set up in state. During this time it is visited by relatives, friends and acquaintances who come to take a last farewell of the deceased[602]. It is during this time, too, that the deceased's friends and relatives bring clothes, their contribution toward the dressing up of the corpse and preparing it for its journey. Every member of each group usually touches the cloth they bring on his or her head and touches his or her breast with it, the last person to do so puts the cloth by the feet of the corpse by which is usually a plate in which sympathizers drop money and other presents all of which are meant as a token of respect and friendship to help the deceased on its voyage to the spirit-world; a sign of sympathy with the relatives bereaved and sometimes as settlement of any debt owing to the deceased or that person conducting the burial[603]. There are even some mythical stories purporting that the deceased during their journey have to cross the "River of death" and others that they have to pay tribute in order to be helped to identifying their group in the spirit-world[604]. Still, while the body is laid in state, four large yams are placed on the roof of the house in which the body of the deceased lies. (Normally this is done by the son or daughter of the deceased.) A person specially chosen by the deceased (or a diviner as the case may be in some cases) takes the yams inside the hut, and places them on the ground; two at the feet of the deceased and one close to his right and left side, so that his hands touch the yams. While the person selected does this he says: "These yams are for you. When you return to the world may your yams be as big as these. And may we during our life-time be successful growers of yams. It is not by my wish that I place these yams in your hands but by yours. See to it that I do not suffer any harm in consequence". This rite is known as 'Ekpama' or 'Ekpawa Ji na-aka' - the placing of yams in the hand and was formely so performed at Owerri[605].

Next is the rite known as 'Eku-ihu-ocha' (making the face of the dead man white or radiant). Women of the deceased's kindred (Umu-ada) bring a cock (normally a white one) fastened to a string of cowries; and one of the women who is considered lucky (e.g. one whose children are all alive) or some person previously indicted by the deceased, holds or hangs the cock over the dead man's head. When the cock shakes its wings (in which case it is a sign of acceptance by the deceased) it is taken out and hung at the door of the house or on a branch of an 'oterre' tree in the compound. After a while it is taken down and its neck is drawn, the blood is allowed to drop on the ground at the threshold of the house. The fowl is then cooked and eaten by female relatives of the deceased[606]. Meanwhile funeral dirges are sung and danced. During this time two suggestive rites are performed: one is a ritual dance, in which the deceased's age-group sing war songs, dirges and praises of the deceased and appreciation of the contribution he/she made to the community. They dance and search the village for elusive death to avenge the wrong he had done them and if possible wrest from him his victim. Carrying sticks, matchets, guns, small branches and twigs, they dance round the village, peering into nooks and corners[607]. The other is a rite known as "EWA-ANYA", opening the eye. It is performed with a dog or a cock. The sacrificial victim is brought to the compound with a rope of palm leaves tied round its neck.

Drums are beaten and guns fired. During the drumming known as the "OGU NDU", a fight of life or "NKWA-IKE", a drumming that gives strength, a man specially appointed and renowned for his bravery carries the dog to the deadman's chamber accompanied by the members of his age-group, and extends the dog to the corpse saying: "I am doing this not by any wish of mine but by yours. And I do it in order that you may be a man of bravery in your next life - but a man of bravery merged with discretion". Having said this he and the others run out at full speed towards the drummers, who immediately cease drumming when the dog is held up in the air. This is done three times, but at the fourth time the man appointed to perform the rites stabs the dog in the throat at the door of the deadman's hut. (Formally it was customary to pour some drops of the dog's blood into the dead man's eyes but nowadays it is poured on the four leaves of an 'abosse' tree, the leaves being placed beside the corpse.)[608] The dead body of the dog is carried at a run[609] to the drummers who stop their drumming but soon recommence. Dancing is begun, guns are fired and songs are sung; the first song being: 'Oh, where is the dog, and where are they ?' The body of the dog is handed over to the senior member of the deceased kindred[610]. After these activities, the remains are carried to its last resting place. The corpse is carefully straightened in the grave and laid flat on the back facing the rising sun. The face must remain uncovered[611]. Some of the deceased's personal belongings, e.g. weapons of the chase and tools of his profession are also buried with him[612]. The relatives and others take up positions at the sides and foot of the grave. They must avoid standing at the head of the grave. (Meek remarked: "As, when the earth is thrown in, the dead man's soul - Nkporo-obi[613], i.e. heart-soul - is thought to take its departure from the head of the grave"[614]). The person who throws in the first earth shouts out while he does so: "Avoid the earth", i.e. "begone before the earth touches you"[615]. In case of any young man or woman who dies in the prime of youth, the people often say: "When you go to Chukwu declare to him who killed you and return to take vengence", or simply: "Take vengence on whoever caused your death"[616]. When the grave is filled up, guns are fired and all go home[617]. The grave diggers and all who came in contact with the corpse must purify themselves by taking a bath (in a river or in some water poured into a hole in the ground and lined with leaves of coco-yam or in a bowl) and rubbing their bodies with various concoctions, for in consequence of mortuary contagion, they are polluted and socially changed[618].

Some days after burial, a rite known as 'Eto-ewu-ikwu' is performed. But this provided the deceased has children. The members of the deceased age-grade assemble. A goat is provided by the deceased's heir. A person is chosen by divining; he takes the goat and pushes it backwards and forwards towards the deadman's house four times. He then kills it saying: "I do this for you that in your next life you may beget children who will remain alive and that you may have a long life ! The last drops of the goat's blood are sprinkled on two 'Ogirisi' leaves which are placed on the deadman's house. The goat is cooked; some pieces of the cooked flesh are deposited on the grave by the senior son of the deceased or by the Okpala of the deceased's kindred, if the senior son is still a minor. Also a libation of palm-wine is poured on the grave. The meat is eaten by all present[619].

Mourning and final funerary rites

As for the relatives of the deceased, they feel in themselves the blow that has struck one of them: a ban separates them from the rest of the community. And those who are most directly affected (e.g. wives, husbands, sons, daughters etc.) a ban is imposed on them and it affects their way of life: they are set apart from the rest of the community; they can therefore no longer live as the others do. For instance, they may not follow the way of dressing or adornment and arraying the hair, which are proper to individuals who are socially normal and which are signs of the community to which (for a while) they no longer belong. In short they are subjected to a number of mourning taboos and special prescriptions[620].

Apart from the mortuary rites and the mourning taboos and prescriptions, they are other rites coupled with pompous and sumptuous festivities. (We shall concern ourselves here with the religious significations of these rites.) These are the Igbo 'Ikwa Ozu' rites - the so called 'second burial'. With very few exceptions where they are performed a few days after the mortuary rites and in which case it is called 'Ikwa Ozu Ndu', they usually take place several weeks or months afterwards; and even in some cases some years may have elapsed before they are performed[621]. The responsibility for performing these rites falls on the principal heir - Okpala - of the deceased. In some cases it may be the responsibility of the family-group[622]. In the night of the appointed day, when all lights are out, the initiated men who impersonate the spirits of the ancestors gather at the compound of the village head. Iron gongs sound and a powerful flute blows a high-pitched blast. Then comes the falsetto, guttural and awesome voices of the "Okoroshi" or "Egwugwu" or "Ayaka" masqueraders impersonating the ancestral spirits. The gongs sound again and the flute is blown once more. The 'Okoroshi' house is now a pandemonium of quavering voices. The spirits of the ancestors emerge from the earth (as they are believed to do) greet themselves in their esoteric language, walk out of the compound and round the village singing doleful tunes throbbing with awesome and guttural responses. All throughout the night they keep a watch. Meanwhile, the person chosen to impersonate[623] the 'dead man-coming-back' comes to the family of the deceased. He consoles and comforts the family, assures them of his continued existence, happiness and interest in their welfare. He then asks the living members for something, e.g. a chicken, or simply for some edible. (Some of my informants say it is normally what the deceased while alive used to like.) The living members on their part show he is welcome by giving him what he asks of them[624]. Three categories of Dibia (professional priests) namely "Dibia-na-agba-aja"; "Dibia-na-akpu-aja", and "Dibia-na-ago-mmuo", are employed in this rite. The first performs the real "ichu-aja", as the Igbo understand it. The second purifies the house or the compound because death defiled it; while the third offers the sacrifice the Igbo term "igo mmuo"[625].

The religious significance of this rite is "the bringing the spirit of the deceased into the house". By this it is believed the survivors of the deceased will again be able to have intimate intercourse with the deceased[626]. It is a symbolic way of "reviving", "summoning back", "inviting the departed" and thus renewing contact with him in the next world and partly declaring a formal resumption of life. Perhaps one might go so far as to regard it as the Igbo's symbolic and ritual celebration of man's conquest over death, which has disrupted and not destroyed the rythm of life. It indicates that the departed are not really dead but "living", and can be contacted, invited back and drawn into human circles[627].

At break of day or night previous to the funeral day, a wicker-work coffin (Ibudu) is constructed, placed on two forked sticks and is covered with grass mat and then with white cloth; thus enshrounded, it serves as the substitute containing the real body of the deceased. This is placed in a position where it can be viewed by the assembled folk. By late in the morning, the invitees, relatives and friends of the deceased's kindred assemble. Various ritual dances are performed. The heir (or the person on whom the responsibility of performing the rites falls) presents two goats. The first is "Ewu-Ofo" - the goat of Ofo because every person has a personal Ofo by which he is integrated into the living community; the second is called "Ewu Mkpulu-obi" or simply "Ewu Obi" - the goat of the marrow of the soul, i.e. the goat which is sacrificed to strengthen the man's soul which has become weakened through separation. It is sometimes called "ewu-inye-obi-ike" - the goat that gives strength to the heart, or the goat that gives endurance, because it is meant to confer endurance in the journey to the next life[628]. The throats of these goats are slit (normally by a man whose father had died)[629] in front of the wicker-work coffin. The blood is collected in a vessel, the remaining drops are smeared on the cloth covering it[630]. The goats are singed and cut up in the traditional manner. Any mistake in the cutting-up of the goat meat means a fine, payable to the elders by whoever was responsible for the mistake[631].

These two rites are laden with politico-religious significance.By offering the victim known as "Ewu-ofo", the heir of the deceased abolishes the deceased's existing authority, and establishes his right over whatever used to be regarded as the deceased's. He takes possession of the deceased's ofo - the Igbo instrument of symbolic embodiment of the spirits of the ancestors and their authority, the guarantee of truth as well as of unity and indestructibility of the individual or group possessing it[632]. Acquiring this symbol the heir, incorporates in himself politico-religious powers as the rightful authority-holder: namely as the representative and mouthpiece of his family and their ancestors. He succeeds the deceased not only physically but also spiritually, i.e. he succeeds to the continuation of the family priestly character or "child-dead-father-family priestly relation"[633]. This explains why the senior of the kindred in the rite of dispatching a soul to the spirit world, always appeals to his/her predecessors in office not to harm him/her for he/she is their rightful successor in office[634]. By sacrificing the victim known as "Ewu Obi" or "Ewu-inye-obi-ike", the ancestors are propitiated and disposed to accept the deceased who had once represented them and acted as the rallying point between them and the living members of the community, the invisible counterpart of which they form. The ancestors thus propitiated and the soul of the deceased is strengthened and emboldened, as it were, and rightfully rejoins his forefathers and regains its former existential relationship; or as Robert Hertz puts it: "In rejoining his forefathers, the deceased is reborn, transfigured and raised to a superior power and dignity."[635]

After the afore-mentioned rites comes the final severing of the existing connections with the deceased whose final ceremonies are being performed. A live cock and a live ram (in some cases with an iron bell on its neck) are tied to a pole with strips of cloth and hoisted in front of the compound, and blown to pieces by gunmen. Then the senior of the unit (sometimes any "Dibia-na-agba'aja" is employed in this) goes before the wicker-work coffin. He is handed a kola-nut which he breaks into cotyledons and puts into the coffin. The Chi-symbols (or in some areas Ikenga-symbol) of the deceased are put into the coffin. (In some places this is destroyed on the day of death.) He cuts a small piece of wood into a small plate, puts some food into it, and puts the plate and its contents into the coffin. Then he pours in some drinks. All these operations are performed strictly with the left hand The coffin is lifted at each end; moved towards the wall of the deceased's house and struck gently on it. This striking is done seven times. At each strike the priest pours water on it. At the end of the seventh, the coffin is carried out, followed by dancing groups, each singing its song and playing its instruments. When the procession reaches where the deceased is buried, the grave is opened deep enough to contain the wicker-work coffin, which is gently deposited into it and covered up again. With this rite, the final rites - the real "Ikwa-Ozu" are ended[636].

It is significant that until the 'Ikwa Ozu' ceremonies are completed, no food can be offered to the spirit of the deceased inside the house or compound. The spirit is said to be complaining that he cannot enter his house because he has not been welcomed. The fulfilment of these rites enables the deceased, the people believe, to take up his residence in the "Okpensi" which is the collective word for the memorials set up in the house in honour of the departed relatives. Some Igbo communities call it "Mkpulu-Chi"[637]. It is before them that appeals are made to the ancestors and to all the departed relatives recognized as having joined the community of the ancestors.

8.1.3 Dreams and appearances

Apart from these rites, the Igbo believe that the deceased can be seen in dreams or trances and they can impart information or explanation or give instruction on any matters about which the family is in a serious predicament. They can also consult the dead through mediums[638]. Along the road or in lonely places or during the night, it is believed that the deceased can appear to a person either to give guidance or aid or to molest[639].

8.1.4 Communion with Ndichie (Ancestors)

8.1.4.1 Who are the ancestors ?

Death, according to the Igbo, is sometimes spoken of as "a going-home to join the ancestral community". But who are the ancestors ? In the theogonical conception of the Igbo we said that ancestors are men who while on earth founded lineages, were good and popular, died without blemish after a good old age and received proper burial. Here we intend to explicate more these terms so that we can grasp the full implication of their speaking of death as a going-home to join their ancestral community.

Founding lineages

To found a lineage, one must have, at least a male child to succeed one after one's physical death. For as we saw earlier a man who has no one to succeed him quenches the fire of life, and becomes forever dead since his line of physical continuation is blocked[640]. Likewise the spiritual continuation. It is, therefore, not necessarily "children" that matter; some of them must be male. These males are essential to continue the family priestly character which is essential in the child-dead-father (ancestors) relation[641]. To put is negatively and in the words of Professor Ilogu, "it is a calamity both to the living and the dead if no sons remain alive to offer prayers and libations of wine and sacrifice either of kola-nuts, or of pieces of food to the ancestors every day"[642]. But the begetting of sons, though essential, does not overrule good moral life. In fact, many a wicked man with several sons had died but was not acknowledged as an ancestor. Among some Igbo (e.g. the Okigwi), when a man, publicly known as "wicked" (ajo mmadu) dies, the people cover his eyes with a bag (Ikpuchi akpa n' anya) before he is buried. This is done to prevent him from seeing. Obviously the people's aim is to impede him from coming back again to harm his fellows. Such a man is excluded from the ancestral group no matter how many sons he left behind him ![643].

Good Moral life

So an ancestor is one who is by the 'vox populi' estimation an upright and popular man. This is necessary if the dead man was to be a guardian of public morality: "the ancestors who are also under the control of Ale, act as her agents, as guardians of morality"[644]. This privilege is accorded to them because they themselves, in their earthly lives, had been models of righteousness: "They had laid the social foundations of goodness, truth and purity and they, now dead and in the spirit world, would want such goodness to continue. It is by doing what the ancestors would approve,that is, by being loyal to traditional code of morality, that the tribe or extended family could survive."[645] And one would like to add: those to join their community must have to attain these prerequisites. That this is necessary to join the ancestral community in the next world, is clear from the distinction the Igbo make: Ndi Akaliogoli or Ndi Ohuogoli are dead people who lived bad lives here on earth; whereas the dead man who were good morally while they lived here are termed Ndichie ('canonized' saints)[646]. The former have no place in the ancestral community. They are doomed forever[647]. From this, and at least, as far as the Igbo are concerned, it would seem that Meyer Fortes' statement must be rejected, namely that "a man may be a liar or a wastrel, or an adulterer, a quarrelsome neighbour, or a negligent kinsman; he may be a mean and bad-tempered parent who has made his son's life miserable... If he dies leaving a son he becomes an ancestor of equal standing with any other ancestor. To put it in the believer's words, he acquires the power to intervene in the life of his descendants, in exactly the same way as any other ancestors"[648]. One is inclined to think that Meyer Fortes lays more emphasis on the begetting of a son at the expense of good moral life for he continues: "On the other hand, a man may be a paragon of virtues, as parent and as kinsman... if he leaves no son he cannot become an ancestor; or at best, among the Tallensi, if he has a daughter he may become a matrilateral ancestor of secondary worth only, to her sons and their descendants."[649] This observation is not justified by circumstantial evidence and must be rejected as well.

A good ripe old age

The Igbo say: "Ndu bu agu-u, o na-agu onye, o na-agu ibe ya". This is Igbo way of expressing that everybody loves to live long. They drive it home to themselves by making it their daily salutation. In some areas among the Igbo the people simply wish one another long life: "anwula !" - do not die; or in full "anwuchula" - do not die early or young ! Children after meals say to their parents: "anwula" - live long ! This wish, too, is extended to all well-wishers as well as benefactors in gratitude for gifts received. It forms the object of their daily prayer. They say: "Onye sim di, ya di: onye sim nwulu, ya nwulu" - whoever wishes me to die, let him die as well. Sometimes it is proverbially put thus: "Egbe bere, ugo bere, nke si ibe ya ebela, nku kwa ya" - Let the eagle perch, let the hawk perch. Any that wishes the other the contrary, let his wings break !

It appears "the more or less instinctive judgment of the ordinary man", says Josef Pieper, "that everyone knows that to wish someone's death does not mean wishing him a good, but wishing him something evil... For death is the downfall of what is bent on life."[650] But still worse, if not the absolutely worst evil for the Igbo, is to wish someone a premature death. Premature death is very much dreaded by the people. It is known as "onwu ike" - strong

death, that is, forced death. To attain an old age is desired by every Igbo. It is recognized (or believed !) to be not only a sign of wisdom and seat of life experience but more a reward from God for a good moral life, for as we saw in their world-vision, there is nothing that is purely physical but has not its religious significance[651] . So when an old man dies, it "is a moment of joy and not of sorrow !"[652], for the older a man is, the more descendants he has, the higher his rank and prestige, the more acceptable does his death become. The peaceful demise of an old chief with numerous progeny is a much an occasion for rejoicing in his life's achievement as for sorrow"[653].
Therefore if a man lived to ripe old age, he has taken a good pace towards being an ancestor, provided his death is such as would not warrant denying him a proper burial.

Proper Burial

From what has been said so far it follows that founding a lineage, living a morally good life and attaining a good ripe old age (all of which are deemed in one way or the other as Divine confirmation) find their culmination on giving the deceased a proper burial. Needless to repeat here that giving the deceased a proper burial (that is with due mortuary and funeral rites) in itself implies that the deceased does not fall under the category of those-who-must-be denied it. And as such according a deceased due mortuary and funerary rites is tantamount to officially and definitely declaring that such a one has led a life here on earth without 'blemish' and is now inscribed into the community of the ancestors and that his life is accordingly worthy of imitation and the deceased should be venerated with ancestral cult. The practical criterion by which this is asserted is the 'vox populi' estimation of the deceased and his popular fame - i.e. the popular acclamation is the criterion[654]. From this the observations of some authors become intelligible: namely "it appears that death alone is not a sufficinet condition for becoming an ancestor entitled to receive 'worship'. Proper burial, that is, with funerary rites appropriate to the deceased's status and by the person designated by right and duty to see to it, is the sine qua non..."[655]. And indeed, it is the sine qua non, for the mortuary and funeral rites are "the first steps in the transformation of parents into ancestor spirits"[656].

8.1.4.2 Ancestral community - a koinonia of parent-saints

From this, it also goes without saying that the ancestors as well as all those deemed worthy to be admitted into their community are those who "having passed beyond the grave", have "out-soared the shadow of our night",[657] "have only changed this for another" and "in consequence of going into that life, they have been released from all the restraints imposed by this earth". Thus they are ontologically "possessors of limitless potentialities which the people believe, they can exploit for the benefit or to the detriment of those who still live on earth"[658]: they have acquired new powers, those powers may help men, and so men make any sort of appeal that may get succour in time of need."[659] In short the people regard and have them for their "saints"[660]. They are parents, men and women who "have run their course in this world, and gone to their master - the Supreme Being", "and are living with him in the spirit world, where they are endowed with the never-ending life, after the mortuary and funerary ceremonies are performed[661]. But this endowment with never-ending life cannot be until the deceased had passed through the gate into the presence of Chukwu to receive whatever judgment awaits them: for the Igbo say: "Ikpe di na ani muo" - judgment is in the spirit world[662]. Should we call them "parent-saints", because despite death the deceased continue to have the title of relationship which they had borne as heads of families while they were on earth ! They are still spoken of a NNAM (my father) or NNEM (my mother). The Igbo pay them, then, filial duties - honour, reverence and homage[663]. Their cult of ancestors can best be described as "an extension into infinity of the family activities of the earth"; "a manifestation of an unbroken family relationship between the parent who has departed from this world and the offspring who are still here"[664]. For though the deceased are now in Ani mmuo (the spirit-world) they still remain the fathers or mothers which they were before their death, capable of exercising their parental functions and, more, in a more powerful and unhampered way, over their survivors[665]. They are still present with their relatives. They are always 'near' them[666] and ever anxious to intercede for them before God and the spirits[667]. Hence Fr. Anozia remarks: "This explains why the Igbo had a corresponding religious interest in the ancestors, prayed more frequently to them and invited them at every meal to communicate with their children on earth. Both sides, as it appears have vested interest in their approach to each other. While the ancestral spirits see in the cult given them a means for boostering their prestige and social status among less honoured spirits, their children make their effective intercession a condition for continuing their homage, or as the Igbos say for continuing to feed them... And what reception would be accorded an ancestor who had been a little industrious in obtaining the requests of his children ! On the other hand, nobody on earth would like to turn his dead ancestors from loving parents to pestering spirits, specialized in bringing sickness and failure in business. The balance must be kept. This is why Igbo ancestral honour has been rightly described as 'religion based on reciprocity'".[668] In other words both depend on each other - the ancestors for filial piety on the part of the living; those on earth on the ancestors for paternal and maternal protection[665]. And if both depend on each other, then it follows that the gap between them would not be so great as to warrant to one the title 'superior' or 'absolute' and the other 'inferior'. In short there is no basis for either side to 'worship' the other[670].

Sumarily one would like, in this connection, to remark that 'ancestor worship' as this had been commonly known is a wrong nomenclature, for it is no 'worship', but a manifestation of an unbroken family relationship between the parent who has departed from this world and the offspring who are still here"; "an extension into infinity of the family activities of the earth"[671]. Now back to death as "a going-home-to join the ancestral community": we have seen that the ancestral community is a "Koinonia" of "parent-saints"[672]. These parents, while they were on earth, were models of righteousness, "they laid the social foundations of goodness, truth and purity"[673]. Now that they are in the spirit world they become under the control of Ale - the Earth-spirit, agents and guardians of public morality[674]. They would also want that such goodness, truth and purity be continued by their survivors on earth. And as such prerequisites for entry into their community is loyalty to this traditional code of morality[675]. Therefore those deemed worthy to join their community are those whose moral life did not conflict with the traditional code of morality, of which they laid the foundation while here on earth. In other words to go home to join the ancestral community is tantamount to saying joining the "Koinonia" of "parent-saints" - i.e. death is a going-home to join the community of parent-saints. Need we add, too, that ancestral community is "Koinonia of Ndichie" - i.e. "Koinonia of patriarchs" [676].

8.1.5 Ino uwa and Ogbanje (partial reincarnation and metempsychosis ?)

Igbo concept of life-after-death is incomplete, however, without a word on "Ino Uwa" and "Ogbanje". In the ceremony of "Ikwa Ozu" (the so-called "second burial") the rite of the bringing the spirit of the deceased into the house, apart from purporting that the dead men returned to life in order to comfort their families and assure them of their continued existence, happiness and interest in their welfare[677], also insinuates that those who die do not remain in the grave. Their bodies do not 'rot away' indeed. They remain their "essential selves" from the "bodies of the earth". The dead "resurrect" from the grave. But this is not the resurrection of the body in the dramatic and eschatological sense of the graves giving up their dead at the consummation of all things. For the Igbo, whatever takes place happens after death when the ceremonies are performed[678]. And before we go further it is necessary to remark that there is no belief in reincarnation in the classical sense among the Igbo; that is in the sense that reincarnation is the passage of the soul from one body to another; and the lot of the soul in each being determined by its behaviour in a previous life. In Igbo language, two terminologies express what apparently seem like reincarnation. One is Ogbanje and the other is Ino uwa

8.1.5.1 Ogbanje[679]

The Ogbanje are a set of children who, the people believe, form themselves into "clubs" - the "Ogbanje club". Their sole purpose is to be born on earth in order to torment parents by their premature and early death. Ogbanje literally means a "repeater-child". These children are born out of the influence of malignant spirits, the people believe. They are generally very beautiful and endowed with many natural gifts which endear them quickly both to their parents and others; their sudden death is in consequence most painful. While they are on earth they are thought to recognize others who belong to the Ogbanje club at the moment of regularisation. The Igbo have rites whereby children dictated to be Ogbanje are regularised and brought to normal[680]. No parent would like to father or mother an Ogbanje. These children are exceptions to the rule. Perhaps this is the nearest concept among the Igbo which can be termed reincarnation or metempsychosis !

8.1.5.2 Ino uwa

Besides to be Ogbanje, the Igbo have another terminology, that is "Ino uwa" - returning to the earth or another coming to the earth. Generally this is believed to be a reward for those deceased who, while on earth were good persons and were ripe for death when they died. "Ino uwa" is based on the belief that deceased persons do return to the world in the grand-children and great-grand-children. Sometimes the same deceased can be said to have "come-back-to-life" in more than one person at the same time: in several grand-children, great-grand-children, who are brothers, and sisters, cousins, aunts and nephews, uncles and nieces, ad infinitum. Such children, call themselves "agu" - a term which means a little more than the English "namesake, because it also implies a vital relationship of the namesake to the same "principle". It is significant to note that the Igbo continue to address prayers to the deceased known to be already "back to life on earth". Even the very people in whom they are supposed now to 'live' pray to them for help[681]. This means that despite "ino uwa" the people believe the deceased continue to "live" in the "After-life"; they are there with all ancestral qualities unimpaired. In other words, despite "Ino-uwa-concept", the belief of the Igbo is that, those who depart from this world, once they have entered After-life, there they remain and there the survivors and their children after them can keep unbroken intercourse with them. And yet, in spite of the belief that the deceased contrive to remain in full "life" and "vigour" in the "After-life", it is believed also that they "reincarnate" not only in one grand-child and great-grand-child but in several contemporary grand-children and great-grand-children. These "rebirths" seem rather to be interminable ! Notwithstanding, living persons are spoken of as "reincarnating" in some children. From the above it would seem that when the Igbo speak of a coming-back-to-life, they do not mean that a man returns with the same personality, nor do they even mean that he has now a double personality . This is irreconciliable with the facts discussed above: their concepts of individualization as was mentioned in their concept of life and Igbo psychology. All, it rather appears to establish, is the belief in the concrete fact that there are certain dominant lineage characteristics, i.e. physical, moral and spiritual qualities which keep recurring through births and thus ensuring the continuity of the vital existence of the family, Obi or the Umunna, etc. Is it then partial reincarnation ? With Igbo "reincarnation-thought one great difficulty crops up. One often hears people speak of what they hope to be and do in their "next turn of life". Not infrequently, one hears some women say that in their next life they would like to be men, powerful men ! Poor men are heard expressing the hope that in their next life God will make them rich. What strikes most is that they speak with unshakeable conviction that their hopes will be realized during their next turn of life. Even the inconsistency of this way of thinking with their other beliefs does not seem to strike them. The fact that perhaps in their "last-life", they might have expressed the same hope for life which they now live - hopes as yet unrealized - does not diminish their confidence that the future could be better. Is this only expressing what an Igbo name beautifully puts thus: "NKEIRUKA" - "that which the future will bring is still greater" ?

More, it is common that when a person dies, a fowl is killed and the blood is sprinkled on the chest of the deceased and meanwhile the deceased is thus addressed: "You made this or that mistake. Be sure that when you return, you do not repeat those mistakes". Some Igbo common parlance with this view (perhaps !) regard death as a going-back-to Chukwu to take stock. However my informants remarked, and it is interesting that the phrase is applied to men with whose lives on earth their kindreds were not satisfied. But what a contradiction ! Perhaps underneath these desires to return and live again on earth lurks that "desiderium naturae" for a life interminable, the desire to remain "immortal" as mythical tales and "traditions" purport God originally designed human nature. For the Igbo it seems to be a desire to live life to the full, to "accomplish that for which one was created"[682]. Or with Uchendu: "Belief in reincarnation, gives the Igbo hope of realizing their frustrated status goals in the next cycle of life."[683]

But when all these have been said, we must admit in conclusion that there are many things about ourselves which we do not yet know. It may well be that in regard to this matter there are possibilities which are yet beyond our comprehension. We must come back to the point of this discussion, which is not the resolution of the paradoxical phenomena of Igbo "Ino-uwa" or "Reincarnation"-concept, but the fact that there is this apparent paradox which is one of the solid grounds on which the Igbo base their belief in the concrete reality of After-life. Retrospectively, however, one thing seems peculiarly significant: namely, that the Igbo "life-in-the-beyond-concept" is very much concerned with Life (Ndu) - "Desiderium Naturae" - to live a life interminable, i.e. eternal life. We shall see the influence of this desiderium in the next Chapter.

CHAPTER NINE: LIFE AND DEATH AND IGBO SOCIAL CONSCIOUSNESS: THEIR RELATIONSHIPS

Any treatise on the Igbo life and death concepts without a word on their relationship to their social consciousness would be incomplete. So the next pages will be devoted to this.

9.1 The relationship between life and death: Life on earth, an existence-in-relation in quest for a full life

9.1.1 In the socio-religious reality is the fullness of life to be sought

We have already refered to an Igbo ditty which says: "Afia ka anye biara na uwa. Anye zujuru ukpa, anye azujuro ukpa, mgbe oge gwuru onye obuna eburu ukpa ya lawa". This may be rendered as: "We are all buyers and sellers on earth. Whether we buy all we need or not, when the market-day comes to an end, we must pack our commodities and go". This market-metaphor is analogous to Igbo conceptualization of man's existence here on earth. A "market-wish" accompanied by a short ritual which children give to their mothers when they are going to the village-market makes more intelligible this comparison of life on earth to a market-place. As a mother has packed her wares in a rectangular wicker basket and is helped to put the load on her head, her children who are hanging around to give her the "market-wish" come up one after the other and say: "Nne zugbuo ndi afia; Ndi afia azugbula gi", which translated is: "Mother, get the better of the market-people; may the market-people not get the better of you !" As each child gives his market-wish, he spits into the mother's cupped palms. When this ritual is over, the mother rubs her palms together and ritually cleanses her face, thus symbolically ensuring "good face" for the day's bargaining operation[684]. Perhaps those who are foreign to the "time-consuming operation" which takes place in Igbo market-forum may not understand the full significance of this market-metaphor. Among the Igbo market-prices are determined by a rigorous system of bargaining between buyer and seller. To this market-place all come with one common motive, the desire to make profit[685].

But what profit does an Igbo wish to make in his "market of life" ? He wants to attain the greatest of all personal hopes; he wants to live a life morally good according to the code of behaviour established by the ancestors: to live a life full of years and prosperous with many descendants; he has come to live in order to achieve a hierarchical social status; all of which culminate in receiving a proper burial with due mortuary and funerary rites as well as achieving ancestral honour "when the market-day" comes to an end. In other words life on earth is, as it were, a market-place. Yes "a market of life" in which the Igbo believe they have come to bargain for a profit - "to buy a full life", i.e. in pursuit of a full-life, which as was remarked earlier, is the realization of the entire raison d'être, at once heavenly and earthly, eternal and temporal, collective and personal[686].

But the traditional Igboman, like most Africans, does not believe that this quest for a "fullness of life" is to be sought and achieved in isolation. Rather it is to be sought in the social reality which consists of man's fellowship with his parents who gave him birth; the "clan" into which he is born; the village and village-group by which he is identified; the ancestors, the spirits and Chukwu (God) who caused him to be born and direct every moment of his earthly life[687]. Summarily life on earth is an "existence-in-relation" by which the individual is socially, personally and mystically involved in order to seek the fullness of life[688]. This also means that the individual over and above his physical personality must be a social being, a corporate person[689]. But as his existence-in-relation involves him not only with the visible society of his family (also extented), his "umunna" (localised patrilineal group), his village and village-group, but also with the invisible society of the ancestors, the spirits and the Transcendental Power beyond the visible world, Chukwu, the individual has to be brought up, created, trained and gradated so as to be in contact with, and enter into communion with all the inmates of his world, i.e. he is to be ushered into the community of men and spirits[690]. This ushering into or incorporation into the community of men and spirits is a long symbolical process. It is not a single event which can be recorded on a particular date; it is a process which begins from the embryonic state, indeed before the arrival of the individual into this word - and continues thereafter[691].

9.1.2 Pregnancy and Taboos

Children, according to the Igbo, are the buds of society (Nwabuugwu, Nwabuogo, Nwajikolu); and every birth is, thus, the arrival of 'Spring' when life shoots out and the community thrives (Nwabuikenna, Ikenna, Mmadubuanyanwu). The birth of a child is therefore the concern not only of the parents, but of the "Obi"-members, the "Umunna"-grouping, the village and the village-group units[692]. Consequently as soon as a woman is pregnant, she becomes a special person and receives special treatment from relatives and neighbours, because the first indication that a new member of society is on the way, is given[693]. The expectant mother (and in some cases the husband is included) must observe, then, certain taboos and regulations partly because pregnancy in effect makes her ritually 'impure' and chiefly in order to protect her and her child[694]. Throughout pregnancy, among some Igbo communities (e.g. in the Nsukka division) prospective mothers must avoid eating the flesh of 'Nchi' (a rodent). For this animal, it is generally believed, might instill into the pregnant woman its peculiar habit of running forward and stopping; and thus at the time of her delivery the child might come forward and then slip back. Delivery will be impeded or delayed and the danger to both mother and child thereby increased[695]. At Ubomiri in Owerri division a pregnant woman should refrain from eating the flesh of any animal which had died a natural death; otherwise, it is believed, the child will be born dead. She would also avoid eating the neck of any animal; otherwise her child will have boils on its neck. Both she and her husband must avoid eating the meat of any animal which had been killed in honour of a deity and subsequently exposed for sale in the market; otherwise the pregnant woman will abort or give birth to an abnormal child, which will have to be destroyed. In the Agwu division pregnant women are said to avoid eating the flesh of monkeys, lest their children should have a monkey-like appearance. Snails (ejuna) are taboo to all pregnant women, because it is believed the child will stream with water and it will dribble. Likewise the flesh of 'Agalama' - an animal known to be paralysed by light at night - must not be eaten; otherwise when the child is born it would be unable to run away from danger.

Husbands must not shoot hares (Mgbada) while their wives are pregnant, lest the babes should be born with skin like a hare's. They must not attend any burial or even help in carrying a dead animal lest the babe should die in the womb. They are also enjoined not to refuse food cooked by their pregnant wives or the babes when born will refuse food and die. And above all pregnant women should not fight nor must they be fought.

Meek remarked: "None of these taboos are absolute laws, but their breach may entail censure if things subsequently go wrong."[696]. And there may or may not 'be scientific truths in the beliefs concerning foods' and these regulations. But they have developed as a result of people's experiences and imaginations and above all are meant to safeguard the health and safety of the mother and the new bud of society[697].

9.1.3 Prayers and rituals for expectant mothers

Igbo communities do not rest satisfied with making laws for their expectant mothers. They pray for them too; prayers are made to God, to the ancestors and to the spirits to ensure the protection and safety of their prospective wives and children. Thus in the village-group of Mboo, a woman who conceives for the first time don a special cloth known as Agbale (known as ipeteri in Egbema) and wear it for a period of a month. This cloth seems to be regarded as a mark of affiliation with Ala, the Earth-spirit[698]. Before, however, she puts on the cloth, her husband summons an old woman, the wife of a member of his kindred and hands her a pup. The old woman holding the pup says: "Today this young wife is about to don the Agbale cloth, in order that evil spirits may be driven away. For we have no desire that evil spirits should become incarnate among us. From today the Earth-spirit of Mboo is adopting this woman as one of the wives of the men of Mboo". Having said this she lays the pup on the ground. The husband's brother then cuts the pup in two with his matchet. He also cuts a basket in two and deposits one half of the pup in one half of the basket and the other half of the pup in the other half of the basket. A piece of canwood (ufie) and a piece of the yellow dye known as 'edo' are also cut in two and the halves are deposited in the pieces of the basket. The woman takes the two pieces of basket and proceeds to 'Ajo Ofia' (bad bush), accompanied by the old woman and her husband's brother. Here she leaves the baskets; she then goes to a stream and bathes. On emerging she is given the Agbale cloth. Her old cloth is given to the old woman[699].

At Ache, when a woman becomes pregnant, her husband goes to his wife's village and presents a chicken to the senior priest of Ala (Ezeani). The priest, standing before the shrine of Ala (Ihu Ala) prays as follows: "Ala, this man has married our daughter and has paid the bridewealth to her parents. He has brought this chicken to you as your share of marriage gifts. His wife has become pregnant and we beg you to protect her and to bring forth the child without difficulty"[700].

When the pregnant woman is between her second and sixth month of pregnancy, a more suggestive rite known as 'Aja Nkita' (dog-sacrifice) is perforned. The husband obtains a branch of an 'ogirisi' tree and some gravel from a river-bed. The senior member of the woman's 'Umunna' (the localised-patrilineal group) comes to the husband's home and plants the 'ogirisi' branch beside the husband's barn. The gravel is laid at the base of the 'ogirisi' tree. He then directs the woman to kneel beside these life symbols, and holding a dog (provided by the husband) speaks as follows: "We have come here to perform the rites of 'Aja nkita'. We have planted an 'ogirisi' tree in order that the child to this woman may flourish like the 'ogirisi' tree. We have set gravel from the river-bed beside the tree in order that, as gravel remains when the river dries up, so may this woman's child remain alive after the waters of child-birth have broken". A young man then catches the dog by the head and an old man and an old woman (normally of the husband's kindred) grip it by the body. Together they lift it and wave it round the woman's head. As they do so the officiant says: "May the child you deliver whether male or female, be born alive and remain alive". This is said four times; and at each time the pregnant woman repeats the officant's words. Finally the officiant says: "Bear children, male and female, but let males exceed the females in numbers". The dog is now slain and the blood allowed to pour over the stones. The flesh is cooked, and pieces are deposited on the stones. The liver is cut in two, and one half is given to the husband and the other to the wife. The officiant then addresses the wife saying: "You and your husband must agree to be 'sweet-mouthed' to one another". The wife says: "We do agree, even as we are about to eat a sweet thing together". She then places a piece of the liver in her husband's mouth, and he places a piece in hers. Having eaten the liver they embrace each other[701]. In Egbema a similar rite is performed. It is called "Iwu-Ahzi". It is performed between the fith and the seventh month of a woman's first pregnancy.

9.1.4 The Actual Birth

Traditionally birth usually took place outside the house and there were women specialists who helped women in labour[702]. When labour begins, an old man of the husband's family (or the husband himself) takes a seed-yam with which he draws a straight line down the woman's forehead and abdomen (thus wishing that the birth be 'straight', i.e. without complications). As he does so he says: "Obasi-di-na-enu (O God, Lord of the sky) and Ala (the Earth-spirit) help this women (my wife) to deliver freely". He then goes to the threshold of the compound and praying he says: "Chukwu Abiama, come I pray you, and help this woman (my wife) deliver safely. Let not the child die in her womb". He then cuts the yam into two (Meek says that the yam is sometimes cut into four pieces) and lays the pieces on the ground saying: "Anyanwu (the Sun-spirit), take this yam to Obasi-di-na-enu. Obasi, it was you that made the child and placed it in the womb. Come and undo the wrapper which you tied. Ancestors, our fathers and Ala, come ye and help this woman (my wife) to deliver her child safely."[703] As soon as birth is safely given, the womenfolk announce the event with songs praising the bravery of the mother and invite her husband to come and see 'ifeoma di mma' (the best of all goodness). He replies to their song with shots from a gun and meets them with gifts of kola-nuts. They in their turn paint his right hand (if the child is a male) or his left (if it is female) with chalk. This is followed by festive jubilation among the Umunna who manifest their own solidarity to the family by presenting the mother with material gifts or money; the last person throws a coin into a bowl containing fresh water[704].

9.1.5 The placenta and umbilical cord, objects of special treatment

The placenta and umbilical cord are symbols of the child's attachment to mother, to motherhood, to the state of inactivity; and as such they are objects of special treatment in Igbo communities, as in most African societies[705]. So after birth they are severed and buried by women of the husband's compound in a special place[706]. Physically, the placenta and the umbilical cord symbolise the separation of the child from the mother; but this separation is not final since the two are still near each other. However, the child has begun its journey of being incorporated into the community, so that the separation between the individual mother and the child continues to widen as the child's integration increases. The disposal of the placenta and umbilical cord indicates then the child has died to the state of pregnancy and is now alive in another state of existence. It has died to the stage of being alone in the womb of the mother; but now it has risen to the new life of being part of human society. Thus paradoxically the child is near the mother and yet begins to get away from the individual mother, growing into the status of being: "I am because we are and since we are, therefore I am[707] (Ikeumunna, the strength of patrilincal group; Umunnabuike, the patrilineage is my strength). In short it becomes a public property. It belongs to the entire community and is now no longer the exclusive property of one person and ties to one person or one household are symbolically destroyed and dissolved in the cutting of the umbilical cord and burying it with the placenta in a special place by women of the husband's compound.

9.1.6 Circumcision

In normal circumstances, on the 8th day after birth, the child, whether male or female is circumcised[708]. Thus is the custom among the Egbema village-group and their neighbours. Some Igbo communities, e.g. Oguta and a number of village-groups in the Nsukka division and those on the Western bank of the Niger Basin, do not circumcise females until shortly before marriage or after the first or second menstruation[709]. In this later case circumcision seems certainly to be a rite of introduction into adult status or matrimony. But in the former, it has not this clear-cut meaning. Nevertheless as a general rule, circumcision which 'has the authority of custom', apart from being an introduction into the adult status, is also a token of membership and association with the community[710].

9.1.7 Seclusion and purification

Formerly it was a custom that after birth the woman and child lived in a booth alongside the walls of the house, which is constructed for the purpose of sheltering her and her new-born babe, or simply indoors in a house but sleeping on 'Mgbo' (a special sleeping-place for both the mother and a newly born baby)[711]. This seclusion lasted for 28 days (Igbo seven weeks). During this period the woman was not allowed into the 'Obi'/'Obu', nor could she communicate or eat together with her husband, let alone leaving the precincts of the compound. At the end of this, everything belonging to the booth, the materials thereof and any mats, cloths and, indeed everything used during these weeks, all were collected, carried off and cast away into 'Ajo ofia' (bad bush)[712]. Then the husband invited all the women of his kindred and a feast was prepared for them. The midwife also attended. During the feast, she or the oldest woman of the man's kindred took a yam and waved it over the head of the mother and child saying as she does so: "May everything that comes into this compound be pleasant and let all evil spirits be gone from this household". She then threw the yam on the ground. Taking a gourd of palm wine, she waved it round the heads of all the women present saying: "May you conceive the very next time you sleep with your husbands"[713].

The young children of the kindred were also invited. Each child brought a potsherd which the husband filled with soup. Each child was given also a cooked-yam. The children took their yams and soup outside the compound and ate their meal there. When they had finished they broke the potsherds to pieces by stamping on them. Afterwards all the children went to a stream and bathed. On their return they smeared themselves with canwood. Then one of the boys (or one of the girls - if the newly born babe is a female) took some water in his mouth and spat it over the fire in the mother's house. This he did until the fire was extinguished. The mother then swept out the house while the boys went and obtained fresh fire from the neighbouring compound. After this rite the boy rubbed some chalk on the child's forehead saying: "If your father or mother sends you on a message do not refuse to go. But if a spirit (Ndi Ajo mmuo) sends you, say that you have no feet. Let not what your parents eat cause you any harm". On the following day the boy or girl who had quenced the fire returned to the mother's compound where an old woman took some camwood in her mouth and spat it over him. The boy then escorted the mother of the newly born babe to her husband's farms, or 'Oba' (a storage place for yams). There she laid her hand on one of the yams saying: "Today the taboo against my touching yams had been removed"[714].

Among some groups (e.g. in Owerri and Orlu divisions) after this the woman went to the market beautifully clad, as it were, to present herself to the people. There she was greeted and embraced by friends and relatives and she receives numerous gifts[715]. This seclusion symbolises the concept of death; separation from society, i.e. 'death' to one state of life and 'resurrection' to a fuller state of living when it is over. It is as if the mother and child 'die' and 'rise again' on behalf of everyone else in the society; they are integrated into the community and the child is now to receive its name - the symbol of its personality[716].

9.1.8 Name-giving ceremony and presentation to the people

The next ceremony after the seclusion is ended and the purification rites are performed is the naming of the child. Igbo names for this rite are "Igu afa" (iba aha), "isa nwa" or "asa nwa". This ceremony is the concern not only of the 'Umunna' but of the whole village. Relatives and friends are usually invited from other villages and even from outside the village-group. The 'Umunna' of the mother of the newly born babe is also specially invited. Parents and grand-parents on both sides are principally concerned in the naming of the child[717]. The day of birth, some special event or circumstance, a 'fancied foreboding' at the time of a child's birth - shortly before or after; all these suggest to the parents names for their children[718]. Since this ceremony is a peace-offering (and as such a festive one) in which the community is come to pray for the child, fowl or goats or even a cow (depending on the means of the parents) are brought. When all are assembled either in the yard or in the 'Obi' (OBU), the head of the Umunna-unit, i.e., the eldest of the husband's localised patrilineal-Unit, takes 'Oji' (Kola-nut) and makes a petition-litany common in most Igbo community gathering. Then he takes the child in his arms and raises it in the air four times, saying, "My son, grow up strong and ever give ear to the behests of your father and mother and be a credit to your ancestors"[719]. He asks the father by which name the child is to be known[720]. When the father gives the name(s), the old man announces it (them) to the public. While doing so (let us say a child is given the name Chukwuma) he looks at the child and says: "Chukwuma - God knows - this is the name by which you shall answer our call". He rubs the child on the forehead and on the right hand with a white phallic chalk saying: "Let no evil spirit cause your untimely death". All along all the people present respond to each invocation with "Ise" or "Eha", i.e., "So be it"[721]. Then the offering gifts are killed, drinks are served and cooking begins

In Enugu-Ukwu, Anambra State, there is yet another suggestive gesture that follows the kola-petition. The Okpala of the group after presenting the child to the people "inserts a hoe and a matchet in the hands of the child saying: "My son, with these farm implements your father lived well. We call on you to acquaint yourself with them properly and be hard working. We wish you good fruits of your labour. Live, grow and wax strong". The drinks and food are served[722].

9.1.9 'Ito-Nwa' - dedication to the family ancestors

This ceremony is principally the concern of the paternal Umunna-unit of the child. It takes place when the child has cut his lower teeth. He is taken by his mother to the head of the Umunna in the presence of the members of the unit. Again the senior of the unit officiates; he deposits kola-nut at the shrine of the collective memorial dead members of the family, called 'Okpensi' or 'Mkpulu-chi'. He calls on all the family ancestors to protect the child, who is verily one of themselves as he has cut his teeth in the proper way[723].

9.1.10 Dedication to the Earth-spirit (Ala)

The next childhood ceremony is the dedication of the child to the Earth-spirit. There is no fixed time for it. It is performed at the convenience of the father. The child is taken to the chief priest (Ezeani) of Ala. A chicken is provided by the father. The priest takes the chicken, waves it round the head of the child saying: "Ala this your child has been brought before you by its parents, in order that you may protect it and that it may be permitted to share in foods offered sacrificially to you without incurring your anger"[724].

9.1.11 Agu (Igba Agu) ceremony

Like the dedication ceremony to the Earth-spirit, there is no fixed time for this performance; and it is not necessarily accompanied by feasting. The father invites a diviner, who names the ancestor whose 'reincarnation' the child is. When this is determined, a big dumb-bell-shaped piece of wood (Okpensi or Mkpulu-chi) is prepared to represent this ancestor of the child. At this memorial, the head of the Umunna takes the offering gift demanded by the ancestor, waves it over the head of the child saying: "So and so, we have come to thank you for being reborn in the child. May you remain long in life and prosper"[725]. Henceforth kola-nut petition-litany, and libations of palm-wine and prayers are said before this shrine on the child's behalf.

9.1.12 The Ofo insignia and Amanwulu ceremony

After this ceremony, the little 'Ofo' is provided for the child. The little 'Ofo' is the ritual staff of each individual in the family. It is given to the child to bring him near to his ancestor who is his spiritual guardian[726]. The next and final ceremony is that called 'Amawulu'. Like the 'Agu' ceremony, there is no fixed time for it. This ceremony permits one to take a title at a later date or join any society of the initiated. It is, the equivalent of a certificate or passport to travel[727].

Remarks

These birth and childhood ceremonies introduce the child to the corporate community; and though they are only an introduction and as yet the child is a passive member, it is, nevertheless, entered into the corporate personality both physically, socially and religiously, i.e., it is already ushered into the community of men and spirits. To become a-de-facto-active-membership of the community, what it is already 'in fieri', i.e., to be 'a credit to its ancestors' is left to it as it lives, grows and waxes strong. This 'credit-becoming-to-its-ancestors', acquiring-active-membership of the community, i.e. to live a morally good life according to the code of behaviour established by its ancestors; live a life full of years and prosperous with many descendants and achieve a hierarchical, social status which culminate in being received honourably by the ancestors when the course here is ended and the deceased 'is sent home' with proper mortuary and funerary rites - all these are what the Igbo conceive life to mean.

So briefly, it may be said that the initiation ceremonies are the various means of divesting a person of his status as a "child" and of investing him with the status of actual or potential and spiritual citizenship. Thus the initiation ceremonies not only offer an explanation for the mysteries of life-living, growing and dying-of which change of status is only a part, but also, as a social phenomenon, they are multi-functional: they are symbolic methods of explaining the nature of certain types of relationships and dramatizing the life cycle of an individual or a group of individuals, as belonging to a larger unit[728].

9.2 Death: A transition and a reintegration

From what has been said above, it goes without saying that "Death is no enemy"[729] but "le change simplement de mode d'existence"[730]; "it is the ecstacy of fulfilment"[731]; "a going home to occupy one's proper place" among the "Koinonia of parent-saints"[732]; shading off humanness in order to gain "Godliness" or full life; in a word "a transition"[733]. The Igbo give vent to this belief when sometimes consoling a bereaved they say: "Nwa nna (or nwa nnem) dibe (or ebezina). Obiara ije nwe una" (be consoled, my brother (my sister); a stranger or a passer-by must one day go home). Still in a deeper sense the Igbo in their songs refer to this world as a pilgrimage. They say: "Enu uwa (obu nke onye ?) obu oliri, onye nosia o naba", which means "life on earth (whose is it ?) is like a promenade; one takes a turn and returns home". Even the same idea is expressed in the market metaphor which compares life on earth to a market-place, namely that "when the market day comes to an end we must pack our commodities and go".

This age-old belief is also confirmed by the formula with which some Igbo communites (e.g. the Ngwa people and their neighbours) used to announce the death of a married woman to her relatives. It is this:

Ogo I meela	Father-in-law, thanks for kola !
Nkea bu udu mmanya n'abo Iji gwa gi na owere onye ahu n'anwu	These are two jars, two pots of wine to tell you that someone was sick.
Nkea bu udu mmanya n'abo Iji gwa gi na <u>mmadu</u> nwuru.	These are two pots of wine to tell you that <u>someone</u> is dead.

The use of "mmadu" (someone) is impersonal. It is equivalent to the usages of "on" in French or "man" in the German language.

Nwokocha remarks, "the people did not speak of 'Mgbafo' who was sick and Mgbafo who is now dead. If they were to speak of Mgbafo dying, they would have declared that the whole being, Mgbafo is dead and would thus implicitly contradict their belief in the life after, i.e., in seeing death as 'a going home'. This however they did neither in intent nor by expression. All they said, if one were to add the name Mgbafo, is Mgbafo has gone home to 'Ani mmuo', leaving behind that which one used to see" (the body - "aru" or "ahu")[734]. In other words life on earth, according to the Igbo, "like a beautiful stroll is only for a while"[735], while death is an "Ina Chukwu" - a-return-home-to-Chukwu[736]. But it is "Ina Chukwu" that bases itself on a fulfilment of the course here on earth[737]. Yet the Igbo view death as the disruptor of relationships. When it occurs a restoration is immediately sought. For just as birth is a cause of social joy and festive jubilation among the community members; just as birth occasions social beliefs, sentiments and rites, so also does death. The spirit of the dead is to be ushered into its new state through burial and funerary rites, because death does not confine itself to ending the visible bodily life of an individual; it also destroys the social being grafted upon the physical individual and to whom the social consciousness attributed great dignity and importance[738]. As we saw, the Igbo society "formed", "trained", "gradated" the deceased member by means of rites of consecration or integration, and has thereby put to work energies proportional to the social status of the deceased: his destruction (death) therefore is tantamount to a sacrilege, implying the intervention of powers of the same order but of a negative nature, "it is a consequence of a sinister plot"[739]. When a person dies in an Igbo society, there is performed a ritual dance in which the living members search the village for elusive death, to avenge the wrong he has done them and if possible wrest from him the victim. Carrying sticks, matchets, guns, and small branches and twigs they dance around the village with a war cry, peering into nooks and corners; they engage in imitating a battle with imaginary foes - the antagonistic forces who violently ejected the deceased from the society[740]. In this ritual dance is inherent the society's belief in itself: the character of permanence. And because it feels itself "immortal" and wants to be so, it imparts its own character of permanence to the individuals who compose it: it refuses to believe that its members, above all, those with whom it identifies itself and in whom it "reincarnates" itself should be fated to die. Thus when a man dies the Igbo society feels it loses in the deceased much more than a unit; it is stricken in the very principle of its life, in the faith it has in itself - indeed, the very basis of its existence seems to be shaken or directly threatened by the presence of antagonistic forces[741]. Therefore they take up arms and engage in imitating a battle with these imaginary antagonistic foes, thus satisfying themselves that they are able "to hold the fort" and "defend the group against all annihilation"[742].

Again just as the social consciousness does not or refuses to believe in the necessity of death, so also does it refuse to consider it irrevocable. "Because it believes in itself a healthy society cannot admit that an individual who was part of its own substance, on whom it has set its mark, shall be lost forever."[743] Therefore this exclusion - the death of the member-unit is not final: the last word must remain with 'Ndu' (life). But the individual will not return to the life he has just left: the separation has been too serious to be abolished so soon[744]. Nonetheless the deceased will rise from the grip of death and will return in one form or another to the peace of human association. This release and this integration constitute the essence, as it is elsewhere remarked, of the Igbo mortuary and funeral rites, so that the deceased may be reunited with those who like himself and those who before him have lived and left this world and gone to the ancestors; so that he may enter this "mythical" society of souls which each society constructs on its own image[745]. However this "mythical" society of souls or what was earlier called "koinonia of parent-saints" is, according to the Igbo, not a mere replica of this earthly city. "By recreating itself beyond death", says Robert Hertz, "society frees itself from external constraints and physical necessities, which here on earth constantly hinder the flight of the collective desire. Precisely because the other world exists only in the mind, it is free of all limitations; it is - or can be - the realm of the ideal..."[746]. "Moreover in some societies, the way in which earthly life ends is a kind of blemish; death spreads its shadows over this world and the very victory that the soul has gained over death opens up for it an infinitely pure and more beautiful life."[747] Therefore there is no longer any reason why the "fulness of life" or, as Hertz again puts it, "why games should not be perpetually abundant in the 'happy hunting-grounds' of the other worlds" or why every day of the life among the "Koinonia of parent-saints" "should not be a Sunday to the Englishman eager for psalms"[748].

The nature of life itself in the beyond is variously conceived by the Igbo people. But all agree that: first, life on earth is a gift, a divinely intended opportunity for the individual in the community. It is a pilgrimage during which the individual has to realize his or her personal, social, moral and spiritual potentialities through his or her response to self, the neighbour and community. Yes, life is "iru oru onye na Chi ya ketara" or as some put it: "iru ife mmadu ketara n'Chi", i.e. to execute or accomplish one's lot from birth. Secondly, life in the beyond is believed to be a much more abundant existence. It transcends this earthly span; and it is characterized by some ontic and epistemic proximity to the Deity and the spiritual beings. Further, the finite and personal achievements, social and moral failures in personal situations, find their ultimate realization for better, for worse. Says P. Anyadioha Ibeawulà: "N'ani mmuo mmadu ezuoani ike afufu uwa; narakwani ugwo ya" (In the Spirit-World one rests from the toils of this world and also receives one's reward for them)[749].

CHAPTER TEN: CHRISTIANITY AND IGBO TRADITIONAL RELIGION: TOWARDS THE THEOLOGY OF THE DISPENSATION OF TRADITIONAL RELIGION

10.1 Summary of salient socio-religious values in Igbo Traditional life and death concepts

In our investigation, we saw that Igbo traditional society is a socio-religious community, which structurally follows a somewhat hierarchico-democratic pattern, in which all share the same egalitarian ideology and which is based on a "mythical" conceptualisation of the blood-ties between the unit-members, with its unit-heads (Okpala, ofo-holder or oji-ofo) as fundamentally the representatives and mouthpiece of their ancestors. Thus each unit-head becomes a rallying-point for his unit in so far as he occupies the senior position traceable to the first (putative) ancestor and eventually to God, from whom the ancestor obtained his power through the intermediary of the Earth-spirit, Ala. Igbo society is one in which the conduct of public affairs is a sacred undertaking and the attainment of material progress and economic growth as well as the welfare of the members of the community depend on conformity to "Omenala", the reward of which is the realization of the entire raison d'être of all its constituent members, namely, at once heavenly and earthly, eternal and temporal, collective and personal[750]. This explains why religion for the Igbo is an affair of the group and their knowledge of God and his worship through intermediaries (acting as dispensers of God's benefits) very strongly reflects their socio-religious structure[751].

Further, the Igbo asserted the eternal self-existence of Chukwu as the Supreme Being, who is the origin and ground of all that is and upon this basic faith rests the superstructure of their belief[752]. The aknowledgement of this Supreme Being is not so much the result of the gamut of metaphysical thinking as an outcome of man's experience of the Divine: human experience of that awesone immanence of the "Wholly Other", who though is invisible to man, yet he is actually present and visible to him in his varied actions, man's experience of that power who dominates and controls the unseen world in which he feels himself enveloped; that same power coming as providence: good and thoughtful of man, giving children to the barren, food to the hungry, perseverance to the despairing, justice to the afflicted and peace to troubled households. And all these shades of human experience are expressed in Igbo names in one form or another, and in their hymns, ritual mime and dancing music; they form subjects for minstrelsy; and they find vehicles in myths and folktales, proverbs and sayings[753].

This Supreme Being is also the Creating-Chi (Chineke). Because he is Life himself (Chukwubundu, Chinwendu,Chibundu) in creating he "apportions" life to other beings[754]. The Life which is allotted is the life-giving principle of every existing being. It is the "Chi-ukwu-within" in everything and it makes that being move, grow, strive, growl and exhibit all sorts of manifestations of life. Above all it "recharges" that being day-by-day and keeps it alive. The "Chi-ukwu-within" which is shared out to every being by the "Life per se", Chukwu, while he is apportioning life, when infused into that composite known as "Aru-mkpulu-obi" edifice, makes it "Mmadu", man, a creature possessing its nature more perfectly in union and sharing in a higher degree in the Divine Life than other creatures; it makes it existentially human, a single and unitary man in the full and unadulterated sense of the word, that is to say, with all the natural endowments that belong to it: personality, physicality, spirituality and sociality[755]. Furthermore because of its nature, man's whole being, his ontic intentional disposition, tends towards Chukwu from whom he got his "Chi-ukwu-within" (its personality-soul, Chi) which also acts as its (man's) own "Directive" (Guardian)[756]. Though every being possesses this "Chi-ukwu-within" in itself, there are some ascending order or degrees of participation of the "Life per se": there is a hierarchy in being[757]. The spiritual beings are manifestations of and symbolize Chukwu: they are his metaphors[758]. Ontologically they are higher than Mmadu (man). But Mmadu, of all other creatures in the visible world, is the synthesis, the sum total, the climax, the culmination of all that Chukwu created and created beautifully and good; he is the crown of Chukwu's creative act, indeed, the "Let-there-be-goodness and peace"[759]. But despite the fact that man is the crown of Chukwu's handiwork in the midst of the world, he is a creature who is rooted in history and yet can never determine with any note of finality the history in which he finds himself, for the ultimate meaning of history always remains under the enactment of Chukwu's command[760]. Hence when Chukwu withdraws the "Chiukwu-within" from man, the breath of life which he has given to each being, and death occurs, man's death is no more a "neutral" process. Rather, mythical tales are brought in to explain why the present phenomenon of man dying, although it is acknowledged as a universal human experience, does not seem to be altogether "natural"; thus, too, implying that man's death is consequent upon either because of a previous culpability or as a result of maltreatment or the failure of the messenger of immortality, that is man's inability to rise again after death. Needless to add, this insinuates something "non-natural" in the "present" phenomenon of man's death and makes Igbo conceptuality of death somewhat ambivalent[761]. This ambivalence is heightened by the fact that the Igbo express the death of man, as "a going-home" (Ina ulo) or "a returning -home-to Chukwu" (Ina Chukwu), which is symbolized by man's last upward breath[762]. This term or phrase, though it is strenghthened by Igbo social-consciousness - the mysterious sense of continuity and solidarity which enables them to think of themselves, living on so long as the group with whom their life had been linked continues to live - tersely expresses Igbo belief in the indestructibility and imperishability of some element of man's composite despite death. This element is the marrow of the personality - soul (mmuo) responsible for the psychic power - the ontic intentional dispositions stored in every human being; this drives man into action to realize himself in society and create his social existential relationship. The "mmuo" returns to "Ani-Mmuo", the spirit-world, as soon as death occurs. But it cannot properly rejoin its forefathers unless it has regained its existential relationship, which the Igbo believe a man retains inspite of it, to his former human existence. This belief is one of the reasons, of the Igbo mortuary and funerary rites[763]. These rites profoundly alter the condition of the deceased: they enable him to resume a serene and secure "social" life again.

Since no one element of a cultural complex can be exhaustively studied and understood in isolation from the rest, Igbo ideas of life and death as reflected in their social consciousness were examined, for in a sense it can be said that ideas and values are not only a mere ideological reflection or superstructure of the social order, but also the social order can be an objective expression of the system of ideas and values[764]. From this examination, it is discovered that for the Igbo life on earth is a "relationship-existence" in pursuit of the "fullness of life", a gift, a divinely intended opportunity for the individual in the community to realize himself personally, socially and spiritually; and death in normal circumstances is a transition from the visible society of the living and a reintegration into the invisible society of one's forefathers, what was called "KOINONIA OF PARENT-SAINTS"[765].

The way the Igbo individual whom I questioned conceives the life in the beyond varies. But on this point they seem to agree. If life on earth is a gift, a divinely intended opportunity for the individual in the community, a pilgrimage during which the individual has to realize his personal, social, moral and spiritual potentialities through his response to self, the neighbour and the community, the life in the beyond is believed to be a much more abundant existence; it transcends our earthly span and is characterized by some "ontic and epistemic proximity" to the Deity. For death is "a returning to Chukwu" or simply "a going home", they insist. Therefore the new life brought about by death opens up new possibilities, perhaps, too, a new qualitative beginning - indeed, a limitless vista of Ndu (life) within which the finite and personal achievements and social and moral failures in personal situations, find their ultimate realization, for better, for worse.

Our investigation into Igbo concepts of life and death in their relationships to Chukwu, God, has been primarily to examine these ideas in their traditional setting. No attempt has been made to reconcile or compare them with the deposit of Christian teaching. Indeed one wonders whether there is any basis for such. I may well have inadequately expressed these concepts of the Igbo. Nonetheless I do hope that through this study a stepping-stone is laid for future and more specialized studies in this field and that these researches will continue to throw more light on these aspects of Igbo religion which are still obscure.

Even the value of this intimate knowledge and application of reason to a subject where only the heart seems competent might well seem both ridiculous and sacrilegious ! But it cannot be denied that the pattern of life within any given society is an expression of the particular view of man held by that society; and the practices of religion and the shape of political life are as much the outcome of that society's doctrine of God as of its estimate of man. More, the supreme and final crisis of life - death - is of the greatest importance among the sources of religion. And, in any case, an insight is given us of Igbo perception of the complicated system of balance which binds together the individual, the community, the ancestors, the spirits and God - in short their visible and invisible word-view; Igbo principle of order, their social organs and civic traditions, the organic unity and continuity of human life, their humanity's ethos and their image of human goal.

10.2 Justification of Traditional Igbo religion in the light of Christianity

Obviously, however, when compared with the more specific and explicit Christian teaching, some of the Igbo ideas of life and death in their relationship to Chukwu, God, may not be "orthodox"; some might with difficulty conform to it, while some still are authentically human values - "Christian" values. These phenomena that Igbo traditional religious thoughts exhibit need not surprise us. Indeed, on the contrary, it would have been strange, if they did not exhibit such.

If the picture of God revealed to us by Jesus Christ is true, as the one who is directly searching for man, not as a subject of condemnation or disdain but as the child of God[766], then the whole of mankind's religion is God's movement towards and his quest for man. "Christianity", like every other religion must be concerned with divine facts or acts which consist in changes that affect mankind and these are changes brought about solely by the power of God. These acts of God would have as their object the uplifting of man. If he who accomplishes them is God, he in whom and for whom they are accomplished, is man; and whatever happens is a happening which concerns man and not a happening which concerns God[767]. Observed Hans Küng: "We can ask what is outside the Church, but the question is difficult to answer. But what is outside God and his plan of Salvation is no question at all. If we look at God's plan of salvation, then there is no extra, only an intra, no outside, only an inside, since God 'desires all men to be saved and to come to the knowledge of the truth. For there is one God, and there is one mediator between God and men, the man Jesus Christ, who gave himself as a ransom for all' (1 Tim. 2,5f).[768]

Furthermore, if attention is drawn to the nature of God's salvation that Jesus Christ revealed, there is a passage in the New Testament with tremendous theological significance. It is a passage in St. Paul's letter to the Ephesians 1,3-14. In this passage it is stated in a most startling metaphor of a time before time (cf. Eph. 1,4), the revelation of God's "Charis", his "Ḥēn" for all mankind - the gratuitousness of God's favour and the way he manifests his glory[769]. It must immediately be said that the source of the "Charis" (Ḥēn or ḥesed) is God's liberality and its purpose is to make his glory appreciated by creatures. In other words, God's "Charis" is primarily the "Charis" God has for all men and that leads him to choose and call them "to be holy"[770] and this includes men's love for God that results from, and is a response to, his own love for men[771]. Otherwise there would be no connection between God's being and his doing - what God is eternally in himself, and what God does, which is necessarily within time. Or, as Karl Rahner puts it: "There could be no serious question of a serious and also actually effective salvific design of God for all men, in all ages and places."[772] More, everything comes from God and everything should lead to him[773]. If the rebirth, as St.Paul in the passage in question insists, is effected by Christ reuniting all the parts of creation in an organism with himself as the head and so to reattach it to God, it is because all the parts are saved by the single act of God[774]. Consequently in a hidden sort of way all men without exception are offered salvation by God, and the means to attain it.

Again, if the prologue of St.John is anything to go by, it is this: that God has always and never for a moment ceased to take a salvific interest in the world. His light has always been among men to show them the way of life. This enlightenment of all men who come into the world (which St. John as a believer ascribed to Christ) is effected in a double manner. First, the word of God works in the spiritual interiority of man, instructing him in mysterious and hidden ways according him grace, actual preparative grace that should lead him to God. No one is excluded from this influence of God's light. Secondly, all these were done by the exterior manifestation of God in the world. For as St.Paul puts it: "God has not left you without some clue to his nature in the kindness he shows"[775]. And again the letter to the Hebrews says: "At various times in the past and in various different ways, God spoke to our ancestors..."[776]. One scarsely needs add the whole world should be seen as a "universe of signs" through which the Spirit of God indicates to man that there exists other realities[777]. Christianity teaches that there are three divine persons in God. If God is one, not many, and is the Creator-God as he is equally the Spirit or Wisdom[778] operative in the whole creation, then he is known, however inadequately and partially; and this knowledge of him is through the outpouring of his Spirit in the world of human beings. This is revelation, that is, God's self-manifestation encountering man wherever he is and at all times[779]. Admirably Hulsbosch sums up God's saving and creative act thus:

> The Son of God made man is the light of the world. He was the eternal wisdom, who, before his becoming flesh and in the time of preparation "in every generation passed into holy souls, and made them friends of God and prophets" (Wis. 7,27). The godly of the old covenant lived by the light, and through his light praised God and his creation. For wisdom does not enlighten only man, but makes creation recognizable as God's creation, by giving it form and order. Before man existed, wisdom already inhabited the universe, and because the Wisdom of God was in all things, nothing was meaningless. Because of wisdom those creatures who were never seen by man were not meaningless. They were there to praise their Creator. But as soon as man is raised by Wisdom to the knowledge of the Creator he becomes the interpreter of the hymn of Creation. (780)

The salvation Hulsbosch has in mind is certainly the salvation willed by God and won by Christ, "the salvation of supernatural grace which divinizes man, the salvation of the beatific vision". But it is to be noted immediately that it is also a salvation really intended for all those millions of Igbo people and others who lived, long before Christ, and also for those Igbo who haved lived after Christ, as for all other nations, cultures and epochs of a very wide range which were and are still completely shut off from the view-point of those living in the light of the New Testament. If really we conceive "salvation" as something specifically "Christian"; if there is no salvation apart from Christ; if according to Catholic teaching the supernatural divinization of mankind can never be replaced merely by good-will on the part of man, but is necessary as something itself given in this earthly life; and moreover, if God has really, truly and seriously intended this salvation for all men, then these two aspects cannot be reconciled in any other way than by stating that every human being is really and truly exposed to the influence of divine, supernatural grace which offers an interior union with God and by means of which God communicates himself whether the individual takes up an attitude of acceptance or refusal towards this grace[781]. If creation and salvation history threaten, as it were, the inner procession of God, that is, if they are really founded on the free decision of God and in such a way that saving history has been the drama of mediation between God and man, then mankind would not have any real arbitrary autonomy and freedom in relation to God. It would seem, indeed, there has always been some illuminating, radical and pervasive presence of the Deity in his creation[782], and man cannot but be a "homo religiosus". Furthermore, it would seem equally strange that man created in the image and likeness of God and destined for salvation could help being unaware of the Infinite Divine Reality, that is, of not standing in some immediate presence of Infinite Power, Infinite Goodness and Love - shall I say - in some direct "epistemic proximity", subjectively, interiorly and religiously"[783]. But it is the teaching of the Catholic Church that every genuine and salutory religious act which proceeds from the human soul is sustained by an intervention of Divine Spirit and constitutes an experience of Christ and is an implicit invocation directed towards him[784].

However man is not merely subjectively and interiorly a "homo religiosus". He is limited by his very nature to time and space. He is born at a certain time in history into a specific community of men living in a certain geographical corner of the universe. He is also by nature, not an island, but a social being and is necessarily brought up within a particular kind of culture having its own religious expression. It is a fact evident to all, that, in the great majority of cases, the religion in which a person believes and to which he adheres, depends, at least initially, upon where and into which family, he is born. Let us take a Nigerian case as an example. At present there are Catholics, Anglicans, Presbyterians, Methodists, Qua Iboe, United African Church, the Seventh Day Adventists, the Aladuras, Moslems, and Traditional Religionists. All these groups have adherents and pockets of concentration in the country. And if someone is born to parents practising any one of these religions, that person is likely to follow the religion of the parents. I would presume that the same holds good for the various world religions. Of course in each of the above-mentioned cases the person may be a fully committed or a merely nominal adherent of his religion. But whether one is a Christian, a Muslim or a Traditional Religionist depends nearly always on to which family one happens to have been born into. Any credible religious faith, must be able to appreciate this circumstance - that man gives expression to his subjective religious dispositions and sentiments in the concrete religion of the people into whom he is born and among whom he passes his earthly sojourn. Granted, therefore, God's universal salvific design which postulates that man enters into a genuine saving relationship with him, and in view of man's social nature and in view of the radical solidarity of men, it is absolutely inconceivable that the individual man could have been able to maintain the relationship with God which he must have and which God does and must make available to him if he is to be saved within absolutely private interiority and apart from the actual religion offered him by his milieu[785]. One must not forget that the present division or separation of state and church (religion) is a modern phenomenon and altogether Western[786]. In fact with Karl Rahner one is compelled to affirm that if man everywhere and always could be and had to be a "homo religiosus", so that as such, he might save himself, then he was this "homo religiosus" within the contemporary concrete religion in which he lived and was forced by nature to live, and from which he could not totally disassociate himself, however much he may have taken up a critical and selective attitude towards this religion. Therefore, if the Igbo always had a saving positive relationship with God, and if they have always had to have it, then they have had it precisely within the religion actually at their disposal as a moment of their existential milieu[787]. And in the concrete, it must contain supernatural, gratuitous elements, and in using this religion they were able to attain God's salvation[788].

John H. Newman says that Revelation properly speaking is a universal, not a local gift, and that in every religion on earth there is something true and divinely revealed, overloaded as it might be and at times stifled by the impiety which the corrupt will and understanding of man had incorporated with it.

> Such are the doctrines, of the power and presence of an invisible God, of His moral laws and governance, of the obligation of duty, and the certainty of a just judgment, and of reward and punishment, as eventually dispensed to individuals ... and the distinction between the state of Israelites formerly and Christians now, and that of the heathen, is, not that we can, and they cannot attain to the future blessedness, but that the Church of God ever has had, and the rest of mankind never have had, authoritative documents of truth, and appointed channels of communication with Him. The word and the Sacraments are the characteristic of the elect people of God; but all men have had more or less the guidance of Tradition, in addition to those internal notions of right and wrong which the Spirit had put into the heart of each individual. (789)

Further he called, "this vague and uncertain family of religious truths, originally from God, but sojourning without the sanction of miracles, or a definite home, as pilgrims up and down the world, and discernible and separable from the corrupt legends with which they are mixed, by the spiritual mind alone, the 'Dispensation of Paganism'"[790].

And rightly so, for revelation, remarks Latourelle, is first of all, essentially, a work of grace. God alone can open himself to man through a gracious gesture which is the work of love. Knowledge of God appears as his gift to those who love him. The Father cannot actually be known. But because He is love and because everything is possible for him, he has granted even this, to those who love him, the power of seeing God. Secondly, revelation is the work of salvation. For those who do not believe, it is judgment, for those who believe it, it is salvation and life; it tends to make man enter into vision and immortality[791].

Nor should it be forgotten that before God called Abraham, he had already made a covenant with mankind, man whom he created in his image and likeness[792], in his alliance with Noah and his descendants after him[793] - indeed with every living creature[794]; a valid covenant forever[795]. And this covenant reverberates through the words of much later prophets and psalmists. God has shown his particular favour in more than one exodus deliverance. "Did not I, who brought Israel out of the land of Egypt, bring the Philistines from Caphtor, and the Aramaens from Kir ?"[796] More than one nation might even have enjoyed the experience of being specially chosen for blessing, and for bringing it to the world. "That day, Israel, making the third with Egypt and Assyria will be blessed in the centre of the World. Yahweh Sabaoth will give his blessing in the words, 'Blessed be my people Egypt, Assyria my creation, and Israel my heritage'"[797]. And in Malachi it is stated that the nations not only recognize the divinity of Yahweh but offer him acceptable sacrifice. "From farthest east to farthest west my name is honoured among the nations and everywhere a sacrifice of incense is offered to my name, and a pure offering too, since my name is honoured among the nations, says Yahweh Sabaoth"[798].

The all-important use of "berit","diatheke" (covenant) to designate the alliance God made with Noah would demonstrate that Israel recognized, at least in principle, the legitimacy of those other religions through which the terms of the covenant were translated into life, even if the abuses were condemned[799]. The certain presence of the supernatural in the Noachite event is also attested in the eulogy which the author of the letter to the Hebrews makes of Noah's faith[800]. It might be argued, however, that Noah's faith was consequent on a very special intervention of God. But what of the faith of those who preceded him, equally praised by the same sacred writer: the faith of Abel and Enoch ?[801] Though the Jahwistic and Elohistic traditions would put the revelation of the divine name later in the Mosaic period[802], a son of Seth, named Enosh, was said to be the first to invoke the name of Jahweh[803]. How, one may ask, did Enosh come to invoke the name of Jahweh ?

The significant place given by the sacred writer to Melchizedek , King of Salen - this King of peace and righteousness - and priest of God Most High[804] would point to the importance of God's covenant with mankind. The priesthood and sacrifice of Melchizedek, a priest, perhaps, of God's first covenant with mankind - was to be a figure of the eternal priesthood and sacrifice of Christ. Both the Old and New Testament would praise him, and to this day the Church of Christ does so[805].

Sacred Scripture seems to give reason to believe that a saving relationship between God and mankind has always existed; that, indeed, there has been a dispensation of World religions; and that this dispensation was delivered to mankind at large, has been continually and secretly reanimated and enforced by new communications from the unseen world[806]. Apart from the injunctions to Noah, the first recorded fact of salvation history after the deluge, there are other clues that God has always spoken to man and told him to a certain extent his duty. The book of Genesis, for example, contains a record of the dispensation of World religions as well as of the patriachal. The dreams of Pharaoh and Abimelech, as of Nebuchadnezzar afterwards, are instances of the dealings of God with those to whom he did not vouchsafe a written revelation[807].

Or should it be said, that these particular cases merely came within the range of the Divine supernatural governance which was in the neighbourhood - an assertion which requires proof ! Let the Book of Job be taken as a more credible (or less suspicious) instance of the dealings of God with mankind. Job was a "pagan" in the sense in which the eastern nations are "pagans" at the present day. He lived among "idolaters"[808]. Yet he and his friends had cleared themselves from the superstitions with which the true creed was beset; and while one of them was divinely instructed by dreams[809], Job himself at length heard the voice of God out of the whirlwind, in recompense for his long trial and his faithfulness under it[810]. Scripture as if drawing back the curtain farther still, contains the story of Balaam. In this instance a bad man and a "heathen" is made the oracle of true divine messages about acting justly, and loving mercy, and walking humbly; indeed, even among the altars of superstition the Spirit of God vouchsafes to utter prophecy[811]. And in the cave of Endor, even a saint (Samuel) was sent from the dead to join the company of - shall I say - an "apostate" king,

Saul, and of the sorceress whose aid he was seeking[812].

"To the Word of God", says Clement of Alexandria, "all the host of angels and heavenly powers is subject, revealing, as he does, his holy office, for him who has put all things under him. Wherefore also all men are his; some actually knowing him, others not as yet; some as friends, others as faithful servants, and others as simply servants. He is the teacher, who instructs the enlightened Christian (the Gnostic) by mysteries, and the faithful labourer by cheerful hopes, and the hard of heart with his keen corrective discipline; so that his providence is particular, public and universal. He it is whom we call Saviour and Lord of all; and persuades all who are willing. For he compels no one to receive salvation from him, because he is able to choose and fulfil from himself what pertains to the laying hold of the hope. He it is who gives the Greeks their philosophy by his ministering angels, for by an ancient and divine order the angels are distributed among the nations (cf. Deut. 32, 8,9). But the glory of those who believe is 'the Lord's portion'. For he is the Saviour not of these or those, but of all, the Lord of those who have not believed, till, being enabled to confess him, they obtain the peculiar and appropriate boon which comes by him."[813] Man alone of all the other living creatures was in his creation endowed with a conception of God; and there is no other better and more suitable government for men than that which is appointed by God. In consequence that which truly rules and presides is the Divine Word and His Providence, which inspects all things, and despises the care of nothing belonging to it. Those, therefore, who choose to belong to him, are those who are perfected through faith[814]. His precepts, both the former and the later, are drawn forth from one fount; those who were before the law, not suffered to be without law, those who do not hear the Jewish philosophy not surrendered to an unbridled course. Dispensing in former times to some his precepts, to others, philosophy, now at length by his own personal coming, he has closed the course of unbelief, which is henceforth inexcusable; Greek and barbarian being led forward by a separate process to that perfection which is through faith. Since all things are arranged with a view to the salvation of the universe, both generally and particularly, the goodness of the great overseeing Judge corrects and compels egregious sinners to repent. Everything which does not hinder a man's choice from being free, he makes and renders auxiliary to virtue and improves as far as practicable, in order that there may be revealed somehow or other, even to those capable of seeing but dimly, the one only almighty, good God - saving from eternity to eternity[815]. And St. Augustine outrightly affirmed that there were righteous men before the Incarnation who were made whole by the future humility of Christ, their King revealed to them through the Spirit. "From these Abraham, a devout and faithful servant of God, was chosen that to him might be made the revelation concerning the Son of God, so that by imitating his faith all the faithful of all nations in time to come might be called his children." These men were "saints" and they were members of Christ's Church, although they lived before Christ our Lord was born according to the flesh. And later he spoke of the "unknown saints" who observed the first covenant of works. In another book of his he tells us that the reality of the Christian religion has never been absent in the history of mankind; it only received its name when Christ came in flesh[816].

Could these give us a gracious insight regarding Igbo Traditional Religion - indeed the variety of religions of mankind - and all those who in those religions sought God with their hearts ? Between Adam and the coming of Christ, how did men arrive at the saving God ? Who can affirm that the faith indispensable for salvation was limited only to those few of whom we read in Sacred Scripture ? And accordingly, that is, if we admit faith outside Christianity, would it be an unreasonable notion that, there could have been poets and sages or sibyls or even prophets outside the Jewish-Christian dispensations, divinely illuminated and organs through which religious and moral truth was conveyed to their countrymen, however faint or defective their knowledge of the Power from whom the gift came, and their perception of the gift as existing in themselves may be ? In fact the New Testament appears to support this: When Paul teaches in Roman (cf. 1, 18 ff.; 2,14 ff.) that human beings can know God through the testimony of the created world and their own conscience, he makes no reference to Christ being involved as the agent or means of this knowledge. When the Book of Acts speaks of the witness to God provided by the seasons and bounty of nature, it does so without invoking Christ (cf. 14,17.22 ff.). It should also be remembered that the functions attributed to Christ by Christians - as agent, model and goal of God's creations - were attributed by Jewish theology to divine Word and Wisdom.

Faith involves belief in the supernatural, and this in turn involves some type of supernatural, definite, and indeed, a determinate relationship[817]. Writes Clement of Alexandria:

> The judgement which follows knowledge is in truth faith. Accordingly faith is something superior to knowledge, and its criterion. ... And as the worksman sees that by learning certain things he becomes a craftsman, and the helmsman by being instructed in the art will be able to steer; he does not regard the mere wishing to become excellent and good enough, but he must learn it by the exercise of obedience. But to obey the Word, whom we call instructor, is to believe him, going against him in nothing. For how can we take up a position of hostility to God ? Knowledge, accordingly, is characterized by faith; and faith by a kind of divine mutual and reciprocal correspondence, becomes characterized by knowledge (818).

To admit the legitimacy of mankind's religious variety does not necessarily imply that the "errors" or short-comings in them should be, or may be made light of or overlooked, for since the various religions extant reflect the historical nature of man - created in the image and likeness of God, sinful yet called to salvation - even so every religion contains simultaneously all human components. Grace and sin, light and darkness exist in every human religion side by side. Not even the Judaic religion which was especially revealed by God was removed from these aberrations. The chequered history of Christianity is too evident in this respect as to need any further comment. Nor must it be understood here that a liberal syncretism is being advocated.

The Fathers of the Church were well aware centuries back that not only Greek philosophy but even the "hated" mysteries have in their elements of human craving and human framework some shadow of the divine. The nocturnal worship of the "pagan", darkened by vice as it was, was still an attempt at worship[819]. But, as is to be expected (as the few references made so far would also have intimated) they saw as the climax of all these dealings of Providence with mankind the coming of Christ in the flesh, and for practical purposes they took sacred Scripture as the depository of the unadulterated and complete revelation of providence to man. Obviously their endeavour was to find connections between "Paganism" or existing systems and Christianity, which existing systems they also laboured to supplant with Christianity.

To link up the Christian truths with the truths contained in the existing systems the Apologists among them elaborated the theory or doctrine of the "Logos Spermatikos" (seminal word) as the meeting point[820]. For them there is a unity between the natural and supernatural order. According to Caperan, until the Pelagian heresy the tendency to find a clear-cut dichotomy between the natural and the supernatural was unknown[821]. Creation is seen by the Apologists in the biblical light as the beginning of the manifestations of God's love in preparation for man with whom he wishes to share his life. But creation and the salvation of man are one declaration - one plan of God, his one tender solicitude for man's salvation, though with two hues. Man's salvation was not something secondarily intended in creation. Rather it was what God willed in creation, namely that "all men should be saved and come to the full knowledge of the truth"[822]. St.Irenaeus admirably put it thus:

> Mundi enim factor vere Verbum Dei est: hic autem est Dominus noster, qui in novissimis temporibus homo factus est, in hoc mundo exsistens; et secundum invisibilitatem

> continet quae facta sunt omnia, et universa conditione infixes, quoniam Verbum Dei gubernans et disponens omnia; et propter hoc in sua visibiliter venit, et caro factum est, et pependit super lignum, uti universa in semetipsum recapituletur (823).

In this paragraph against the Gnostics, Irenaeus, following St.Paul, was at pains to explain the dynamic unity between creation and salvation history, the double role of the Incarnate Word as Creator and Saviour, his visible and invisible operations, his metaphysical place and his physical intervention in the history of humanity. The manifestation or revelation of God to man - the Oikonomia of salvation - passes gradually from cosmic revelation to positive and personal revelation to such personages as Adam, Noah, Abraham, Moses and the prophets, all of whom authoritatively proclaimed the Word of God. But the climax and completion of this manifestation of God to man came when the Word of God himself became man as Jesus Christ and lived among men.

St.Augustine attributed a double role to the Incarnate Word of God. On the one hand he instructs men and reveals to them the living truth which they had not known in their distorted and false approaches to God and thus he leads them into a progressive appropriation of the truth. On the other hand he helps men to their salvation, since without the grace of that faith which is from him, no man can subdue his vicious desires or be cleansed by pardon from guilt[824]. And Christ's coming in flesh gave the reality that already existed a name:

> I said in De vera religione that Christianity is the safest and surest way to God. I referred only to the true religion that now is called Christian. I was not thinking of true religion as it existed before the coming of Christ: I was referring to the name and not to the reality to which the name belongs. For when the apostles began to preach Christ after his resurrection and ascension into heaven and many believed, it was at Antioch, as it is written, that the disciples were first called Christians (Acts 11,26): so I said: Now in our day this is the Christian religion...not that in former times it was not present, but because it received this name at a later date (825).

If everything right from creation to Christ was ordered to the revelation of God's glory, and the perfect image of God is his Word by whom all things without exception were made and directed, then it follows that nothing could possibly manifest God without reflecting him. In every man according to the Apologists, there is ingrained in the intellect a seed of the word (spermata tou logou). All truth is traced back to the Logos. Writes Clement of Alexandria: "And should any one say that it was through human understanding that philosophy was discovered by the Greeks, still I find the Scriptures saying that understanding is sent by God."[826] Philosophy here for Clement (in opposition to the mere lucubrations of the human intellect and in no respect to be accounted divine) is that prerequisite for righteousness, conducive to piety, a kind of preparatory training or preparation, paving the way for him who is perfected in Christ; all good doctrine in every one and all precepts of holiness combined with religious knowledge. In effect all that trained mankind for the fulness of time[827]. All these are God's ways of dealing with mankind for his are all men; he is the Saviour of all and he is the common fount from which all alike draw forth; he leads all forward by separate processes to perfection through faith. His benefience has no beginning; nor is it limited to places and persons; it is not confined to parts[828]. If his dealings with mankind is universal, it is also particular, individual and accommodating[829]. Hence unbelief is inexcusable. But until the Full Light shines forth all is like the touch of a wick which men kindle, artificially stealing the light from the sun. But on the proclamation of the Word all that holy light shines forth[830].

In the thinking of St.Justin transcendent, unknowable invisible, acts through the intermediary of the Logos: through him he created and organized the World; through him he makes himself known; through him he effects salvation in the World and it is for all this that God conceived the Logos: "the son of God, the only one who is properly Son, the Logos existing with him and begotten before all creatures, when, at the beginning, he made and ordered all things"[831]. This generation was bound up with creation and it took place in view of this creation. Justin, in many texts, insists on the absolute priority of the Logos to the whole creation: "as the principle before all creatures, God begot of himself, before all creatures, a certain verbal power"[832]. For Justin the generation of the Logos appears as an activity through which God, before creation, by his power and his will, emits the word as the agent of creation[833]. And since in every human being there is a "seed", "a germ of the Logos" permitting him to come to the partial knowledge of the truth (kata meros) and express it, all truth draws its origin from the Logos of Divine Word[834]. Consequently every right principle that the "pagan" thinkers and legislators discovered and formulated is due to this participation of the Logos - in the human mind. Their errors are due to the fact that they have a partial and not full possession of the Logos in person, as the Christians do[835]. None-the-less the truths that they declared from their obscure and partial participation of the Logos deserve to be called Christian[836]. For Justin, the activity of the Logos embraces all humanity and though it is spread everywhere, it is more fully present among the Jews and the prophets. But it is total only in the person of Christ[837]. Justin identifies the Logos with Christ, and calls him the first-born of the Father, from whom all men partake of their being and are saints if they live reasonably: "Christum primo-genitum Dei esse ac rationem illam, cuius omne hominum genus particeps erat, dedicimus, et supra declaravimus. Et qui cum ratione vixerunt, Christiani sunt, etiamsi athei existimati sunt..."[838]. Having identified the Logos with Christ, Justin calls him our "teacher"[839]; he whom we must prefer to all other teachers[840]; he who enlightens the nations[841] by his lessons, his precepts, his teaching, his maxims[842]; whose doctrine is the doctrine of salvation: the Logos became man "to bring us a doctrine destined to renew and regenerate the human race"[843]; and this doctrine, contained in the memories of the Apostles "which are called Gospels"[844], we all are invited to receive in faith and make our lives conform with them[845]. This adherence finally is worked out in grace, for no one can either see or understand, if God and his Christ do not give him the gift of understanding[846]. In order to stress the unity of God's plan, Justin does not say that the theophanies of the Logos in the Old Testament prepare for the Incarnation; instead he prefers to speak of salvation which groups together the manifestations of the Logos in the Old and New Testament[847]. To do this Justin took over from the Greek philosophers the two concepts of Logos and Nomos (law), and incorporated them in his theology of history. When Christ is called Logos and Nomos and mediator of divine Revelation it is a historical understanding of divine Revelation[848]. Through the uninterrupted work of revelation of the Logos, the history of mankind becomes a carefully planned construction with beginning, purpose and end. In this way Christ, the eternal Dynamis of God[849] is the Nomos of the human race[850]. By him order is brought into a work in which everything has been in confusion. His advent breaks the influence which the demons had exerted in history through the "nomoi" of the peoples.

Theologians may dispute whether Justin attributed supernatural revelation to the non-Christian philosophies as a consequence of their share in the "Logos spermatikos". But one thing seems certain for Justin, and that is, that Revelation is one and progressive and reaches its totality in the God-man. Commenting on Justin's unification of natural and supernatural revelation Harènt notes that the two revelations are not mutually exclusive but complete each other; and that Justin could all the more easily unite the two and consider them as the one illumination of the Word in as such as in Justin's time the distinctions between nature and grace, the natural and the supernatural, were completely unknown[851].

For Irenaeus, the "creator of the best in Tertullian", the "precursor of the mightier Augustine" and the theologian of "redemptive History"[852], God is one and the economy of revelation is one. Revelation is bound up with the broader activity of the Word and the work of salvation. The Word of God is at work from the dawn of humanity. Under his guidance humanity is born, grows and matures up to the fullness of time; through the Incarnation of the Word and his redemptive work, humanity becomes the body of Christ and together with him walks towards the vision of the Father[853]. Thus the Word of God (Logos) is creator, redeemer and revealer[854]. Against the Gnostic-Docetic heresies[855], the new attacks on the "substantia Domini nostri" as he puts it Irenaeus sets out resolutely not to win "pagans", but rather to preserve the "depositum fidei"[856]. This means, above all, the emphasizing of the Unity of God, Christ and Salvation. Irenaeus stressed the unity of the Incarnation of Christ, God and man, and the real centre of unity against all dualism in the cosmos and history and the historicity of the act of redemption. Utilizing the Old Testament as the "regula fidei" and preserving the traditional concept of Christocentricity he resolves the unity of God, Christ and Salvation. In this connection he develops the idea of a universal "Oikonomia" which embraces both creation and end and puts Christ-event in the middle[857]. Creation, the Incarnation of Christ, and Resurrection, belong together as different parts of the one all-embracing saving work of God. The significance of "Anakephalaiosis" (Recapitulation) as an act of Christ is the special contribution which Christ makes to the realization of the one Oikonomia of the Father in Christ and the Spirit. Christ is already revealed and prefigured in the Old Testament and is thus already an object for the faith and the hope of the Old Testament. But in the New Testament, something new has been added by the real coming of Christ, which enriches the knowledge of faith: "Quemadmodam enim in nuovo testamento ea, quae est ad Deum, fides hominum aucta est, additamentum accipiens Filium Dei, ut et homo fieret particeps Dei..."[858]. Nevertheless, this new thing of the New Testament is only there as a result of the "Recapitulation" brought about in Christ. The whole order of the salvation which finds its climax in the Incarnation of Christ (with his passion, his resurrection, his coming again and the resurrection of all mankind and the revelation of salvation) is said to lead to the Recapitulation in Christ.

> Unus igitur Deus pater quemadmodum ostendimus, et unus Christus Jesus Dominus noster veniens per universam dispositionem, et omnia in semetipsum recapitulans. In omnibus autem est et homo, plasmatio Dei: et hominem ergo in semetipsum recapitulans est, invisibilis visibilis factus, et incomprehensibilis factus comprehensibilis, et impassibilis passibilis, et Verbum Dei; sic et in visibilibus, et corporalibus principatum habeat, in semetipsum primatum assumens, et apponens semetipsum caput ecclesiae, universa attrahat ad semetipsum apto in tempore (859).

Just as the Logos is, in the invisible world, already the head of all beings created through him, so now in the Incarnation he becomes the head of the visible and corporeal world, and above all the head of the Church and so draws everything to himself. This represents at the same time a recapitulation of creation, and, above all, of the fallen man Adam, that is a renewing and saving permeation of the whole history of the world and mankind by Christ, the head from beginning to end[860]. In this way, the world, history and man reach their climax, but at the same time they are also brought back by Christ to their principle, God. The whole of God's previous work through the Logos in the world and in man is concentrated in the Incarnation of Christ; it reaches its fullness, and now in Christ fills the whole of the world and the whole of history[861]. For Irenaeus, then, the Incarnation is merely the conclusion in an immense series of manifestations of the Logos which had their beginning in the creation of the world[862], educating and preparing mankind for the salvation whereby all things are recapitulated in Christ. Salvation consists in the manifestation of God and the communication of his life to man. Because man initially was like an infant unprepared for the food of adults (the intuitive vision of God) the Father through the world led man across different theophanies, progressively manifesting himself to man until in Christ that which was invisible of the Father became visible. It is now possible to know God:

> No one can know the Father except the Word of God, that is, unless the Son reveals him; nor the Son except through the good pleasure of the Father. The son accomplishes the good pleasure of the Father. The Father sends, the Son is sent and comes. And the Father, invisible and uncircumscribed with respect to us, is known by his own Word, and since he is ineffable, it is this word which makes him known to us. In his turn, the Father knows only the Word. That is why by the very act of making him known, the Son reveals the knowledge of the Father, for everything is made manifest through the Word (863).

And why does the Father have to reveal himself through the Son ? - "ut per eum omnibus manifestetur, et eos quidem qui credunt ei iusti, in incorruptelam, et in aeternum refrigerium recipiat"- for to believe in him is to do his will (credere autem ei facere eius voluntatem"[864]. The knowledge of God which is brought to humanity through the intervention of the Word gives life - a moral intuitive vision of God. Hence no one but the humble of heart may find that knowledge of God. The proud philosophers did not arrive at a true knowledge of God because they lacked the humility of heart[865]. Humility and purity of heart are indispensable for him who desires to know God. This religious character of revelation which Irenaeus stresses is of great significance, because it points to the fact that simple, untutored and ordinary people may come to faith in the existence of a saving God. Learning is therefore not a prerequisite, and because it is not necessary, the supernatural nature of man's faith comes more to light. What is more, this "revelation" embraces all creation from the angels to men and all the course of human history from Adam to the Incarnation.

Writing on the role attributed to the Logos in revelation according to Irenaeus, Escoula asks: "Should the word 'revelation' be understood in the wide sense, and when talking of revelation through the medium of creation, can one say that Irenaeus just means the traces of God left in creation, perceptible only by the use of the natural light of reason ?" For Escoula it does not seem so because "the revelation in question is an 'ennaratio Patris'... and an instruction of man..., an enlightenment which demands faith..., an 'ostensio Dei' in a life-giving manner and the protagonist of this revelation is the word..., the consequence of this revelation being supernatural, namely eternal life for those who accept it and damnation for those who refuse it..., how can we deny that such a revelation contains supernatural elements ?"[866]

It must also be borne in mind that Irenaeus does not speculate about the possible ways in which God could have manifested himself in the history of salvation. He looked at the concrete reality - that in fact God did reveal himself to mankind. Irenaeus, admiring the marvellous unity and progress in the plan of revelation as manifested in Creation, in the Law and the prophets and finally through the Incarnation, insists that, at all stages no one could know God except God teaches him: "Edocuit Dominus quoniam scire nemo potest, nisi Deo docente, hoc est, sine Deo non cognosci Deum; hoc ipsum autem cognosci eum, voluntatem esse Patris. Cognoscunt enim eum quibus cumque revelaverit Filius". And he significantly adds: "Ab initio eum assistens Filius suo plasmati, revelat omnibus Patrem, quibus vult et quando vult, et quemadmodum vult Pater; et propter hoc in omnibus, et per omnia unus Deus Pater et unum verbum, Filius, et unus spiritus, et una salus omnibus credentibus in eum."[867]

Here, indeed, we find the key idea regarding God and his dealings with mankind all over the earth, namely, that both the "Oikonomia" within and outside God are extremely closely connected. If creation and the history of salvation seem to threaten to become factors in the inner procession of God, it is because the "Oikonomia" is a drama of mediation between God and man; or as some theologians put it, it is the saving history whose origin is to be found in the free decision of God, and whose end will lead to the Son giving back his authority to the Father in the consummation of the ages. Thus one can say that the same God is the creative Word, because he is the basis of knowledge and truth and moral law, the originator of man's thoughts and and the end result of all the dealings of providence towards man[868]. The practical conclusions arising from this have often been ignored by Christianity in its relationship to

Non-Christian religions. When, then, Christ affirms that no one knows the Father excepting the Son and those to whom the Son has revealed him (Mt. 11,27), this holds good for all times, both before and after the Incarnation. "He does not say this of the future as if the Word has begun to manifest the Father only after he was born of the Virgin Mary he is present throughout all time. From the beginning the Word in creation, reveals the Father to everyone, whom he wills, when he wills and as he wills"[869]. Through creation itself the Word reveals God as the creator; through the World, he reveals the creator as the builder of the world; through his work, he reveals the workman; through the Son, the Father is revealed[870]. And Latourelle comments: "Irenaeus does not say whether this testimony that the created world gives to God can be grasped by the light of reason. In the order of fact, where he takes his stand, it is knowledge of a religious character that is in question, a manifestation that involves salvation or judgment."[871]

What we learnt from Justin holds true of Irenaeus: the unity of God's saving plan progressively manifested in history is the dominant idea. They are not concerned with the distinction between nature and grace, natural and supernatural. They are explaining the factual and concrete realisation of God's plan for man. The Incarnation, the unity of God's Word with humanity, is the climax and fullness of revelation. Salvation is already present among us even though directed to its eschatological completion in the vision of God's glory 'facie ad faciem'. It is from the fact that everything before Christ was a preparation for his coming, and that it is only through him that we can know God and be saved, that the Church derives her important role as the "Sacramentum Christi", an instrument for the salvation of humanity[872].

This biblical and patristic view of revelation as the progressive unfolding of God's plan for man's salvation - the communication of his life to man - permeates the Constitution "Dei Verbum" of the Second Vatican Council. The Constitution tells us both the why and the how of revelation; clearly preserving the unity between the two. On the why, the

Constitution says:

> In his goodness and wisdom God chose to reveal himself and to make known to us the hidden purpose of his will (cf. Eph. 1,9) by which through Christ, the word made flesh, man might in the Holy Spirit have access to the Father and come to share in the Divine nature (cf. Eph. 2,18; 2 Pet. 1,4). Through this revelation, therefore, the invisible God (cf. Col. 1,15; 1 Tim. 1,17) out of the abundance of his love speaks to men as friends (cf. Exod. 33,11; Joh. 15, 14 f.) and lives among them (cf. Bar. 3,38) so that he may invite and take them into fellowship with himself (873).

In the same paragraph, the Council teaches that God's revelation is realized both by words and deeds and that in Christ, revelation reached its fullness. As we have just seen, revelation was due to God's initiative, consequent on his goodness, wisdom and love and is directed towards the manifestation of God so that man may share his divine life: "quo homines per Christum...accessum habeat ad Patrem et divinae naturae consortes efficiuntur".

On the how of revelation, the Constitution, following the biblico-patristic tradition, sees revelation beginning with creation and reaching its climax in Christ:

> God who through the Word creates all things (cf. Joh. 1,3) and keeps them in existence, gives men an enduring witness to himself in created realities (cf. Rom. 1,19 f.). Planning to make known the way of heavenly Salvation, he went further and from the start manifested himself to our first parents. Then after their fall, his promise of redemption aroused in them the hope of being saved (cf. Gen. 3,15), and from that time on he ceaselessly kept the human race in his care, to give eternal life to those who perseveringly do good in search of salvation (cf. Rom. 2,6 f.) (874).

Then he chose Abraham and the patriarchs and through Moses and the prophets preached for the coming of the Saviour. But after speaking in many and varied ways through the prophets "now at last in these days God has spoken to us in his Son" (Heb. 1,1 f.). For he sent his Son, the eternal Word who enlightens all men, so that he might dwell among men and tell them of the innermost being of God (cf. Joh. 1,1-18)[875]. Remarkably, the Council does not comment on the "supernatural" nature or otherwise of the revelation by and within creation. It merely places revelation by creation within the history of Salvation as the first of those manifestations of God's loving plan. That alone is sufficiently significant and calls for some reflection.

Also in the Constitution "Ad Gentes", where the Council Fathers advocate and urge respect and reverence for the authentic religious values of non-Christian religions which they regard as "semina Verbi in eis latentia", the influence of the patristic vision of revelation is also reflected[876]. And in asserting her "sincere respect" for non-Christian religions, the Catholic Church in spite of many differences, acknowledges that outside the Christian religion there exist "not infrequently rays of that truth which enlightens all men" (haud raro referunt tamen radium illius veritatis quae illuminat omnes homines)[877]. The Council even exhorts Christians to go out in search of these values which the Church recognizes as God-given for the salvation of all men. Their ontological values derive from their source and purpose.

All through this section it has been my aim, drawing abundantly from Christian teaching and writings, to establish that God's help under the most varied forms, hidden or visible, is offered all peoples of all times and places. Thus every authentic human value or principle found in the Igbo Traditional Religion, the Religion itself as an institution, as well as all non-Christian religions, come in fact, through God's illumination, and like all illumination from God, it is intended for the life of man. If some reject it, this is sinful; if others receive it, this is the result of grace and of their own free will.

10.3 Which way Africa ?

Perhaps, one is already sensitive of Christianity's exclusive claim in relation to other religions. The fallacy of exclusivism, Christianity's bold claim, that it alone provides the true contents for the time being, that is, during this earthly pilgrimage for salvation, is one point against such an inclusive claim for the "Christian God" ! (In heaven there would be no sacraments and no dogmas; faith would have fulfilled its mission.)

Some writers might argue that every religion has its "jealousies" and its parochial theological prejudices - what I personally would regard as human cussedness - and that the exclusivism of Christianity does leave room for other religious faiths in the world. But one fears that its claim to openness cannot be substantiated in more recent times as distinct from earlier times. In fact, it has positively put limitations in practice on its belief and its early teaching to be the mystery of God's plan of salvation for the whole world.

Furthermore, it is becoming increasingly clear that the "Epicycles added to its Ptolemaic theology", as John Hick describes it, in order to accommodate the growing knowledge of other religious faiths and the awareness of the true piety and devotion which these religions sustain, do not solve the problem of mankind's religious variety. There is also the fact that millions and millions of men and women have died and will continue to die outside the reach of the "Gospel message". And in any event, it remains highly questionable whether the basic anthropological situation common to all other existing religions can truly be proved to be theoretically different in Christianity !

These observations, notwithstanding, I find myself obliged for obvious reasons, to be advocating "Christianity" for Igbo land, as also for many other African societies in similar situations. I am sensitive of the fact that this could be construed as a bias in favour of Christianity ! But suffice it to say that the Christianity which is here in question is not a "Christianity with predetermined and arbitrary attitudes", but a Christianity directed to respecting the richer and broader pneumatology of God's self-offering and self-manifestation to all mankind in view of his universal salvific design, a salvific design which is the drama of mediation between God and man, and threatens, so to speak, the divine "Oikonomia" both within and outside God.

It has been said that mankind's religiousness is innate; and it has also been argued that religion will continue in some form so long as human beings remain essentially the same, that is, as long as the question of the ultimate meaning of life cannot be silenced. Have the Igbo people and many other African peoples not been accused of being "notoriously" religious ? Igbo traditional society and many other African societies have been greatly disturbed by the contact with Western civilization. Within the past three generations many changes have occurred. Some of these changes are accepted, some rejected. Fundamentally, too, the Igbo traditional world-view remains unchanged. Its egalitarian, individualistic and success-orientated ideology still manifests itself in various ways in contemporary society. The traditional religion is increasingly on the downward incline. But its hold is still remarkable. Native religious susceptibilities must have to be filled up somehow. In fact there is some fear that in the future the Igbo people may be "ifilifi" - faceless faces, if the present trend of events continues unchecked. I personally and seriously doubt whether any Igbo man would like to go back to the Traditional Religion qua tale, not even the adherents of "Godianism"[878]. And for some obvious reasons Islamic religion has never really attracted most Southern People of Nigeria. There does not seem to be any evidence that it will do so in the future, unless there is some drastic political and religious upheaval in Nigeria.

In a sense "Christianity" can be said to be quite a different kind of religion. Its history has shown that it has in its very nature a syncretistic openness in all directions, and for centuries this openness and receptivity has been its glory. With Paul Tillich one can really say that Christ "crucified the particular in himself for the sake of the universal"[879]; or, paradoxically, that Christianity acts "irreligiously" and "atheistically" against political religions and idols of countries and nations, following the crucified Christ for the sake of the Absolute[880]. This liberates it from bondage to particularisms and leaves it open to whatever is good in every man and in every culture. Further, it illustrates the authentically human character of its religious ideal which appeals only to the simplest, the most general, the most personal and spiritual need of man[881]. From being a Jewish sect, de-orientalized, hellenized and westernized, Christianity became the religion of all Europe. Yet the Christianity which has grown in the territory of the Greek and Latin antiquity and among the Celtic, the post-Latin and Teutonic races is different from the Christianity of the oriental peoples - the Jacobites, Nestorians, Armenians, Abyssinians; and that of the Russians is, indedd, a world of its own. Historically, Christianity has provided the foundation for the European political system and for western civilization. Its "secular" concepts of human dignity and of the equality of rights for all men as well as the notions of the freedom of man and community responsibility for the material welfare of all, as the appropriate ideals for improving the quality of life in the state, were all derived from Christianity[882]. In other words, the Christianity that is being advocated here for our society should not be opposed to legitimate change, temporal or spiritual, nor should it off-handedly reject the inner dynamism of Christianity towards a continual self-purification and self-deepening. It should eschew the purely historical, individual and relative accents which it has at one time assumed in the territories where it developed and from where it was brought to us.

In this regard I am referring primarily to the overt and covert hostility or intolerance and ideological rivalry between the various Christian churches in our society, and also to the materialistic tendencies which oftentimes disregard the traditional Igbo world-view. The Christian bodies should strive to break down barriers, to close up gulfs and recognize, indeed, that they all are children of the universal Father, and are seeking and finding him, and are being sought and found by him. In fact all the religious bodies should endeavour to work towards a community that turns its constituent members into a total "we", as was the case in the Igbo

Traditional Religion, though on a more parochial level: Christianity has brought home the fact that "Mother-Earth" is the universal Mother of all mankind. Faith in a God "crucified" for the salvation of all peoples should enjoin on us "productive tolerance" and openness to other peoples and their ways !

The German dramatic and art critic, Gotthold Ephraim Lessing (1729-1781), has an interesting parable to illustrate the need for "productive tolerance" in human society. It is embodied in his "Nathan der Weise" (Nathan the Wise), an ideal Jew of serene tolerance, benevolence and generosity. According to the story, a sultan had three sons. As he was approaching death, each son desired their father's opal ring, which possessed magic power, and was a symbol of their father's authority. The sultan loved all his three sons and did not know how to decide which of these sons should have his ring. He finally decided on a plan. He had two counterfeit rings made that duplicated the appearance of the original in every way. Each son was given one of the three rings, and after the sultan's death, each claimed that he had received the authentic ring. After much tension the sons approached a wise man called Nathan, who gave them the following advice:

> Accept the matter wholly as it stands.
> If each one from his father has his ring,
> Then let each one believe his to be
> The true one. - Possibly the father wished
> To tolerate no longer in his house
> The tyranny of just one ring ! - And know:
> That you, all three, he loved; and loved alike;
> Since two of you he'd not humiliate
> To favour one. - Well then ! Let each aspire
> To emulate his father's unbeguiled,
> Unprejudiced affection ! Let each strive
> To match the rest in bringing to the fore
> The magic of the opal in his ring !
> Assist that power with all humility,
> With benefaction, hearty peacefulness,
> And with profound submission to God's will !
> And when the magic powers of the stones
> Reveal themselves in children's children's children:
> I bid you, in a thousand thousand years,
> To stand again before this seat. For then
> A wiser man than I will sit as judge
> Upon this bench, and speak (883).

It may be noted that Lessing's play and parable therein took as their subject the medieval world, which was very much concerned with the relation among three basic religions: Judaism, Christianity and Islam. From Lessing's point of view there are many more "rings" today. But it must also be said that Lessing was not criticizing the different subjective modes of faith for their certainty; he criticized their dealings with one another. It is my contention that all the "rings" brought to light have in common an inkling of an identical truth about the divine Reality and of an identical ultimate goal for human existence.

More, it has been said that in the depth of every human religion there is a point at which the religion itself loses its importance, and that to which it points breaks through its particularity[884]. We have already noted that the truth itself, the underlying reality is undemonstrable : at present the real hidden truth is partially discovered in the ethos of humanity. And this discovery of the truth is a continual striving, an on-going process or activity; and it entails some risk of error[885].

If all these observations are true, then the duty of Christianity in Igbo society is to continue to penetrate the Igbo ancestral perception of the complicated systems of balance, their principle of order, social organs and civic traditions, their organic unity and continuity in the next life. Indeed our Christianity has got to elevate to spiritual freedom, and with it to a vision of the spiritual presence in other expressions of the ultimate meaning of man's existence, the Igbo human ethos, their picture of humanity and the image of its goal, "the ore in which the true metal is found"; in short the undemonstrable reality, which has been relativized, absolutized and transmitted to us in the Traditional Religion. It goes without saying that our Christianity has to traverse into areas as yet strange and unfamiliar and joining the traffic, as it were, across the borders beyond which it has not yet ventured.

To do this effectively our Christianity has to be syncretistically open - or should I say, "open-ended" - to all aspects of Igbo good, true and beautiful values and principles which it will heighten, correct and perfect in itself. Thus, too, our Christianity is indirectly "infected" by Igbo ideas, values and principles; shall I use that portentuous word: incarnated in our soil. That is, the mission of the Igbo - Gospel - carrier is not merely to communicate something but to receive something as well. Unfortunately this has hardly been the case !

ABBREVIATIONS

AAS Acta Apostolicae Sedis. Roma 1909 ff.

ANCL Ante-Nicene Christian Library. Edited by A. Roberts and J. Donaldson. 25 Volumes. Edinburgh 1867-1897.

DS H. Denzinger/A. Schönmetzer, Enchiridion symbolorum, definitionum et declarationum de rebus fidei et morum, Barcinone - Friburgi/Brisgoviae [35]1973.

DThC Dictionnaire de théologie catholique. Initiated by A. Vacant, continued by E. Mangenot and E. Amann. 15 Volumes. Paris 1903-1950.

LThK Lexikon für Theologie und Kirche. Edited by J. Höfer and K. Rahner. 2nd. Edition. 10 Volumes. Freiburg/Breisgau 1957-1967.

PG J.P. Migne (Editor), Patrologiae cursus completus, series graeca. 161 Volumes. Paris 1857-1866.

PL J.P. Migne (Editor), Patrologiae cursus completus, series latina. 221 Volumes. Paris 1844-1855.

REFERENCES

CHAPTER ONE

1 Cf. Onwuejeogwu (4) 221-224.

2 Cf. S.Leith-Ross, African women. A study of the Ibo of Nigeria. London 1965; Evans-Pritchard (1) 7.

3 Cf. Evans-Pritchard (1) 109.

4 Ibid. 108; cf. Hick (1) VII.165-179.

5 Schmidt 6; cf. Evans-Pritchard (1) 121.

6 Cf. Hick (4) 167f.

7 Newman 76.

8 Ibid. 75.

9 Ibid.

10 Hick (1) 100-102.

11 Irenaeus, Adv.Haer.III 12,13.

12 Hick (1) 175.

13 Evans-Pritchard (1) 4f.

14 Cf. M.Ward, Early Church Portrait Gallery. London-New York 1959, 25.

15 A.Leonard, The Lower Niger and its tribes. London 1968, 6.

16 Cf. Newman 67; Clement of Alexandria, Strom.I 1,7.

17 Quoted by J.O'Gara, Theology of the laity. In: New horizons in Catholic thought. London 1964, 69.

18 Cf. Vatican Council II, Nostra Aetate 1; Idowu (1) 169; S.Sidhom 113.

19 Bronislaw Malinowski as quoted by Goody 13. Goody himself adds: "Many of the early contributors to the comparative sociology of religion, especially Edward Taylor and Herbert Spencer, saw in the institutions that centre upon death-funeral ceremonies, cults of the dead and beliefs in an after-life the kernel of their studies." (ibid.).

20 E.W.Smith, The religion of the Semites. London [3]1927, 2.

21 Newman 85.

22 Cf. K.Rahner, Schriften zur Theologie V, Einsiedeln [2]1964, 137.

23 Cf. Encyclopedia Britannica, Book of the year 1978, 616.

24 Smith, W.C. (4) 93.

25 Samartha (6) 153.

26 It is said that there are about 600,000 Muslims in Canada and the United States of America, 120,000 of them clustered around New York city. There are about 500,000 Buddhists in the U.S.A., 8000 in Germany and 5000 in England (cf. Samartha [6] 170, note 8). Since the 1950s Asian immigration from India and Bangladesh has brought sizeable Muslim, Hindu and Sikh communities to many cities in Britain, adding three more

non-Christian groups to the Jews who had already been there for more than two centuries. Observes Hick (2) 71f.: "By their very existence these non-Christian communities presented the Church with a number of new questions, which it has generally chosen to see as difficult problems. Should we try to help the Muslims, Sikhs and Hindus to find suitable premises in which to worship ? Should local religious broadcasting include or exclude them ? Should we try to insist that all children in the state schools shall receive Christian religious instruction, regardless of the religion which they or their parents profess ? And so on." - These questions all have theological implications. Behind the questions there lies the fundamental theological question of the Christian attitude to other world faiths. What positive part is played by those other religions in God's providence ? - In Nigeria various states are taking over the schools formerly known as Voluntary Agency schools. With the take-over of these schools and the establishment of Federal Government Schools to foster the spirit of oneness among Nigerians the problem is taking a new dimension. One hesitates to say that the Christian Churches have not worked out a plan to meet the new situation. In some parts of the federation it is over a decade since the schools were taken over by the State governments. A broader conception of divine initiative towards mankind may help us come out of our uncomfortable and unstable state to face the problem more realistically.

27 W.A.Visser t'Hooft, Pluralism, temptation or opportunity ? In: Ecumenical Review 18 (1966) 149.

28 Cf. Secretariatus pro non-christianis 14.

29 Christianity, despite its own origin in history, views itself to be the visible sign of the realization of God's plan for mankind. It claims that it is, for the whole world, the universal and efficacious sign of salvation. Ever since it has claimed this absoluteness, it has also been confronted with the problem of the salvation of those men and women who lived and died before it began, as well as those who do not, nor wish to, belong to it. Time and again, it has added some previso or cautela; - or as some theologians have described it, "epicycles added a Ptolemaic theology" - , while it still makes its bold claim namely "Extra Ecclesiam nulla salus" (cf. DS 1305.2429.3860-3880, esp. 3860-387; Encyclical "Corporis Christi Mystici" [1943]; Lumen Gentium 16 for the various ways of belonging to the Church). Origen, it would seem, was the first to formulate the axiom. In his "In Jesu Nave homiliae", written between 249 and 251, he writes: "Nemo ergo sibi persuadet, nemo semetipsum decipiat: extra hanc domum, id est extra ecclesiam, nemo salvatur; nam si quis foras exierit, mortis suae ipse fit reus" (Let no one persuade himself, no one should deceive himself: outside this house, that is outside the Church, no one shall be saved; for, if any one should go out of it, such a person shall be guilty of his death cf. MG 12,841). Later Cyprian would say that one cannot have God as father who no longer has the Church as mother ("habere iam non potest Deum patrem qui ecclesiam non habet matrem" [cf. Cyprian's "De ecclesiae unitate" in: ML 4,502]). The notion is repeated by the Latin Church Fathers, especially Jerome and Augustine. The Church defined it as a revealed truth. It is contained in Pseudo-Athanasian Symbol (cf. DS 75f.) and embodied in the

decree which was imposed on the Waldenses by Pope Innocent III (cf. DS 792-802). It has ever since remained one of the most basic points of the Church's teaching. - The clearest statement is in the Bull "Unam Sanctam" of Bonoface VIII (1302): "Unam sanctam ecclesiam catholicam et ipsam apostolicam urgente fide credere cogimur et tenere, nosque hanc firmiter credimus et simpliciter confitemur, extra quam nec salus est nec remissio peccatorum... Porro subesse Romano Pontifici omni humanae creaturae declaramus, dicimus, diffinimus omnino esse de necessitate salutis." (cf. DS 870.875). The decree was repeated in the Council of Florence (1428-1445): "The Holy Roman Church...firmly believes, acknowledges and proclaims that no one outside the Catholic Church, neither heathen nor Jew nor unbeliever, nor anyone separated from the unity, will partake of eternal life, but that he will rather fall victim to the everlasting fire prepared for the devil and his angels, if he does not adhere to it before he dies." (cf. DS 714) - At this time it may be noted, Christianity was the Imperial Religion. The crusades, the Albigensian wars , and the political persecutions of the groups mentioned were both the presuppositions and the result of the declaration. In 1854, Pope Pius IX in an allocution said: "It must, of course be held as a matter of faith that outside the apostolic Roman Church no one can be saved, that the Church is the only ark of salvation, and that whoever does not enter it will perish in the flood..." (cf. DS 1647). It is to be noted that Pius IX was the first to refer to invincible error in explaining the axiom: "On the other hand, it must likewise be held as certain that those who are affected by ignorance of the true religion, if it is invincible ignorance, are not subject to any guilt in this matter before the eyes of the Lord." (cf. ibid.) - In the Dogmatic Constitution on the Church, "Lumen Gentium", it is stated: "This holy Council...basing itself on scipture and tradition...teaches that the Church, a pilgrim now on earth, is necessary for salvation: the one Christ is mediator and the way of salvation; he is present to us in his body which is the Church. He himself explicitly asserted the necessity of faith and baptism (cf. Mc 16,16; John 3,5) and thereby affirmed at the same time the necessity of the Church which men enter through baptism as through a door. Hence they could not be saved who, knowing that Catholic Church was founded as necessary by God through Christ, would refuse either to enter it, or to remein in it." (LG 14). - The Protestant equivalent of this has been the firm assumption, not however explicitly stated as an article of faith in any of the great Reformed, Lutheran or Anglican confessional declarations, that outside Christianity there is no salvation. This note, however, is to be heard not only in older missionary statements but also in declarations made within very recent years from the fundamentalist evangelical groups. For example, the Frankfurt Declaration of 1970 spoke to the non-Christian world, saying: "We therefore challenge all non-Christians, who belong to God on the basis of creation to believe in him [Jesus Christ] and to be baptized in his name, for in him alone is eternal salvation promised to them." (Christianity Today, 19th June, 1970, paragraph 3) Again: "The adherents of the non-Christian religions and world views ...must let themselves be admitted by belief and baptism into the body of Christ" (ibid. paragraph 6). - In the same spirit the Wheaton Declaration of 1966 pledged its supporters to work for "the evangelization of the world in this generation" (cf. H.Lindsell [edit.], The Church's worldwide mission. Proceedings of the Congress on the Church's worldwide mission, 9-16 April 1966 at Wheaton College, Wheaton Illinois, 237). And in one of the messages delivered at the Congress on World Mission at Chicago in 1960 it was said that "in the years since the war, more than one billion souls have passed into eternity and more than half of these went to the torment of hell fire without even hearing of Jesus Christ, who He was, or why He died on the cross of Calvary" (cf. J.O.Percy [edit.], Facing the unfinished task. Messages delivered at the Congress on World Mission. Chicago-Illinois 1961, 9). - If one is asked how one knows the faith of people in other tradition to be false, one is rather stumped. Observes W.C.Smith (4) 101: "Most people who make this kind of statement do not in fact know much about the matter. Actually the only basis on which their position can and does rest is a logical inference. It seems to them a theoretical implication of what they themselves consider to be true, that other people's faith must be illusory." One thinks that this is to put far too much weight on logical implication. For there have been innumerable illustrations of man's capacity for starting from some cogent theoretical position and then inferring from it logically something else that at the time seems to him persuasive but that in fact turns out on practical investigation not to hold. It is far too sweeping to condemn the great majority of mankind to lives of utter meaninglessness and perhaps to hell, simply on the basis of what seems to some individuals the force of logic (cf. ibid. 101f.). - Further, as soon as one meets and comes to know people of other faiths a paradox of gigantic proportions becomes disturbingly obvious. As a Christian one is taught to believe that God is the God of universal love, the creator and father of all mankind, that he wills the ultimate good and salvation of all men. But one has traditionally maintained that the only way to salvation is the Christian way. And one knows that the large majority of the human race who have lived and died up to the present moment, have lived and died either before Christ or outside the borders of Christendom. Can one then accept the conclusion that the God of love who seeks to save all mankind has nevertheless ordained that man must be saved in such a way that only a small minority can in fact receive this salvation ? Can God really have so restricted his saving encounter with humanity ? Or why has he given the majority of mankind only inferior opportunities to know him and only a second-class status in relation to himself, less truly his children ? Observes Hick (1) 102-104: "I do not think it is an exaggeration to say that traditional Christian theology simply ignored the greater part of the human race ! For it has had only after thoughts to offer concerning God's purpose for all those hundreds of millions of men and women who have lived and died since man began either before the birth of Christ or beyond the borders of Christendom. To this extent our theological tradition is not so much monotheistic as henotheistic, and is ripe for important further development and enlargement." Furthermore, the Old Testament writers knew of the religions of their neighbours, and the early Church knew of the defunct mystery cults of the Roman Empire. Neither the Old nor the New Testament writers knew of any of the world faiths beyond Judaism and Christianity. And therefore no application of biblical statements to African Traditional Religions, Islam, Hinduism, Buddhism, etc. can possibly claim to represent the original meaning of the texts. It cannot be maintained by noting that the Bible only speaks of God's saving activity within Judaic-Christian history, and concluding from this that people of other faiths have no 'absolute' and valid experience of a saving encounter with God; that God-in-relation-to-man has not encountered other men in other ways.

30 Cf. Editorial comments in London Quarterly and Holborn Reviews (London: Epworth Press, January 1959); see too Idowu (1) 31; (3) 25. Parrinder (3) 192f., remarks: "If other religions speak the truth, the Christian must see that this truth comes from God...all truth and light come from the Word of God. By the word of God - this is to say by Jesus Christ - Isaiah and Plato, Zoroaster, Buddha and Confucius uttered and wrote such truths as they declared. There is only one Divine Light and every man in his own measure is enlightened by it... Isaiah was not a Christian, but he has always been regarded by Christians as a forerunner of their faith, and his words are in our Bible. Plato's Greek philosophy gave the basis for most Christian thinking. Zoroaster is akin to some Hebrew prophets...the truth that they declared must come from God if God is one..." (see also: Evans-Pritchard [1] 2f.; Dickson/Ellingworth 19; Hick [1] 101f.; Hick [2] 77).

31 Troeltsch (1) 30. See also: Newman 75f.; Hick (1) 101ff.; Clement of Alexandria, Stromateis VI,8; Irenaeus, Adv.Haer III 12,13.

32 Newman 80f.

33 Augustine, De Baptismo V,38.

34 Augustine, De vera Religione VI,2.

35 Cf. Panikkar 126ff.

36 Latourelle (2) 105f.

37 Fragments from Irenaeus: quoted by Maximus Confessor from Irenaeus treatise to Demetrius, Deacon of Vienna. On the faith which (he says) commences "seeking God" cf. Library of the Fathers of the Holy Catholic Church. Anterior to the Division of East and West. Translated by members of the English Church. Oxford-London 1872, Vol.4, 542.

38 Clement of Alexandria, Strom.II,2 (cf. Ante Nicene Christian Library [ANCL]. Edited by A.Roberts and J.Donaldson. Edinburgh 1869, Vol.12, 4.

39 Strom.II,4 (cf. ANCL, Vol.12, 10).

40 Strom.II,2; VII,2 (cf. ANCL, Vol.12, 4.409-414).

41 Cf. Rahner (2) for the notion of the "anonymous Christian". See also G.Gispert-Sauch (edit.), God's Word among men. New Delhi 1973. - For Hans Küng's "ordinary and extraordinary means of salvation" cf. Neuner, Christian revelation 52ff.; cf. Schlette (2) for similar ideas; see also Fransen (1) and DThC VII 1726-1930.

42 Cf. Hick (1) 120ff. and (2) 75-77.

43 Smith, W.C. (4) 100.

44 Cf. Clement of Alexandria, Strom.I,15; see also Newman 82.

45 Troeltsch (2) 25f.

46 Smith, W.C. (4) 105.

47 Panikkar 142.

48 Cf. W.Barclay, The plain man looks at the Apostles' Creed. London 1975, 16.

CHAPTER TWO

49 The Igbo are grouped into five sub-cultures: (1) The Southern Igbo (or what used to be known as Owerri Igbo, namely, Isuama, Oratta, Ikwerre, Ohuhu-Ngwa, Isu-Item) are centred around Owerri-Ngwa. They have the distinctive cultural features of the absence of elaborate title and mmuo societies and the presence of Mbari temples. (2) The Northern Igbo (the so-called Onitsha Igbo) are centred around Nnewi-Nri-Awka-Nsukka. Their distinctive features are the Ozo title and an elaborate ancestor temple system, Obu. This area is the heart of Nri hegemony. As recent archaelogical finds show, the kings of Nri, Eze Nri, built a political and ritual hegemony around 1000 A.D. which was probably at its peck between the 12th and 17th centuries and was liquidated by 1911 as a result of British and missionary intervention. (3) The Eastern Igbo or the Cross-River Igbo (embracing Ada-Edda, Abiriba, Abam, Ohafia and Arochukwu) have the distinctive features of an elaborate age-grade system and inheritance through the male and female lines. The Aro are patrilineally organized; and they developed one of the greatest monopolies in Atlantic trade with Europeans in the 18th and 19th centuries. (4) The North-Eastern Igbo (Afikpo, Abakaliki, Ezza, etc.) have a distinctive horse title system and ancestor 'cult' associated with graves. (5) The Western Igbo are characterized by having either a centralized Kingship authority suerimposed on hierarchies of patrilineages as in Agbor, Aboh, Oguta, Ogwashi-uku, or a gerontocratic centralized system as in Ibusa, Egbema and Okpanam (cf.:Onwuejeogwu [4] 178; Forde/ Jones 9f.,29ff.; Meek [5]; see also the map of Igboland Figure III).

50 Cf. Uchendu (2) 47-56.

51 Ibid. I. Cf. Introducing Biafra. Published by the Government of the Republic of Biafra and reproduced in Britain by the Britain-Biafra Association. London 1967, 5; see also: Schwarz 15; Floyd 28; Onwuejeogwu (4) 178. - I should like to add that none of these figures is reliable. The population of the Igbo may well be more than nine million.

52 Onwuejeogwu (4) 178.

53 Green (1) 149-165; Dike 43-46; Introducing Biafra (see note 51) 7f.; Talbot, Vol.I, 234; A.Leonard (see note 15) 34f.

54 Cf. J.H.Greenberg, Studies in African linguistic classification. The Niger-Congo-Family. In: South-Western Journal of Anthropology 5 (1949) 79-100. See also: Floyd 28, Meek (5) 4; Shaw (7) 93ff.

55 Uchendu (5) 3f.

56 Ibid. 2. Cf. Floyd 29.

57 Ojike 105.

58 Anene (1) 12; Floyd 29.

59 "Biafra la fin" - Art. in: L'Express (7-13 Oct., 1968) 25, rue de Berri, Paris.

60 Uchendu (5) 2.

61 Ibid.

62 Introducing Biafra (see note 51) 6. Cf. Shaw (1) - (7); see also the following articles of Shaw: The mystery of the burried bronzes. Discoveries at Igbo-Ukwu (Eastern-Nigeria), in: Nigeria Magazine 92 (1967) 55-74; The Africans. An Entry to cultural history. London 1969, 94. Cf. Hartle (1) and (2).

63 Onwuejeogwu (4), esp. 38-52.178ff.; Shaw (7) 1978.

64 Cf.: S.Johnson, History of the Yorubas. London 1921; Lucas; Biobaku; Ike, A.; J.O.Nzekwu, Onitsha. In: Nigeria Magazine 50 (1956) 200-223; Williams (1); Basden (3) 411ff.; Talbot, Vol.1, esp. 1-32; L.Frobonius, The voice of Africa. London 1913, esp. 322ff.; Jeffreys (4) and (6).

65 Davidson (2) 25.

66 Ibid. 95; C.O.Ojukwu, Principles of Biafran Revolution. In: Markpress News feature service (Geneve), June 1969, 13.

67 Davidson (2) 95.

68 Uchendu (5) 42; Davidson (2) 92; Obi (2) 4.

69 Ojike 232; cf. Onwuejeogwu (4) 179.

70 Anene (1) 1-25, esp. 2.12.14; Green (1) 14ff.

71 Leith-Ross (see note 2) 67.

72 Onwuejeogwu (4) 1.

73 Dike 43; cf. Anene (1) 1-25.

74 Herskovits (1) 36; cf. Dike 43.

75 As quoted by Dike 43; cf. G.V. Childe, Social Evolution. London 1951.

76 Anene (1) 2.

77 K.O.Dike, History and self-government. In: West Africa 34 (1953) 36-73 (cf. Dike 43).

78 Cf. below chapters 3 and 5.

79 P.Akoi, Religion in African social heritage. Rome 1970, 4; cf. Mbiti (1) 22ff. See also chapters 3 and 9 below.

80 Ezeanya (4) 1-9; Uchendu (2); Basden (3), esp. chapters VI and VIII; Anene (1) 13ff.; Introducing Biafra (see note 51) 9ff.; Obi (2) 20ff.105; Mbiti (1) 2ff.; Akoi (see note 79) 4.51-56.

81 Cf. Onwuejeogwu (4) 179

82 Ibid.

83 Uchendu (5) 39ff.81-83.

84 Onwuejeogwu (4) 180ff.

85 Uchendu (5) 39; Anene (1) 1-25.

86 It must be noted that the accepted anthropological definition of a family (simple or elementary) does not do justice to the Igbo connotation of this terminology. "EZI na ulo" or "Di na Nwanye na umu fa (ha)" would be Igbo equivalent to an elementary or simple family; and this in traditional Igbo societies included a man and his wife (wives, if a polygynous family),their sons both married and unmarried, however old, their daughters (less the married ones) as well as their dependants, if any (cf. Obi [2] 17; P.Akoi [see note 79], text at the back of the book). Against this traditional background the term "nuclear family" (simple or elementary) and its "nuclear founder" (original) or simply "ancestor" will be employed in this work.

87 In a polygynous family a man had and still has more than one wife and it was and still is, legally and socially permitted. The present tense will be used in this section because some of the things described here are still in practice, though their functions and importance may not be the same as in the past

88 Obi (2) 17; cf. note 86 above.

89 Ofo is a piece of wood carved out of a brachlet of the "Deterium senegaalense". It derives its sacredness and importance from the legend that this tree was specially created and set aside by Chineke (the Creating Chi) as a symbol of truth and righteousness (cf. Ezeanya [7] 38; E.Ilogu (Ofo. A religious and political symbol in Iboland. In: Nigerian Magazine [Lagos] 82 [1964] 234f.) writes: "No one knows how the world first began, but when first men came, ofo came too. One of the special features of this tree is that the branches pluck themselves off from the parent trunk when they are grown. They are not cut; it is believed that Chukwu (the great God) purposely created this tree to be sacred, and by the manner its braches fall off unbrocken, he [Chukwu] symbolises the way families grow up and establish new extended family lineages". Cf. Nzekwu (2) 33 for different kinds of ofo and how it is acquired; see also Uchendu (5) 90f.

90 Ilogu (1).

91 Obi (2) 17f.; O.Dilim, Nigerian villager in two worlds. London 1965, 32.

92 Dilim (see note 91) 37.

93 Ibid.; cf. Uchendu (5) 40.85.

94 Uchendu (5) 40. The emphasis is on locality rather than on persons. The point of departure between "nuclear family" and "obi" is very small. Both coincide rather early.

95 Obi (2) 14; Uchendu (5) 31ff.

96 In societies where ozo-title is in vogue, "no one can really officate", Onuora Nzekwu says, "as a priest who has not taken the ozo title". This title is "equivalent to ordination to the Holy Orders". Ofo is a means whereby the priest comes in contact with ancestral spirits and comunes with them. So whoever takes charge of the ofo is regarded as the embodiment of ancestrals spirits. In other societies there are some other initiation ceremonies wherby one acquires the ofo and thereby can officiate as a priest. Ofo, as a symbol of authority and a guarantee of truth, becomes also an "emblem of unity and indestructibility for the individual or the group possessing it". Thus the compound head or any other unit-head commands the obedience and respect of all in his unit (cf. Nzekwu [2] 32ff.; see also Ilogu [1] 234f.). But Uchendu (5) 90ff., seems to imply that ozo titled men have secular roles whereas ofo holders have politico-religious duties. However, there is danger in generalisation, for there is no rigid distinction between titled men and ofo holder. Cf. also Meek (5) 63ff.

97 Nzekwu (2) 32; Ilogu (1) 234f.; Dilim (see note 91) 36ff.

98 Uchendu (5) 40.85.

99 Ibid. 40.

100 Obi (2) 17. See also Introducing Biafra (see note 51) 9ff.; Green (1) 87ff.; Uchendu (5) 39f.; Nkem 50f.

101 C.K.Meek, and ten years after him M.M.Green used 'kindred' and 'lineage' to translate this term. S.N.C.Obi is of the opinion that these terminologies are ambiguous. He preferred 'localised patrilineage' as 'an improvement' (cf. Meek [5] 34; Obi [2] 15f.; cf. Uchendu [5] 39-41). Forde/Jones 15 used also 'localised patrilineage' to translate 'Umunna'.

102 Obi (2) 16.

103 Ibid.

104 Ibid.

105 Meek (5) 104.

106 Uchendu (5) 40; Obi (2) 16; Nzekwu (2) 32; Meek (5) 104ff.

107 Uchendu (5) 40f.; Obi (2) 16; Forde/Jones 15ff.; Green (1) 17. Uchendu (5) 91 observes: "The Okpala (okpara) of the Umunna holds the "big ofo" while the smaller ones are held by the senior males of the minor umunna (minor lineages). The distribution of ofo among various segments shows that ritual and secular authority among the Igbo is not unified but evenly distributed."

108 Uchendu (5) 91; Meek (5) 105.301.

109 Ref. to what was said about political legislative processes and maintenance of law and order in the section on Obi-unit.

110 Cf. Obi (2) 16f.; Meek (5) 105; Nkem 155-159.

111 Cf. Obi (2) 13.

112 Cf. Green (1) 15; Obi (2) 14; Forde/Jones 16.

113 Green (1) 15 equates village with Umunna.

114 Obi (2) 15.

115 Cf. Obi (2) 14.

116 Ibid.; cf. Onwuejeogwu (4) 180.

117 Obi (2) 14; Green (1) 58-60.149-165.

118 Nzekwu (2) 31ff.

119 Uchendu (5) 41.90; Ojike 232; Nkem 45.

120 See above "Obi - Umunna Units".

121 Uzodimma 11.

122 Uchendu (5) 44ff.

123 Cf. Onwuejeogwu (4) 180.

124 Cf. Uchendu (5) 41; Obi (2) 15. See also Chinua Achebe's "Arrow of god" (= Achebe [3]) and Uzodimma's "Our dead speak".

125 Obi (2) 14; Achebe, esp. the characters of Ezeulu and Ogbuefi Nwaka.

126 Uchendu (5) 41f.

127 Ibid. 42.

128 Anene (1) 12f.; Uchendu (5) 42; Basden (3), Chapter VII; Parrinder (1) 49; Green (1) 112f.,132-138; Meek (5) 88-115.

129 Uchendu (5) 43; Anene (1) 13.

130 Obi (2) 24; cf. Uchendu (5) 43.

131 Ibid.

132 Green (1) 119.145; Meek (5) 88-115; Anene (1) 13f. See also Achebe (1), Chapter X and Leith-Ross (see note 2) 19-39.105-110.

133 Cf. Achebe (1). For the personality of Okonkwo and for the personality of Dike and his successor cf.: Uzodimma 12; Anene (1) 14

134 Anene (1) 14; Green (1) 200; Uchendu (5) 43.

135 Meek, Green and some other writers (including some Igbo writers like Uchendu) use village-group for the Igbo socio-religious unit called obodo (mba or ala). In official documents and colloquilally it is called town. Obi thinks that one is justified to employ "town". He remarks that in practice as well as in theory in such towns as Onitsha there is a sharp distinction between Onitsha town and Onitsha township; and that the boundary is well defined (cf. Obi [2] 12). However we shall use both village- group and town. But we should bear in mind that this latter term, town, when employed in this work is not understood to be the English sense of an agglomeration of contiguous houses. For this we shall retain the term, township or urban area. Cf. also Onwuejeogwu (4) 180-185, for some other terms of the same concept.

136 Obi (2) 12.

137 Green (1) 11.

138 Okafor-Omali 33ff.; Jeffreys (10) 119ff.

139 Cf. Obi (2) 12.

140 For the person and role of Ezeulu cf. Achebe (3). For Ada Ani's person in the village cf. Uzodimma.

141 Obi (2) 13; cf. Nwapa (1).

142 Obi (2) 13; Uchendu (5) 44ff.; Onwuejeogwu (4) 38-51.

143 Obi (2) 13.

144 Uchendu (5) 44f.; cf. Nzekwu (2), esp. 22ff.

145 Uchendu (5) 45.

146 Anene (1) 15-18; Uchendu (5) 45.90ff.; Basden (1) 208f. - Ref. also to Anene (2) and (3), and to Simmons.

147 Jones (3) 5; Uchendu (5) 45.

148 Uchendu (5) 45f.

149 Anene (1) 12ff.

150 Uchendu (5) 12ff. - See too Onwuejeogwu (4) 44f.

151 Ref. to Talbot, Vol.2, 263; Basden (1) 113ff. and (3) 269ff.

152 Ref. to Obi (2) 16.24; Uchendu (5) 90f.

153 Cf. Uchendu (5) 90ff.; Davidson (2) 95; Principles of Biafran Revolution (see note 66) 13.

154 Uchendu (5) 42f. - According to "Omenala" the Igbo believe in the sanctity of the life of a constituent unit-member. His person is sacred. Wilful and wanton destruction of any human life of its unit-member is not only a grave crime but an abomination, Aru (Alu or Nso Ala), for his life is holy and sacred being protected by the Earth-spirit (Ala), the parochial principle of brotherhood of all unit members. Thus murder (homicide), Ochu is an offence against the Earth-spirit for which the murderer is required to hang himself. After that Umu ada, or Umu Okpu (daughters of the unit-group) perform the rite of 'izafu ntu ochu' - sweeping away the ashes of murder. If the murderer has fled, his extended family must also flee, and the property of all is subject to raids. But if it is a manslaughter (Ochu Oghum) the culprit must flee the town or village into exile. Cf. also Basden (3) 259-261; Correia (2); Th.Northcote, Anthropological report on the Ibo-speaking people of Nigeria. Part I: Law and custom of the Ibo of Awka neighbourhood. London 108f.

155 Anene (1) 13.

CHAPTER THREE

156 Mbiti (1) 1; Parrinder (1) 9.

157 A.G.Leonard, The Lower Niger and its tribes. London 1968, 429.

158 Cf. Basden (3) 33; Meek (5) 20.

159 Mbiti (1) 15.

160 Leonard (see note 15) 429.

161 Correia (2) 889.

162 Cf. Mbiti (1) 15.

163 Cf. Gravard 23.

164 Basden (3) 33.

165 Cf. Gravard 23; Mbiti (1) 57.

166 Basden (3) 33.

167 Cf. Akoi (see note 79) 4.51f.; Mbiti (1) 21ff.; Ezeanya (4) 1-9; Uchendu (2) 47-50; Green (1) 47-49; Basden (3), Chapters VI-VIII; Anene (1) 13ff.; Introducing Biafra (see note 51) 9; Obi (2) 11ff.; Meek (5) 20ff.

168 Cf. Onwuejeogwu (4) 125.

169 The terming of tradition in Igbo Catechism "Osi-Na-aka-fere-aka-wee-rua-anyi-aka" as distinct from Omenala or custom seems to be of modern provenance. Probably this term was coined under the influence of missionaries (cf. Shelton (7) 31.

170 The Igbo distinguish today between Omenala (custom) and Iwu (law); but it is difficult to trace the origin on this distinction.

171 The traditional Igbo society was not a literate society and did not seem to have possessed an "institutionalized literati" or "specialized groups" such as among the Dahomey, Manding, Tswana and Yoruba. In so far they lacked that institution it is not surprising that "an extensive body of culturally dispersed oral literature and tradition are shared by members of Igbo communities" and less so that these were subject to modification where necessary (cf. Shelton [7] 31ff.).

172 Cf. Shelton (7) 31.

173 Cf. Anozia 14; Nwokocha 173.

174 Cf. Shelton (7) 37.

175 Cf. Idowu (1) 7.

176 Cf. Pratt, Chapters I and II.

177 Cf. Idowu (1) 7; Th.F.O'Dea, The sociology of religion. New Jersey 1966, 8-11.

178 Talbot 14ff.40-54; Horton (2) 17-28; Parrinder (1) 94ff.; Jordan 55f.; Williams (2) 185-235. (The material for this work is, according to the author, consisted of answers to questionnaires sent out to missionaries and government agents in different parts of Africa.); Anozia 14. - Miss M.M.Green, who found no evidence of this has treated Igbo religion in a more or less cursory way and her study has been criticised in some respects (cf. Review of the 1964 Reprint of her "Igbo Village Affairs" by Dr.A.E.Afigbo in Journal Hist. Society. Nigeria 1967, 186ff.

179 Literally, he answered the call and went to help himself with excrement. (Other traditions say, he was licking oil. In another tradition, the dog reached Chukwu early and was handed an answer to man's demand in a bag. But returning, he went to drink water and left the bag containing the message of life and death on the shore. A snake came and stole the bag.).

180 Some traditions have chameleon (ogwumagala) as the messenger.

181 There are various versions of this story: cf. Beier (5) 56; Nwokocha 53; Basden (1) 23 and (3) 431f.; Ojike 185f.;

Meek (5) 53. Many a time, the story concerning origin of death is told separately from that of the creation of the world. The story was first told to my hearing in 1947 when I was in Infant II during what used to be called vernacular lesson. Some ten years later, in 1957 (this time outside the locality I heard the story first) it was told by a child of 11 years in standard two while I was supplying for a teacher who was ill. This time, the child added that Chukwu created the universe in two parts: First, the Heavens and then the Earth. He created Anyanwu and Onwa (the sun and the moon) to be his messengers ("ka ha na agara ya ozi"). This seems to confirm the tradition story Horton (2) recorded (cf. ibid. 17-28).

182 Cf. Shelton (7) 30f.

183 Ibid. 31.

184 Cf. Jeffreys (8) 162-167 and (10) 119-131.

185 By "prescientific" I mean a man or a child, lacking the INSTRUMENTS of precision to observe and calculate; a man who knows no exploration of geology, astronomy and their sister sciences.

186 Cf. Horton (2) 17-28. See also the myths on the origin of spiritual beings: Chapter Five, note 318.

187 This gives rise to the belief prevalent in some areas that ANI is the wife of Igwe (some of CHUKWU himself). Ref. Talbot, Vol.2, 43.

188 Ibid. 43ff.; cf. Green (1) 52. Some have interpreted Meek as implying that "CHI" and "EKE" are two different powers (see Meek [5] 143).

189 Shelton (5); Talbot 43f.

190 Except the sole remark of Dr. Talbot on the IKWO,OHAFIA, NGBO and OKPOSSI AWAZARA (Igbo communities) of whome he wrote regard ALE as the creator/creatrix of "the earth as also the rivers and seas" (cf. Talbot, Vol.2, 43f.; cf. also Isichei 124.

191 Cf. Horton (2) 17-28; Jeffreys (8) 162-167.

192 Cf. Basden (1) 283.

193 Cf. The myth being analysed and the various versions.

194 Baumann 203.

195 Anozia 2-4; Arinze 75.

196 Other variants of the word are mmanu, madu or manu.

197 Cf. Ezenwadeyi, Izuzuchukwu in interview with Fr.Raymond Arazu. The former was nearly 100 years when Arazu interviewed him on various aspects of Igbo religious belief. Arazu said that he attended elementary school with Mr. Ezenwadeyi's grandson. The interview was tape-recorded, transcribed and translated into English. The manuscript fills 69 pages of typedscript. See also Anozia 158f.

198 Ezenwadeyi with Arazu in Interview: Cf. ibid.

199 Ibid.

200 Cf. Azorji 13 and Onwuejeogwu (4) 248f.

201 Cf. Shakespeare's Hamlet, Act 2, Scene 2 (Hamlet to Rosencrantz and Guildenstern).

202 Shelton (5).

203 Cf. Anozia 159.

204 Uchendu (2) 18.

205 Ibid.

206 Basden (1) 283 (and [3] 431f. for another story narrating the origin of diseases); cf. Ojike 185 for the origin of evil on earth.

207 Leonard (see note 15) 139-141.188.

208 Anozia 7.

209 Leonard (see note 157) 140.

210 Ibid. 139.

211 Shelton (5); cf. Onwuejeogwu (4) 251.

212 Ojike 183.

213 Cf. Obiego, "Uli uli mmu, Lucerna explained". In: Lucerna [Bigard Memorial Seminary publication, Enugu] 2 (1981) 5ff.

214 Shelton (5).

215 Cf. Anozia 7, esp. note 7; Onwuejeogwu (4) 251.

216 Ojike 183f.

217 Obiefuna 33.

218 Nwanodi 61f.

219 Obiefuna 31.

220 Cf. Chapter IV below: "Classification and significance of names"; Obiefuna 35-42; Anozia 200-204.

221 Obiefuna 35.

222 Cf. the myth that is being analysed and note 181.

CHAPTER FOUR

223 Woelfel 499-504, esp. 499.

224 Anozia 105-153; Ezeanya (3) 2-8.

225 Wieschhoff 212-222.

226 Cf. Anozia 89.235; Leonard (see note 15) 548ff.

227 Cf. Anozia 89.

228 Ibid.

229 Azorji 22.

230 See Anozia 89. Leonard (see note 15) devoted 12 pages to the mentality and humanity of names. I regret, however, to say that this treatment is highly superficial. See also I. Coker, The romance of African names. Lagos 1964.

231 Azorji.

232 Anozia 87.

233 Idowu (1) 33.

234 Leonard (see note 15) 548.

235 Ibid.

236 Anozia 87-89.94f.

237 Cf. Azorji 5-7.

238 Cf. Coker 30.

239 Obiefuna 22f.

240 Ibid. 23.

241 Ibid. 24.

242 Leonard (see note 15) 548; cf. Wieschhof and Obiefuna 36.

243 Anozia 89.

244 Leonard (see note 15) 548.

245 Anozia 88f.

246 The inverted comas on Spirit are mine. Anozia treated this term in a perspective that this investigation finds rather defective. Reasons will be seen as the term is examined.

247 Anozia 28.

248 Talbot, Vol.2, 278.

249 Ibid. 280.

250 Ojike 183.

251 Meek (6) 109; cf. Meek (5) 55; Forde/Jones 26 describes "Chi" in almost the same words as Meek. - Munonye 55 writes: "Do you think it is you who guards him ? Don't forget that his Chi goes about with him always." Nzekwu (2) 96 writes: "Chi, according to our traditional religious doctrine, was a genius, a spiritual double connected with every individual's personality. Every individual has a Chi, a guardian angel." Okeke 56: "The duty of the personal Chi can be campared with the duty of angel guardian of the Christians." Anozia 7 (cf. ibid. 28-34) treated Chi primary as a gurdian angel. Likewise Ezenaya (7) 43; see too Ilogu (2) 304-308. Ezekwugo in his Thesis: "Chi, the true God in Igbo Religion" regards "Chi" as the correct Igbo word for "God" and attempts to prove that "Chi" and "Eke" (Agu, Aka, Okike/Okuku) are co-creators of man: "Chi" being the God-head while "Eke" is the personal deity, a "mediator between human being and Chi" whose duty it is to fix particulars of the child to be born: viz. its sex, its term of life, its social and economic standing, its occupation and trade" (cf. Ezekwugo 140-180). Ezekwugo's contention is precarious. However some expressions in common parlance and some proper names either of gratitude or petition seem to give reason for this surmise of the possibility of "Chi" and "Eke" being two different entities. For example one often hears old people rebuking a child who is rather slow in carrying out a message thus: Kedu ife (ihe) i na-eme ? Ina achoo chi gi ka ina achoo eke gi ? What are you doing ? Are you seeking for your "Chi" or your "Eke" ? I have often suggested to many Traditional Religionists whom I interviewed that Chi and Eke are different

entities; that Chineke means "Chi and Eke"; and that it does not mean the Creator-God. All emphatically retorted that Chi is a shortened form of Chineke and that Eke is usually the short form of Chukwu in such names as Ekechukwu or Ekechukwuka. I also interviewed some people whose family name is Eke. They all said that the full name is Ekechukwu or Ekechukwunyere or Ekechukwuka. Three of them, told me that Ebereeke, i.e. Ebere nke Eke or Eberechukwu is their full name. Ebereeke or Eberechukwu means "the mercy that Chukwu has shown". Some even narrated the background surrounding the giving of the name. Further, I asked numerous men and women to explain to me: "Ina achoo Chi gi ka ina achoo eke gi". Some elderly people again remarked that Chi and Eke are shortened forms for Chineke and Chukwu, who is invisible. When someone is asked whether he or she is looking for his or her Chi; for his or her Eke, it is a way of asking the person whether he or she is searching for an invisible object (ife adi afufu); or, why is the object so difficult to find ? Another interesting idiom in this regard is "Okuku si na ya kpachara Chi, kpaani eke, beazi ikpani onwe ya, Chi ejinari ya - A fowl says that it catered for Chi and for Eke, but got benighted as it came to provide for itself". Many observed that the meaning of the idiom depends on the context in which it is used. But, generally it is a way of questioning a hard luck that confronts someone in life; a protest to the invisible forces for any imputation of fault or negligence on one's part. In short, why should the invisible forces permit such a hard luck to come one's way ? There are many more such expressions that seem to support Ezekwugo's view. The following are a few examples. Uwa di-na-eke (earthly life is in Eke); Eke-nwe-uwa (to Eke belongs the earth); Eke-bu-ndu/Ndubu-eke (life is Eke); Eke-ji-uwa (Eke holds the earth); Okike-ndu (Okike is life); uwa-bu-eke (earthly life is Eke); Enebe-eke (let us keep on looking upon Eke); Eke-kwe (if Eke permits); Ana-ekpere-eke (let us keep on begging Eke); Eke-je-ekwu (Eke will finally say); Eke-ji-okwu (Eke has the final decision); Eke-gozie (may Eke bless or Eke has blessed); Belu-eke (cry to Eke); or Beluso Eke (if it were not for Eke); Rapulu Eke (leave it to Eke); Eke-kwe-m (if Eke permits me); Elebe-eke (let us look up to Eke); Ekeleme (Ekeneme-eke) or eke-neme (Eke has done it); Ekeledo/Eke-nedo (Eke arranges fittingly); Eke-kima (Eke plans well enough); Eke-buzo (Eke goes in front); Okparaeke (son of/from Eke); Uba-bu-eke (increase or wealth is from Eke); Eke-emezie (Eke has redressed); Eke-nenye (Eke gives); Ife-eke-neme (what Eke does [in goodness]); Adu aka (off-spring of Aka). Aka is a dialectical variant for Eke or Agu.

252 Nzekwu (2) 96; Nwokocha 52.

253 Forde/Jones 26; Meek (5) 35.

254 Shelton (5) 15-18.

255 Meek (5) 55.60; cf. Parrinder (2) 15.

256 Ojukwu 27. See also Chapter III above.

257 In daily parlance, one hears the following for example: A weakling is called "onye adighi ndu" (one who is not alive) or equally "onye-ike-gwuru" (one who lacks energy, an exhausted one); a sick man speaks of himself as "ike adighi m".

(there is no more strength or force in me) or very often "aru (ahu) na-anwu m" (my body is dying). Recovering of health implies that one is filled with "ike" life, or strength again - "Onwetala ike" or "ahu adi-na ya".

258 Jordan 125.

259 Meek (5) 292; Anozia 112.

260 Jordan 125.

261 Cf. Chapter 3.3.

262 Cf. Leonard (see note 15) 139f.; cf. Chapter 3.3.

263 Ojike 183.

264 Anozia 3-6; Uchendu (5) 20f.; E.G.Parrinder, African mythology. London 1970, 15.

265 In the light of this explanation such translations of "Chiukwu" (Chukwu) as "the Supreme Spirit" or "The High-God" seem to me to be defective and fraught with misunderstanding. For contrary to the opinion of earlier writers and those who thought that Chukwu of the Igbo is a withdrawn high God, a deus otiosus, it must be reiterated that Chukwu is always in one sense or the other immediately present to the Igbo. He is not so far as the cult of him would seem depict. On the contrary , he is immanent i.e. he is so 'near' that the Igbo can and do in fact establish contact with him. In short, he is worshipped (cf. Shelton [5] 15-17; Ezeanya [6]; Idowu [1] 48ff.; Anozia 50-66; Nwokocha 56f.191-197.

266 Cf. Chapter 4.2.

267 Cf. Anozia 3-6; Uchendu (5) 20f.; Parrinder (see note 264) 15.

268 Idowu (1) 38.

269 A.C.Bouquet, Comperative Religion. London 1945, 19.

270 Idowu (1) 39.

271 Meek (5) 20ff.

272 Cf. Ezeanya (7) 39; Talbot seems to imply that this terminology, "Chineke" appears to have come into use of late and in many parts only after the introduction of the Christian religion. The old word seems to have been "Chi", sometimes called Chiukwu, the great-Chi (cf. Talbot, Vol.2, 52). Miss Green, seems to follow Talbot in this surmise and even goes to the extent of doubting Igbo conception of a universal creator-God (cf. Green [1] 52; see also O'Donnell 54-60). Though there are no written data to argue against these doubts, nonetheless Igbo attitude to Chukwu in sacrifices, in daily prayers shows that even if he (Chukwu) was not originally known as "Chineke" until Christianity was introduced to them the idea of a crator-God was native and indigenous to them. It must, also, be said that those who doubt the indigenous origin of this terminology do not substantiate their doubts with any reasons. They merely make the assertions, as if it were so self-evident. Besides some dialectical variations like "Chileke" commonly used among the elderly Igbo in Ikwerre and Egbema areas; or "Ezechitoke", "Anyanwu-Ezechitoke" or "Chukwu-okike" commomly

used in the natives' sacrificial and other ritual rites still survive and they should eliminate such surmises as Green's.

273 "Chi" used without any further qualification can mean either the apportioned life-principle, especially man's - "God-within" or personality-soul; or an abbreviation for Chineke or Chiukwu, God (cf. Anozia 112.136, note 115). "Eke" can be the present particle of "okike" or "ike" - "to apportion" , "to divide", "to share", "to form". In my interview the people reiterated that "Eke" is invariably an abbreviation for "Chineke" and it stands for such names as Ekechukwu or Ekechukwuka - the share or lot God gives is greater or better. See also note 251.

274 Cf. Meek (5) 143 and his footnote on p.57 on the ceremony of "Ero chi". It is also to be noted that some expressions in common parlance seem to give reason for this surmise of the possibility of "Chi" and "Eke" being two different entities.

275 It has been claimed that the term Osebuluwa was not wide-spread among the Igbo before the coming of Christianity. According to Correia, the indigenous learned committe who helped Vogler to produce the first Igbo Catechism adopted the term to translate "Lord". It is also reported that at Abuchi (Awuchi), the home-town of some of the translators, "Ose" is represented as a "fetish" carrying the world on its back; hence Osebu-uwa or Osebuluwa - Ose who is carrying or supporting the world (cf. Correia [1] 360-366). - It may be observed that the translators were searching for a term to translate "Lord" and not for a word to translate God or Creator-God. It is possible that the Abuchi people might have taken their local terminology for the Creator-God to represent Lord for the Igbo. So instead of weakening our argument, it strenghtens it in the sense that the idea of God creating and supporting the world is native to the Igbo. Furthermore, it may be observed that there are today evidence that the term "Ose" or "Olisa" as God-concepts might well be native and wide-spread among many Igbo communities, even before the coming of Christianity into Igboland. There are many names derived from Ose or Olisa. Such names are: Nwosa, Nwolisa, Ossai, Oseka, Olisaemeka, Oseloka, Osakwe, Olisakwe, Osegbo, Osefoh, Osunoh, Olisabunoh. These names are common among the Umuoji people in Anambra state. The term is also connected with "Osu" system. There are also patrilineage shrines known as "Okwu Olisa" or "Okwu Iyakiya". Before these shrines patrilineage segments offer yearly sacrifices. It is said that the priest or the head of "Okwu Olisa" or "Okwu Iyakiya" must be someone who has been to Aro-Chukwu or has obtained his authority from a person who had been there. It would seem that the influence of Nri ritual hegemony might have spread the term into many parts of Igboland (cf. Onwuejeogwu [4] 38-52, esp. 28).

276 Cf. Meek (2) 60; cf. also Meek (5) 21.

277 "Chukwu-Abiama": "Abiama" may mean "abea" and "ama". "Abea" means "to come", "to appear", "to approach", "to come within sight". "Ama" is "to know", "to recognize"; with "Igba" prefixed to "ama" it means "to reveal", "to unveil", "to make something hidden came to light". So latent in the name "Chukwu-Abiama" seems also to be: God (Chukwu) who reveals

or come to clearer light as he manifests himself in the cosmic phenomena. In this respect, too, he is called "Ama-ama-amacha-amacha" (ama-ama-amasi-amasi), known but not fully comprehended.

278 Chidube (m) or Chukwudube (m): It is usually the Igbo etiquette to accompany one's visitor some yards away from one's house. This is called "Ndupu" from "idu edu" meaning to accompany or escort. "Chukwudubem" or "Chidubem" as contained in that imagery enunciates not just "May God lead or guide me"; it says: "May God while accompanying me guide or lead me".

279 O'Connell. Shelton (cf. [2] and [3]) wrote two articles in refutation of this theory.

280 Idowu (1) 18f.; cf. Idowu (2) 9.

281 The word "Ike", in addition to the above listed meanings, means "bottom" or "I" (first personal pronoun). For instance "Obu" Ike m ka i na abpure" ? (Is it I that you are abusing or are you abusing me ?).

282 "Chiagbaoso" or "Chukwuagbaoso": God does not run or God does not desert his own, or God is faithful to his own; he is firm and steady. Various reasons may suggest the giving of the name to a child. First, families might have constantly experienced God's protection or blessing, whenever there has been some global disaster, famine or even civil strife in a given area. In consequence they would name their child: "Chiagbaoso" or "Chukwuagbaoso" - thereby enunciating their belief that God always comes to the aid of his people; he does not desert the people he loves. - Secondly, it is of bitter common human experience that human beings may disappoint; even spirits, when there is a difficult situation. But God "stands firm and can never disappoint; cannot run away from danger, for he is all powerful and creator of all things - Ikechi; and therefore fears nothing. Again "Chiagbaoso" is his name. Furthermore, in a proverbial and metaphorical sense "Chiagbaoso" or "Chukwuagbaoso" means that God is too big and bulky to run - a feat rarely accomplished by any bulky person. In that conception God would be unable to move and even one could hardly imagine his bulkiness. Hence the Igbo say "Chiagbaoso", that is to say the "unmoved Chi", "the unreceived Chi" or philosophically expressed "unmoved mover". In giving this name to a child, there lurks therefore, in the mind of the parents either an expression of gratitude to God for not deserting them in the time of disaster, suffering or difficulty; or an assertion of God's omnipotence and fidelity to his people or even a demonstration that God is the "unmoved mover", on whom depends all things.

283 The possible origin of this terminology in Igbo Catechism and consequently its spread among the Igbo has been mentioned earlier (cf. Chukwu as creator, note 275).

284 Idowu (1) 60.

285 Onwuejeogwu (4) 38-52; see also note 275.

286 Mbiti (1) 30 and (3) 3.

287 Ezenwadeyi in the interview with Arazu; cf. Isichei 122-134.

288 Arinze 258ff.; Mbiti (1) 37f. - In this context one can

understand why the Igbo insisted that a murderer (homicide) should kill himself; not however for a unwilful or accidental murder (manslaughter).

289 Mbiti (1) 38.

290 Chukwunweobo - to revenge is God's. It might be remarked that Igbo traditional religion strongly believed in giving an eye for an eye, a tooth for a tooth. That is why the poor who could not avenge themselves of injustice done to them by more powerful people, looked up to God for vengeance.

291 See Chapter V.

292 Izuchukwu - The decision of God; the plan of God; that which comes out of God's plan or decision. To bring out the force of this name, let us examine the imagery which it contains. "Izu" is a decision or a plan reached after the discussion of a group of people done tête-a-tête. Anyone who is familiar with the democratic spirit of the Igbo, can imagine what goes on in an "Nzuko ndi Igbo" - a gathering or meeting together for some project - before a decision is reached. A plan or decision agreed on, becomes seriously binding on all. Private advice given by one or two or even more men to another is called "alo" or "ndumodu". This is more liable to err than that reached after a serious deliberation by a group - "Izu". Perhaps it is because of the weight given to "Izu" that the same word sometimes is used for Wisdom. An Igbo name says "Izukanne" - "Wisdom is greater than the multitude". When the Igbo, then, name a child "Izuchukwu", they assert thereby that that, which God has decided and suggested is wise and has behind it the strength of the all-wise and all-knowing and all-seeing planner (cf. Anozia 122f.).

293 "Ama-ama-amasi-amasi" - known but not fully known or comprehended. It is a curious phenomenon that the Igbo have no particular figure or image representing Chukwu. He is aniconic in character (imageless) for though the Igbo see him in all manifestations of natural phenomena or forces, none of these manifestations can claim exclusivity of his nature.

294 Arinze 106f.

295 "Onye" in Igbo is used for persons only, namely for a being that is rational. It is not used for animals or things.

296 The inverted commas on pagan are mine.

297 Anozia 116f.; cf. ibid. 117f.

298 Chukwukanero (kanelo) - God thinks it out best. "Ilo ililo" in Igbo means thinking and weighing ideas drawn from the past in preparation for the future.

299 "Chigbo" or "Chigboo" (gboo is prolonged and thus pronounced gives the idea of the immemorable past for example "oge gbo" or "gboo" - "in diebus illis", "unaccountable times").

300 Anozia 107.

301 Uchendu (5) 95; Talbot, Vol.2, 40; Nwokocha 53.

302 "Obasi" is probably a term borrowed by the Igbo from their Efik-Ibibio speaking neighbours.

303 Nwokocha 53.

304 See note 282 above.

CHAPTER FIVE

305 Mbiti (1) 57; cf. Gravrand 23-25.

306 Mbiti (3) 8.

307 Mbiti (1) 56; Ezeanya (7) 35f.

308 Mbiti (1) 56; cf. Isichei 122-134.

309 Ezenwadeyi in Interview with Rev. Fr. R.Arazu, C.S.Sp. (unpublished manuscript) 14-18; cf. Isichei 124; Ezeanya (7) 35f.; Gravrand 25f.; Mbiti (1) 56ff.

310 Mbiti (1) 57.

311 Cf. Gravrand 23.43-45; Pope Paul VI, Message of his Holiness Pope Paul VI to the hierarchy and all the peoples of Africa (Africa terrarum, No.8) 15f.; Westermann, The African today and tomorrow. Oxford 1949, 83; Ezeanya (7) 36; Mbiti (1) 75.

312 The inverted comas on tribal are mine. The Igbo were organized by the British administrators under recognized chiefs. They never regarded themselves as a tribe before then; nor were they barbarous, as Basden (3) 33 would have us believe.

313 Ibid.

314 Jordan 124.126.

315 Uchendu (5) 20; cf. ibid. 11f.; Anozia 2f.

316 Ezeanya (7) 35.

317 Origin of the spirits vary from place to place. Two accounts from Imo and Anambra states will be given here. First from Ngor-Okpala in Imo state. The parent-spirits (ALusi) were created by Abiam (Chineke) himself. But the later became parents of the smaller alusi. All parent-Alusi or spirits were god-man in character, i.e. they were divine and human. They have spiritual qualities as well as human characteristics. The first children of the spirits were equal to their parent-gods; they enjoyed the same qualities. But with time the offsprings of their children's childrens degenerated because they constantly violated the rules of their nature. The parent-gods in consequence broke away from their offsprings, became more spiritualized and pure spirits. They shaded off all their human and materialistic potentialities. They never died; they did not suffer from disease or sickness as human beings do. The constant violation of their code of conduct by their children's children resulted in the quick propagation of many more and less pure spirits; they brought sickness and death to man. Before they became pure spirits, they were visible, used their corporeal parts in the exercise of their duties. Their strength was limited, but above human powers. They bore children as men do. But when they broke off from their children's children, they became invisible, their spiritual powers increased; they ceased to bear children directly. Rather they have control over child-bearing and determine the number of children that come into their territory. (Extracted from Rev. Fr. Clifford Maduike's interview with Mr. Nnadi Madu Ugbala of Umuogi Village in Ngor-Okpala; a traditional priest and a Dibia; the oldest man in the village; he might well be over 90 years of age at the time of interview.) - The other is narrated by Madam Akanya Okwnenu of Umuoba-Anam, a chief-priestess of Ani-Spirit in interview with Rev. Fr. Michael Ndive (19th April 1980). It

reads: "The Almighty Governor of the whole universe, whom we call God has two sons whom he used to send on errands. The first was sent to the world of men to look after them. He was to return to God after some time and report to him the happenings on earth. While among men he grew wicked; and instead of doing the work he was assigned to do by his Father-god, he began to molest men. To worsen matters he refused to return to his Father-god when he was asked to give account of his stewardship on earth. His Father-god having waited in vain for him came in person to look for him. And as this bad and wicked son saw his Father-god coming he ran away and fell into the sea and disappeared. But before this happened he had already married and after his fall he strted breeding many of his type in the sea. Knowing very well that he is unworthy to see his Father-god again, he chose to persist evil and wickedness all through his life, he and his family, and their descendants, even unto this day. - This wicked and fallen son of God and his offsprings are very powerful on the seas; and they can and do cause harm to humanity, if they are not placated. That is why they are called "Alusi mmili" - do not violate the water; "Onye-ukwu" - the great one; "Idenyi omu nwa" - Great elephant who bears children; "Ogalanya afo julu" - rich man of immense wealth; "Eze-oka-aka" - king of kings or king of mighty hands. - All these praise names or titles are given him in order to keep him happy and self-contented; and lest he attacks humanity as he always is wont to, and boasts of through the oracles. God finally cursed this wicked son of his and as he fell into the sea he be became evil-spirit. Because the first messenger failed, God decided to send a second son to men. He came into the world and was very good. Because the first messenger, scandalized men very much, the second son had to stay long on earth in order to heal whatever wounds the first messenger caused, and to promote peace and order in the world. This second son did a lot for humanity: he even died shedding his own blood on account of justice. In a similar legend it is said that the second son is called "Nwachieji-eji-nwachiaboo-aboo" - the son of perpetual light, because on the day he shedded his blood for justice there was neither dawn nor darkness; everything stood still.

318 Anozia 2f.; Onwuejeogwu (4) 179.248; Uchendu (5) 11ff.; Mbiti (1) 75.

319 Horton (2) 18.23; Ezeanya (7) 41.

320 Some traditions tell of Chukwu sending Igwe, the Sky-spirit, to pregnant the earth; another speaks of Chukwu creating Anyanwu and Onwa to his messengers (cf. Horton [2] 18; Talbot, Vol.2, 43f.; see also note 317).

321 Onwuejeogwu (4) 5-7.

322 Spirit: the equivalent in Igbo language in the context is in the plural (spirits - ndi mmuo) which means literally "the spirits". We have been accustomed to translate "ndi mmuo" in the singular to correspond with the English word, "spirit". But according Ezenwadeyi the spirits that are worshipped can be numbered but each of them is said to be ""ndi mmuo". Equally interesting was the answer to the question "whether Chukwu and Ana were 'mmuo'". He retorted: "Obu Chukwu bu ndi mmuo" - it is God who is the spirits (cf. Arazu with Ezenwadeyi in interview 52f.).

323 Ibid. 52ff.

324 Onwubia Mmara in interview with Rev. Fr. Michael Ndive on the traditional priesthood in Anam. Onwubia Mmara is a native of Umueze, Anam, and a native priest and "dibia" (native doctor).

325 Uchendu (5) 95.

326 Cf. Basden (3) 36f.; Anozia 27.

327 Meek (5) 21; cf. Talbot, Vol.2, 46.

328 Cf. ibid. 42-45.

329 Stories abound of how the sacred days and places originated. An example of such myths may suffice. It is told by Mr. Amadi Eke, a native of Amafor. He is a Dibia. He is more than 70 years. The interview was conducted by Rev. Fr. Clifford Maduike. The myth is: "Imeri was a polygamist god-man who was very fond of women. One day he seized and deflowered the daughter of the River-god by name 'Arungu'. Arungu in consequence harassed him and his household. Finally he was forced to marry the woman he deflowered. But before this agreement was reached Arungu ordered his agents to attack the wives and children of Imeri. Imeri's household and his agents took to hiding. Unfortunately, it was during the famine season. - The agents of Imeri, devised a means: some took the form of monkeys (ewe). As monkeys they were able not only to spy on the invaders from Arungu, but also to go to other territories and farm-lands to steal yams, maize and other edibles to feed the family of Imeri, while at the same time they continued to negotiate for Imeri's release. - Eventually an agreement was reached. Imeri was released on the condition that he married the daughter of Arungu whom he deflowered. His family returned to their home. With time the day of his release and the return of his family from their hiding place and their hiding place become sacred. Monkeys (ewe) became also a sacred animal, and was added to Imeri as a suffix, hence "Imeriewe" became the name of their town. Meanwhile the daughter of Arungu, popularly known as "oyoyo" begot children. She refused to accept as sacred both the place and the day the Imeriewe community commemorates in its history. She chose to live beside the river, where she has selected as a meeting place between her and the people of her parental home. Other wives of Imeri followed suit. Hence there is no single day or place regarded as sacred by the whole Imeriewe community. Only Umuoge-village retains the original sacred place and day of their ancestor-father, Imeri.

330 Cf. Onwuejeogwu (4) 5-7; Uchendu (5) 95; Talbot, Vol.2, 43-45.75-86.104-113.

331 Cf. Uchendu (5) 95.

332 Cf. Chapter II above.

333 Cf. Isichei 122.

334 Cf. Talbot, Vol.2, 43; Uchendu (5) 95; Meek (5) 24.

335 Cf. McKenzie (2) 107.

336 Cf. Isichei 124.

337 Cf. Talbot, Vol.2, 43; Uchendu (5) 95.

338 Madam Akanya Okwuenu of Umuoba-Anam observes: "A set of my

spirits complains very often that Ani, who is the Lord of all spirits always leaves criminals unpunished, and as such crimes multiplies day in, day out". However, all the spirits acknowledge that they are often ignorant, why Ani is so merciful and so silent in the face of many crimes. Ani knows better than the other spirits (cf. Ndive in Interview with Okwuenu, 17.4.80).

339 Cf. Uchendu (5) 96-97; Parrinder (1) 29. Practically all the Igbo consider her to be feminine. Talbot said that some of the "Ika Igbo" consider her androgynous" and some others (whom he did not specify consider her the wife of Chukwu by whom she bore mankind, animals and plants, every living thing on earth. And some traditions regard her as the wife of of Igwe, the Sky-spirit. Cf. Talbot, Vol.2, 43; Nkokocha 186. See also Forde/Jones 25; cf. Meek (5) 25.

340 Cf. Meek (5) 26; P.A.Talbot, Some Nigerian fertility cults. London 1967, 60.

341 Cf. Uchendu (5) 96.

342 Parrinder (1) 49; Obiefuna 54.

343 Meek (5) 25.

344 Cf. Uchendu (5) 42; see Chapter II above; cf. Meek (5) 25.206ff.; Nwapa (2) 144ff.

345 Cf. Uchendu (5) 95; Meek (4) 210.

346 According to an Agbaja (a town in Mbano) tradition, the people originated from a pair of ancestors, a man called Ngalaba, and a woman called Okpoite. Both were created by Chineke on the spot which the people claim is the centre of Agbaja. It is today the central Agbaja market place. Near it is a piece of sacred bush which is dedicated to the ancestors. The couple had eleven sons. The sons are the founders of the eleven villages making up Agbaja, as it is known today (cf. Green [1] 52; especially for allusion to this myth).
The Ezinihitte (in Aboh Mbaise) tradition has it that Chineke created the 16 villages making up Ezinihitte and the villages of Isiala Ngwa on an orie day, and the spot known today as "Orie ukwu market". Some times it is referred to as "Chileke Orieukwu". The spot is to date called "Ihu-Chileke", the face or presence of God, i.e. the place where God manifested himself to their ancestors. On this spot an annual festival called Oji-Ezinihitte takes place. The people of Ngwa who live on the other side of the Imo River, (they are supposed to have migrated to their present home-land from Ezinihitte) celebrate this same feast in remembrance of their ancestral home. - The Anam (of Anambra) tradition validating the priesthood of Ana has it that a native doctor (dibia) prepared some medicine for the people to foster a spirit of oneness and to help them withstand the occasional raids of the Abos, the Adas and possibly from neighbouring villages. The dibia asked the people to get a male and a female slaves. The slaves were required, the dibia explained, because a slave is one who has experienced hardship and therefore is ruthless with whomsever annoyed or displeased him/her. And this ruthlessness would be necessary in dealing with any criminal who violates the law of the land. All the people consented to the advice,

provided it would put an end to the crimes committed among them. The elders were assembled by the Dibia under the grove. The slaves were brought in. A big pit was dug in the grove. The slaves were lowered into the pit; they stood erect. The dibia asked the elders of the people to enumerate their needs. Meanwhile the Dibia squeezed some herbs and roots and mixed them together; he held some sticks in his hand while he did this. Later he gave the sticks to the slaves to hold. The elders enumerated their needs, the sumtotal of which was to put an end to the crimes the villagers committed against one another and that peace and harmony might reign among them, and that they might win their battles against the enemy. - The Dibia, then, took the sticks from the slaves and with the sticks made seven counts on their hands. He then commanded that the pit be filled up again with clay. In this way all the villagers were bound together one to another. Further, the Dibia instructed that the first settlers should be custodians of the medicine and the shrine. The person who takes charge of the shrine becomes Eze-ani, chief priest of the Ani-spirit; he has to offer sacrifices to the spirit of Anam-land on behalf of all in Anam. - Each village in Anam had to collect some earth from the shrine, bring it to its settlement. There the Spirit is placated and planted. The cult of carrying home the clay from the shrine is called "Ijulu Ani Anam", i.e. the imbibing of the Spirit of Anam in our locality. Every village appointed its priest after an oracle has been consulted. These priests in collaboration with Eze-ani, the chief-priest of Ani-Anam, have to ensure that moral rectitude is observed; and when there is a breach of moral law or defilement of the land, they have to ensure that equilibrium is restored immediately (Extracted from a series of Interviews conducted by Rev. Fr. Michael Ndive in preparation for a long essay on the "Traditional Priesthood among the Anam in Anambra Local Government Area". Those interviewed included Messers Alfred Onuorah, Onwubia Mmara, Paul Ezeolise and Madam Akanya Okwuenu. The interviews were protracted. They were from 1978 - 1980.).

347 Cf. Meek (5) 25.

348 Cf. Talbot, Vol.2, 45; Parrinder (1) 45; Meek (5) 25.

349 Cf. Talbot, Vol.2, 43.

350 Ibid. 45; cf. Meek (5) 25.

351 Cf. Uchendu (5) 96.

352 Cf. Obi (2) 13.

353 Cf. Uchendu (5) 96.

354 Cf. ibid.

355 Cf. Horton (2) 23-36.

356 Cf. ibid. 23.

357 Cf. Evans-Pritchard (1) 109.

358 Cf. ibid. 108.

359 Cf. Forde/Jones 25; Ezenwadeyi in Interview cit. p. 11-24.

360 Cf. ibid. 14-18; Isichei 124. "Ubu" is the name of a river-spirit which has a cult at Ihiembosi (some 24 miles from Onitsha). Agwu'nsi is the spirit that gives knowledge of the power of herbs, roots and other material objects used

in curing diseases and divining hidden phenomenon, in making charms, etc. - Ogwugwu is a spirit paid a cultural reverence at Ukpor, a neighbouring town to Ihembosi. Poultry - farming is dedicated to him; every year the people offer him a fowl. Aro (Aho) is the year force. There is a ceremony or feast known as "Ichu Aro", it is done on the eve of every new year. From my own knowledge it is equivalent to what the Austrians and Germans call "Silvester-Tag" and the features are the same (31st December).

361 Cf. Ezenwadeyi 19f.; cf. Isichei 124.

362 Cf. ibid. 24.

363 Cf. ibid. 21-23; Isichei 124.

364 EKWE is an instrument and a sine qua non for a funeral ceremony for adult males.

365 Ezenwadeyi 24f.; cf. ibid. 38-41.

366 Cf. Horton (2) 23-26; Meek (5) 21.

367 Cf. ibid. 23.

368 Cf. Uchendu (5) 96; Horton (2) 23.

369 Cf. Ezeanya (7) 37; Meek (5) 221.

370 Nwokocha, C.C. 185.

371 Ezeanya (7) 38; Meek (5) 221.

372 Onwuejeogwu (4) 6.

373 Cf. Nwokocha, C.C. 185.

374 Cf. Ezeanya (7) 37; Meek (2) 60; Shelton (5).

375 Cf. Uchendu (5) 96.

376 Cf. Forde/Jones 25; Ruel 295-306.

377 Cf. Uchendu (5) 96.

378 Cf. Meek (5) 221.

379 Cf. ibid. 221.

380 Cf. Jeffrys (4) 93-111.

381 Cf. Chapter 4.3 above.

382 Cf. Talbot, Vol.2, 46.

383 Cf. Uchendu (5) 97.

384 Cf. P.A.Talbot, Some Nigerian Fertility Cults (see note 340) 57.

385 Cf. Anozia 36.

386 Cf. Talbot (see note 340) 52.

387 Cf. Uchendu (5) 96.

388 Cf. Talbot, Vol.2, 47; Uchendu (5) 97.100ff.

389 Cf. ibid. 100ff.; Anozia 36.

390 Cf. Meek (5) 21; Isichei 124; Ezenwadeyi (interview cit.); Onwuejeogwu (4) 6; see also Mbiti (1) 75ff.

391 Some Igbo Communities, e.g. at Oguta say when they are going afishing: "Ejejem oku". Some refer to farming in similar expression.

392 Talbot, Vol.2, 144.

393 Ibid.

394 Basden (1) 147; cf. Meek (5) 16.

395 Ibid. 147.

396 Jeffreys (10) 119-131; cf. T.W.Northcote, Anthropological Report (see note 154) 137f.

397 Uchendu (5) 99; Basden (1) 147.

398 Uchendu (5) 99.

399 Ibid.

400 Cf. Talbot, Vol.2, 145-147; Uchendu (5) 99; Anozia 37.

401 Cf. Uchendu (5) 99; Anozia 216.

402 Basden (1) 148; cf. ibid. 216.

403 Uchendu (5) 99; Anozia 150.

404 Uchendu (5) 99.

405 I refer to the servitors of Agwu as 'specialists' because of their specialised offices, knowledge and skill in religious matters.

406 Uchendu (5) 98.

407 Mbiti remerked that traditional doctors are "the specialists who have suffered most from European-American writers and speakers who so often and wrongly call them 'Witch-doctors' - a term which should be buried and forgotten forever" (cf. Mbiti[1]166). Likewise one would wish that such terms as "Juju-doctors" or "Juju-Priests" should be buried.

408 Basden (1) 54f.; Okeke 119. It must be said that many a time the same specialist plays a role of both, e.g. a 'Dibia-na-agba-afa' and a 'Dibia-na-agwo-ogwu' (meaning diviner and traditional doctor respectively). So there is too great a danger in an academic distinction (see Mbiti [1] 171; Basden [1] 55).

409 Okeke is of the opinion that because 'magicians' have no Igbo equivalent, and because the Igbo regard them with abhorrence the office of magicians is not Igbo in origin. It is foreign. I am inclined to disagree with this view. For we cannot say for certain the difference between 'magicians' and 'mediums' or even the wonderful performances of Dibias (see Okeke 119).

410 See Uchendu (5) 98; Mbiti (1) 166-168.173ff.; Parrinder, West African Religion. London 1961, 75-94; Okeke 71-87.

411 Mbiti (1) 166.

412 Ibid. 169. See also what was said on the reality of the spiritual dimension of existence among the Igbo, Chapter 5.1.

413 See Mbiti (1) 166.193.

414 Uchendu (5) 97.

415 Mbiti (1) 77.

416 Basden (1) 217.

417 Ibid.; cf. Meek (5) 18.

418 Uchendu (5) 97.

419 See Arinze 31f. for more such water-spirits.

420 See Uchendu (5) 97f.

421 Talbot, in his 'Tribes of the Niger Delta' (see p.59) recounts such stories; see also pp. 57ff. for more of such water-spirits.

422 Anozia 149.

423 Nwapa (1) 149.

424 Talbot, Vol.2, 43; Uchendu (5) 95; Meek (5) 24.

425 Uchendu (5) 95.

426 Davidson (2) 95; Ojukwu (see note 66) 13.

427 Isichei 124.

428 Ezenwadeyi in Interview with Fr. Arazu (see note 197); Isichei 124; Mbiti (1) 56f.

429 Cf. ibid. 77.

430 Cf. ibid. - "Duduludu" means time immemorial. Some Igbo, for example, say that "Chukwu or Chineke dili be anyi duduludu; anyi na akpalu ya ugbo - God has been among us from time immemorial; we weave sacrificial boat for him, i.e. we offer him sacrifices.

431 Cf. Onwuejeogwu (4) 248.

432 Mr. Pius Anyadioha Ibeawula is the oldest man in my patrilineal unit (Umunna). He is the oldest surviving brother of my grandmother. He is between 75 and 80 years old. He is not a Christian. I often engaged him in conversation on many aspects of the Traditional Religion. I once asked him if he would not become a Christian, and he told me it is his duty to feed our ancestors, i.e. to offer sacrifices in their honour.

433 "O dimkpa na anye ga-na enye nna anyi na ndi mmuo nile nri, na asopulu wee, na akpuku wee, na adoni wee ishi-ala, na atuni wee egwu, makana alawe eledidi anye anya, na eche anye nche, na edu anye. Nke yahu bu oru ekeri wee ka alawe aru. Mana oge anye na enye wee ife ndia yahu anye na enye kwani ya Chileke, onye kere anye na wee. Ife enyere nwatiri, o kpa obu ile ya na nna ya ka enyere ya - It is necessary that we feed our ancestors and all the spirits; that we honour and reverence them; that we invoke them, adore and respect them, because they watch over us, protect and guide us. This is the duty assigned to them. But when we perform all these duties towards them, we perform them also toward God, who created both us and them. For whatever gift that is given to a child is also given to its parents" (In conversation with Mr. Pius Anyadioha Ibeawula in 1977).

434 Whether the predication of Chukwu and the created but non-human spiritual beings as Mmuo was originally Igbo is a difficult question.Onwuejeogwu seems to hold the contrary opinion: 'Alusi' are metaphysical forces that have attributes of men, but they are neither human beings (Mmadu) or dead-human beings (Mmuo); they are being forces (cf. Onwuejeogwu [4] 6). Arazu regards such predications with misgivings. He calls them "phenomenal" and "metaphysical adaptations" (pp. 2f. of his manuscript entitled "The Pagans"). See also note 317 above.

435 See Mbiti (1) 79; see also Chapter 4.2.2 above.

436 Mbiti (1) 80.

437 See Chapter 5.2.1 above.

438 Onwuejeogwu (4) 6ff.

439 Among the Igbo "canonized" spirits are classified according to family, Obi (extendedfamily), Umunna, village and town. All these correspond to the various socio-religious units. Those given communal rite of libation are those chiefs, priests, and men of various categories of life, who traditionally have distinguished themselves in times of difficulty as valiant defenders of the rights of the village or village-group. Each paterfamilias has every liberty and even the duty to pay particular homage and devotion to the "canonized spirits" of his immediate line of descent, esp. to his father and grandfather (see Anozia 10).

440 Ibid.; Nwokeocha, C.C. 168-172.

441 Meek (5) 105; Onwuejeogwu (4) 6f.; Anozia 9-12.

442 Meek (5) 61.

443 Anozia 11.

444 Ibid. 12f. - See Chapter 3.1 (Omenala).

445 Ilogu (2) 307. See also 'Omenala', Chapter 3 (cf. Onwuejeogwu [4] 125).

446 Ezeanya (7) 44, footnote 32,reported that in some parts of Igboland, like Orareri, Ekwensu is regarded as one of the good spirits. They use Akaliogeli to denote the evil spirits (see also Isichei 124f.; Arazu [unpublished Mss. "The Pagans"]). The whole cult of Ekwensu requires more investigation. Much about it today is obscure.

447 Onwuejeogwu (4) 6f.

448 See Basden (3).

449 The Igbo make subtle distinctions in their sacrificial rites. Broadly their sacrifices can be divided into: 1) Petition and thanksgiving sacrifices - Ilo Mmuo - principally a communion service (peace offering); 2) Expiatory sacrifice (Ikpu ala or Igbu aja) which is more a purification rite. Its aim is atonement and cleansing a defilment 'committed' either by animals or men (see Arinze 75-78); 3)Sacrifice to ward off molestation from unknown evil spirits or known but uncertain for waht reason the sufferer is molested. This is the Igbo 'Ichu aja' and 'Igo Mmuo'. 'Ichu aja', is offering made wholly and entire only to malevolent and malignant spirits. It means literally 'to drive away evil'or'to drive out the devil'. The articles used in this sacrifice are normally ugly, rotten and disreputable or worthless. They are never eaten, i.e. no sacrificial meal. Usually they are deposited on cross roads or at the junction where three or more paths intersect at a spot outside the confines of the village or they are thrown into the 'bad bush' - Ajo ofia - the supposed dwelling place of disgruntled spirits. - In my view one cannot, strictly speaking, call 'Ichu aja' a sacrifice. For as Basden (3) 55-60, rightly pointed out: It does not spring from any inherent desire to give nor from any spontaneous love to render honour or worship . Rather it

is the only way to escape from their evil designs. Though outwardly, all Igbo sacrificial rites appear to be alike the underlying principles both in their purpose and in method of offering are different. Thus one may find it difficult to grasp the difference between Ichu aja and Igo Mmuo. 'Igo Agogo' means 'to deny', 'to protest', 'to avow innocence', 'to consecrate', 'to offer something to a spirit' (see Arinze 113, also 112-117, for the division of Igbo sacrifices). So the principle underlying Igo Mmuo is inarticulate protestation or question regarding the 'injustice' namely : if I have done no known wrong - i.e. if I have not trespassed against the law of the land or against the communitiy, why then has this evil or misfortune befallen me? But because the Igbo recognise man's insufficiency and his inability to walk uprightly, he adds in a still undertune and begs the intermediaries and all familiar spirits, if however by any chance he has sinned inadvertently, he now makes this offering as an atonement for the unknown misdeeds (see Basden [3], Chapter II). It is mainly aimed to quieten or placate these spirits. Perhaps the logic behind this offering might be strange to people foreign to the Igbo. As was noted earlier, the Igbo are very conscious of the spiritual dimension of existence. For them, therefore nothing is purely natural or physical. Everything has always its spiritual aspect. When therefore an Igbo is troubled by illness or misfortune, he sees in it not only as a physical occurrence but also as a religious experience. He might be unable to trace any definite reason for which such vengeance is executed upon or punishment meted out to him. In fact whether by omission or commission he may be unable to state, nonetheless he accepts the verdict and meekly submits to whatever befalls him; though inwardly he may protest (see Arinze 74-195, for fuller treatment of Igbo Sacrifice).

450 Anozia 37f.

451 See Chapter 2.2.

CHAPTER SIX

452 Cf. Chapters 3, 4 and 5.

453 Basden (3) 37.

454 Meek (6) 112f. (cf. Meek [5] 20).

455 Unegbu 12.

456 O'Connel 67-69.

457 Ladurie Marie Le Roy, Pâques Africaines. De la communauté clanique a la communauté crétienne. Paris 1965, 60.

458 Uchendu (5) 94f.

459 Cf. Mbiti (3) 203ff.; Shelton (5) 15-17; Ezeanya (7) 37; Idowu (2) 48ff.; Anozia 50-66; Nwokocha, C.C. 56f.,191-197.

460 Cf. Chapter 4.2.2 and note 278 above.

461 Nzekwu (2) 34.

462 Jordan 221; Achebe (1) 70.

463 Okeke 31.

464 Ojiako 77.

465 C.T.Young, The idea of God in Nyasaland. In: African Ideas of God (1966) 41.

466 Ojike 6.

467 Fortes (1) 37.

468 Cf. Meek (5) 292.

469 Shelton (5) 16.

470 Sabatier says: "Religion is an intercourse, a conscious and voluntary relation entered into by a soul in distress with a mysterious power which it feels itself to depend, and upon which its fate is contingent. This intercourse with God is realized by prayer. Prayer is religion in act; that prayer is real religion." (Quoted from James, W. 453; otherwise cf. A.Sabatier, Esquisse d'une philosophie de la religion. 2nd. edit., Paris 1897, 24-26).

471 Mbiti (3) 194.

472 Smith, E.W. 15; Mbiti (3) 220.

473 Smith, E.W. 14f.

474 Ilogu (2); Smith, E.W. 14. - I am not insinuating that among the Igbo no one can have a faith which is more personal and spiritual than that of the others of his group. What is being empphasized is that religious awareness is based more on social traditions than on individual reflections. Man gives expression to his subjective religious dispositions and sentiments in the concrete religious convictions of the people into whom he is born and among whom he passes his earthly life.

475 Mbiti (3) 2.

476 Cf. Chapter 2.2.

477 Cf. Mbiti (3) 227ff.

478 Meek (5) 299ff.; Uchendu (5) 95 (cf. Conclusion of Chapter 2.2); Onwuejeogwu (4) 119-122.

479 Ibid. 121f.

480 Uchendu (5) 95.

481 Idowu (2) 141.

482 Otto 13.

483 Ezeanya (4) 1.

484 Ibid. 1f.

485 Ibid. 3 (cf. Chapter 5.2.1).

486 Ezeanya (5) 3.

487 Alutu 238.

488 Obi or Obu is a single-roomed house whose door is the main entrance to a family compound. An Igbo family lives in two or more houses with the father living in one house, his wife (wifes) and grown-up children in the others. All the houses are surrounded by a wall whose entrance is the same as that of the Obi. The Obi is used for morning prayers, for breakfast, for receiving visitors. It is the general assembly

house for the family and sometimes for the villagers. It served as court-house where minor criminal and civil disputes were heard and settled (cf. Ojike 24).

489 Ibid. 17; Arinze 49; Nwokocha, C.C. 108-118.

490 P.A. Talbot, Tribes of the Niger Delta. London 1967, 69; cf. Achebe (1) 27-29.

491 Cf. Talbot (see note 490) 67.

492 Cf. Achebe (1) 27-29; see section on Earth-spirit (Chapter 5.2.1).

493 This phrase is often put in this proverb: "Ikpele ani ka eghu ji anu nne ya ara"; the young goat suchs its mother's breasts on its (young goat's) knees.

494 Basden (3) 67f.

495 Achebe (3) 77ff.

496 Uchendu (5) 99.

497 Meek (2) 24.

498 Uchendu (5) 100; Achebe (3) 82 ff.

499 See Chapter 5.2.2; Meek (2) 60; Shelton (5); Talbot, Vol.2, 45.

500 Meek (2) 221; Forde/Jones 25.

501 Nwokocha, C.C. 186.

502 The sun is often associated with good fortune, wealth and good luck in new enterprise (cf. section on Anyanwu: Chapter 5.2.2; Forde/Jones 25; Nwokocha, C.C. 184).

503 Meek (2) 221 (cf. Meek [5] 289).

504 Ezeanya (7) 38.

505 See section on the Igwe and Amadioha Spirits: Chapter 5.2.3.

506 Ezeanya (7) 37f. - It is believed that Amadioha like Ale and the Aro-Chukwu "Juju" is against all those who act contrary to custom. The thunder God sends down his bolt to strike such sinners; so when a man is killed by lightning, people always know that he has done some bad thing (cf. Talbot [see note 340] 57). - Sometimes such prayers may be only simple gesture of the hand, a gesture, which symbolises and implies an appeal to the Supreme Being. "It may be a mother who behind her hut in the early morning when the village is still quiet, raises her first-born to heaven to present it to the Supreme Being, while murmuring a prayer of offering or filial request; or again a father who when his son is leaving the paternal roof for a long journey, invokes the help and protection of the Most High during the journey till the day of return home." (ibid. 60).

507 Ibid. 44.

508 Ibid. 46; cf. Meek (5) 288.

509 Ibid. 24.

510 Ezeanya (7) 37; Forde/Jones 25; Uchendu (5) 94f. - The inverted commas on Gods are mine.

511 Parrinder (1) 24.

512 Ojike 190.

513 Van Bulk 17-33; Parrinder (1) 35; Meek (5) 21.

514 Talbot, Vol.2, 40.

515 Nwokocha, C.C. 193; Parrinder (1) 38.

516 Ezeanya (7) 38f.

517 Ibid. 40.

518 Goody 33.

519 Ezeanya (7) 39.

520 Ibid. 40.

521 It is significant that elements for sacrifices to Chukwu are mostly, if not always white. Thus the Igbo imply that Chukwu is holy and his offering, must be undefiled, pure and clean (see Basden [3] 61).

522 The Kola-Nut (Oji) and the white phallic chalk (NSU) are of great religious significance to the Igbo. The kola is a symbol of friendship, love and unity. To present it to a guest is to express these sentiments to the guest. In Igbo hospitality, it is a "sine qua non". To refuse to share the kola with one is tantamount to declaring that one is an enemy. For more elaborate treatment of the kola cf.: Nwokocha, C.C. and P.I. Anozia, La liturgia degli Igbo. In: Rocca 12-15 (1967) 22. - The white phallic chalk (nsu) is a symbol of peace. To rub it on the hand or eyebrows of a visitor is to give him a transit "Passport". Members of the village will know him as a friend. In offering these to God, the same sentiments are expressed to him.

523 Ezeanya (7) 40.

524 Ibid.

525 Meek (5) 40. Shelton witnessed, too, such sacrifices among most villages of Nsukka where the "Onyisi" accompanies the suppliant to the village square and makes the sacrifice - which is less important economically than spiritually consisting usually of kola and palm oil during which the Onyisi invokes Eze Chitoke to intervene and bring the suppliant out of his miseries (cf. Shelton [5]).

526 Ezeanya (7) 40f. - Anozia described a simolar rite commonly known among the Oguta people and their allied Oru people (riverians) as "Iruma Chukwu" which means "Implatation of God" (in the compound). According to these groups, Iruma Chukwu is another name for Aja Eze Enu. The elements for this rite are practically the same as that for Aja Eze Enu (cf. Anozia 60-68).

527 DUDULUDU means time immemorial - in diebus illis. No word brings out more clearly and forcefully the meaning except that the priest intended to emphasise that what he has just done is altogether indigenous and as old as the town itself.

528 Sacrificial boat is a boat-shaped receptacle prepared from palm-frond and used for holding part of the victims for sacrifice. To weave sacrificial boat is simply another way of saying that sacrifice is offered (cf. Ezeanya [7] 41; also footnotes 24.25 on the same page); cf. Meek (5) 285f., 289f.

529 Shelton (5) 17.

530 Ibid. 16.

531 A better translation is the "Mouth of Chukwu" i.e. the Shrine of God.

532 Shelton (5) 17.

533 Ezeanya (7) 39.

534 Ibid. - One of my informants remarked that during "Ili Agba Chukwu" - eating of the covenant of God, God is specifically thanked for all his blessings, favours; and especially for the help they got from him in producing the new yams. They ask him for long life and atone for the offences they committed in the land during the year.

CHAPTER SEVEN

535 Cf. the "Declaratio de Ecclesiae habitudine ad Religiones non-christianas 'Nostra aetate'" of the Second Vatican Council.

536 Cf. Idowu (2) 169.

537 Sidhom 113 (cf. "Nostra aetate", No. 2).

538 Cf. Anozia 188.

539 Cf. Plato's Symposium.

540 Cf. Anozia 187.

541 Cf. Nwapa (2) 211.

542 See the myth on the origin of death (cf. note 181 of Chapter 3.1). - Beier (5) 56; Nwokocha, C.C., 53; Basden (1) 283 and (3) 431f. The idea of man commiting some 'sin' for which he is punished is contained in all these stories cited. In addition, some Igbo myths explaining the present distance between man and Chukwu seem to allude to this 'primordial guilt' (see Anozia 163, footnote 124). Ojike 185f., narrates: "In the beginning there was no evil in the world. Death, war, pestilence, famine, flood, hurricane and accidents were unheard of. Whenever man wanted anything, he went to the hillside, called upon God and obtained his requests. There was no struggle for existence or for higher standards of living either. Life was easy, bed of roses. One day, a woman was preparing an evening corn meal, and instead of sitting down as was customary she stood up and went on beating the corn. The wooden pestle which she was using was so tall that its top end pierced the sky; immediately rain and diseases and sin and death and all sorts of evil poured down on earth: Life became a struggle and so it will remain until one dies and returns his spirit to God who gave it." (cf. Meek [5] 53).

543 Pieper 62.

544 Ibid.

545 Cf. Nwapa (2) 211-213.

546 Uchendu (5) 12.

547 Noon 638-654; Leonard 171ff.

548 Cf. Chapter 3.1 and Chapter 5.1; Mbiti (1) 155f., 169.

549 Hertz 77.

550 Mbiti (2) 164.

551 Talbot, Vol.2, 298.

552 Basden (3) 280.

553 Basden (1) 118.

554 Cf. Nwokocha, C.C., 174f.

555 Cf. Basden (1) 118; Nwokocha, C.C., 174ff.

556 Cf. Anozia 158ff. (see also Chapters 3.3 and 4.2 above).

557 Cf. Anozia 40 (see also Chapters 3.3 and 4.2).

558 See Chapter Three above.

559 Cf. Chapter 3.3.

560 Cf. Chapters 3 and 4.

561 Talbot, Vol.2, 263ff.; Basden (3)278; Leonard 184; Uchendu (5) 12.

562 Anozia 11.23; Okeke 28; Nwokocha, C.C., 30.

563 Jordan 137; cf. Uchendu (5) 12.

564 Cf. Ahunanya 56.

565 Sidhom 102.

566 Nwokocha, C.C., 14.20; Mbiti (1) 2.110ff.

567 Luykz (2) 133-143.

568 Nwokocha, C.C., 202.

569 Jordan 31ff.

570 Talbot, Vol.2, 263; Basden (3) 278; Leonard 184; Uchendu (5) 12.

571 Some elderly Igbo, even among them were some Christians, with whom I had the opportunity to discuss this point grimly remarked: "One wonders how happy one could be in heaven without one's immediate relationships". "Perhaps", they added, "this sounds materialistic. But ...".

572 Mbiti (1) 26.

573 Ibid. 133.142.

574 Ibid. 26.148.

575 Ibid. 133. Mr. Igbokwe in answers to the questionnaire on the structure of the council of elders remarked: An okopolo (bachelor) is not yet fully initiated into the community; he is not counted a complete person. He may not take a title (e.g. ichi ozo or igbu ichi). During new-yam festivity, he may not carry children to the presence (ihu) of a shrine dedicated to local spirit; and of course, he is not allowed to acquire a personal ofo. Some of these prohibitions are applicable to a married man who has no male children. But all these, notwithstanding, I would be inclined to think that Mbiti's remark that he who does not participate in it [marriage] is underhuman is oversweeping, if not wholly exaggerated (cf. Mbiti [1] 133). Likewise the observation of Basden and Onuora Nzekwu that celibacy is an impossible prospect for the Igbo (cf. Basden [1] 68; Nzekwu (2) 57).

576 Mbiti (1) 133.148.

577 Ibid. 133.

578 Cf. Anozia 193f.; Mbiti (1) 133ff. See also Mbiti (2) 164ff.

579 While interviewing some Igbo in Austria, Britain, Germany, Italy and Switzerland, some of them remarked on this issue that: The psychological gratification - despite the modern concept of the dignity and importance of the individual person - with which parents identify themselves with their children or even of teachers to live vicariously in the careers of their students, seems to be reckoned with in the happiness of the individual, even if the whole structure of heaven and beatific vision were utterly immaterial - a structure where there shall be "neither marrying nor giving to marriage", but where all will have for "their fathers, Abraham, Issac and Jacob".

580 Cf. Mbiti (2) 182f.; see also Lepp 173ff.

CHAPTER EIGHT

581 Hertz 27.

582 C. Achebe in interview with Francis Wyndham for "The Sunday Times" (27 July 1969, p.13, entitled: "Conversations in Biafra").

583 Cf. Chapter VII; Basden (1) 118; Nzekwu (2) 131.

584 Ibid. 142.

585 I still remember my grandfather on my father's side saying that his father (my great-grandfather) before his dead said that 'it was time for him to go home'.

586 Achebe (see note 582).

587 Basden (1) 117f. and (3) 282.

588 Talbot, Vol. 3, 470; Basden (1) 119 and (3) 283; Nzekwu (2) 111.131.

589 Cf. Nwapa (2) 146f.

590 Talbot (see note 490) 255ff.; Basden (1) 114.119 and (3) 276; Ojiako 5 (see also Chapter 5.2 and 5.3 above).

591 The main works on this are: Basden (1), esp. Chapter X; Basden (3), esp. Chapter XX (here esp. pp. 263ff.); Meek (5) 303ff.; Talbot, Vol.3, 468ff.; Talbot (see note 490), esp. Chapters XIX and XX (here esp. pp. 231ff.); Major Leonard (see note 15), esp. 139ff.; Th. Northcote, Some Ibo burial customs. In: The Journal of Royal Anthropological Institute (1916) 166-213; Ahunanya.

592 Basden (3) 277.

593 Cf. Chapters 3.3 and 7.

594 Cf. Chapter 7; Leonard (see note 15) 140f.

595 Cf. once more Chapter 7 and also Chapter 3.3.3.

596 A. van Gennep, The rites of passage. London 1960, 146.

597 Cf. in this Section the remarks on "Communion with Ndichie (ancestors)".

598 Nzekwu (2) 131.

599 Hertz 37f.

600 Ibid. 38.

601 Nzekwu (2) 131f.

602 Talbot, Vol.3, 473.

603 Basden (3) 271.273; Nzekwu (2) 131f.; Talbot, Vol.3, 47 471.493ff.; Meek (5) 318; Talbot (see note 490) 263ff; O'Donnell 54-60 (for allusion to this belief in the conversion of the three condemned murderers before their execution). Likewise Nwapa (2) 149.210.217f.

605 Meek (5) 308.

606 Ibid. 303f.

607 Cf. Nzekwu (2) 131. - See Chapter 9.2 below for the interpretation of this dance.

608 Cf. Meek (5) 305, footnote 4.

609 The two runnings symbolize the dash to attack in war.

610 Cf. Meek (5) 305. - Some told me that the meat is cooked and eaten; others says that the body is buried with the corpse. The significance of this rite seems to be the same inherent meaning as the first ritual dance. However the former allowing of the blood drip into the eyes of the dead seemed to symbolise that his eyes should 'be open' in order to make a safe journey; the drumming is to strengthen his soul to overcome the trials on the way to the next life.

611 Cf. Meek (5) 307.

612 Cf. Jordan 136; Basden (3) 113.

613 The right spelling of the word is 'Mkpuru-obi' or 'Mkpulu-obi'.

614 Meek (5) 307.

615 It is believed that it is at this time that the marrow of the soul-Mmuo finally leaves the remains of its human existence.

616 Cf. Nzekwu (2) 134; Meek (5) 307-309.

617 Among some Igbo communities e.g. at Mboo in Awgwu Division, when the grave is filled up, branches of palm are laid over the soil, which is then trampled down hard, to prevent the occurance of cracks. If a crack appears in the grave a diviner must be consulted, and if the diviner declares that the crack is due to anger of ALA, the earth goddess, on account of some offence committed by the deceased, the grave is opened and the body thrown away into the 'bad bush' - 'Ajo-ofia'. After the inhumation, all who had taken part enter a stream and bathe. They throw some water over the right shoulder, facing the direction from which the stream comes. The next face the direction in which the stream goes and do the same. This is to purify themselves from the pollution of death (cf. Meek [5] 307f.).

618 Cf. ibid.

619 This ceremony and the bringing of the spirit of the deceased into the house, which we shall soon see in 'Ikwa Ozu' rites, show the great religious importance of marriage and procreation in Igbo society. The son

plays a leading role in continuing and keeping up the memory of the deceased. An unmarried person or a person married but without an issue is not given this ceremony. And this means that the unmarried is in effect partially conquered by death.

620 Cf. Meek (5) 310.

621 Cf. ibid. 314.

622 Cf. Nzekwu (2) 130; Nkem 200.

623 Immedialtely a person is dead the height of the deceased is measured with a bamboo stick and is hidden away. The person who is to impersonate the 'dead-man-coming-back' is to be of the same height. With this stick too, is used to construct a wicker-work coffin (Ibudu), which serves as the substitute for the coffin containing the body of the deceased on the 'Ikwa-Ozu' day.

624 Cf. Talbot, Vol.3, 494.

625 See Chapter 5, note 449.

626 See Idowu (1) 190f.

627 Cf. Mbiti (1) 152; Idowu (1) 191f. - Hertz 74, on this writes: "The final ceremony thus profoundly alters the condition of the deceased: it awakes him from his bad sleep and enables him to live a secure social life again. It makes a wondering shade into a 'Father'. This transformation does not differ essentially from a true resurrection."

628 Cf. Meek (5) 315.

629 Cf. Nzekwu (2) 135.

630 Cf. ibid.

631 Cf. ibid. and Meek (5) 315, for the procedure and the sharing of the sacrificial meat.

632 Cf. Ilogu (1) 234f. and (2) 304-308; Meek (5) 61ff.; Ezeanya (7) 37.

633 Cf. Nwokocha, C.C., 171; Ilogu (2); Meek (5) 63ff.

634 Cf. Mortuary rites: Nzekwu (2) 131.

635 Hertz 79f. - Robert Hertz calling this "transfigured rebirth", "a true resurrection" adds: "Only what was elsewhere the achievement of the group itself, acting through special rites, here becomes the attribute of the divine being, of a saviour who by his sacrificial death has triumphed over death and freed his disciples from it; resurrection instead of being the consequence of a particular ceremony, is a consequence postponed for an intermediate period of God's grace. Thus...the notion of death is linked with that of the resurrection; exclusion is always followed by a new integration." (cf. Hertz 74.78f.; see too D. Haignere, Des rites funèbres dans la liturgie romaine. Boulogne-sur-Mer 1888, 23.60ff.).

636 Cf. Nzekwu (2) 136.

637 Cf. Basden (3) 281.284.

638 Uzodimma 130ff.

639 Nzekwu (2) 141.

640 Cf. Chapter 7.1.2.

641 Nwokocha, C.C., 171.

642 Ilogu (2) 306.

643 Nwokocha, C.C., 170f.

644 Forde/Jones 25.

645 Ilogu (2) 307; cf. Goody 407f.

646 Cf. Onwuejeogwu (4). See also the theogonocal notions of the Igbo: Chapter 5.3.

647 Cf Chapter 4.2.3.

648 Fortes (2) 133.

649 Ibid.

650 Pieper 50.

651 Cf. Chapters 3 and 5; Nwokocha, C.C., 168; Esua Cornelius Fontem, Towards an African Spirituality. In: Lux (Review of the African Association of St.Augustine), No. 2/3 (1969) 292-308.

652 Nwokocha, C.C., 169; Anozia 191.

653 Bradbury 97.

654 Cf. Leonard (see note 15) 187.

655 Fortes (2) 116. The inverted commas on worship are mine.

656 Fortes (1) 29.

657 Parrinder (1) 66.

658 Idowu (1) 192.

659 Parrinder (1) 66.

660 Anozia 26; Nwokocha, C.C., 181.

661 Basden (1) 119.

662 Basden (3) 282; cf. Chapter 4.3.5.

663 Uchendu (5) 102; Parrinder (1) 65ff.

664 Idowu (1) 192.

665 Ibid.

666 Nwokocha, C.C., 180ff.

667 Anozia 26.

668 Ibid. 26f.

669 Cf. Nwokocha, C.C., 181.

670 Ibid.

671 Cf. ibid. 180ff.; Anozia 23ff.; Idowu (1) 192; Parrinder (1) 65ff.; Uchendu (5) 102.

672 Koinonia is the same as the ancestral community.

673 Ilogu (2).

674 Forde/Jones 25; cf. Ilogu (2).

675 Ibid.

676 Onwuejeogwu (4) 5-7.

677 Talbot, Vol.3, 494.

678 See Chapter 8.2.1 - 8.2.3 (burial and funeral rites).

679 Cf. Achebe (1) 70ff.

680 Cf. ibid. 72-77.

681 Cf. Anozia 19f.; Idowu (1) 194.

682 Anozia 22.

683 Uchendu (5) 102; cf. Chapter 9, note 758.

CHAPTER NINE

684 Uchendu (5) 15f.

685 Ibid. 16.

686 See Igbo-socio-religious structure (Chapter 2.2, esp. the Conclusion); Uchendu (5) 11ff.; Anene (1) 12ff.; Akoi (see note 79) 183ff.

687 Cf. ibid. 177ff.; Sidhom 102; Nwokocha, C.C., 14.202.204; Mbiti (1) 2.110ff.; Luykx (2) 133-143.

688 Cf. Akoi (see note 79) 176ff.; Mbiti (1) 110ff.

689 Ibid. 110; Sidhom 104.

690 Akoi (see note 79) 184.

691 Ibid.; Mbiti (1) 110.

692 Cf. ibid. 110. The section on Igbo social consciousness and the religious significance of marriage and procreation (Chapter 7.2.2.2).

693 In many Igbo communities, e.g. in Egbema, as in most African societies, marriage is not fully 'recognized' or 'consumated' until the new wife has become pregnant and given birth. This becomes the final seal of marriage, the sign of complete integration of the woman into her husband's family and kinship circle. Little wonder there is, then, for the concern of the group - and no less the unhappy state of the wife herself and her people - when a new wife remains childless after a considerable time in marriage wedlock, for she become the dead end of human life not only for genealogical line but also for herself in both worlds (cf. Nwapa [1] and [2]; Mbiti [1] 110ff., 113ff.; Ojike 6. see also Igbo concept of immortality, the social consciousness and the religious significance of marriage and procreation [cf. Chapter 7.2]).

694 Mbiti (1) 111. - It must be immediately remarked that the prohibitions vary in different Igbo communities. But they are general all over Igboland (cf. Basden [3] 168ff.; Meek [5] 288f. and Talbot [see note 490] 161ff.)

695 Cf. Basden (3) 169; Meek (5) 288f.

696 Ibid. 289.

697 Mbiti (1) 111. - For more of the taboos, see Meek (5) 288f.; Basden (3) 168ff.

698 Formerly if it were not worn the woman's child would be destroyed at birth, so my informants told me (cf. also Meek [5] 284).

699 Cf. Meek (5) 285.

700 Ibid.

701 Ibid. 286 (cf. ibid. 286-289 for more rites); see also Talbot (see note 490) 161ff.

702 Okafor-Omali 42; Meek (5) 290; Basden (3) 172.

703 Meek (5) 289f.

704 Cf. Nwokocha, C.C., 118f. - Water for the Igbo is a symbol of life. Hence they refer to a healthy man as a man who has a 'water-oozing-body' (onye aru na-ata mmiri).

705 Mbiti (1) 113.

706 Meek (5) 292. - A priest of Ala (the Earth-spirit) must be one whose mother's placenta with umbilical cord is buried in the land and whose parents are free people, i.e. they must be "Diala"; cf. Uchendu (5) 96.

707 Mbiti (1) 113. See Igbo concept of immortality and their social consciousness as well as the religious significance of marriage and procreation (Chapter 7.2).

708 Meek says it is between the fourth and eighth or twelveth day after birth (see Meek [5] 292); Basden (3) 176, says it is between the fourth and the eighth day; Okafor-Omali says between the eighth and the twelveth day after birth for the Enugu-Ukwu-village-group (cf. idem 43).

709 Meek (5) 293; Basden (3) 176; Talbot (see note 490) 168. Among the Eha-Amafu village-group and neighbours it used to be an offence punishable by a heavy fine and payable by the male paramour and the girl's parents, for any girl to conceive before she has been circumcised (cf. Meek [5] 293).

710 In the olden days and practically in all Igbo communities, an uncircumcised person would be a shocking 'phenomenon', and a title of contempt. Even no normal Igbo would venture contract marriage with an uncircumcised (cf. Basden [3] 176).

711 Okafor-Omali 42; Anozia 100.

712 Basden (3) 172.

713 Meek (5) 293.

714 Ibid.(cf. also pp. 294f. for other similar rites).

715 Ibid. 294; cf. also Anozia 100.

716 Mbiti (1) 114f.; cf. Nwokocha, C.C., 119; Uchendu (5) 60.

717 Okafor-Omali 45.

718 Cf. I. Coker, Romance of African names. Art. in Sunday Post (April 5th, 12th, 19th, ff.), Lagos 1964; Okafor-Omali 46; Basden (3) 174ff.

719 There is no set formula for this prayer. It is like the impromtu chant in the funeral rites but the thought-patterns are the same.

720 It is to be remarked that each of the parents may give a name to the child. Any other person approved by the family is also at liberty to give a name to the newly born baby and will also present special naming gifts to it. As they give

the names the head announces them to the public (cf. Okafor-Omali 45).

721 Meek (5) 295; Anozia 100ff.; Nwokocha, C.C., 119ff.

722 Okafor-Omali 44f.

723 Cf. Meek (5) 297. Among most Igbo communities to cut the upper teeth before the lower ones was regarded by the people as unusual. Treatment meted out to such children used to be varied (cf. ibid 297).

724 Ibid. 297.

725 Ibid. 296.

726 Okafor-Omali 47.

727 Ibid. 48

728 Onwuejeogwu (4) 264-268.

729 Sidhom 112.

730 Vindu 15-25.

731 Sidhom 112.

732 Cf. Jordan 138; Basden (3) 118.

733 Nwokocha, C.C., 174ff.

734 Cf. Ahunanya 56 and Nwokocha, C.C., 174-176.

735 Anozia 223.

736 See Chapter 7 ("Death of Mmadu ...").

737 Jordan 138. - Perhaps the conceptualisation of death as a fulfilment of life here on earth may well explain why those who die young, children, young men and ladies before they get married and become fathers and mothers; married men and women who have no issues are believed to remain 'children', 'men and women without honour or unworthy of attention' in both worlds. They are regarded as having lived a frustrated life (cf. Uchendu [5] 16; Meek [5] 314; Nwapa [2] 148f.). And for the relatives of these, the belief in "Ino Uwa" - partial reincarnation or whatever that meant to individuals, gives some consolation, because as Uchendu says, "it provides the 'idea system' that rationalises, interpretes, accomodates...as well as tolerates certain character traits". It gives them hope that such deceased members of theirs "will realize their frustrated status goals in the next cycle of life" (cf. Uchendu [5] 16.102). Whether this "idea system" is realizable or not, that is another question. All the same it does offer a "prop" - call it "faith", if you like; and through it some energy is mustered; there is offered some vision, resolution and capacity to survive disappointment, namely that "nke iru ka" - that which the future has in store is still greater. And this is socially important, because the sense of loss might drive someone without such a "prop" to extremes (see B. Spencer/F.J. Gillen, Northern tribes of Central Australia. London 1904, 516; M.H. Kingsley, Travels in West Africa. London 1897, 463). On the other hand whether belief in 'Ino Uwa' is necessarily a result of the "deep lacuna in Igbo Traditional Religion", namely "that the concept of heaven where men dwelt eternally with God was unknown to Igbos", as Anozia 23.223.229f., seemed inclined to affirm, remains an open question.

738 Cf. Hertz 76f.

739 Ibid. 77. Perhaps this helps to explain why death whenever it occurs is regarded to have defiled the Earth-spirit (Ala).

740 Nzekwu (2) 131; see also Meek (5) 304f.

741 Cf. Hertz 78ff.

742 Ibid.; Sidhom 112.

743 Hertz 78.

744 Ibid. 79.

745 Ibid. 79. See the mortuary and funerary rites of the Igbo (Meek [5] 303ff.).

746 Hertz 79.

747 Ibid.

748 Ibid.

749 Anyadioha Ibeawula in Conversation with Rev. Fr. Cosmas Okechukwu Obiego. - I should like to add that some ambivalence is exhibited here! When I asked some people which of the two lives they would prefer, this or the next life, many invariably retorted, "Onye jechara lota? Ndi lotara uwa adighi ekwu ife a furu wee!" - "No one has come back from the spirit-world (to tell). Those who are reincarnated never speak of their experiences!" - However, a few said: "Nna nna anyi wee se na onwu bu ina Chi, ina ulo. Onye laruo ulo o toruo ume ani zuo ike. Anye kwere; O kwa alala wee; K'anyi lakwuruni wee, i.e.: "Our forefathers said that death is a returning to Chukwu, a going home. When one returns home one relaxes and rests oneself. We belief, our ancestors are gone; let us rejoin them!"

CHAPTER TEN

750 See Chapter 2.2.

751 Cf. Chapters 5 and 6.

752 Cf. Chapters 3 and 4.2.

753 Cf. Chapters 3 and 4.

754 Cf. Chapter 4.1.

755 Cf. Chapters 4.1, 4.3 and 3.3; see also Chapter 7.1.

756 Cf. Chapter 3.3.

757 Cf. ibid. and Chapter 4.1.

758 Cf. Chapters 3, 4.1 and 4.4.

759 Cf. Chapters 3 and 7.

760 Cf. ibid.

761 Cf. Chapter 7.

762 Cf. Chapters 5.2 and 7.

763 Cf. Chapters 3.3, 7, 8 and 9.

764 Cf. Evans-Pritchard (1) 7; Hertz 7; R. de Vaux, Ancient Israel. New York 1965, VII ff.; A.N. Whitehead, Religion in making. London 1927, 6.

765 Cf. Chapters 8 and 9.

766 Cf. Luke 15,1-10.

767 Cf. J. Danielou, Christ and us. London 1961, 45.

768 H. Küng, Christenheit als Minderheit. Einsiedeln 1965, 36.

769 Cf. Exod. 24,16f.

770 Cf. Col. 3,12; 1 Thess. 1,4; 2 Thess. 2,13; Rom. 11,28.

771 Cf. Rom. 5,5; 8,14f.; Gal. 4,4f.

772 K. Rahner, Christianity and non-Christian Religions. In: Christianity and other Religions. Selected Readings. Edited by John Hick and Brian Hebblethwaite. Glasgow 1980, 70.

773 Taylor (3) 223, observes "that there is no such thing as merely being, not even in God. One is only what one has done, or what one is inwardly and irrevocably committed to doing... To say that a person is loving or just is actually meaningless until that person is committed in particular acts of love and justice. It is by acting truly and consistently at moments when the opposite is a real alternative that one comes to be truthfull and reliable. Action creates being - not the other way round. No person and not even God can be merciful and forgiving in the abstract or in a timeless vacuum where there is nothing and no one to forgive.".

774 Cf. Eph. 4,10f.

775 Acts. 14,17.

776 Heb. 1,1.

777 Cf. J. Danielou, Le mystère du salut des nations. Paris 1948, 33.

778 Without going into the history of the Logos, suffice it to say that the concept of personified creative Wisdom as identified with the Word of God was gradually developed in the sapiential literature of the Old Testament especially during the post-exilic period and later was to receive its full appreciation and decisive completion in the New Testament application of the same concepts to the person of Jesus Christ, the Word Incarnate and Wisdom of God. - The fundamental notions as found in the sapiential books could be summed up as follows: Wisdom has distinct existence and is desirable in itself (cf. Job 28; Baruch 3,9-4,4); Wisdom preexists all things created and is endowed with divine nature (cf. Prov. 8,22-31; Wisd. 7,22. 25-27); Wisdom has the role of giving men life, instructing them in God's will, and finally of leading them to God (cf. Prov. 8,31.35f.; Wisd. 7,23.27; 9,10); Wisdom is God's creative power by which all things are called into being and it is she who continues to order and rule the universe (cf. Wisd. 7; 12,21; 8,1.6). - It may be noted as well that the Old Testament Wisdom literature and conceptions are very closely connected with those of the Ancient Near East. Comperative studies of these documents make it clear that there is substantial resemblance, even though important

modifications are introduced in the Old Testament. For example, the Wisdom literature alone in the Old Testament directs attention explicitly to the problems of the individual person, and draws attention, thereby, to the importance of the business of daily life of the man who is not so very important; and it lays emphasis on the fact that life is unity and integrity which must be preserved from the disintegration of folly. (See also Wisdom Chapters 10-19, where God's wisdom is manifested in creation and his guidance of nations and individuals.) - More it should not be forgotten that the process of thought free from presuppositions was unknown to the Hebrews. God and divine revelation were accepted as fixed points. Accordingly, all that was aimed at was merely to penetrate deeper into the contents of what was given and to define it more precisely. Nor is the form of "Hokhma" (Wisdom) that of school speech; it is popular. Its problems concern questions dealing with the practical wisdom of life or with godliness.

779 Cf. Wisd. 13,1. - Karl Barth has said that the revelation of God in the outpouring of the Holy Spirit is the judging but also reconciling presence of God in the world of human religion, that is, in the realm of man's attempts to justify and sanctify himself before a capricious and arbitrary picture of God. He maintains that religion is really unbelief, and that revelation is God's self-offering and self-manifestation, and that it encounters man on the presupposition and in conformation of the fact that man's attempts to know God from his own standpoint are wholly and entirely futile because of a practical necessity of fact. In revelation God tells man that he is God, and that as such he is his Lord. In telling him this, revelation tells him something utterly new. If it is true that God is God and that as such he is the Lord of man, then it is also true that man is so placed towards him, that he could know him. But this is the very truth that is not available to man, before it is told him in revelation. If he really can know God, this capacity rests upon the fact that he really does know him, because God has offered and manifested himself to him. Furthermore, the truth that God is God and our Lord and that we could know him as God and Lord, can only come to us in a neutral condition but in an action which stands to it, as the coming of truth, in a very definite, indeed a determinate relationship. That is to say, it reaches us as religious men, namely, it reaches us in the attempt to know God from our standpoint. It does not reach us, therefore, in the activity which corresponds to it. The activity which correponds to revelation would have to be faith; the recognition of the self-offering and self-manifestation of God. Revelation is the act by which in grace God reconciles man to himself by grace; it is also the radical assistance of God which comes to us as those who are unrighteous and unholy (cf. Barth [2] 32.36-39; see also Heb. 11,6).

780 Hulsbosch 98f.

781 Rahner (see note 772) 63; see also ibid. 61; see also St.Augustine, De catechizandis rudibus. In: Patristic Studies of the Catholic University of America. Vol.8, Washington 1926, 31-33; Hick (1) 145; R. Otto, Mysticism East and West. New York 1957, 131.

782 Cf. A. Orbe, La uncion del Verbo. Estudios Valentinianos 3 (= Analecta Gregoriana 113), Roma 1961, 211f.; Schillebeeckx, (2) 1-4.6-9. - Rahner remarks that if it is true that the eternal word of God became flesh for the sake of our salvation and despite our guilt died the death of sin, then the Christian has no right to assume that the fate of the world still travels in its own way in the "no" of man, that the history of the world is just as it would have been if Christ had not come. Christ and his salvation is not simply one of two alternatives offered to man's freedom of choice, but rather the act of God which victoriously opens and redeems man's false choice. In Christ God gives not merely the possibility of salvation which still must be worked out by man himself, but the actual salvation itself, however much this includes a right decision - precisely as given by God - of human freedom. In other words, where once sin ruled, grace reigns in superabundance; and not only is grace offered outside the Christian Church but to a great extent it achieves a victory in man's acceptance, an acceptance effected by grace itself (cf. Schriften zur Theologie 5, Einsiedeln 1964, 146; see also Vatican Council II, Lumen Gentium, No. 2.).

783 Tertullian in his Apologetical Works (Ad nationes, Apologeticum, De testimonio animae, Ad Scapulam, Adversus Iudaeos) appealed to the Roman administrators and populace for the toleration of Christianity. Following the example of Hellenic philosophers like Posedonius, Philo, Chrysippus, Seneca and others to derive the knowledge of God from macrocosm and microcosm side by side, from the great universe and the little world of the human soul, he rebutted pagan superstition and endeavoured to use the soul not ruined by 'education' as witness for the existance and attributes of God, for the life after death, and for reward and punishment in the world beyond the grave. There is no need for philosophical reflexion and instrüction; all these truths are present to the soul. Nature pure and simple is the teacher of the soul to the effect that she is an image of God, a better witness to truth also, and so he writes: "Would you have the proofs from the works of his hand, so numerous and so great, which both contain you and sustain you, which minister at once to your enjoyment, and strike you with awe; or would you rather have it from the testimony of the soul itself? Though under the oppressive bondage of the body, though led astray by depraving customs, though enervated by lusts and passions, though in slavery to false gods, yet, whenever the soul comes to itself, as out of surfeit, or a sleep, or a sickness and attains something of its natural soundness, it speaks of God; using no other word, because this is the peculiar name of the true God. 'Great God!', 'Good God!', 'Which may God give!' are the words on every lip. It bears witness, too, that God is judge, exclaiming, 'God sees!', and 'I commend myself to God' and 'God will repay me'. O noble testimony of the soul by its very nature Christian (cf. Apologeticum 17,4-6). - This argument of the Apologeticum, the "testimonium animae naturaliter Christianae", was expanded and treated in a special work entitled "The Testimony of the Soul" (De testimonio animae), written in the same year (197) as the Apologeticum.

Johannes Quasten noted that the phrase "anima naturaliter christiana" means the spontaneous awareness of the Creator as derived immediately from the universe and from experience and as evidenced in the daily exclamations of the people." Thus common sense tells us of the existence of a Supreme Being (cf. Patrology, Vol.2, Utrecht - Antwerp 1953, 266). And I should like to add that this awareness of God is more than a suggestion of that 'transcendental experience' of God analysed by K. Rahner (cf. LThK 1 [1957] 564f.). - St.Augustine also seems to allude to this spontaneous awareness of the Creator when he writes: "Laudare te vult homo, aliqua portio creaturae tuae. Tu excitas ut laudare te delectet, quia fecisti nos ad te, et inquietum est cor nostrum donec requiescat in te (cf. Confessions, Bk. 1, Chapt. 1). And St.Thomas writes that man feels that he is obligated by some sort of natural prompting to pay, in his own way, reverence to God from whom comes the beginning of his being and of all good. Man's cult of God is called 'religion', because in some way man binds himself by such acts, so that he will not wander away from God (cf. Contra Gentiles III, 7; see also M. Schmaus, Katholische Dogmatik, Vol.1, 2nd. edition 1940, 92; Clement's of Alexandria "Protreptikos pros Hellēnas", Chapt. 3).

784 Concilium Arausicanum, DS 373-378; Vativan Council II, Verbum Dei, No. 5 (cf. also the Dogmatic Constitution on Catholic faith of the First Vatican Council [DS 3000 -3045, esp. 3010]).

785 Cf. K. Rahner, Art. in: The church. New York 1963, 122f.

786 Dawson 49.

787 Rahner (see note 785) 128; cf. idem, Schriften zur Theologie 5, Einsiedeln 1964, 151.

788 Rahner (see note 772) 73.

789 Newman 80.

790 Ibid. 81. And Clement of Alexandria (cf. Stromateis VI 8) writes: "The Lord is on many waters (cf. Ps. 29,3), not the different covenants alone, but the modes of teaching, those among the Greeks and those among the Barbarians, conducing to righteousness. And already clearly David, bearing witness to the truth, sings, 'let sinners be turned into Hades, and all the nations that forget God' (Ps. 9,17). They forget, plainly, him whom they formerly remembered and dismiss him whom they knew previous to forgetting him." This dim knowledge of God, Clement further observes, contains all things that are necessary and profitable for life; and it came from God and was given as a particular covenant, being, as it is, a stepping-stone to that which is according to Christ. And in the same book (cf. Chapter V) he says that in the Christian dispensation God made a new covenant with mankind, the Greek and Jewish covenants being old. We who worship in a new way in the third form are Christians. For clearly, he says, the one and only God was known by the Greeks in a Gentile way, by the Jews judaically, and in a new and spiritual way by us. And furthermore, the same God who furnished the various covenants trained different peoples by different covenants as well (cf. ANCL, Vol.12 [see note 38 above], pp. 327f., 340-342; see also Irenaeus, Adv. Haer. III 12,13 and cf. the notes 38-40 of Chapter One above).

791 Cf. Latourelle (2) 104.

792 Cf. Gen. 1,26. Cf. also Stromateis VII 2, where Clement says that the saving God would never neglect his own work, because man alone of all the living creatures was in creation endowed with a conception of the Deity. Now that which truly rules and presides is the Divine Word and his providence, which inspects all things, and despises the care of nothing belonging to it; so that those who choose to belong to him are those who are perfected through faith, by him, the Son of the almighty Father, the cause of all things, being the first efficient cause of motion - a power incapable of being apprehended by sensation (cf. ANCL, Vol. 12, pp. 411f. - In another work of his (cf. Paidagogos I 3 in: ANCL, Vol.4, 118f.) Clement says: "The Lord ministers all good and all help, both as man and as God: as God, forgiving our sins; and as man, training us not to sin. Man is therefore justly dear to God, since he is his workmanship. The other works of creation are made by the word of command alone, but man he framed by himself, by his own hand, and breathed into him what is peculiar to himself. What, then, was fashioned by him, and after his likeness, either was created by God himself as being desirable on its own account, or was formed as being desirable on account of something else. If, then, man is an object desirable for itself, then he who is good loved what is good, and the love-charm is within even in man, and is that very thing which is called the inspiration (breath) of God; but if man was a desirable object on account of something else, God has no other reason for creating him than that unless he came into being, it was not possible for God to be a good creator, or for man to arrive at the knowledge of God. For God would not have accomplished that on account of which man was created otherwise than by the creation of man; and what hidden power in willing God possessed, he carried fully out by the forthputting of his might externally in the act of creating, receiving from man what he made man; and whom he had he saw, and what he wished that came to pass. Man, then, whom God made, is desirable for himself, and that which is desirable on his account is allied to him to whom is desirable on his account; and this, too, is acceptable and liked." Clement sums up saying that man is loved by God: "For how shall he not be loved for whose sake the only-begotten Son is sent from the Father's bosom, the Word of faith, the faith which is superabundant; the Lord himself distinctly confessing and saying, 'For the Father himself loves you, because you have loved me'." - And man, Clement observes elsewhere (cf. Protreptikos III in: ANCL, Vol.4, 92), has been constituted by nature so as to have fellowship with God. His peculiar and distinguishing characteristics - born, as he is, for the contemplation of heaven, and being, as he is, a truly heavenly plant - invite him to the knowledge of God, counselling him to furnish himself with what is his sufficient provision for eternity, namely, piety. But he also emphasizes that man is not compelled to do this, just as the horse is not compelled to plough or the bull to hunt, but is set to that for which he is by nature fitted.

793 Gen. 8;9;11.

794 Gen. 9,10f.; 16.

795 Gen. 9;12;16 (cf. Is. 24,5).

796 Amos 9,7.

797 Is. 19,24f.

798 Mal. 1,11. - Catholic exegetes generally follow patristic tradition and the Council of Trent's interpretation of the prediction of a pure oblation offered by the nations in the the messianic age as referring to the Eucharistic Sacrifice of the Holy Mass (cf. DS 1742). There are also some Catholics who hold that only the typological sense refers to the messianic sacrifice of the Mass, while its literal sense refers to the 'pagan' worship of Malachy's day (cf. A. Gelin, Introduction à la Bible, Vol.1, Paris 1959, 573). In any case it has to be noted that the prophet speaks of a universal sacrificial worship; he does not specify what is to be offered.

799 Cf. Gen. 9,8; 11,12; 13,15; 16,17.

800 Cf. Hebr. 11,7.

801 Cf. Hebr. 11,4f.

802 Cf. Exod. 3,14; 6,2f.

803 Gen. 4,26.

804 Hebr. 7,1 (cf. verse 2); Gen. 14,17-20; Ps. 110,4.

805 Cf. Eucharistic Prayer (the Roman Canon) of the Mass!

806 Newman 81 (cf. also Clement, Strom. VII 2 in: ANCL, Vol.12, 410-414).

807 Cf. Gen. 20,1-18. See also Gen. 12,10-20; 41,1-32; Daniel 2,1-45; 4,1-34.

808 Cf. Job 31,26-28.

809 Cf. Job 4,13f.

810 Cf. Job 38,1; 42,10f.

811 Cf. Num. 22-24.

812 Cf. 1 Sam. 28,3-25.

813 Stromateis VII 2,in: ANCL, Vol.12, 409-411.

814 Ibid. 411.

815 Ibid. 412-414 (cf. also Strom. VI 8, in: ANCL, Vol.12, 340f.; cf. Newman 83).

816 Cf. St.Augustine, De catechizandis rudibus 19,33 (Text and translation in: Patristic Studies [see note 781] 80-86; see also ibid. p. 97: "And so he made manifest a new covenant of everlasting inheritance, wherein man, renewed by the grace of God, might lead a new life, that is, the spiritual life; and that he might show the first covenant to be antiquated, wherein a carnal people living after the old man (with the exception of a few, patriarchs and prophets and some unknown saints, who observed it), and leading a carnal life, eagerly desired of the Lord God carnal rewards and received them as symbols of spiritual blessings."; cf. also Augustine's Retractationes 1,12,3 in: PL 32, 603 and De Civitate Dei 1,18 in: PL 41, 609).

817 Cf. Barth (2) 36.

818 Clement of Alexandria, Stromateis IV (cf. ANCL, Vol.12, 10).

819 Cf. Maisie Ward, Early Church Portrait Gallery. London - New York 1959, 36. See also the Chapters 6 and 7 of Clement's Protreptikos in: ANCL, Vol.12, 69-75; cf. Newman 80.

820 It may be noted that the expressions "sperma tou logou" and "spermatikos logos" were all Stoic terminologies. For the Stoics the Logos, as immanent fire, is the principle of all reason (ratio). Reason in the individual is merely an aspect of it. By virtue of the activity of the Logos, all men are capable of forming certain moral and religious concepts. They are called "physikai ennoiai" or "koinai ennoiai", or even "spermata tou logou" as distinct from "spermatikos logos". The spermata are participations in the Logos by the human spirit. They derive from the activity of the Logos which therefore sows knowledge in the human reason. Consequently, the Logos as an active principle or source of all partial knowledge is called spermatikos logos. Where there are only seeds of the Logos, the Logos is present partially (aro meros). But in the end he is the subject of all knowledge.

821 Cf. Caperan 68.

822 Cf. 1 Tim. 2,4; Irenaeus, Adv. Haer. V 18,3 (cf. in: PG 7, 1174). See also Fransen (1) 37f.

823 Irenaeus, Adv. Haer. V 18,3 (cf. in: PG 7, 1174): "For the maker of the world indeed is the Word of God; and this is our Lord, who in the last times was made man, existing in this world: who invisibly contains all things that were made and is established in the whole creation (has a fixed place), as being God's Word, governing all things: and therefore into his own he came visibly, and was made flesh and hung upon the tree that he might sum up all into himself." In a Preface (cf. PG 7, 1120), where, after summarizing the main points of the first four books (Exposition of all the heretics and their doctrines and refutation of their impious opinions) Irenaeus gives the aims of book five, namely, to form arguments from the teaching of our Lord and from the Apostolical Epistles against the gainsayings of the heretics; to draw back them that err, and convert them to the Church of God; to conform also the mind of the novices, that they may keep unshaken the faith which they have received thoroughly guarded from the Church; that in no wise may they be perverted by such as endeavour to teach them amiss and to lead them away from the truth. He advises that it is necessary to read carefully the first four books in order to be conversant with the arguments with which he refuted the heretics; but above all so that one will "find answer to them ready...to take up; their opinions... to cast away, as dung, by the faith which comes from heaven, and him alone (to follow), who is the true and strong Teacher, the Word of God, Jesus Christ, our Lord, who for his immense love's sake was made that which we are, in order that he might perfect us to be what he is.".

824 Cf. Augustine, Epistola CXXVII 12; Confessiones IV 12.

825 Idem, Retractationes (see note 816); De Civitate Dei (see

note 816). Cf. also Ambrose, Expositiones in Psalmum 118 (see PL 15, 1318) and Jerome, In Epistolam ad Galatas (see PL 26, 326).

826 Clement of Alexandria, Stromateis VI 8 (cf. ANCL, Vol.12, 340). And he also describes "understanding as the free gift of God, who accepts in every nation anyone who fears him and is righteous and grants many and varied paths to himself, not only the different covenants, but the modes of teaching, which is conducive to righteousness, for he is good and saves in many ways. He made a most startling statement when he said that "the absence of respect of persons in God is not only in time, but from eternity." For God's beneficence has no beginning, and it is not limited to places and persons, nor confined to parts. God has made different covenants with mankind, he argues. He has variedly taught men and led them to righteousness. Therefore anyone who forgets God plainly forgets him whom he formerly remembered, and dismisses him whom he knew previous to forgetting him (cf. ANCL, Vol.8, 339-344; Vol.2, 366-375).

827 In Stromateis I 16, Clement of Alexandria rejects the view which held that the Hellenic philosophy apprehended truth accidentally, dimly and partially, because it was set going by the devil. "But if the Hellenic philosophy", he argues, "does not comprehend the whole extent of the truth and, besides, is destitute of strength to perform the commandments of the Lord, yet it prepares the way for the truly royal teaching; training in some way or other, and moulding the character, and fitting him who believes in Providence for the reception of the truth." (cf. ANCL, Vol. 4, 400-405. In Stromateis VI 7, Clement describes philosophy really and strictly as the "systematic wisdom which furnishes acquaintance with the things which pertain to life"; and defines it "to be certain knowledge, being a sure and irrefragable apprehension of things divine and human, comprehending the present, past and future, which the Lord has taught us, both by his advent and by the prophets." Later he terms this wisdom or this sure and irrefragable apprehension of things divine and human as a "rectitude of soul and of reason, and purity and life, which is kindly and lovingly disposed towards Wisdom, and does everything, and does everything to attain to it." Wisdom itself is the creator and teacher of all things, that is, the Son of God. Since the "unoriginated Being is one, the Omnipotent God", one, too, is the God who formed the beginning of all things; who "is called Wisdom by all the prophets; who is "the Teacher of all created beings"; "who foreknew all things"; and who "from above, from the first foundation of the world, 'in many ways and many times' (Heb. 1,1) trains and perfects" all peoples. Further, the apprehension is irrefragable by reason, in as much as it has been communicated by God, and is wholly true according to God's intentions, as being known through the means of the Son. In consequence, "in one aspect it is eternal, and in another it becomes useful in time. Partly it is one and the same, partly many and indifferent, partly without any movement of passion, partly with passionate desire, partly perfect, partly incomplete." Besides, if Christ himself is Wisdom, and it was his working which showed itself in the prophets, by which the gnostic tradition may be learned, as

he himself taught the apostles during his presence, then it follows that the gnosis, which is the knowledge and apprehension of things present, future and past, which is sure and reliable, as being imparted and revealed by the Son of God, is Wisdom (cf. ANCL, Vol.12, 335-339).

828 Cf. Clement of Alexandria, Stromateis VI 8. See also note 827.

829 Cf. Clement of Alexandria, Stromateis VII 8; 9. See also ibid. VI 2; 8. In an earlier book (Strom. I 5), Clement remarked that "the way of Truth is therefore one. But into it, as into a perennial river, streams flow from all sides". Commenting on Prov. 4; 10f., 21, he observed that "not only did (God) enumerate several ways of salvation for any one righteous man, but he added many other ways of many righteous, speaking thus: 'The path of the righteous shine like the light' (Prov. 4,18). The commandments and the modes of preparatory training are to be regarded as the ways and appliances of life". Further, the expression " "how often" (cf. Mt. 23,37; Lu. 13,34) "shows Wisdom to be manifold; and in every mode of quantity and quality, it by all means saves some, both in time and in eternity." (cf. ANCL, Vol.4, 366-370).

830 Cf. Stromateis VI 8; VII 2; Ward (see note 14) 32

831 Justin, Apologia II 6,3 (cf. PG 6, 454).

832 Justin, Dialogus cum Tryphone 61,1 (cf. PG 6, 416).

833 Cf. G. Aeby, Les missions divines de Saint Justin a Origène, Fribourg (Swisse) 1958, 14.

834 Cf. Justin, Apologia II 13 (PG 6, 446-467). See also Clement of Alexandria, Stromateis VI 17; Protreptikos VI; VIII.

835 Justin, Apologia II 8; 10 (PG 6, 458f.).

836 Justin, Apologia I 46 (PG 6, 398).

837 Justin, Apologia I 5; 46 (PG 6, 335; 398). In Apologia II 10, he writes: "...for whatever either lawgivers or philosophers uttered well, they elaborated by finding and contemplating some part of the Word. But since they did not know the whole of the Word, which is Christ, they often contradicted themselves...". And in Chapter XIII he adds: "For all the writers were able to see realities darkly through the sowing of the implanted word that was in them. For the seed and imitation imparted according to capacity is one thing, and quite another is the thing itself, of which there is the participation and imagination according to the grace which is from him." (cf. PG 6, 459.466f.); cf. Clement of Alexandria, Stromateis II 18f.; VI 8.

838 "We have been taught that Christ is the first-born of God, and we have declared above that he is the Word of whom every race of men were partakers and those who lived reasonably are Christians, even though they have been thought atheists" (cf. Justin, Apologia I 46 [PG 6, 398]).

839 Justin, Apologia I 12,9; 21,1 (PG 6, 342.359).

840 Justin, Dialogus cum Tryphone 142,2.

841 Justin, Dialogus cum Tryphone 122,4.

842 Justin, Apologia I 14,3f.

843 Ibid. 23,1f.

844 Ibid. 66,3.

845 Ibid. 61,2; 67,3f.

846 Justin, Dialogus cum Tryphone 7,3.

847 Cf. Latourelle (2) 91. Thus Justin, calling Christ the eternal dynamic of God (cf. Apologia I 33,1ff.) said that the Incarnation is the last link in the chain of events during which the Logos had earlier already appeared on earth in other circumstances to reveal the will of the Father (cf. Dialogus cum Tryphone 75,4); and that the Logos maintains this function of being mediator of revelation until the end of the world. It comes to an end in the second parousia, a phrase which he coined (cf. Apologia I 52,3 and Dialogus cum Tryphone 14,8).

848 Cf. S.C. Anderson, Logos und Nomos. Berlin 1955, 312-314.

849 Justin, Apologia I 33,1f.

850 Ibid. 40,5f.; 39,1 (cf. Dialogus cum Tryphone XI-XXV; see also Ps. 1,2 and Is. 2,3f.).

851 Cf. S. Harent, Art. Infidèles. In: DThC 7 (1927) 1807: "Ces deux révélations, l'une naturelle, l'autre positive, ne s'excluent pas, mais se complètent; la seconde présuppose la primière; puisque la foi devine, que la révélation positive tend à obtenir, suppose nécessairement la connaissance naturelle des préambules de la foi, c'est-à-dire la révélation naturelle. ... L'infidèle de bonne foi qui n'a que cette révélation naturelle, est déjà, quoiqu'à un degrée inférieur, participant du Verbe; et ce qu'il possède de lumière morale et religieuse, s'il ne l'éteint pas et s'il y conforme sa vie, l'achemine d'ailleurs vers une révélation plus haute. En ce sens 'la semence du Verbe est innée dans tout le genre humain.' [Justin] ... Et ces deux révélations, vraiment connexes, Justin pouvait d'autant plus facilement les unir et les prendre comme une seule illumination du Verbe, qu'alors on ne connaissait guère les distinctions de nature et de grâce, de naturel et de surnaturel."

852 Cf. Ward (see note 14) 49; O. Cullmann, Christ und die Zeit. Zürich 1962, 65 (cf. the English tradition: Christ and Time. London 1962, 56f.).

853 Cf. Irenaeus, Adv. Haer. IV 38,3.

854 Cf. Escoula (1) 385-400.

855 Pre-Christian in its origin, Gnosticism has two main tenets - that matter is evil, and that salvation comes not from love but from knowledge, a secret knowledge available only to the chosen few. Claiming to put upon them a deeper interpretation, it seized on the pagan mystery religions, Judaism, and ultimately Christianity; so that there was a pagan Gnosticism, a Jewish Gnosticism, and a Christian Gnosticism. There are hints of the beginnings of Christian Gnosticism before the death of St. Paul. These we find in his condemnation both of vain talk about genealogies and of those who forbade marriage. Christian Gnosticism came into clear

prominence in the second century. In Christianity, the movement appeared at first as a school (or schools) of thought within the Church; and it soon established itself in all the principal centres of Christianity, and by the end of the second century, the Gnostics had mostly become separate sects. In some of the later books of the New Testament forms of Gnostic teaching are denounced, though less developed than the gnostic systems of teaching referred to by second century writers. Certain features are common to Gnosticism as a whole: a central importance is attached to gnosis, the supposedly revealed knowledge of God and of the origin and destiny of mankind, by means of which the spiritual element in man could receive redemtion. The source of this special "Gnosis" was held to be either the Apostles, from whom it was derived by a secret tradition, or a direct revelation given to the founder of the sect. Gnosticism took many different forms, commonly associated with the names of particular teachers, e.g. Valentinus, Basilides and Marcion. In Valentinus' system, God above is separated from the world below by the pleroma, a mid-world built up in a complicated way. Between the lower and the upper world (pleroma) a drama of salvation is played out, a drama which is to liberate the divine spark imprisoned in man. Christ is an aeon who descends to redeem man (cf. F.M.M. Sagnard, Gnose Valentinienne. Paris 1947, 387-415). This Christ of the upper world unites himself with the Jesus of the lower world, who is not, however, the Jesus of the Gospels. For any union of the divine with the material is unthinkable, as the latter is radically evil. The words and actions of the earthly Christ are no more than signs of the realities which are being played out in the upper world of middle beings. Salvation does not consist in the return of the earthly and visible world and of the fallen fragments of divinity. Salvation is effected by knowledge. The Ptolemaeans, who developed from the Valentinians wished to make a complete fragmentation of Christ by assigning different objects to the differing sayings of the Johannine prologue. One was the Logos, one the Only-begotten, another the Saviour and Christ. Marcion characterised by his extreme dualism, in the "Antitheses" assumed the existence of two Gods: one God of the Old Testament and another of the New Testament. Jesus is the son of the God of the New Testament but is seen by Marcion in an almost modalistic nearness to the Father. Jesus is the good God in person, clothed in the form of man. He needs only to lay this aside to become once again pure Godhead. Finally, Jesus died a real death on the cross by which he redeemed men from the creator God and his domination, the God whose work Christ has come to destroy.

856 A. Grillmeier, Christ in Christian Tradition. London 1965, 116.

857 A. Benoit, Saint Irénée. Introduction à l'étude de sa théologie. Paris 1960, 219-227; A. D'Ales, Le mot oikonomia dans la langue théologique de Saint Irénée. In: Revue des Etudes Greques (Paris) 32 (1919) 1-9; Grillmeier (see note 856) 47-119.

858 Irenaeus, Adv. Haer. IV 28,2 (cf. PG 7, 1061f.: "For as in the New Testament, that faith of man (to be placed) in God has been increased, receiving in addition (to what was already revealed) the Son of God, that man too might be a partaker of God...".

859 "There is therefore, as we have pointed out, one God the Father, and one Christ Jesus, who came by means of the whole dispensational arrangements (connected with him), and gathered together all things in him (Eph. 1,10). But in every respect, too, he is man, the formation of God; and thus he took up man into himself, the invisible becoming visible, the incomprehensible being made comprehensible, the impassible being capable of suffering, and the Word being made man, thus summing up all things in himself: so that as in the super-celestial, spiritual and invisible things, the Word of God is supreme, so also in things visible and corporeal. He might possess the supremacy, and taking to himself the preeminence as well as constituting himself Head of the Church he might draw all things to himself at the proper time." (Adv. Haer. III 16,6 [cf. PG 7, 925f.]).

860 Grillmeier (see note 856) 120.; see also G.T. Amstrong, Die Genesis in der Alten Kirche. Tübingen 1962, 63-67.

861 A. Houssian, La christologie de Saint Irénée. Louvain 1958, 220f.

862 Adv. Haer. III 18,3; cf. ibid. IV 20.

863 Ibid. IV 6,3 (cf. PG 7, 973).

864 Ibid. IV 6,5 (cf. PG 7, 989).

865 Cf. Adv. Haer. III 11,25 (PG 7, 752; cf. PG 7, 799) where Irenaeus writes: "If, however, anyone does not discover the cause of all these things which become objects of investigation, let him reflect that man is infinitely inferior to God; that he has received grace only in part, and and is not yet equal or similar to his Maker; and moreover, that he cannot have experience or form a conception of all things like God; but in the same proportion, as he who was formed but today, and received the beginning of his creation, is inferior to him who is uncreated, and who is always the same, in that proportion is he, as respects knowledge and the faculty of investigating the causes of all things, inferior to him who made him. For thou, o man, are not an uncreated being, nor didst thou always exist with God, as did his own Son; but now through his preeminent goodness, receiving the beginning of thy creation, thou does gradually learn from the Word the dispositions of God who made thee."

866 Escoula (1) 555.

867 Adv. Haer. IV 6,4 (PG 7, 988): "For the Lord taught us that no man is capable of knowing God, unless he be taught of God, that is, that God cannot be known without God: but that this is the express will of the Father. For they shall know him to whomsoever the Son has revealed him." - Adv. Haer. IV 6,7: "For the Son, being present with his own handiwork from the beginning, reveals the Father to all; to whom he wills, and when he will, and as the Father wills. Wherefore, then, in all things, through all things, there is one God, the Father, and one Word, and one Son, and one Spirit, and one salvation to all who believe in him."

868 Cf. Orbe (see note 782) 211f. and Grillmeier (see note 856) 133.

869 Adv. Haer. IV 6,7 (PG 7, 990).

870 Cf. ibid. IV 6,6 (PG 7, 989); II 6,1; 27,2 (PG 7, 724.803); III 25,1 (PG 7, 986); V 18,3 (PG 7, 1174).

871 Latourelle (2) 100; see also Schillebeeckx (2) 6f.

872 Schillebeckx (2) 5f.

873 Concilium Vaticanum II, Dei Verbum, No.2 (cf. AAS 63 [1966] 818).

874 Dei Verbum, No.3 (cf. AAS 63 [1966] 818).

875 Ibid., No.4 (cf. AAS 63 [1966] 818).

876 Concilium Vaticanum II, Ad Gentes, No.11 (cf. AAS 63 [1966] 60).

877 Concilium Vaticanum II, Nostra Aetate, No.2 (cf. AAS 63 [1966] 741).

878 Godianism is the term given to the Traditional Religion now being revived and practised by some intellectuals who are opposed to the exclusive claim of Christianity as the only one and valid way of salvation. Arguing against the exclusivism of Christianity in an Enugu Television Debate on "Religion" (1981), moderated by Mr. Chris Adigwe, Lecturer at I.M.T., Enugu, Anambra State, Nigeria, under the general title: "Philosophy and Life", Dr. Enyeribe Onuoha (a godianist) asked his colleagues: If Christianity is the only valid religion for the whole world and is meant for all mankind, what, then, could be said regarding the fate of millions of people who had lived and died before the coming of Christ?

879 Cf. Tillich (3) 111.

880 Moltmann 197.

881 Troeltsch (2) 21.

882 Cf. D.J. Dietrich, Johann Baptist von Hirscher. The Kingdom of God in the Revolution of 1848. In: Église et Théologie 9 (1978) 304. See also Ch. Dawson, Progress and Religion. London 1945; Religion and the Modern State. London 1935; Mediaeval Religion. London 1934.

883 Gotthold Ephraim Lessing, Nathan the Wise. New York 1955, 79f.

884 Cf. Tillich (3) 121.

885 Cf. Hick (1) 92f. (see also Moltmann 199).

SELECTED BIBLIOGRAPHY

Abrahamsson, H., The origin of death. Studies in African mythology. Uppsala 1951.

Achebe, C. (1), Things fall apart. London 1958.

- (2), No longer at ease. London 1960.
- (3), Arrow of God. London 1962.
- (4), Sacrificial egg and other short stories. Onitsha 1962.
- (5), The role of the writer in a new nation. In: Nigeria Magazine 81 (1964) 157-160.

Adelgbola, E.A., The theological basis of ethics. In: Biblical revelation and African beliefs. Edited by K. Dickson and P. Ellingworth. London 1969, 116-136.

Adigwe, H., The beginnings of the Catholic Church among the Ibos of South-east Nigeria. Unpublished dissertation. Wien 1966.

Afigbo, A.E. (1), The warrant chief system in Eastern Nigeria 1900-1929. Unpublished dissertation. Ibadan 1964.

- (2), Oral tradition and history in Eastern Nigeria. In: African Notes (Ibadan) 3 (1966) 12-20; 4 (1966) 17-27.
- (3), Revolution and reaction in Eastern Nigeria 1900-1929. The back-ground to the women's riot 1929. In: Journal Historical Society (Ibadan) 3 (1966) 539-557.
- (4), The warrant chief system in Eastern Nigeria: direct or indirect rule ? In: Journal Historical Society (Ibadan) 3 (1967) 683-700.

Ahunanya, T., Igbo pagan funerals studied in the light of catholic Christian funerals. Unpublished dissertation. Roma 1965.

Ajayi, J.F., Christian missions in Nigeria 1841-1891: The making of a new elite. London 1965.

Akpunonu, P.D., The religion of the Ibos yesterday and today. In: Lux (Review of the African Association of St. Augustine, Rome) 1 (1965) 85-94.

Alan, B., History of Nigeria. London 1929.

Albright, W., From the stone age to Christianity. New York 1957.

Alutu, J.O., A ground work of Nnewi history. Enugu 1963.

Anderson, J.N.D., Christianity and comparative religion. Illinois 1970 - London 1971.

Anene, J.C. (1), Southern Nigeria in transition 1885-1906. London 1966.

- (2), The protectorate government of Southern Nigeria and the Aros 1900-1902. In: Journal Historical Society (Ibadan) 1 (1956) 20-26.

- (3), Nigeria, Inside Arochukwu. In: Nigeria 54 (1957) 273-288.

Anozia Ifeanyichukwu, P., The religious import of Igbo names. Unpublished dissertation. Roma 1968.

Ardener, E.W. (1), The kinship terminology of a group of Southern Ibo. In: Africa 24 (1954) 83-98.

- (2), Lineage and locality among the Mbaise Ibo. In: Africa 29 (1959) 113-133.

Arinze, F.A. (1), Ibo sacrifice as an introduction to the catechesis of Holy Mass. Unpublished dissertation. Roma 1960

- (2), Sacrifice in Ibo Religion. Ibadan 1970.

Auer, A., The changing character of Christian understanding of the world. In: The Christian and the World. Readings in Theology. New York 1965, 3-44 (Translation of Auer's "Gestaltwandel des christlichen Weltverständnisses". In: Gott in Welt. Edited by J.B. Metz and others. Vol.1, Freiburg 1964, 333-365).

Auvray, P., Création. In: Vocabulaire de Théologie Biblique. Edited by X. Léon-Dufour. Paris 1964, 171-178.

Ayandele, E.A., The missionary impact on modern Nigeria 1842-1914. A political and social analysis. London 1966.

Azorji. E., The socio-religious significance of Igbo traditional personal names. Unpublished dissertation. Enugu 1980.

Bane, M.J., The popes and Eastern Africa. An outline of mission history (1460s-1960s) New York 1968.

Banton, M. (Editor), Anthropological approach to the study of religion. London 1966.

Barth, D. (1), The doctrine of creation (=Church Dognatics III/1) Edinburgh 1958.

- (2), The revelation of God as the abolition of religion. In:

Christianity and other religions. Selected readings. Edited by J. Hick and B. Hebblethwaite. Glasgow 1980.

Bascom, W.R., West Africa and the complexity of primitive cultures. In: American Anthropology 50 (1948) 18-23.

Basden, G.T. (1), Among the Ibos of Nigeria. London 1921, ^{2}1966.

- (2), Notes on the Ibo country and Ibo people. In: Southern Geographical Journal 55 (1925).

- (3), Niger Ibos. London 1938, ^{2}1966.

Baumann, H., Schöpfung und Urzeit des Menschen im Mythos der afrikanischen Völker. Berlin 1936.

Baumann, H./Westermann, D., Les peuples et les civilisations de l'Afrique. Paris 1948.

Beier, U.H. (1), Art in Nigeria Igbo. London 1960.

- (2), Ibo and Yoruba Art. A comparison. In: Black Orpheus (Ibadan) 8 (1961) 46-50.

- (3), Osezi festival in Agbor. In: Nigeria Magazine 78 (1963) 184-195.

- (4), Agbor dancers. In: Nigeria Magazine 83 (1964) 240-248.

- (5) (Editor), Origin of life and death. African creation myths. London 1966, ^{2}1968.

Betbeder, P., Traditional African religions in their relation with christianity. In: Lumen Vitae Studies. Brussel 1956.

Biafra. Introducing Biafra. Published by the government of the Republic of Biafra and reproduced by the Britain-Biafra Association. London 1967.

Biobaku, S.O., The origin of the Yoruba. Broadcast (Nigeria) 1955.

Blomjous, J.J., Mission and liturgy. London 1960.

Bopp, L., The salvific power of the word according to the church. New York 1964, 147-167.

Boros, L., Mysterium mortis. Der Mensch in der letzten Entscheidung. Olten 1963.

Boston, J.S. (1), Alosi shrines in Udi division. In: Nigeria 61 (1959) 157-165.

- (2), Notes on contact between the Igala and the Ibo. In: Journal Historical Society (Ibadan) 2 (1960) 52-58.

- (3), Some nothern Ibo masquerades. In: Journal Royal Anthropological Institute (London) 90 (1960) 54-65.

- (4), Ceremonial iron gongs among the Ibo and Igala. In: Man 64 (1964) 157-165.

Bouchaud, J., L'église en Afrique noire. Paris - Genève 1958.

Bradbury, R.E., Father and senior son in Edo mortuary ritual. In: African Systems of thought. London 1965, 96-121.

Brown, P., Pattern of authority in West Africa. In: Africa 21 (1951) 261-278.

Bühlmann, W., The necessity for liturgical renewal in Africa today. In: Liturgy and the Missions. London 1960, 103-111.

Buess, E., Geschichte des mythischen Erkennens. München 1953.

Burton de Witt, E., Spirit, soul and flesh. Chicago 1918.

Cairns, D., Image of God in man. New York 1953.

Caperan, L., Le problème du salut des infidèles. Paris 1912.

Carrol, K., Nigerian traditions and adaptations. In: Exit (Ibadan) 5 (1964) 26-28.

Cassirer, E., Philosophie der symbolischen Formen II, Darmstadt 1957.

Christensen, J.B., The role of proverbs in Fante culture. In: Africa 28 (1958) 232-243.

Chu, P.A.K., The church's attitude towards native culture. In: The Torch (Enugu) 24 (1961) 12-15.

Chubb, L.T., Ibo land tenure. Ibadan 1942.

Cogan, B., Ibo catholicism. A tentative survey. In: Afer 8 (1966) 346-358.

Coker, I., A grammar of African names. Lagos 1964.

Congar, Y. (1), Vaste monde, ma paroisse. Verité et dimension du salut. Paris 1959.

- (2), "Ecclesia ab Abel". In: Abhandlungen über Theologie und Kirche. Festschrift für Karl Adam. Düsseldorf 1952, 79-108.

Cornelis, E., Valeur chrétienne des religions non chrétiennes. Paris 1965.

Correia, P.J.A. (1), L'animisme Ibo et les divinités de la Nigeria. In: Anthropos 16/17 (1921/1922) 360-366; Un totem Nigeria. Ibid. 960-965.

- (2), Le sens moral chez les Ibos de la Nigeria. In: Anthropos 18/19 (1923/1924) 880-889.

- (3), Vocables religieux et philosophiques des peuples Ibos. In: Bibliotheca Africana I, 1925, 194-113.

Daly, J., Boy's age-groups in Eastern Nigeria. In: Afer 6 (1964) 262-266.

Dander, F., Schöpfung nach der Lehre des heiligen Thomas von Aquin. In: Zeitschrift für katholische Theologie 53 (1929) 1-40.203-246.

Danielou, J., Les saints païens de l'Ancien Testament. Paris 1955.

Danquah, J.B., The Akan doctrine of God. London 1944.

Davidson, B. (1), Old Africa rediscovered. London 1959, ²1965.

- (2), The Africans. An entry to cultural history. London 1969.

Dawson, C., Religion and culture. London 1948.

Deissler, A./Koch, R., Man. In: Encyclopedia of Biblical Theology. Edited by J.B. Bauer. Vol.2, London 1970, 542-551.

Delmond, P., De l'imposition de nom de personne aux africains. In: Bulletin de l'Institut Francais d'Afrique Noire 15 (1953) 453-460.

Deschamps, H., Les religions de l'Afrique noire. Paris 1954.

Dickson, K./Ellingworth, P. (Editors), Biblical revelation and african beliefs. London 1969.

Dike, K.O., Trade and politics in the Niger delta 1830-1885. London 1956.

Doncell, J.F., Philosophical anthropology. New York 1967.

Durueke, J.A. (1), Egwu Onwa. London 1948.

- (2), Elə ətətə nwanye n'ala Igbo. London 1948.

Duschak, W.J., The possibilities of forms of the mass in mission territories. In: Liturgy and the Missions. London 1960, 128-744.

Edwards, P. (1), Embrenche and Ndichie. In: Journal Historical Society (Ibadan) 2 (1962) 401-402.

- (2) (Editor), Equiano's travels. London 1967.

Eichroth, W., Man in Old Testament. London 1951.

Ekwensi, C.O.D. (1), Ikolo, the Wrestler and other Igbo tales. London 1947.

- (2), Ezunaka, the legend of Nkwelle. In: Nigeria Magazine 18 (1963) 176-183.

Eliade, M. (1), Myths, dreams and mysteries. The encounter between contemporary faiths and archaic reality. London 1960, [2]1968.

- (2), From primitives to zen. A thematic source book on the history of religions. London 1967.

Enechukwu, L., Olili Ji (The new-yam festival). In: The Pylon 24 (1967)

Eneli, G., The place of ancestral worship in the religious belief of the Ibo. In: The University Herald (Ibadan) 4 (1951) 16.

Epelle, E.M.T., Chieftaincy titles in Igbo land and church membership. In: West African Religion (Nsukka) 5 (1966) 3-6.

Escoula, L. (1), Le verbe sauveur et illuminateur chez saint Irénée. In: Nouvelle Revue Théologique 66 (1939) 385-400.551-567.

- (2), Saint Irénée et la connaissance naturelle de Dieu. In: Revue des Sciences Religieuses 20 (1940) 252-271.

Ezenwa, P.A., Marriage customs in Asaba division. In: Nigerian Field 13 (1948) 71-81.

Esike, S.O., Aba riots of 1929. In: African Historian (Ife) 1 (1965) 7-13.

Evans-Pritchard, E.E. (1), Theories of primitive religion. Oxford 1965, [2]1969.

- (2), Zande blood - Brotherhood. In: Africa 6 (1933) 369-401.

- (3), The Neur conception of spirits in its relation to the social order. In: American Anthropologist 52 (1953) 201-214.

Ezeanya, S.N. (1), The place of the supreme God in the traditional religion of the Ibo. In: West Africa Religion 2 (1963) 1-4.

- (2), Christian and pagan morality. In: Afer 5 (1963) 318-319.

- (3), The use of Igbo names. In: West African Religion 3 (1964) 2-8.

- (4), The "Sacred Place" in the traditional religion of the Igbo of eastern group of provinces of Nigeria. In: West African Religion 6 (1966)

- (5), Religion in Igbo society. In: The Leader (Catholic newspaper, published by Assumpta Press, Owerri)

22 October 1966, p.3.
- (6), The Osu (cult-slave) system in Igboland. In: Religion of Africa (Leiden) 1 (1967) 35-45.
- (7), God, spirits and the spirit world. In: Biblical revelation and African beliefs. Edited by K. Dickson and P. Ellingworth. London 1969, 30-46.

Feret, H.M., Das Mysterium des Todes. Frankfurt 1955, esp. 13-126.194-218.

Feuillet, J., La connaissance naturelle de par les hommes d'après Rom I,18-29. In: Lumière et Vie 14 (1954) 207-222.

Floyd, B., Eastern Nigeria. London 1969.

Forde, D. (1), African worlds. Studies in the cosmological ideas and social values of African peoples. London 1954, [2]1968.
- (2), Tropical African studies. In: Africa 35 (1965) 30-97.

Forde, D./Jones, G.I., The Ibo and Ibibio-speaking peoples of South-eastern Nigeria. London 1950.

Fortes, M. (1), Oedipus and Job in West African Religion. Cambridge 1959.
- (2), Some reflections on ancestor worship in Africa. In: African systems of thought. London 1965, 122-144.

Fraine, J. de, The Bible and the origin of man. New York 1961.

Frankfort, A.I./Wilson, A./Jacobsen, T., The intellectual adventure of ancient man. Chicago 1946.

Fransen, P. (1), Divine grace and man. 2nd. revised edition. New York 1965.
- (2), Man and freedom. In: Man before God. Readings in theology. New York 1966, 68-89.

Friedrich, M., Description de l'enterrement d'un chef a'Ibouzo. In: Anthropos 2 (1907) 100-106.

Geary, W.M.N., Nigeria under British rule. London 1927.

Geertz, C., Religion as a cultural system. In: Anthropological approaches to the study of religion. Edited by M. M. Banton. London 1966.

Gelin, A., The concept of man in the bible. London 1968.

Goode, W.J., Religion among the primitives. Illinois 1951.

Goody, J., Death, property and the ancestors. London 1959, [2]1962.

Gravrand, H., Meeting the African religions. Roma 1969.

Green, M.M. (1), Igbo village affairs. London 1947, [2]1964.

- (2), The unwritten literature of the Igbo-speaking people of South-eastern Nigeria. In: Bulletin of the School of Oriental and African Studies of the University of London 12 (1948), parts 3-4.

Green, M.M./Igwe, G.E., Akuko Ife nke ndi Igbo. Folk stories of the Igbo. London 1962.

Grottanelli, V.L. (1), Pre-existence and survival in Nzema beliefs. In: Man 61 (1961) 1-5.

- (2), Asongu worship among the Nzema. A study in art and religion. In: Africa 31 (1961) 46-60.

- (3), Leben, Tod und Jenseits in den Glaubensvorstellungen der Nzima. In: Réincarnation et vie mystique en Afrique noire. Paris 1965.

- (4), Nzema high gods. In: Paideuma. Mitteilungen zur Kulturkunde 13 (1967) 32-41.

Groves, C.P., The planting of Christianity in Africa. London 1948.

Guillet, J., Leitgedanken der Bibel. Luzern 1954.

Gutbrod, W., Die paulinische Anthropologie. Stuttgart 1934.

Hartle, D.D. (1), Bronze objects from Ifeka garden site, Ezira. In: West African Archaeological Newsletter (Ibadan) 4 (1966) 25-28.

- (2), Archaeology in Eastern Nigeria. In: Nigeria Magazine 93 (1967) 134-143.

Hastings, A., Church and mission in Africa. London 1967.

Herskovits, M.J. (1), Myth of the negro past. New York 1941.

- (2), African gods and catholic saints in new world negro beliefs. In: American Anthropologist 39 (1937) 635-643.

Hertz, R., Death and the right hand. Aberdeen 1960.

Hick, J. (1), God and the universe of faiths. Essays in the philosophy of religion. London 1973, 2nd. revised edition Glasgow 1977.

- (2), The centre of Christianity. London 1977.

- (3), God has many names. London 1980.

- (4) (Editor), The myth of incarnate God. London 1977.

Horton, R. (1), The Ohu system of slavery in a northern Ibo village-group. In: Africa 24 (1954) 311-336.

- (2), God, man and the land in a northern Ibo village-group. In: Africa 26 (1956) 17-28.

- (3), African traditional thought and western science. In: Africa 37 (1967) 50-70.155-187.

Hulsbosch, A., God's creation. London 1965.

Idigo, M.C.M., The history of Aguleri. Yaba (Nigeria) 1955.

Idowu, B.E. (1), Olodumare, God in Yoruba belief. London 1962.

- (2), God in Nigerian belief. Lagos 1963.

- (3), Towards an indigenous church. London 1965.

Ike, C.V., Toa for supper. London 1965.

Ike, A., Origin of the Ibos. Aba (Nigeria) ^{2}1951.

Ilogu, E. (1), Ofo: a religious and political symbol in Iboland. In: Nigeria Magazine 82 (1964) 234-235.

- (2), Christianity and Ibo traditional religion. In: Nigeria Magazine 83 (1964) 304-308.

Ilozue, E.O., The Umuoji cultural heritage. Onitsha 1972.

Imegwu, C., The Aros and the oracle. In: African Historian 1 (1965) 43-46.

Isichei, E., Ibo and Christian beliefs. Some aspects of a theological encounter. In: African Affairs 68 (1969) 122-134.

James, E.O. (1), Myths and ritual in the ancient Near East. London 1958.

- (2), Marriage customs throughout the ages. New York 1965.

James, M., Religion en Afrique - Présence Africaine. Paris 1959.

James, W., The varieties of religious experience. A study in human nature. Glasgow 1981.

Jeffreys, M.D.W. (1), The divine Umundri king. In: Africa 8 (1935) 346-354.

- (2), Sacred twinned vessels. In: Man 39 (1939) 137-138.

- (3), Dual organisation in Africa. In: African Studies 5 (1946) 82-105.

- (4), The winged solar disk or Ibo it (ichi) facial scarification. In: Africa 21 (1951) 93-111.

- (5), The degeneration of the ofo Anam. In: Nigeria Field 21 (1956) 173-177.

- (6), Ikenga: the Ibo ram-headed god. In: African Studies 15 (1956) 132-147.

- (7), The Anam Ofo. A cult object among the Ibo. In: Africa Journal of Science 53 (1956) 227-233.

- (8), The origin of the names of the Ibo week. In: Folklore (London) 67 (1956) 162-167.
- (9), Some Ibo proverbs. In: Folklore (London) 67 (1956) 168-169.
- (10), The Umundri tradition of origin. In: African Studies 15 (1956) 119-131.

Jensen, A.E., Mythos und Kult bei Naturvölkern. Wiesbaden 1951.

Jones, G.I. (1), Dual organisation in Ibo social structure. In: Africa 19 (1949) 150-156.
- (2), Ibo land tenure. In: Africa 19 (1949) 309-323.
- (3), The Jones report. Report on the status chiefs, Eastern Nigeria. Enugu 1956.
- (4), Ecology and social structure among the North-eastern Ibo. In: Africa 31 (1961) 117-134.
- (5), Ibo age organisation with special reference to the Cross river and North-eastern Ibo. In: Journal of the Royal Anthropological Institute 92 (1962) 191-211.

Jordan, J.P., Bishop Shanahan of Southern Nigeria. London 1939, ^{2}1965.

Kümmel, W.G., Man in the New Testament. London 1963.

Kibongi, R.B., Priesthood. In: Biblical revelation and African beliefs. London 1969, 47-56.

Läuchli, S., Monism and dualism in the Pauline anthropology. In: Biblical Research 3 (1958) 15-27.

Latourelle, R. (1), Revelation, history and incarnation. In: The Word. Reading in theology. New York 1964, 27-63.
- (2), Theology of revelation. Cork 1966.

Leonard, A., Toward a theology of the word. In: The Word. Readings in theology. New York 1964, 64-89.

Lepp, I., Death and its mysteries. London 1969.

Le Roy, A., La religion des primitifs. Paris 1910.

Levi, J./Semmelroth, O., Man and the mystery of Christ. In: Man before God. Readings in theology. New York 1966, 199-226.

Lisner, I., The African. In: American Ecclesiastical Review 31 (1904) 136-147.

Lubac, H. de, Catholicism. London 1962.

Lucas, J.O., The religion of the Yorubas. Lagos 1948.

Lufuluabo, F. (1), Les religions africaines traditionnelles. Paris 1962.

- (2), Valeurs des religions africaines selon la Bible et selon Vatican II, Kinshasa 1967.

Lunea, A., L'histoire du salut chez les pères de l'église. Paris 1964.

Luykx, B. (1), Adaption of liturgy in the missions. In: Liturgy and the missions. London 1960, 78-88.

- (2), Christian worship and the African soul. In: Afer 7 (1965) 133-143.

Lyonnet, S., The redemption of the universe. In: The church. Readings in theology. New York 1963, 136-156.

Malinowski, B., Magic, science and religion and other essays. New York 1948, ²1954.

Mangematin, B., "Thou shall not have strange Gods beside me". In: Afer 6 (1964) 17-23.

Marie-Andre, S. du, Social structure of native customs confronted by Christianity. In: Lumen Vitae Studies. Brussels 1956.

Mba, C., Matrimonial consent in the marriages of the Igbo of Nigeria. Unpublished dissertation. Roma 1964.

Mbiti, J.S. (1), African religions and philosophy. London 1969.

- (2), Eschatology. In: Biblical revelation and African beliefs. London 1969, 159-184.

- (3), Concepts of God in Africa. London 1970.

McKenzie, J.L. (1), The two-edged sword. London 1955, ²1965.

- (2), Myths and realities. London 1963.

Meek, C.K. (1), Intelligence report. Enugu 1930.

- (2), Nigeria. An ethnographical report on the peoples of the Nsukka division. Lagos 1931.

- (3), Report on the social and political organisation in the Owerri division. London 1933.

- (4), Ibo law. London 1934, 208-226.

- (5), Law and authority in a Nigerian tribe. London 1937.

- (6), The religions of Nigeria. In: Africa 14 (1943) 113-117.

Mendelsohn, J., God, Alla and Juju. New York 1962.

Messenger, J.C., Reinterpretations of Christian and indigenous belief in a Nigerian nativist church. In: American Anthropologist 62 (1960) 268-278.

Metz, J.B., A believer's look at the world. In: The Christian and the world. Readings in theology. New York 1965,

68-100 (Translation of "Weltverständnis im Glauben", in: Geist und Leben 35 /1962/ 165-184).

Mitchison, L., Nigeria: Newest nation. London 1960.

Moltmann, J., Christianity and the world religions. In: Christianity and other religions. Glasgow 1980.

Moore, G./Beier, U.H., Mbari houses. In: Nigeria 49 (1956) 184-198.

Morel, E.D., Nigeria, its peoples and its problems. London 1911.

Mulago, V., Un visage africain du christianisme. Paris 1962.

Munonye, J., The only son. London 1966.

Neuner, J. (Editor), Christian revelation and world religions. London 1967.

Newman, J.H., The Arians of the fourth century. London 1876.

Nkem, N., Danda. London 1964.

Noon, J.A., A preliminary examination of the death concepts of the Ibo. In: American Anthropologist 44 (1942) 638-654.

North, R., Teilhard and the creation of the soul. Milwaukee 1967.

Nwanodi, G.O., Ibo proverbs. In: Nigeria Magazine 80 (1964) 61-62.

Nwapa, F. (1), Efuru. London 1966.

- (2), Idu. London 1970.

Nwokocha, C.C., The Kola-Igbo symbol of love and unity. A valuable starting point for the study of the Eucharist. Unpublished dissertation. Roma 1969.

Nwokocha, J., African women today. London 1964.

Nzekwu, O. (1), Awka, town of smiths. In: Nigeria 61 (1959) 138-156.

- (2), Wand of noble wood. New York 1961.

- (3), Blade among the boys. London 1962.

- (4), Highlife for lizards. London 1965.

Nzimiro, F.I. (1), Family and kinship in Ibo land. A study in acculturation process. Unpublished dissertation. Köln 1962.

- (2), Oguta. In: Nigeria Magazine 80 (1964) 30-43.

Obi, S.N.C. (1), Women's property and succession thereto in modern Ibo law. In: Journal of African Law (London) 6 (1962) 6-18.

- (2), Ibo law of property. London 1963.

- (3), Modern family law in southern Nigeria. Lagos 1966.

Obiefuna, A., The Christian education of Igbo moral conscience. Unpublished dissertation. Roma 1966.

O'Connel, J., The withdrawal of the High God in West African religion. An essay in interpretation. In: Man 62 (1962).

O'Donnell, W.E., Religion and morality among the Ibos of southern Nigeria. In: Primitive Man 4 (1931) 54-60.

Ogbalu, F.C. (1), Ilu Igbo (The book of Igbo proverbs) Onitsha 1961.

- (2), Omenala Igbo. The book of Igbo custom. Onitsha [5]1965.

Ojiako , J., Bride price among the Igbos of south-eastern Nigeria. Unpublished dissertation. Innsbruck 1966.

Ojike, M., My Africa. New York 1946, 2nd edition London 1955.

Ojukwu, E., The Ahiara declaration. Genève 1969.

Okafor-Omali, D., A Nigerian villager in two worlds. London 1965.

Okeke, S., Priesthood among the Igbos of Nigeria studied in the light of catholic priesthood. Unpublished dissertation. Innsbruck 1967.

Okoli, J., People of Anambra. In: African Historian 1 (1963) 19-22.

Okoreaffia Chinyere, O., Elements of Igbo language studies. Onitsha 1966.

Onwuejeogwu, M.A. (1), The cult of the Bori Spirits among the Hausa. In: Man in Africa. Edited by M. Douglas and P.M. Kaberry. London 1969.

- (2), An outline account of the dawn of Igbo civilization in the Igbo culture area. In: Journal of the Odinani Museum. Nri (Nigeria) 1972.

- (3), The traditional political system of Ibusa. Onitsha 1973.

- (4), The social anthropology of Africa. An introduction. London 1975.

Onwuteaka, V.C., The Aba Riots of 1929 and its relation to the system of "Indirect rule". In: Nigerian Journal of economic and social studies 7 (1965) 274-282.

Onyenacho, B.M., Education amongst the Mbaise-Ibo. In: African Historian 1 (1965) 34-37.

Opara, E.O., Ilu okwu Ibo (Igbo language proverbs). Aba (Nigeria) 1950.

Ottenberg, S. (1), Ibo oracles and intergroup relations. In: South-west Journal anthropology 14 (1958) 295-317.

- (2), Ibo receptivity to change. In: Continuity and change in African cultures. Edited by W.R. Bascon and M.J. Herskovits. Chicago 1959, 130-143.

- (3), Double descent in an Ibo Village-group. In: Men and cultures. Edited by A.F.C. Wallace. Philadelphia 1960, 473-481.

Otto, R., Das Heilige. München 1963 (first published Breslau 1917).

Oyolu, C., Native culture and the catholic religion. In: The Torch 24 (1961) 8-11.

Panikkar, R., The unknown Christ of Hinduism. In: Christianity and other religions. Glasgow 1980.

Parrinder, E.G. (1), African traditional religion. London 1962.

- (2), West African psychology. London 1963.

- (3), What world religions teach. London 1968.

- (4), Religion in Africa. London 1970.

Parsons, R., Religion in an African society. The Kono of Sierra Leon. Leiden 1964.

Paulme, D., Two themes on the origins of death in West Africa. In: Man 2 (1967) 48-61.

Perham, M., Native administration in Nigeria. London 1937.

Pidoux, G., L'homme dans l'ancien testament. Neuchâtel 1953.

Pieper, J., Death and immortality. London 1969.

Pratt, J.P., The religious consciousness. New York 1946.

Quelle, G., Die Auffassung des Todes in Israel. Leipzig 1925.

Rahner, K. (1), Anonymous Christianity and missionary task of the church. In: Theological Investigations, Vol. 12, London - New York 1974.

- (2), Observations on the problem of the "Anonymous Christian". In: Theological Investigations, Vol. 14, London - New York 1976.

- (3), Anonymous and explicit faith. In: Theological Investigations, Vol. 16, London - New York 1979.

- (4), Order and redemption within the order of creation. In: Mission and Grace. London 1963, 59-113.
- (5), The unity of spirit and matter. A Christian understanding. In: Man before God. Readings in theology. New York 1966, 25-51.
- (6), Weltgeschichte und Heilsgeschichte. In: Schriften zur Theologie, Vol. 5, Einsiedeln 1964, 115-135.
- (7), Das Christentum und die nichtchristlichen Religionen. In: Ibid., 136-158.

Rahner, K./Ratzinger, J., Das Christentum und die nichtchristlichen Religionen. Nürnberg 1965.

Robinson, A.R., The vitality of the individual in the thought of Ancient Israel. Cardiff, 1949.

Robinson, G.W., The Christian doctrine of man. Edinburgh 1911.

Robinson, J.A.T. (1), The body. London 1952.
- (2), Truth is two-eyed. London 1979.

Ruel, M.J., Religion and society among the Kuria of East Africa. In: Africa 25 (1965) 295-306.

Samartha, S. (1) (Edit.), Dialogue between men of living faiths (Ajaltoun 1970). World council of churches. Geneve 1971.
- (2), Living faiths and the Ecumenical Movement. World council of churches. Geneve 1971.
- (3), Towards world community (Colombo 1974). World council of churches. Geneve 1975.
- (4), Dialoque in community (Chiang Hai 1977). World council of churches. Geneve 1977.
- (5), Guidelines on dialogue with people of living faiths and ideologies. World council of churches. Geneve 1979.
- (6), Dialogue as a continuing Christian concern. In: Christianity and other religions. Glasgow 1980.

Sawyerr, H., Sacrifice. In: Biblical revelation and African beliefs. London 1969, 57-82.

Schäfer, K., Der Mensch in paulinischer Auffassung. In: Das Bild vom Menschen. Düsseldorf 1934, 25-35.

Scheffczyk, L., The meaning of Christ's Parousia for salvation of man and the cosmos. In: The Christian and the world. New York 1965, 130-157.

Schillebeeckx, E. (1), Revelation in word and deed. In: The word. Readings in theology. New York 1964, 255-272.
- (2), Christ the sacrament. London 1965.
Schilling, O., Das biblische Menschenbild. Köln 1961.
Schlette, H.R. (1), Die Religionen als Thema der Theologie. Freiburg 1963.
- (2), Towards a theology of missions. London 1966.
Schlier, H./Mouroux, J., The heart of faith as a dialogue in love between God and man. In: Toward a theology of Christian faith. Readings in theology. New York 1968, 55-104.
Schmidt, W., The origin and growth of religion. New York 1931.
Schnackenburg, R., Man before God. Toward a biblical view of man. In: Man before God. Readings in theology. New York 1966, 3-24.
Schwarz, W., Nigeria. London 1968.
Secretariatus pro non-christianis, Religions. Fundamental themes for a dialogistic understanding. Roma 1970.
Seligman, C.G., Races of Africa. London 1967.
Semmelroth, O., God's word and man's reply. In: The word. Readings in theology. New York 1964, 273-285.
Shaw, C.T. (1), Bronzes from Eastern Nigeria. Excavations at Igbo-Ukwu. In: Jornal Historical Society (Nigeria) 2 (1960) 162-165.
- (2), Excavations at Igbo-Ukwu, Eastern Nigeria. An interim report. In: Man 60 (1960) 161-164.
- (3), Further excavations at Igbo-Ukwu, Eastern Nigeria. An interim report. In: Man 65 (1965) 181-184.
- (4), Spectographic analyses of Igbo and other Nigerian bronzes. In: Archaeometry (Oxford) 8 (1965) 86-95.
- (5), Radio carbon dates for Igbo-Ukwu. In: West African Archaeological News-Letter 4 (1966) 41; and: Africa Notes 3 (1966) 21.
- (6), Igbo-Ukwu. London 1970.
- (7), Nigeria. Its Archaeology and early history. London 1978.
Shedd, R.P., Man in community. London 1958.
Shelton, A.J. (1), The offended Chi in Achebe's Novels. In: Transition 13 (1964) 36-37.

- (2), Behaviour and cultural value in West African stories. Literary sources for the study of culture contact. In: Africa 34 (1964) 353-359.
- (3), On recent interpretation of Deus Otiosus. The withdrawn high god in West African psychology. In: Man 64 (1964) 53-55.
- (4), Departure of the Nshie. A North Nsukka Igbo origin legend. In: Journal of American Folklore (Philadelphia) 78 (1965) 115-129.
- (5), The presence of the "withdrawn" High God in North Ibo religious beliefs and worship. In: Man 65 (1965)
- (6), The meaning and method of Ifa divination among the Northern Nsukka Ibo. In: American Anthropologist 67 (1965) 1441-1456.
- (7), The articulation of traditional and modern in Igbo literature. In: Conch 1 (1969) 30-49.

Shorter, A.E.M., Is there an African culture? In: Afer 7 (1965) 158-167.

Shropshire, D., Ancestor Worship. In: Man 34 (1934)

Sidhom, S., The theological estimate of man. In: Biblical revelation and African beliefs. London 1969, 83-115.

Simmons, D.C., Notes on the Aro. In: Nigerian Field 23 (1958) 27-33.

Smith, E.W. (Edit.), African Ideas of God. London 1966.

Smith, W.C. (1), The meaning and end of religion. New York 1963, London 1978.
- (2), Questions of religious truth. New York 1967.
- (3), Religious diversity. New York 1976.
- (4), The Christian in a religious plural world. In: Christianity and other religions. Glasgow 1980.
- (5), Towards a world theology. London 1980.

Spico, C., Dieu et l'homme selon le Nouveau Testament. Paris 1961.

Spiro, M.E., Religion. Problems of definition and explanation. In: Anthropological approach to the study of religion. London 1966, 85-124.

Spoerndli, J., Marriage customs among the Ibo. In: Anthropos 38/39 (1942) 113-121.

Stacey, W.D., The Pauline view of man. London 1958.

Swiderski, S., Le problème de l'adaptation vu par l'église. In: Tradition et Progrès 5, Brazzaville (Congo) 1966.

Talbot, P.A., The peoples of Southern Nigeria. 4 Vols. (1926), London 1969.

Talbot, P.A./Mulhall, H., The physical anthropology of Southern Nigeria. A biometric study in statistical method. London 1962.

Tanner, R.E.S., Ancestor propitiation ceremonies in Sukamaland Tanganyika. In: Africa 27 (1958) 225-231.

Taylor, J.V. (1) (Edit.), Primal world views. Christian dialogue with traditional thought. Ibadan 1970.

- (2), The primal vision. Christian presence and African religion. Philadelphia 1963.

- (3), The theological basis of interfaith. In: Christianity and other Religions. Selected Readings. Glasgow 1980.

Tempels, P., Bantu philosophy. In: Présence Africaine. Paris 1959.

Thils, G., Propos et problème de la théologie de religions non-chrétiennes. Paris 1966.

Thomas, N.W., Totemism in Southern Nigeria. In: Anthropos 10/11 (1915/1916) 234-248; 14/15 (1919/1920) 543-545.

- (2), Anthropological report on the Ibo-speaking peoples of Nigeria. London 1913.

- (3), Some Ibo burial customs. In: Journal Royal Anthopological Institute (1917) 166-213.

Tillich, P. (1), Christianity and the encounter of the world religions. New York 1963.

- (2), The future of the religions. London 1966.

- (3), Christianity judging itself in the light of its encounter with the world religions. In: Christianity and other Religions. Glasgow 1980.

Troeltsch, E. (1), The absoluteness of Christianity (1901), Atlanta 1971, London 1972.

- (2), The place of Christianity among world religions. In: Christianity and other Religions. Glasgow 1980.

Turner, V.W., Ritual symbolism, morality and social structure among the Ndembu. In: African Systems of thought, 79-95.

Uchendu, V.C. (1), The status implications of Igbo religious beliefs. In: Nigerian Field 29 (1964) 27-37.

- (2), Kola hospitality and Igbo lineage structure. In: Man 64 (1964) 47-50.
- (3), Livestock tenancy among Igbo of Southern Nigeria. In: African Studies 23 (1964) 89-94.
- (4), Concubinage among Ngwa Igbo of Southern Nigeria. In: Africa 35 (1965) 187-197.
- (5), The Igbo of South East Nigeria. New York 1965.

Unegbu, M., Ibos and Christianity. In: Missionary Annals 2 (1954) 12.

Uzodimma, E.C.E., Our dead speak. London 1967.

Van Bulk, G., Existence and significance of African monotheism. In: Lumen Vitae Studies. Bruxelles 1966, 17-36.

Vindu, E., Rites funèbres chez les Lari. In: Tradition and Bulletin pastoral et culturel 5 (1966) 38-58.

Vodopivec, J. (1), L'église - Continuation du Christ. In: Euntes Docete 7 (1954) 312-325.

- (2), Unity in diversity. In: Euntes Docete 13 (1960) 458

Wach, H., General revelation and the religions of the world. In: Journal Biblical Religion (1954) 869-887.

Westermann, D., Africa and Christianity. Oxford 1937.

Whitehouse, A.A., Note on the "Mbari"-Festival of the natives of the Ibo Country. In: Man 4 (1904) 162-164.

Wieschhoff, H.A. (1), The social significance of names among the Ibo of Nigeria. In: American Anthopologist 43 (1941) 212-222.

- (2), Concepts of abnormality among the Ibo of Nigeria. In: Journal American Oriental Society (Boston) 63 (1943) 262-272.

Williams, J.J. (1), Hebrewisms of West Africa (from the Nile to Niger with the Jews), New York 1930.

- (2), Africas God. In: Anthropological Series of the Boston College Graduate School 1 (1936) 185-233.

Woelfel, D.J., Die Religionen des vorindogermanischen Europa. In: Christus und die Religionen der Erde. Edited by F. Koenig. Wien 1951, 499-504.

Young, C.T., How far can African ceremonial be incorporated into the Christian systems? In: Africa 8 (1935) 210-217.

Zaehner, R.C., The Catholic Church and World Religions. London 1964.